AF714370

Making Our Ideas Clear

Pragmatism in Psychoanalysis

A volume in
Advances in Cultural Psychology: Constructing Human Development
Jaan Valsiner, *Series Editor*

Making Our Ideas Clear

Pragmatism in Psychoanalysis

edited by

Philip Rosenbaum

Haverford College

IAP

INFORMATION AGE PUBLISHING, INC.

Charlotte, NC • www.infoagepub.com

Library of Congress Cataloging-in-Publication Data

Making our ideas clear : pragmatism in psychoanalysis / edited by Philip Rosenbaum, Haverford College.
pages cm. – (Advances in cultural psychology : constructing human development)
ISBN 978-1-62396-868-7 (hardcover) – ISBN 978-1-62396-867-0 (pbk.) – ISBN 978-1-62396-869-4 (ebook) 1. Psychoanalysis. 2. Pragmatism. I. Rosenbaum, Philip, editor.
BF173.M356458 2014
150.19'5–dc23

2014038453

Cover by Ilana Simons

Copyright © 2015 Information Age Publishing Inc.

All rights reserved. No part of this publication may be reproduced, stored in a retrieval system, or transmitted, in any form or by any means, electronic, mechanical, photocopying, microfilming, recording or otherwise, without written permission from the publisher.

Printed and bound by CPI Group (UK) Ltd, Croydon, CR0 4YY

CONTENTS

SECTION II

APPLYING PRAGMATIC THEORY TO CONTEMPORARY QUESTIONS

SECTION III

PRAGMATIC METHODOLOGY IN CLINICAL WORK

SERIES EDITOR'S PREFACE

CONNECTING CULTURAL PSYCHOLOGY WITH PSYCHOANALYSIS

How Pragmatism Matters

What our readers encounter in *Making our Ideas Clear: Pragmatism in Psychoanalysis* is important. Psychoanalysis—in its various brands that have proliferated in European societies since late 19th century—has been at the forefront of creating theoretical models of complex and dynamic aspects of human psychological functioning. Psychoanalysts have not been afraid of starting at that end of psychological phenomena where all other psychologists have been shy to enter—the abnormal and quasi-abnormal cases that nevertheless represent our very normal ways of being. Psychology is a science of human beings—rather than a master narrative based on white rats or salivating dogs.

In the case of psychoanalysis, we can observe the usual tension for any science between what is known and not yet known. Psychoanalysts' ideas have been a good example of "non-dogmatic dogmatism" (see Chen's commentary, this volume)—crossing the established borders of the social norms and meaning systems (i.e., countering existing dogmas) while arriving at new dogmatisms of their own. Opposites become each other—liberating

Making Our Ideas Clear, pages ix–xii
Copyright © 2015 by Information Age Publishing
All rights of reproduction in any form reserved.

the human mind leads to new bondage from which the next system of ideas could liberate the mind, anew. And so we move towards the infinity of human understanding of ourselves.

The reader of this volume has a unique access to an innovation in the psychoanalytic thought. One can learn here to appreciate the dialogue between two major Old and New Worlds' traditions of thought, and to see how both of these turn out to have filled major—yet interesting—epistemological gaps for contemporary cultural psychology. The psychoanalytic tradition of continental Europe has become a major source of social representations that focus on the role of sexuality in the human *psyche* and play the role of reorganizing the borders of sociomoral norms. As such, psychoanalysis has been highly pragmatic as a tool in the development of Occidental societies—far beyond its limited use on the therapist's couch. Yet in that success is also a failure—the fascination with the "forbidden topic" of sexuality that was liberated from its religious confines by Sigmund Freud has not led to the next logical step—to view in sexuality a form of alimentation. Perhaps this step is left for cultural psychology to take. Thinking in terms of utility, the act of eating is by far more profound for human existence than that of sexual intercourse. Or—before the reproductive success—the beloved idea of evolutionary psychologists—can ever happen, the offspring need to be fed.

A parallel system of thought to psychoanalysis that revolutionized occidental societies over the past century was born in the New World in the 1890s—*pragmatism* (William James) or *pragmaticism* (Charles S. Peirce) brought into social focus the general notion of usefulness in understanding our actions and forming our thoughts for clear communication. On the pages of the present volume these two traditions meet—albeit after both have been muddled by the so-called "post-modernist" flow of fascinating fashionable discourses that mix up society and knowledge, and politics and science (Valsiner, 2009). The present volume collects the pieces that remain—on both sides of the Atlantic—and enters into the discourse of building a new version of psychoanalytic thought that is linked with our newly developing cultural psychologies.

TRAJECTORIES FOR THE FUTURE

The present volume continues the investigation into the ideas of psychoanalysis that in our series was started by Salvatore and Zittoun (2011). Both of the editors of that volume are contributors to this one—joining in with the European voices into the otherwise North America-centered discourses about postmodernism, pragmatism, and psychodynamics. A number of themes in this volume could be the beginning for a new version of psychodynamic perspectives—perhaps to be labeled cultural-dynamic psychoanalysis. First of all, the reader encounters the impending relevance of two psychoanalysts who break with the older traditions—the celebrated English tank commander and psychoanalyst Wilfred Bion (1897–1979) and the Chilean psychoanalyst Ignacio Matte-Blanco (1908–1995), whose work is by far more connected with Italy than with his native land. In both cases the unconscious becomes presented as abstracted out of time—striving towards truth (Bion) or symmetrization (Matte-Blanco). The ideas of Melanie Klein have been productive in triggering new theoretical sophistication in psychoanalysis.

Bion's focus on *truth* brings his version of psychoanalysis to play a part in the cultural psychology of today. For cultural psychologies, the notion of *truth* is an abstracted meaning that operates within a society as a social representation (in Moscovici's terms) or as a hypergeneralized field-like sign (Valsiner, 2014). Bion's perspective is thus of interest for further development—both of cultural psychologies and of psychoanalytic theories. In contrast, Matte-Blanco's focus on symmetry <> asymmetry dynamics in the human mind is in contradiction with our contemporary cultural psychology. In psychoanalysis we can observe conceptualization of how inevitably asymmetric life experiences become symmetrized, with the mind becoming freed from the irreversibility of time. Such ontologization is a way of creating necessary cultural tools for surviving within the flow of the present. So—symmetry is set up in the service for real-life necessary asymmetry—between past and future. At the same time the reality of living is asymmetric, yet its account in psychoanalysis is not. As Orgav and Neuman (this volume) remind us, "[A] living organism exists on the boundary of symmetry and asymmetry, order and chaos. For the organism, whether on the biophysical level or the mental level, the ultimate phase of symmetry is death" (p. 280).

The pragmaticism of Charles Sanders Peirce is a convenient connection point of psychoanalysis and cultural psychologies. In his focus on the semiosis, which is a constant process of transformation of the interpretant we can see the ways in which the ontologization of the signs takes place. Salvatore (Chapter 6) emphasizes the recursive nature of sense-making, oriented to the unknown future:

> We can and must always interpret because no interpretation is conclusive: each triggers a further one, just as any step towards the horizon moves the horizon itself ahead. *Sensemaking is the incessant tension of filling the emptiness between language and the world.* (p. 159)

Recursivity in cultural psychological theory building will be a special target of analysis in our series (Beckstead, in press). The problem with that concept is its non-temporality—yet it is precisely the focus on temporality that cultural psychologies are after (Simão, Guimarães, & Valsiner, in press). We may need to think of *precursivity* instead—recursive processes that unfold in the direction of the not yet known future,

Sensemaking is oriented towards the future—hence, instead of truth and usefulness, we may need to focus on *imagination* and *generativity*. By bringing the notion of generativity into the theoretical discourse, Salvatore provides the core idea of how psychoanalytic thinking can innovate itself without losing touch with its orthodox pasts. The move from past to future goes through the negotiation of the actual and the possible—which is further covered by the Trajectory Equifinality Approach (Sato, Mori, & Valsiner, in press; forthcoming in 2015 in this series).

The main value of the present volume is to take a new look at the psychoanalytic enterprise through the lens of cultural psychologies of self and bring the question of interpersonal enactments in therapy to the focus of our attention. Together with the previous volume on psychoanalysis in this series (Salvatore & Zittoun, 2011), it fortifies the interest of cultural psychologies in the psychoanalytic phenomena. Yet the new theory of cultural psychoanalysis has not yet emerged—the ideas of Sigmund Freud, Melanie Klein, Wilfred Bion, Ignacio Matte-Blanco, Harry Stack Sullivan and others—remain there to be developed further. How such further development might happen is still unclear, but the goal orientation is set. Cultural psychologies have much to learn from various versions of psychoanalysis—except for the tendency of turning productive idea systems into orthodoxies.

—**Jaan Valsiner**
Aalborg, Denmark

REFERENCES

Beckstead, Z. (Ed.). (in press). *Cultural psychology of recursive processes.* Charlotte, NC: Information Age.

Salvatore, S., & Zittoun, T. (Eds.). (2011). *Cultural psychology and psychoanalysis: Pathways to synthesis.* Charlotte, NC: Information Age.

Sato, T., Mori, N., & Valsiner, J. (Eds.) (in press). *The trajectory equifinality approach.* Charlotte, NC: Information Age.

Simão, L. M., Guimarães, D. S., & Valsiner, J. (Eds.). (in press). *Temporality: Culture in the flow of human experience.* Charlotte, NC: Information Age.

Valsiner, J. (2009). Integrating psychology within the globalizing world: A requiem to the post-modernist experiment with *Wissenschaft. IPBS: Integrative Psychological & Behavioral Science, 43*(1), 1–21.

Valsiner, J. (2014). *Invitation to cultural psychology.* London, UK: Sage.

ACKNOWLEDGEMENTS

This project grew from a discussion with Jaan Valsiner in the winter of 2011. At the time, we were discussing my fascination with the influence that early American pragmatism had on Harry Stack Sullivan and interpersonal psychoanalysis. As I was a Postdoctoral Fellow at the William Alanson White Institute, I was just beginning to immerse myself in Sullivan's writing. Having been familiar with pragmatism from my undergraduate studies, helped me feel comfortable at the Institute, and made for an easier transition. So when Jaan suggested I compile and edit a book relating the two, it felt like a natural extension of my interest, even if I had never edited a book, or really thought about doing so before.

It is lucky that I had not, since at the time I did not realize what an endeavor it would be and that it would span the better part of four years. During this time, life, as it is wont to do, continued on. My wife and I moved from New York to Philadelphia, I began working at Haverford College, went from being a Postdoctoral Fellow, to an analytic (now fourth year!) candidate, got a dog, and had a child. The book and my relationship to it and its authors, has been a steady and constant (though at times stressful) companion throughout this time. Its ability to mark time and change makes its publication very meaningful to me.

It is also fortunate, that during this process I have had the support and encouragement of a number of people. I'd like to thank Jaan, first and foremost, for suggesting and backing the idea. I cherish his mentorship and guidance, from college and onward. My wife, Michelle has put up with this project for years. Her questions and comments have helped sharpen and clarify the ideas, and I am grateful for her continuous love and inspiration.

Making Our Ideas Clear, pages 1–2
Copyright © 2015 by Information Age Publishing
All rights of reproduction in any form reserved.

My parents and sister have rooted this project onward, despite not always understanding what it is about.

The book itself would not have been possible without the contributions of the fabulously talented (and patient) authors, whose work brings to life the concepts embedded throughout. I am also specifically thankful to Jonathan Weidenbaum, David Schweichler, and Mayer Bellehsen, for reading edits of chapters, introductions and conclusions. Being able to discuss many of the ideas in the book with them helped me develop a better understanding of the topics explored. The editing team at Information Age Publishers has been very helpful in ensuring the flow of the chapters. Lastly, I'd like to thank Ilana Simons whose incredible artwork graces the cover of this book. It was the final piece and one of my favorite parts!

Thank you!

—Philip Rosenbaum
Philadelphia, PA

INTRODUCTION

THE EFFECTS OF THE "POSTMODERN" TURN IN RELATIONAL PSYCHOANALYSIS

Philip J. Rosenbaum
Haverford College

THE POSTMODERN TURN IN RELATIONAL PSYCHOANALYSIS

For the past 30 years, psychoanalysis has incorporated insights from postmodern philosophy, including feminism and queer theory (Benjamin, 1988; Butler, 1990), deconstructionism (Fairfield, 2001), chaos theory (Harris, 2005), systems theory (Beebe & Lachmann, 2003), field theory (Fiscalini, 2007), and hermeneutics (Stern, 1997), undergoing a widely acknowledged "postmodern" or "relational" turn. Specifically, relational psychoanalysis has given greater emphasis to the ways interpersonal phenomena, including linguistic and discursive practices, structures and gives shape to how individuals interpret reality and their lived experiences. As the basis of meaning making, interpretation and subjective experiencing are strongly influenced by familial and cultural norms as well as societal

Making Our Ideas Clear, pages 1–20
Copyright © 2015 by Information Age Publishing
All rights of reproduction in any form reserved.

power structures. Broadly stated, relational psychoanalysis thus considers the ways relationships, culture, and context shape individual psychology and pathology (Greenberg & Mitchell, 1983).

While the broadness of relational psychoanalysis makes it difficult to concretely define, its emphasis on the social and cultural has clearly breathed new life into theoretical and clinical practice. Recent developments have applied postmodern ideas to analytic enterprises. These include studying the impact that trauma and dissociation have on self organization and experiencing (Bromberg, 1998; Stern, 1997; Stolorow, 2007), exploring the ubiquity of enactments within the analytic relationship (Levenson, 1979/2005), emphasizing the importance of individual subjectivity and intersubjectivity (Benjamin, 1988; Stolorow & Atwood, 1992; Stolorow, Atwood, & Orange, 2002), and democratizing of the analytic relationship (Aron, 1990, 1991).

The increasing acceptance and establishment of relational psychoanalysis has recently enabled authors to shift their attention to the consequences and challenges of relational psychoanalysis, rather than arguing for its viability as a theory (Boston Change Process Study Group, 2007; Bromberg, 2012; Shedler, 2010; Stern, 2012; Tublin, 2011). This trend is an important step in the development of relational practice and paradigm (Greenberg, 2001; Kuhn, 1962/1996). Adopting any philosophical perspective entails certain theoretical and practical commitments regarding how phenomena are experienced, understood, and studied. In other words, theory determines which phenomena are brought into greater focus and which fade into the background. Taking stock of these effects engages critics and helps prevent a theory from becoming stagnant through exploring thorny issues and areas of confusion, and specifying directions of future research and growth. Current efforts at assessing the state of relational psychoanalysis have focused on the theoretical and clinical consequences of applying relational theory.

Theoretical Questions and Controversies

Regarding the former, offering a comprehensive, nonreductive theory of how the self develops through interactions with real or imagined Others is the central theoretical problem of relational analysis (Benjamin, 1990; Mitchell, 1988; Target & Fonagy, 1996). Having successfully argued against the isolated and atomic self (Stolorow & Atwood, 1992), relational theorists are presently working to explain the self and its capacities in a way that avoids both upward reduction towards social and linguistic forces (Frie, 2011; Harris, 2011) and downwards reduction towards biology and drives. For example, critics have asked how relational theorists account for the existence of a self (Busch, 2001; Eagle, 2003; Mills, 2012). They reason that if language and culture structure the self, as often claimed by relational theorists, then what happens to the independent self that acts as an agent with free will? Instead, would not the self be a product of these cultural forces, stripping the idea of selfhood to at best an organism reacting to external forces? Building off this idea, critics also wonder if relational theorists are even able to speak of distinctly separate subjects and objects, when all meaningful development occurs within an interpersonal and now intersubjective context (Mills, 2012). In other words, what are the consequences of intersubjectivity becoming a theory of ontology (being)? Furthermore, considering the self a product of social relationships and language and not of *a priori* biological structures, how does relational theory account for embodied experience, or the way that our bodies provide us with the basis of an experiencing and acting self in the world (Frie, 2008)? Finally, when stripped of its driving developmental and causative power, what happens to the unconscious?

The efforts of relational thinkers to respond to these questions have led to admirable attempts at integrating recent advances in neuroscience, attachment literature, sociology, psychology, and phenomenology (Bromberg, 2003; Stolorow, 2009; Stolorow & Atwood, 1992). Complex theories attempt to account for the co-constructed or bidirectional relationship between self and other and self and environment (see, for instance, Harris, 2005). While theoretically sophisticated, they are often dense, unwieldy, and abstract, leading to criticisms of creating more confusion than clarity (Mills, 2012).

Clinical Questions and Controversies

These theoretical questions have practical consequences. For instance, without a traditional conception of a self, how do relational psychoanalysts understand the process of therapeutic change and growth? While relational thinkers would likely argue that change occurs within and through the two-person analytic relationship, how this happens remains to be answered. After all, recognizing the uniqueness of treatment, that truly no two treatments are the same (Bromberg, 2012), has led to a dismantling of classical technique, to the point where some analysts have wondered whether any specific technical guidelines are maintained at all (Tublin, 2011). Furthermore, as the importance of the analysts' subjectivity and feelings towards the patient are increasingly considered transformative, authors are still exploring how to utilize this insight (see, for instance, Stern's 2004 discussion and interesting resolution of this topic).

The uncertainty about what is transformative within the clinical context has led critics to question the applicability of relational theory (Aragno,

2011; Frank, 1998). Specifically, they have attacked the postmodern appeal to contextual forms of knowing, rather than universal truths, as reflecting a lack of theoretical comprehensiveness and rigor, ultimately leading to a situation where all knowledge becomes relative to context (Mills, 2012). They fear that the practical effects of the postmodern turn weaken the analytic enterprise. For example, if analyst and analysand are mutually creating each other, as some analysts suggest, then what happens to analytic authority (Busch, 2001)? Do analysts really not have some knowledge of what ails their patients and how to help? Similarly, what becomes of analytic technique in the postmodern world? If analysts do not know if certain interventions or approaches work better than others, what does this mean for teaching and justifying analytic treatment methods in the contemporary age of managed care?

These questions and critiques are germane to relational psychoanalysis interests in providing effective clinical practice and a philosophically robust theory. As stated earlier, they reflect the philosophical and practical issues that relational thinkers and their critiques are currently grappling with. However, rather than signal the need to abandon ship (as some critics suggest), they indicate areas needing greater clarity and elaboration, as well as the possibilities of dialogue and growth. As should be clear, a willingness to engage in dialogue and embrace a multitude of theories and perspectives is one of the hallmarks of postmodern philosophy and the relational turn in psychoanalysis (Fairfield, 2001). Accordingly, this book continues that tradition by reintroducing the voice of American pragmatism.

WHY PRAGMATISM?

History of Pragmatism and Psychoanalysis

There are a number of reasons to apply American pragmatism to contemporary psychoanalysis. First, pragmatism played a historically important role in the development of relational psychoanalysis. According to Mitchell and Harris (2004), pragmatism is the foundation of American thinking about psychoanalysis. They argue that the theories of pragmatism and semiotics (signs) described primarily by William James and Charles Sanders Peirce (and to a lesser extent George Herbert Mead and John Dewey) contributed significantly to the interpersonal school of psychoanalysis, and then again later to relational psychoanalysis (Greenberg & Mitchell; 1983; Harris, 2011; Mitchell & Harris; 2004). Pragmatic ideas of self, the role of experience, epistemology (how the world is known), and theories of mind were important to Harry Stack Sullivan (Evans, 1996; Harris, 2011; Perry, 1982). As one of the first analysts to create an alternative to classical

Freudian analysis, Sullivan articulated the centrality of the interpersonal field for understanding individual psychopathology. This enabled him to successfully work with schizophrenics, a population that up until then was not considered appropriate for analysis (Greenberg & Mitchell, 1983). Sullivan's work grounded later interpersonal and relational ideas, and in this sense, while his pragmatic background has been relatively forgotten, it has left a lasting imprint.

That pragmatism has largely been forgotten from psychoanalysis speaks more to the difficulties of engaging the early pragmatic writings than necessarily theoretical differences or unbridgeable gulfs. The writing and works of the notable pragmatists, including Peirce, James, Mead, and Dewey, are rarely systematic or comprehensive. Indeed, the pragmatists do not always share the same essential beliefs about what they key tenants of pragmatism are, or which ideas are more important than others. This makes it difficult to present a central pragmatic canon or dogma. Finally, despite their efforts to be clear and practical, much of their writing is complicated, dense, and abstract.

Similarities and Differences

Despite these difficulties, pragmatic theory is a voice old and familiar—new and different. Readers familiar with relational psychoanalysis will likely recognize many of the central themes of pragmatism (Harris, 2011). As will be discussed more thoroughly in the following section, pragmatic theories consider individuals actively interacting within the world. They emphasize the importance of creativity, imagination, indeterminacy, and uncertainty as well as the centrality of individual experience and of multiple forms of knowing (pluralism). Pragmatic theories also do not consider the self as an isolated and unitary entity, but social and fragmented.

At the same time, pragmatism differs considerably from contemporary postmodern perspectives. Indeed, these differences make dialogue between the two fields worthwhile. For instance, as indicated by the title of this book, pragmatism considers the importance of making ideas clear. While this is not to say that postmodernism does not value clarity, what exactly clarity means and how to achieve it are important questions within the current climate that extols the importance of not knowing and ambiguity. That ideas can be clear speaks to the pragmatic consideration of an objective reality. There are different pragmatic ideas of how one experiences reality, such as Peirce's semiotic mediation and James's radical empiricism, but pragmatists generally agree that reality exists and is interpreted and understood through active participation. Thus, they differ from views that consider reality independently waiting to be discovered, as for Freud, but also from the radical versions of social constructionism endorsed by some postmodernists and psychoanalysts (for instance, Hoffman, 1983, 1991).

Pragmatism provides an alternative way to conceptualize phenomena of interest to contemporary psychoanalysts. As an established and comprehensive philosophy, pragmatism also provides a solid basis for how these phenomena are understood and, in turn, how they can inform clinical practice. This helps to address some of the current philosophical issues and critiques while not having to adapt an entirely new theoretical outlook.

Structure and Aims

In the following section, a number of important pragmatic ideas and thinkers are introduced. Given the lack of central pragmatic canon, these ideas are not meant to provide a comprehensive overview of pragmatic theory, or even a survey to all the different pragmatic thinkers (see Thayer, 1982; Stuhr, 2000; and Menand, 2002 for introductions), but rather introduce the reader to the themes and ideas that underlie the chapters of this book. Notably, given the influence that Peirce and James had on the field of pragmatism and on psychoanalysis, the introduction focuses primarily on their thinking. When appropriate, book chapters are matched to the main aspect of pragmatic theory used by the author.

The book itself is divided into three sections. Beginning with an overview of the history of pragmatism in psychoanalysis, the first section shows how contemporary thought can be grounded within pragmatic theory and method. Doing so contextualizes important clinical theories and demonstrates pragmatism's continued relevance for today's climate. Building off this, the second section applies pragmatic thinking to contemporary questions, arguing for its usefulness in understanding important philosophical problems, such as epistemology, free will, and meaning-making processes. The final section explores at how pragmatic method can inform clinical practice. These chapters demonstrate the usefulness of pragmatism in working with borderline patients, dreams, clinical technique, and finally for integrating with neuroscience. Commentaries follow each of the three sections, taking up key issues and ideas of some or all of the specific chapters, providing dialogue and the opportunity to explore some of the ideas in depth.

By both providing an overview of important principles of pragmatic theory and also an in-depth look at their application, this book demonstrates how pragmatic philosophy helps address important practical and philosophical questions. Exploring pragmatism's influence on seminal thinkers and on contemporary issues this book explicates in some detail the influence that pragmatism has had on early analysis. In this respect, while pragmatism often is mentioned as a guiding influence on psychoanalysis, this has been rarely spelled out in as much detail as accomplished in these chapters. Finally, in addition to responding the challenges described earlier, this book's aim is to help analysts be able to take a pragmatic perspective to future clinical and theoretical questions.

PRAGMATIC BEGINNINGS

The Pragmatic Maxim

As the well-known story goes, pragmatism is the most original American philosophy.[1] Its founding in the late part of the 19th century grew from the now infamous discussions of the metaphysical club—a group of Harvard-educated men who met in Cambridge, Massachusetts to discuss philosophical issues in the 1870s (Menand, 2002; Thayer, 1982). At the time, the prevailing philosophical and metaphysical conflict focused on the ongoing discussion between the newer scientific studies of men and the older moral and religious accounts. Science was seen as offering a more factual and data-driven explanation of experience, but not fully grasping the richness and complexity of lived experience. Alternatively, religious and moral accounts were more aesthetically pleasing, but not rigorous. They were also overly reliant upon *a priori* categories and ideas that could not be convincingly demonstrated (Thayer, 1982). Interestingly, the conflict between scientific and religious claims that preoccupied philosophers since the time of Descartes continues through the present day. Its echoes resound in contemporary discussions of whether to use manualized and empirically validated treatments considered more "scientific," or to provide a more holistic and aesthetic therapeutic experience. Much like today, arguments between philosophers frequently dissolved into intractable positions that were rarely resolved. Perhaps suitably, pragmatism began as a method intended to resolve these differences of opinion[2] and also clarifying abstract ideas.

Charles S. Peirce, an original member of the metaphysical club (and subject of a number of chapters in this book) addressed this question in his seminal paper and inspiration of this book's title, "How to Make Our Ideas Clear" (1878/1982). In this article, Peirce argues that clarity results from successfully considering the practical effects of having a certain conception or belief. Specifically, he stated what later became the pragmatic maxim:

> It appears, then, that the rule for the attaining the third grade of clearness of apprehension is as follows: consider what effects which might conceivably have practical bearings we conceive the object of our conception to have. Then, our conception of these effects is the whole of our conception of the object. (p. 88)

In emphasizing the effects of thought, Peirce argued that what matters are its practical consequences such as the actions it enables or limits. For instance, Peirce (1878/1982) discusses the question of how to define hardness. He states, "Evidently that it will not be scratched by many other substances. The whole conception of this quality, as of every other, lies in its conceived effects. There is absolutely no difference between a hard thing and a soft thing so long as they are not brought to the test" (p. 88). In framing the question this way, Peirce highlights that our conception of hardness depends upon considering the effects (not being scratched) as well as the practical circumstances in which we need something hard, like when we use a hammer to bang in a nail. He further notes, that it would not be illogical to "modify our questions, and ask what prevents us from saying that all hard bodies remain perfectly soft until they are touched, when their hardness increases with the pressure until they are scratched" (p. 89). However, he concludes that while from a logical perspective this would not necessarily be false, in considering the effects of a conception and not the arrangement of facts roundabout thinking is avoided.

The pragmatic maxim resolves the dispute between science and morality by considering them each important and necessary aspects of human conduct. The clarification of the different questions, hypothesis, and meanings they ask dissolves the conflict between them (Thayer, 1982). Rather, they are both forms of inquiry into experience. In her chapter comparing William James and Sigmund Freud, Tania Zittoun discusses the role of pragmatism for clarifying ideas and generating knowledge. She discusses how, despite their theories being worlds apart, the pragmatic approach and methodology of these two men link them in profound ways. She reminds us of how both Freud and James constantly updated and evolved their theory to account for new data and the limitations in their existing theories. Although Freud was interested in creating a total system, he remained flexible enough in his thinking to continuously accommodate new phenomena. While at times this gives an impression of inconsistency, it also reflects the legacy of psychoanalysis as focused on a understanding a problem and a willingness to adapt. In her commentary, Katharina Rothe locates the pragmatic maxim for Freud at the juncture between scientific research and clinical healing.

Some General Features and Differences of Pragmatism

The pragmatic maxim has been applied to phenomena that interest psychoanalysis, while retaining an attitude of inquiry, investigation, and theoretical rigor well suited to today's postmodern climate. In this respect, the common refrain that pragmatism is overly practical, providing a bare-bones philosophy, does not take into account the diversity and creativity of the pragmatists. However, before moving on to the more specific pragmatic thinkers and their ideas, there are some general pragmatic ideas and themes worth highlighting.

Active Meaning Making: Thinking as a Tool

Perhaps most important is the recognition of the "inseparable connection between rational cognition and rational purpose" (Dewey, 1931/1982, p. 24). Peirce, James, and Dewey all believed that thought is both experimental and purposive (Thayer, 1982). For instance, Peirce emphasized that rational thought must have a concrete effect upon an individual's lived conduct. Alternatively, James and Dewey considered thought as a tool used as part of the meaningful striving of human actions, adaptations, and adjustments to reality.

The purposeful and experimental nature of thought ensures for both men that individuals are not passive receptors of reality. Rather, individuals are active participants who are engaged in the process of interpreting behavior as part of purposefully adapting and pre-adapting to the future. The pragmatists had different considerations of how this occurs, but each considered it a product of the ongoing interaction between an individual and their environment.

Future Orientation

In considering thought in this manner, the pragmatists emphasized that thinking is directed towards the future (Peirce, 1905/1982). How well active meaning making prepares individuals to engage in future activity provides a way to evaluate the effectiveness of an idea. This ensures that the pragmatists are not total relativists. Although they maintain different standards of evaluating ideas' effectiveness, their concern is very much with lived reality and experience.

Truth and the Importance of Fallibility

This speaks to a corresponding value—namely, the role of doubt, error, and not knowing for generating greater knowledge. For instance, Peirce believed that truth was derived from consensual agreement of a group of inquirers who arrived at the same conclusions. Since agreement hardly ever is 100 percent, his theory emphasizes the role that error has in motivating further understanding. Alternatively, James broadly considers truth as practical. Truths are effective at influencing future experiences. Error can play an important part in modifying beliefs, furthering inquiry, and expanding knowledge. Locating doubt and indeterminacy within a process of generating new knowledge provides a counterpoint to the charge of contemporary psychoanalysis that claims that the emphasis on not knowing makes a virtue out of a vice.

Rejection of the Atomistic Self

Lastly, the pragmatists were unified in rejecting the concept of the isolated and atomic self. Some of this is apparent in Peirce's ideas of a community of inquirers who set truths and then for the most part forget them (later elaborated as conventional signs like language). Moreover, in rejecting the consideration of *a priori* categories of experience, while embracing an altered form of empiricism that considered individuals active in their construction of reality, the pragmatists, and especially James, moved away from philosophy that kept the self split off and isolated from experience.

Whatever Works or Does It? Peirce's Pragmatism

Scientific Process

Peirce utilized the pragmatic maxim from the perspective of a logician, a mathematician, and a scientist. His interests were in how it makes ideas clear so they can be tested and logically studied. Accordingly, the common translation of considering the effects of "doing whatever works" is a gross misrepresentation and reduction of the pragmatic enterprise as defined by Peirce (Harris, 2011). Specifically, while the statement emphasizes that something had a practical effect, namely, it worked, it fails to locate it within a logical scientific process of inquiry. Peirce considered humans as naïve scientists, continuously revising their beliefs and ideas of the way things work to account and prepare for new experience.

He argued that among the different methods of establishing and fixing belief, the most effective at resolving inconsistent beliefs was the method of science (Peirce, 1877/1982). For Peirce, beliefs lead to action. It follows that inactivity stems from an experience of doubt. Interestingly, in arguing for the method of science, Peirce acknowledged that individual beliefs could become set in nonrational and inconsistent patterns, leading to doubt and uncertainty. While these ideas may have been useful for a period of time, the experience of doubt indicates that they are no longer effective at enabling activity. The painfulness of the experience of doubting stimulates individuals to develop new, hopefully more effective beliefs. Peirce deemed the method of science the most effective form of fixing a belief, because it enabled an experimental process whereby individuals could work with real-world consequences. In his system, individuals are active, creating hypotheses and then, based upon their experienced effects, revising beliefs and ideas as necessary.

Scientific inquiry generates a process of consensual validation of hypotheses, which in turn establishes truths. In other words, for Peirce, truth emerges from the consensual validation of a community of inquirers who through inquiry reached the same conclusions. As such, truths do not have to correspond with the objective world but are verified through agreement of effects as part of an ongoing process of investigation. He identified a series of logical inferences used to develop beliefs and truths, including abduction, induction, and deduction, which are not discussed here.

The view of science that Peirce offers has important implications for contemporary psychoanalysis. In considering hypothesis generating and testing to be central, he not only identifies an implicit clinical process, but also suggests a way for clinicians to investigate its empirical claims. This answers the charges of relativism by locating the acquisition of knowledge within a scientific process. However, unlike the scientism of today, it provides a sufficiently supple process to accommodate a wide swath of experiences.

For example, in her chapter, Jean Knox argues for the importance of the scientific method for psychoanalysis. She draws from contemporary neuroscience and empirical research to verify the assumptions of the relational mode. She pays particular attention to the role that trauma has in limiting the ability of the self to imagine and how relational therapy can help restart this process.

Georgia Lepper applies the pragmatic method more directly in her analysis of transcripts of analytic sessions. She uses conversation analysis to follow the turn taking that occurs in analytic sessions, concluding how open-ended questions lead to increased dialogue and collaboration between patient and analyst. Since analysts value a specific type of dialogue, from a pragmatic perspective, these types of questions have more of a payout than others.

Actions and Enactments

Action is clearly central to the process of inquiry. Hypotheses are attempts at making sense of phenomena, behaviors, and experiences. To the extent they are useful they lead to new beliefs that enable future actions. However, Peirce did not consider pragmatisms purpose, solely the production of action, but rather the fulcrum to generating future meanings. Actions are in other words, intermediaries between attributing meaning to an idea and then observing and experiencing the consequences of it (Dewey, 1931/1982). Sergio Salvatore builds off this insight to argue for a pragmatic view of meaning making that considers how meanings are constructed as consequence of action and thus cannot exist prior to them. This idea differs from the classical idea in psychoanalysis that considers meanings existing *a priori* in the world prior to acting. Drawing both from pragmatic theory and the analytic theory of Matte Blanco, he develops a dynamic model that articulates the process where meanings develop through interaction.

Considering action as central to meaning making fits the interpersonal tradition that values the importance of enactments in generating therapeutic growth and change (Levenson, 1979/2005). Pragmatic theory agrees with the interpersonal insight that speaking with the patient is also acting with them. Change results from being able to identify habitual actions and ways of making meaning, or perhaps in Peirce's language, how beliefs had previously been fixed, and then using the analysis as an experimental playground to generate new styles (Greenberg, 1991). This idea is consistent with research that has found insight less likely to precede change and more likely to follow it. However, it refutes the solely behaviorist ideas of only generating actions ("whatever works") instead, needing to be located within the patients unique meaning making system.

Signs and Intersubjectivity

Pragmatism goes further in offering an account of how words and language function as actions. Specifically, Peirce considers them as conventional symbols, a category of signs, and part of his semiotic or sign-based theory of meaning making. He developed his theory as a logical account of how meaning is made based upon the continual interpretation of signs. He intended that his theory would apply to all organisms, and thus the interpreter does not necessarily have to be human (it could also be a plant, for instance); however, for our purposes we will consider how his theory relates to thinking and feeling as well as interpersonal relationships and intersubjectivity (Harris, 2011).

Peirce's semiotic theory provides a complicated and technical account of the way a sign relates to both an object and an interpreter. Recall, that he did not consider thought as passively mirroring or picturing objects in the world, but of generating beliefs and habits to enable activity. He thus included an interpreter in his definition of a sign, broadening it from the definition that depicts a relationship between an object and its representation, or what stands for it. When considering human sign usage, he defines the sign as "something which stands to somebody for something in some respect or capacity" (quoted in Lincourt & Olczak, 1974, p. 82). The sign represents some aspect of the object to a person, in this case the interpretant.

As the interpretant only knows the sign, or the aspect of the object being represented, subsequent to the act of interpretation, the interpretant itself becomes a sign (specifically, an object) open for interpretation. Signification continues onwards in this manner, until the object is known (Lincourt & Olczak, 1974; Rosa, 2007). This occurs since knowledge of the original sign–object relationship only becomes known through subsequent interpretations (the effects) about that relationship. Considered within an interpersonal context, Peirce's structure "distinguishes between the word, its meaning for the speaker, and its distinct but overlapping quasi shared meaning for the listener" (Mitchell & Harris, 2004, p. 171).

Accordingly, Peirce's semiotic theory offers a philosophical basis of intersubjectivity (Mitchell & Harris, 2004). In discussing how signs function between individuals, he argues that the aspect of the object being represented by the sign comes to exist for the interpreter in a real way (Lincourt & Olczak, 1974). Peirce reasons that since individuals are members of a shared community, they acquire the consensual meaning of signs (which can be thought of as symbolic but also habitual) through interpersonal interactions. During communication, the shared meanings echo and overlap with the more idiosyncratic ones such that the listener experiences the thoughts and feelings of the speaker. Indeed, in this respect, Peirce, who along with other pragmatists argued against the isolated and atomic self, considered others crucial for the development of the self-symbol that allows individuals to experience themselves in a unified and consistent manner.

Semiotics influences a number of chapters in this book. Philip Rosenbaum considers how Peirce's semiotic theory can be applied to Sullivan's clinical theory of different forms of experience providing a philosophical basis for interpersonal analysis. Robert White is interested in whether and how the semiotic process stops, particularly as it relates to Wilfred Bion's concept of the infinite. Finally, Matti Keinänen draws on the different categories of signs articulated by Peirce to develop his model of psychosemiosis as a way of conceptualizing the mind–body problem. Drawing from Peirce, he offers a treatment model for working with a Finnish population of borderline college students through which they learn to internalize the symbolic function of their therapist.

Expansion and Contraction: James's Pragmatism

Peirce's unique contributions to pragmatism were his attempts at employing the pragmatic maxim in a logical and scientific manner to a number of phenomena. However, despite the richness of his theories, pragmatism only became popular when William James defended it in 1897, some twenty years after Peirce's original papers. While some of this likely had to do with a combination of Peirce's writing being overly technical and his social failings, James's interests as an educator and humanist played a role in his appropriation of pragmatism into a more accessible theory.

Specifically, James differed from Peirce in what he felt was the usefulness of disambiguating questions and clarifying concepts (Dewey, 1931/1982). As a humanist, James argued that the pragmatic maxim could be used to determine how certain philosophical problems and questions influenced individual conduct. James emphasized the practical, the particular, and the experiential. Accordingly, his developments limited the generalizing principle of the pragmatic maxim[3] but expanded its utility to looking at a plurality of actions (Dewey, 1931/1982).

Pluralism

When applying the pragmatic method to the study of and different claims of truth, James famously concluded that truth was determined by the relative benefit of the practical consequences of an idea to its relative demerit. For instance, he applied the pragmatic method when comparing monism to pluralism. In evaluating the consequences if monism were to be true, he concluded that it is the same as a closed universe where everything is completed and fixed, leaving no room for the future and for growth. This leads to a rationalistic attitude and dogmatically rigid beliefs. Alternatively, he equates pluralism to the open universe, which takes the possibility of an undetermined and malleable future into account. A pluralistic universe allows for empiricism and values indeterminacy, novelty, and growth (James, 1907/1982).

This view informed his ideas of pluralism or that there can be many truths, whose value depends to some extent on whether they contribute to ones fulfillment and value in the world. Pluralism honors the multiple intersections and forms of knowing, including public knowledge and experiential, religious, and spiritual knowing (Harris, 2011). Notably, it does not lead to a type of "anything goes" perspectivism. Rather, for James, truths must be consistent with previous truths. When they clash and conflict with each other, the disagreement needs to be resolved through either rejecting a previous truth, stretching a current one, or establishing a new truth.

Of course, James's idea of truth that honors varying forms of knowing leading to satisfaction differs considerably from more authoritative models of knowing. In this respect, it is consistent with the contemporary ethos that values multiple forms of knowing. In his chapter, Michael Mance explores the different ways pragmatic theories of knowledge are expressed in psychoanalysis. Mance discuses the specifics of analytic knowledge, such as they way analysts learn about the inner lives of their patients.

Radical Empiricism

James's commitment to multiple forms of knowing and pluralism inform his theory of radical empiricism. As a committed empiricist (even before being a pragmatist), James valued the individual's experience of the particular above accounts of the abstract and the general (James, 1997). In applying his pragmatic perspective of truth to empiricism, he felt that he was extending it to its logical limits (Dewey, 1931/1982) and in this respect considered personal experiences as the only material worthy of philosophic debate (James, 1997; 1890/1950). Briefly, his doctrine of radical empiricism argues that individuals directly perceive and experience reality through a continuous process of relating it to their experience. They perceive not just the sense data of reality (perceptions), as described by traditional empiricists, but also how they connect and relate to other aspects of experience. James considered these experienced relationships as creating a thick and rich universe that is real and can be meaningfully studied. Parts of connection hold together from moment to moment creating a coherent structure and leading to knowledge of the world.

In his wide-ranging chapter on the continued relevance William James's philosophy for psychoanalysis, Jon Weidenbaum discusses the importance of radical empiricism for the development of James's thinking. Specifically, he describes how James's philosophy embraces embodied experience and processes of change while retaining a view of the self as an active agent in the world. Through doing so, Weidenbaum provides psychoanalysis with an alternative to phenomenological accounts of the self, addressing many of the concerns about contemporary analysis.

Multiple Selves and Subjectivity

The centrality of active meaning making in James's theory (as well as Peirce's) refutes claims that pragmatism considers the mind a blank slate waiting for experience to be written on it. Perception does not function passively, taking in the world as an idle spectator, but actively as an agent. In an individual's experience of the world, James argues that observation always entails selection, relating current experience to previous experiences, desires, expectations, and so forth. One cannot perceive without acting. According to James, what we see is guided by our interests, passions, and beliefs. Indeed, one of the values of the pragmatic maxim is to make these clear so that we can act and perceive with greater discipline and awareness.

This viewpoint distances pragmatism from both spectator and correspondence theories of reality. As we have seen earlier with Peirce, truth reflects consensus and not definition, while James finds truth in the satisfaction and plurality of practices. Both of these, though particularly James's, lead to a pragmatic view of the self quite different from the atomistic and isolated versions. In this view, the self does not exist prior to experiences, but develops through and after them. The importance of activity in the development of mind can be found in the distinction between an internal "I" self and a social "me" self, made by Peirce, James, and George Herbert Mead. Each of them considered the social "me" developing before the reflective "I." Of the three, Mead provided the most comprehensive theory of this process (Wiley, 1994). He described the importance of the generalized other, noting that through role-playing games, children first learn to take the general role of other as their own. This view exists before the child learns to distinguish the differences in intent, goals, expectations, and so forth of the different parties, in respect to him- or herself (Gillespie, 2003; Mead, 1967). By first positing the existence of the generalized other, the child eventually develops the capacity to recognize himself or herself as a unique and embodied individual.

A dialogical relationship has been hypothesized as existing between the external "me" selves and the internal "I" that has been elaborated into theories emphasizing the multivoiced self, or in other words the theory of multiple self-states (Bromberg, 1996; Hermans, 2001; Hermans & Kempen, 1993; Stern, 2004). These popular theories provide an account of how the self sensitively responds to differences in context and relationships. Clinically, they emphasize the process of dissociation as a way of explaining how the self can know and experience something, such as trauma, but not be aware of knowing it. As Mayer Bellehsen discusses, dissociation cuts the feedback loop of activity that the social self uses to develop. In his exploration of the effects of trauma upon couples, he describes how spouses serve the role of "Other" in restarting this process so that the trauma can be integrated.

Of course, dialogue can also occur internally, within the self, though self-talk, thoughts, and dreams. The question of how the voices of others are internalized and identified has long been important to psychoanalysis. Using Bion's idea that individuals sleep in order to dream, Yair Neumann and Yariv Orgad generate a novel approach to dream interpretation focusing on how the dream language works to integrate experience. Through analyzing the dream reports of kindergarten students, they develop a theory of the unconscious processes that occur during dreaming and sleep through which children internalize the voice of the other as part of the development of self.

CONCLUSIONS

Pragmatism offers a constructive, effective, and also novel way to consider many of the important aspects of contemporary psychoanalysis. As discussed throughout this introduction, the pragmatic emphasis on the usefulness and functionality of ideas leads to comprehensive theories about ideas that interest contemporary analysts. For example, pragmatic thinking offers an account of intersubjectivity considering the individual as always existing within relationships mediated by signs that are knowable and usable as a result of the effects that they have. The pragmatic concern of being able to minutely detail this relationship can be applied to understanding not only infant–mother communication but ongoing processes of relating between adults (i.e., Muller, 1996).

Indeed, the utility of pragmatic theory and the pragmatic method is demonstrated in the variety of topics covered throughout this book. Ranging from the historical to the theoretical, clinical, and integrative, the chapters display how pragmatism can lead to novel and creative ideas. As achieving imaginative ways of thinking and playing has become increasingly important to contemporary analysis (Bromberg, 1996; Stern, 1997, 2004; Stolorow, Atwood, & Orange, 2002), it is clear that pragmatism has had and continues to have a lot to offer.

NOTES

1. Dewey (1931/1982) considers this idea false, noting that Peirce drew pragmatism from a distinction made by Kant between *pragmatic* and *practical*, with the latter referring to *a priori* moral laws and the former to experience and learned behaviors.
2. In many respects, that resolving disputes among a group of gentleman provided the basis for a new philosophy is oddly suitable for a discussion of pragmatisms influence on psychoanalysis. Moreover, as Michael Mance notes in his chapter, it is interesting to note the role that groups and the relationship between members played in the development of pragmatism, psychoanalysis ("the inner circle") and interpersonal theory ("the animal names").
3. The different uses and directions that James took pragmatism infuriated Peirce so much that he later renamed his own philosophy "pragmaticism," a name so intentionally ugly that no one would adopt it.

REFERENCES

Aragno, A. (2011). Listening with a third ear, a second heart, and a sixth sense: Standing on the shoulders of Theodor Reik. *Psychoanalytic Review, 98*, 183–204.

Aron, L. (1990). One and two person psychologies and the method of psychoanalysis. *Psychoanalytic Psychology, 7*, 475–485.

Aron, L. (1991). The patient's experience of the analyst's subjectivity. *Psychoanalytic Dialogues, 1*, 29–51.

Beebe, B., & Lachmann, F. (2003). The relational turn in psychoanalysis: A dyadic systems view from infant research. *Contemporary Psychoanalsyis, 39*(3), 379–409.

Benjamin, J. (1988). *The bonds of love: Psychoanalysis, feminism, and the problem of domination.* New York, NY: Pantheon Books.

Boston Change Process Study Group (BCPSG). (2007). The foundational level of psychodynamic meaning: Implicit process in relation to conflict, defense, and the dynamic unconscious. *International Journal of Psychoanalysis, 88*, 843–860.

Bromberg, P. M. (1996). Standing in the spaces: The multiplicity of self and the psychoanalytic relationship. *Contemporary Psychoanalysis, 32*, 509–535.

Bromberg, P. M. (1998). *Standing in the spaces.* Hillsdale, NJ: The Analytic Press.

Bromberg, P. M. (2003). Something this way comes: Trauma, dissociation, and conflict: The space where psychoanalysis, cognitive science, and neuroscience overlap. *Psychoanalytic Psychology, 20,* 558–574.

Bromberg, P. M. (2012). Stumbling along and hanging in: If this be technique make the most of it! *Psychoanalytic Inquiry, 32,* 3–17. doi: 10.1080/07351690.2011.553161

Busch, F. (2001). Are we losing our mind? *Journal of the American Psychoanalytic Association, 49,* 739–751.

Butler, J. (1990). *Gender trouble: Feminism and the subversion of identity.* New York, NY: Routledge.

Dewey, J. (1982). The development of American pragmatism. In H. S. Thayer (Ed.), *Pragmatism: The classic writings* (pp. 23–40). Indianapolis, IN: Hackett. (Original work published 1931)

Eagle, M. N. (2003). The postmodern turn in psychoanalysis: A critique. *Psychoanalytic Psychology, 20,* 411–424.

Evans, F. B. (1996). *Harry Stack Sullivan: Interpersonal theory and psychotherapy.* New York, NY: Routledge.

Fairfield, S. (2001). Analyzing multiplicity: A postmodern perspective on some current theories of subjectivity. *Psychoanalytic Dialogues, 11,* 221–251.

Fiscalini, J. (2007). The coparticipant field: Commentary on a paper by Juan Tubert-Oklander. *Psychoanalytic Dialogues, 17,* 133–141.

Frank, G. (1998). The intersubjective school of psychoanalysis: Concerns and questions. *Psychoanalytic Psychology, 15,* 420–423.

Frie, R. (2008). Fundamentally embodied: The experience of psychological agency. *Contemporary Psychoanalysis, 44,* 367–376.

Frie, R. (2011). Situated experience: Psychological agency, meaning, and morality in worldly contexts. *International Journal of Psychoanalytic Self Psychology, 6,* 340–351.

Gillespie, A. T. (2003). Supplementarity and surplus: Moving between the dimensions of otherness. *Culture & Psychology, 9,* 209–220.

Greenberg, J. R. (1991). *Oedipus and beyond: A clinical theory.* Cambridge, MA: Harvard University Press.

Greenberg, J. R. (2001). The analyst's participation: A new look. *Journal of the American Psychoanalytic Association, 49,* 359–381.

Greenberg, J. R., & Mitchell, S. A. (1983) *Object relations in psychoanalytic theory.* Cambridge, MA: Harvard University Press.

Harris, A. E. (2005). *Gender as soft assembly (Relational perspectives book series).* New York, NY: Routledge.

Harris, A. E. (2011). The relational tradition: Landscape and canon. *Journal of the American Psychoanalytic Association, 59,* 701–735.

Hermans, H. J. M. (2001). The dialogical self: Towards a theory of personal and cultural positioning. *Culture & Psychology,* 7, 243–281. doi: 10.1177/1354067X017300

Hermans, H. J. M., & Kempen, H. J. G. (1993). *The dialogical self: Meaning as movement.* San Diego, CA: Academic Press

Hoffman, I. Z. (1983). The patient as interpreter of the analyst's experience. *Contemporary Psychoanalysis, 19,* 389–322.

Hoffman, I. Z. (1991). Discussion: Towards a social-constructionist view of the psychoanalytic situation. *Psychoanalytic Dialogues, 1,* 74–105.

James, W. (1950). *Principles of psychology: Volumes I & II.* Mineola, NY: Dover. (Original work published 1890)

James, W. (1982). The tigers in India. In H. S. Thayer (Ed.), *Pragmatism: The classic writings* (pp. 245–248). Indianapolis, IN: Hackett. (Original work published 1895)

James, W. (1982). Pragmatism's conception of truth. In H. S. Thayer (Ed.), *Pragmatism: The classic writings* (pp. 227–244). Indianapolis, IN: Hackett. (Original work published 1907).

James, W. (1997). *The meaning of truth* (Great books in philosophy). Amherst, NY: Prometheus Books.

Kuhn, T. S. (1996). *The structure of scientific revolutions.* Chicago, IL: University of Chicago Press. (Original work published 1962)

Levenson, E. A. (2005). *The fallacy of understanding.* New York, NY: Routledge. (Original work published 1979)

Lincourt, J. M., & Olczak, P.V. (1974). C. S. Peirce and H. S. Sullivan on the human self. *Psychiatry, 37,* 78–84.

Mead, G. H. (1967). *Mind, self and society: From the standpoint of a social behaviorist* (Works of George Herbert Mead, Vol. 1). Chicago, IL: University of Chicago Press.

Menand, L. (2002). *The metaphysical club: A story of ideas in America.* New York, NY: Ferrar, Straus, and Giroux.

Mitchell, S. (1988). *Relational concepts in psychoanalysis.* Cambridge, MA: Harvard University Press.

Mitchell, S. A., & Harris, A. (2004). What's American about American psychoanalysis. *Psychoanalytic Dialogues, 14,* 165–191.

Mills, J. (2012). *Conundrums: A critique of relational psychoanalysis.* New York, NY: Routledge.

Muller, J. P. (1996). *Beyond the psychoanalytic dyad: Developmental semiotics in Freud, Peirce and Lacan.* London, UK: Routledge Publications.

Peirce, C. S. (1982). The fixation of belief. In H. S. Thayer (Ed.), *Pragmatism: The classic writings* (pp. 61–78). Indianapolis, IN: Hackett. (Original work published 1877)

Peirce, C. S. (1982). How to make our ideas clear. In H. S. Thayer (Ed.), *Pragmatism: The classic writings* (pp. 79–100). Indianapolis, IN: Hackett. (Original work published 1878)

Peirce, C. S. (1982). What pragmatism is. In H. S. Thayer (Ed.), *Pragmatism: The classic writings* (pp. 101–120). Indianapolis, IN: Hackett. (Original work published 1905)

Perry, H. S. (1982). *Psychiatrist of America: The life of Henry Stack Sullivan.* Cambridge, MA: Belknap Press.

Rosa, A. (2007). Acts of psyche: Actuations as synthesis of semiosis and action. In J. Valsiner & A. Rosa (Eds.), *The Cambridge handbook of sociocultural psychology* (pp 205–237). Cambridge, UK Cambridge University Press.

Shedler, J. (2010). The efficacy of psychodynamic psychotherapy. *American Psychologist, 65,* 98–109. doi: 10.1037/a0018378.

Stern, D. B. (1997). *Unformulated experience: From dissociation to imagination in psychoanalysis (Relational perspective book series).* New York, NY: Routeldge.

Stern, D. B. (2004). The eye sees itself: Dissociation enactment and the achievement of conflict. *Contemporary Psychoanalysis, 40,* 197–237.

Stern, D. B. (2012). Implicit theories of technique and the values that inspire them. *Psychoanalytic Inquiry, 32,* 33–49. doi: 10.1080/07351690.2011.553163.

Stolorow, R. D. (2007). *Trauma and human existence: Autobiographical, psychoanalytic and philosophical reflections (Psychoanalytic inquiry book series).* New York, NY: Routledge.

Stolorow, R. D. (2009). Individuality in context. *International Journal of Psychoanalytic Self Psychology, 4,* 405–413.

Stolorow, R. D., & Atwood, G. E. (1992). *Contexts of being: The intersubjective foundations of psychological life.* Hillsdale, NJ: Analytic Press.

Stolorow, R. D., Atwood, G. E., & Orange, D. M. (2002). *Worlds of experience: Interweaving philosophical and clinical dimensions in psychoanalysis.* New York, NY: Basic Books.

Stuhr, J. J. (2000). Introduction: Classical American philosophy. In J. J. Stuhr (Ed.), *Pragmatism and classical American philosophy* (2nd Edition, pp. 1–12). New York, NY: Oxford University Press.

Target, M., & Fonagy, P. (1996). Playing with reality: II. The development of psychic reality from a theoretical perspective. *International Journal of Psychoanalysis, 77,* 459–479.

Thayer, H. S. (1982). Introduction. In H. S. Thayer (Ed.), *Pragmatism: The classic writings* (pp. 11–22). Indianapolis, IN: Hackett.

Tublin, S. (2011). Discipline and freedom in relational technique. *Contemporary Psychoanalysis, 47,* 519–546.

Wiley, N. W. (1994). *The semiotic self.* Chicago, IL: The University of Chicago Press.

SECTION I

PRAGMATIC BEGINNINGS: A HISTORICAL OVERVIEW

CHAPTER 1

COMPATIBILITY BETWEEN EARLY PSYCHOANALYSIS AND PRAGMATISM

Tania Zittoun
University of Neuchâtel, Switzerland

INTRODUCTION

Sigmund Freud was the founder of psychoanalysis. His proposition was to create a psychology—a science of human psyche—which would account for the mysteries of mind by addressing specifically psychological processes and not physiological ones. In parallel, some types of psychological troubles could be cured by a psychological technique developed on such understanding. In some basic sense, then, psychoanalysis was to be considered a serious theory because it could actually be used to understand and ameliorate people's lives—that is, "freeing someone from his neurotic symptoms, inhibitions and abnormalities of character" (Freud, 1937/2001, p. 216). That a person would be relieved from such symptoms was thus one marker of the end of the analysis (Freud, 1937/2001)—and in that respect, the disappearance of the symptoms represents a pragmatic way of assessing the value of psychoanalysis. However, and although the theory was contemporary to his work, Freud apparently never explicitly mentions pragmatism as

Making Our Ideas Clear, pages 23–42
Copyright © 2015 by Information Age Publishing
All rights of reproduction in any form reserved.

it has been defined by Charles S. Peirce, John Dewey and William James. Nevertheless, tracing back Freud's educational background, I will show that his intellectual journey has deep similarities to James's—which might have brought the two men to a comparable epistemological stance. Hence, I will suggest that Freud's intellectual work can be said to reflect a basic pragmatist stance, very close to that formulated by James, and visible through the psychoanalyst's constant effort to maintain a generative dialogue between a general theory and the diversity of always new empirical facts.

PSYCHOANALYSIS

Trained as a medical doctor who first specialized in physiological troubles (aphasias, etc.), Freud was soon to be confronted by the hysteric patient. After trying different curing techniques developed in his time—suggestion, hypnosis—Freud came to realize the importance of discourse for understanding and taming the causes of the patient's sufferance. Most psychic pain and hysteric symptoms thus appeared to not have physiological causes, but psychological ones. Freud hence developed his *psychoanalysis*, designating by the same term three aspects of his work (Freud, 1922/2001): a theory of the psychic apparatus, a method for investigating the mind and developing such theories, and a setting and a technique to cure specific types of patient—at that time, mainly neurotic ones.

Freud's ambition was to develop a general psychological theory, the study of pathological cases being a way to contribute to the understanding of healthy functioning, with an emphasis on the "weak points" of mind (Freud, 1939). The core aspects of this theory, as they are presented in Freud's final theoretical contribution, *An Outline of Psychoanalysis* (1938/2001) can be summarized:

First, from a topological perspective, Freud's model of the "psychic apparatus" consists of the *ego*, in which is localized our experience of ourselves, and which maintains itself "between" the demands of the drives issued from the body (constituting the *id*) and the demands of reality. In addition, it has to act under the guidance of the *superego*—resulting from internalized social and cultural norms and rules. The ego, like a chevalier on an untamed horse—the id—has to stay on the road of reality, while dealing with clouds of disturbing birds—suggestions of others, social demands and obstacles, and of the superego.

Second, from a more economical perspective, the drives, which represent in the mind the demand of the organism, are of two main types: the libido, or *Eros*, and a destructive drive, the *death drive*. The first one aims at more psychic linking, complexity, and stability; the other tends toward the destruction of such links and thus to inertia and immobility. In most human action these two drives are combined: eating demands the decomposition of food and its recombination within the body; sexuality demands some aggressive moves aiming at physical reunion. Yet one can dominate the other, or be overly repressed or bent out of its normal course.

Third, Freud's theory includes recognition of the importance of sexuality in a broad sense, from infancy and early childhood on, leaving durable traces in the stabilization of one's later inclinations: Sexuality here includes the pleasure taken from early food intake, excretive functions, or the explorations of one's own body. In this broad sense, the strong attachment the child has for his or her mother or mothering figure and the frustration of sharing it with another all-powerful person—the father figure—can also be considered of a sexual nature. With its very elementary psychical capacities, the child is very sensitive to these needs, but especially to how the others—parents, caregivers—repeatedly react to them (with anger, fear or punishment), in such a way that it might durably shape the person's relationship to his needs or the objects of his liking. Note that Freud insists on this sexual aspect of his theory first because it was the only way to account for the symptoms of most of his patients in an extremely Victorian environment, and second, because sexuality was absolutely absent of the pathology and psychology of his time.

Fourth, from a dynamic perspective, Freud's investigations led him to distinguish three main modalities of representations or ideas: representations that are conscious, those that are preconscious—that are at the periphery of our consciousness or that can easily become conscious, for example, when they are put into words—and representations that remain unconscious. Conscious and preconscious ideas take place in the *ego*; the *id* gives rise to unconscious representations. Unconscious representations are associated through processes that Freud called *primary*—an extremely rapid way of chaining ideas and representations, contrasting with *secondary processes*—the laborious way of elaborating ideas and representation in conscious thought and mainly language, accordingly to the demand of reality and culture. Through his study of people's remembrance of dreams, Freud could identify some of the processes by which such unconscious dynamics take place (see also Freud, 1900/2001). These could then be used to analyze how more generally unpleasant or culturally unacceptable ideas can be transposed or transformed in people discourse and actions. Such a conception of the psychic apparatus accounts for many of people's unhappy dealing with life events. Too-strongly internalized parental or social and cultural rules (a severe superego) might prevent a person's many desires or appetites to come to consciousness. These repressed desires, now unconscious, might remain active, however, and find substitutive forms at a conscious level—through dreams, symptoms, or obscure anxieties. Yet the person who can acknowledge these desires and conflicts expands his consciousness and might use this energy in work or in contributions to the culture.

Freud's psychology is thus located above its organic basis. It is an attempt to account for the psychological dynamics by which people handle the demands of their needs and of interpersonal situations in a given social and cultural environment. Freud's personal psychology also gave him a basis to venture in a more social psychology, accounting for group and cultural phenomena of his time (see, for instance, Freud, 1921/2001, 1927/2001). Altogether, he proposed a conceptual system to represent psychic invisible processes out of which one could only see the outcomes—discourse, symptoms, or actions. He also tried to account for the social and cultural nature of human psyche—as the organization of minds, the conflicting forces that people deal with, internalized rules and obligation, symbols through which one can express oneself or represent one's inner life, come from the culture (see also Salvatore & Zittoun, 2011).

But how did Freud develop such a model, and with what precautions against pure speculation? In what sense is his work, as he claims, science, and not poetry? In other words, what is his epistemological stance, and out of which roots did it grow?

PHILOSOPHY IN MIND: FREUD'S FORMATIVE YEARS

In order to capture Freud's epistemological stance, it might be useful to go back to his formative years. His meeting with the work of two philosophers might have played a significant role in his thinking: Franz Brentano and John Stuart Mill.

A talented and well-read pupil, driven by an intense need to know and some personal ambition, young Freud decided to study medicine at the University of Vienna. This choice was partly made against his own interest for philosophy and taste for speculation—which he forbid himself out of fear of losing himself in imagination (Gay, 1988). Having read Goethe and Darwin, his curiosity seems to have had human mind and culture as an object, rather than the body, and many of his autobiographical comments underlie his wish to understand mind and culture and his ambivalence towards medicine as such (Gay, 1988).

Freud started his medical studies at the University of Vienna in 1873, yet he also kept reading philosophy. A long-time admirer of Ludwig Feuerbach—atheist, against philosophy as speculative enquiry (Gay, 1988)—Freud eventually attended the lectures given by Franz Brentano. In effect, Brentano was teaching as a full professor in Vienna from 1874 to 1880, after which he resigned, before working again as associate professor (*Privatdozent*)

(Merlan, 1945, p. 375, note 4). Freud, who received his MD degree in 1881, thus followed Brentano's classes from 1874 to 1976:

> The results [of an in investigation] show that Freud was enrolled in the following courses given by Brentano: in Freud's third, fourth, and fifth semesters (Winter 1874/75, Summer 1875, and Winter 1875/76 respectively), "Readings of philosophic writings"; in addition, in his fourth semester (Summer 1875), "Logic"; in his sixth semester (Summer 1876), "The philosophy of Aristotle." (Merlan, 1949, p. 451)

In addition, Freud might have developed some more personal relationship with Brentano. Commentators and biographers have emphasized the durable impact Brentano's education might have had on Freud. First, Freud might have had heard for the first time about the idea of the unconscious in *Psychologie vom empirischen Standpunkt* (Brentano, 1874/1995), where the idea is discussed twice and retraced to Thomas Aquinas (Merlan, 1945). Second, Freud's life-long strong separation between a psychological explanation and a physiological one might have found its root in Brentano's work (Fancher, 1977; Merlan, 1945). In addition:

> In psychological theory, both men stressed the motivated nature of thought and a conception of a "psychological reality" that is superior to "material reality." Both saw consciousness of one's own mental activity as arising retrospectively and having a calming effect on emotions. Both emphasized a process of "judgment" or "reality testing," made possible only by the presence of a strong unity of consciousness or ego. (Fancher, 1977, p. 207)

Finally, Freud seems to have agreed with Brentano's methodological proposal, according to which "the retrospective analysis of subjective experience is the principal tool of psychology" (Fancher, 1977, p. 207).

After his studies, Freud had to do his military service in 1879–1880. During this time, through the recommendation of Brentano, he was asked by Theodor Gomperz to translate four essays by John Stuart Mill for the German translation of the complete works (Gay, 1988): *Enfranchisement of Woman* (*Uber Frauenemancipation*), *Plato* (*Plato*), *Thornton: Labour and its pain* (*Arbeitfrage*), *Socialismus* (*On socialism*) (Merlan, 1945, p. 375, note 3).[1] Freud seems to have appreciated this work to escape the dullness of his military assignment, and he might have read more of it. In any case, Mill was part of his internal dialogue. Some mentions of it can be found in his letters to his fiancée (Adams, 1992, pp. 451–452) and deeper influences in various aspects of his work (Govrin, 2004; Molnar, 1999).

Engaging in his medical work, Freud clearly decided to leave the shore of purely speculative philosophy and metaphysics. However, in the background of his work (Gay, 1988), and coming to the fore at the end of his life (Freud, 1938/2001), Freud might have seen his work as a contribution to philosophy—yet a contribution based in the empirical world of facts, human thinking, and activity. However, it is hard to know how much philosophy Freud actually read after his formative year—in 1920, when a colleague pointed his attention to a text by Schopenhauer, Freud declares he has "read very little" (Gay, 1988).

In the frame of his scientific work, Freud was very well informed of current debates—his major books are always based on exhaustive and up-to-date bibliographies, in fields as diverse as neurological disorders (Freud, 1891/1953), dream processes (Freud, 1900/2001), or anthropological facts (*Totem and Taboo,* Freud, 1913/2001). It is thus while preparing some of his contributions on sexuality that he came across some of William James' writings.

THE MEETING THAT ONLY HALF HAPPENED: FREUD AND JAMES

Sigmund Freud (1856–1939) was a bit younger than William James (1842–1910), yet they were active in parallel for some years of their working life. Both marked the history of psychology in their respective continents, and far beyond. Although their sociocultural origins differ, and although they only had a couple of brief encounters, their core theoretical and epistemological stances have deep similarities. The two men share a deep interest for psychological processes (and not outcomes), a methodology based on introspection, the assumption of a constant flow of consciousness of which some aspects might become unconscious, the idea that thinking is posterior to embodied emotional experience, and so on. Mainly, I will argue, Freud's implicit empiricism is extremely close to James' declared pragmatism. Is such similarity just a historical coincidence, or the result of some shared *Zeitgeist*?

A person's ideas and knowledge are the product of ongoing dialogues and personal creation. A person becomes who she is not only through her family and immediate social and cultural environment, but also, as she dialogues with specific, significant others, whether these are present, remembered, or only imagined (Marková, 2005; Perret-Clermont, 2008; Zittoun, Perret-Clermont, & Barrelet, 2008). In what follows, I argue that James and Freud shared two similar significant "others": the admired ones (Brentano and Mill) and the ones against which they positioned their work (the partisans of a physiological, experimental psychology, loosing the specificity of mind). The fact that the two men were dialoguing with such common friends and enemies might thus explain some commonalities of their intellectual journeys.

On the one hand, everything seemed to oppose Freud and James's journey. Their national, sociocultural, and family backgrounds were highly contrasting. Freud's father was a relatively modest wool merchant in Moravia (at that time in the Austro-Hungarian empire), and he grew up in blended Jewish family. On the other side, James's father was a wealthy intellectual American theologian, acquainted with writers and artists. The two men's educational trajectories also differed: Freud studied medicine, while James was educated as a humanist (partly in Europe and Berlin in particular; Goodman, 2009), then as physician before working as a naturalist. Both eventually became interested in the secrets of the human mind, so what is there in common in their intellectual trajectories?

On the other hand, a striking aspect of comparison between the two thinkers' trajectory is the fact that the "others" with whom they entered into dialogue as they developed their own theories were at least partly the same. If Freud studied with Brentano, James' work closely engages with the same philosopher's ideas. Hence for instance, in his *Principles of Psychology* (1890/1981), the classification of psychic phenomena is directly inspired by Brentano's (Kersten, 1969). Also, if Freud developed a close knowledge of John Mill through his work as a translator, James obviously was very familiar with John Mill (as an author if not as a person[2]) to whom he dedicated his studies on *Pragmatism. A new name for some old way of thinking* (1907) with the words "To the memory of John Stuart Mill, from whom I first learned the pragmatic openness of mind and whom my fancy likes to picture as our leader were he alive to-day." The fact that James found an inspiration in Mill did not prevent him from questioning some of his propositions (Throntveit, 2011)—yet this suggests that, as was the case for Freud, Mill was one of the real and internalized "others" with or against whom some of his ideas were developed.

Then, regarding the development of their psychologies, both James and Freud spent some times in Paris where they visited Jean-Martin Charcot—James in 1882 (Goodman, 2009) and Freud in 1885 (Gay, 1988)—who was working at that time with hysteric patients and developing his hypnotic method. They also both were acquainted with the work of Pierre Janet, learned a lot from him, and then took some distance from him (for instance, Freud, 1894/2001).

These parallel formative years were probably playing a very important role in each of these men's thinking, and more than the actual knowledge that each had from the other. There is no trace of a real correspondence between the two men; they scarcely quote each other, and traces of their meetings cannot be interpreted unequivocally. Chronologically, according to Taylor (1999), James read Freud's publication, from the early 1880s in the *American Journal of Insanity*. The two men then met at the First International Congress of Experimental Psychology, held in Paris in 1889. James read Breuer and Freud on hysteria in 1894 (Gay, 1988). On his side Freud "was also familiar with what James had written on the perversion of the instincts in *Principles of Psychology*" (Taylor, 1999, p. 466) and on sexual pathology in the 1890s, either firsthand or through the accounts of other authors (for a detailed account, see Sulloway, 1998). It is quite likely that Freud read more than these chapters of James's work—although supporting information is missing.

What is also known is that the two men met during Freud's visit at Clark University in 1909, a trip organized by Brill, an American psychoanalyst who spent some time in Europe with Freud, during which Freud received a doctorate *honoris causa* – a first international public acknowledgement of his work (see Figure 1.1). This is were the relation between the two men becomes difficult to interpret: biographers report that Freud was impressed by James as a man (Dadoun, 1992), who brought him back to the train station, partly because of his stoicism in front of his approaching death (Gay, 1988). At this moment James is reported to have said, "The future of psychology belongs to your work" (Jones, 1955, quoted in Taylor, 1999, p. 469). This might be heard as supporting the empirical, yet not experimental, (see next paragraph) psychological investigation of what is beyond consciousness. Contrasting with this apparent positive attitude, James also expressed more negative judgments toward Freud's analysis of dreams and symbolism in letters sent in 1909 (Evans & Koelsh, 1985, p. 947; Gay, 1988). Finally, there are some indications that James went to Vienna to consult

Figure 1.1 A conference at Clark University in 1909. Included, in the first row, William James, third from left; Sigmund Freud, fourth from right; and Carl G. Jung, third from right. *Source:* http://www.nytimes.com/2008/01/20/books/review/Prochnik-t.html, Courtesy of Clark University.

Freud in March 1910, shortly before his death (Taylor, 1999, p. 466)—a fact that rather supports the idea of a reciprocal admiration.

To sum up, then, there has been no similar background in the life of the two men, and if they knew each other, it seemed to have been in a relatively limited way. However, their intellectual journeys share much more in common. In the first place, Freud and James's thinking were developing with the same philosophical roots, encouraging them to develop an authentic psychology of human intentionality. Through their medical and naturalist studies and especially through their visit to Charcot, they were taught to exercise a close observation of empirical case studies. Later in their life, they both developed their theories on the basis of a clinical practice, first as hypnotists and then as psychotherapists (Taylor, 1999). Finally, and more important for our matter here, they both in parallel took a strong stance against a reductionist, positivistic, physiological, experimental psychology as was emerging during their lifetime (Taylor, 1999). Rather,

> Both James and Freud, however, saw psychology as a form of phenomenology—thinking that no objective science could exist without factoring into the equation the scientist's state of consciousness that defines science in the first place. For James, the basic datum of psychology was pure experience in the immediate moment, before the differentiation of subject and object. For Freud, it was the content of consciousness that was determined in large part by the dynamic processes of the unconscious. We may think of psychology in this sense as *Erkenntnistheorie*—that is, as epistemology, or as the way by which all knowledge comes to us as immediate experience. The reality of an object is always dependent on someone's consciousness somewhere. (Taylor, 1999, p. 468)

Beyond their many differences and their contrasting psychologies, James and Freud thus carried their work through dialogues with the same positive others, and against comparable enemies. They developed a very similar basic philosophical framework, a comparable thirst for an understanding of complex psychological phenomena seen as located in their world of culture, and both were ready to develop a patient empiricism of which they were also part.

This leads to another question: If they refused the positivistic and experimental paradigms developing in their times, how could the two men hope to achieve some type of scientific knowledge? James devoted an important part of his work to defining a new epistemology—pragmatism—likely to bring about such knowledge, and without being so articulate about his epistemological stance, Freud actually applied such pragmatism.

WILLIAM JAMES' PRAGMATISM

Following his psychological work, and contemporary to the developments of psychoanalysis, James was also very much engaged in philosophical debates of his time. In 1907, that is, almost 20 years after the *Principles of Psychology* (1890) and little after his work on religion (1902), James published his book *Pragmatism* that presents and summarizes his positions on pragmatism, an idea introduced by Peirce in 1878 and developed by him, James and others (John Dewey, Ferdinand C. S. Schiller) during the following years (Madelrieux, 2007). In this book, James presents and clarifies the different views on the term "pragmatism"—as a method, as an epistemological principle, as a modality of conferring some space to metaphysics.

These three modalities are presented in the paper called "What Pragmatism Means" (James, 1904). James first presents the "pragmatic method" as a way to settle metaphysic disputes, which is actually a criterion to evaluate the relevance of notions: "What difference would it practically make to any one if this notion rather than that notion were true? If no practical difference whatever can be traced, then the alternatives mean practically the same thing, and all dispute is idle" (James, 1904, p. 2). In his discussion, James moves from examples in which the pragmatic method consists in observing the real, actual consequence of ideas in the world, to examples in which notions are useful if they add something to or modify our relationship to reality. The first variation of "practical differences" concerns actual action or utility upon the world. James here reports, as a counter example, that there is no difference in the fact that yeast enables the dough to grow, whether it is due to a brownie or an elf—in any case, the dough grows with yeast. Also, the pragmatist "turns towards concreteness and adequacy, towards facts, towards action and towards power" (James, 1904, p. 3): The pragmatist method invites one to work with notions that extend one's activities and power, in the real world, thus distancing him from idealist metaphysician who developed arguments that only mattered in the pure world of thoughts. The second variation concerns our ideas—here the pragmatist method invites us to retain ideas that expand our understanding of the world and to keep the movement of thinking and searching alive. In that sense, continues James, "*Theories thus become instruments, not answers to enigmas, in which we can rest.* We don't lie back upon them, we move forward, and, on occasion, make nature over again by their aid" (James, 1904, p. 4, original emphasis).

From this point naturally follows a second acceptation of pragmatism as epistemology, as a "genetic theory of what is meant by truth" (James, 1904, p. 8). Here, James explains how knowledge grows: If new facts are presented to the observer, the notions have to be adjusted so as to account both to the older state of knowledge and for these new observations.

> The process here is always the same. The individual has a stock of old opinions already, but he meets a new experience that puts them to a strain. Somebody contradicts them; or in a reflective moment he discovers that they contradict each other; or he hears of facts with which they are incompatible; or desires arise in him which they cease to satisfy. *The result is an inward trouble* to which his mind till then had been a stranger, and from which he seeks to escape *by modifying his previous mass of opinions.* (James, 1904, p. 6, emphasis added)

A *truer* notion or theory is, in that sense, a theory that results from the dynamic movement of resolving an "inward trouble," and as a consequence, adjusting to a new diversity of facts. It participates in the developmental process of knowledge building—personal or shared.

> That new idea is truest which performs most felicitously its function of satisfying our double urgency. It makes itself true, gets itself classed as true, by the way it works; grafting itself then upon the ancient body of truth, which thus grows much as a tree grows by the activity of a new laver of cambium. (James, 1904, p. 7)

In contrast, a false theory is in that sense one that would neglect new facts in order to preserve an old theory.

The truth of a scientific enquiry is thus to be found in a dynamic of abduction (Valsiner, 2000): a systematic dialogic process between initial ideas and notions that might bring the person to observe facts or reflect on existing knowledge, which might lead to new observations and realization, which will eventually demand a revision of these initial ideas. In addition, these ideas might themselves demand new organizations into new hierarchies—pragmatism wishes to develop general ideas on the basis of a multiplicity of cases. "The pragmatist clings to facts and concreteness, observes truth at its work in particular cases, and generalizes" (James, 1904, p. 8)—until new facts create some trouble again. Knowledge development is in that sense a never-ending story.

Finally, the third acceptation of James' pragmatism is that of conciliating his radical empiricism with the possibility of metaphysical beliefs. Here, referring to his work on the psychology of religion, James pushes pragmatism to some limit:

> *If theological ideas prove to have a value for concrete life, they will be true, for pragmatism, in the sense of being good for so much. For how much more they are true, will depend entirely on their relations to the other truths that also have to be acknowledged.* (James, 1904, p. 10, original emphasis)

James here is exposed to the problem that these ideas—such as believing in God or afterlife—are true if they make a person's life easier; yet in that sense they are *good.* So is any idea which is "good" true? This is where James brings back the principle of inner consistency of beliefs—an idea is true as long as it is also compatible with other ideas held as true, or as formulated in a less radical way, "what is better for us to believe is good is true *unless the belief incidentally clashes with some other vital benefit*" (James, 1904, p. 12, original emphasis). With this nuance James can allow people to believe whatever they want as long as their beliefs neither harm themselves nor others.

PRAGMATIST GESTURES IN FREUD'S WORK

Freud had chosen to leave the shores of philosophy to avoid the swamps of speculation. However, his initial training, as well as his hunger for the recognition of psychoanalysis as a science, brought him to adopt a certain number of epistemological choices. Although Freud does not present them explicitly and systematically, his extremely reflective way of writing frequently contains commentaries about the movement of his thinking and truth-building. In what follows, I suggest that Freud can be said to work as a pragmatist, in the triple acceptation of the term (for a review of all occurrences of empiricist/pragmatist statements, see Delrieu, 2008, pp. 333–347). In order to do so, I will quickly present one of Freud's early and seminal papers.

In his early paper, "The Neuro-Psychoses of Defence (An Attempt at a Psychological Theory of Acquired Hysteria, of Many Phobias and Obsessions and of Certain Hallucinatory Psychosis" (1894/2001), Freud starts by recalling the currently admitted explanation for hysteria, proposed by Pierre Janet, and recalls a first objection made by himself and Breuer. But then Freud brings about a series of other clinical cases that cannot be explained with such hypothesis and that call for a wider, more powerful explanation. Here, rather than ignoring these cases or considering as untreatable (as was the dominant tendency, which for example led scientists to deny the existence of male hysteria, which simply did not fit in the definition of the time; Mitchell, 2000), Freud decides to question and expand his theories. This is how he moves from the idea of hysteria explained by physiological factors to an explanation of neurotic phenomena due to psychological dynamics, as the subtitle of his communication suggests. Freud finishes his paper with the hypothesis itself:

> The hypothesis, which, incidentally already underlies our theory of "abreaction" in our "Preliminary communication" ([Breuer & Freud,] 1893), can be applied in the same sense as physicists apply the hypothesis of electric fluid. It is provisionally justified by its utility in coordinating and explaining a great variety of psychical states. (Freud, 1894/2001, p. 61)

The new explanation of these various pathological states is that some idea in the mind, or some affects attached to ideas, are not acceptable for the person; and in some cases, the affect becomes detached from the idea and turned into a somatic expression (what Freud will call "conversion"), while in other cases, the affects will be attached to other ideas, eventually charging them with such intensity that they will become obsessions. The idea itself to which the affects was attached then becomes "repressed."

How Can We Read This as Illustrating a Pragmatist Stance?

First, we can apply the pragmatic method to the new notion of "repression." What can it enable one to understand or to do, that could not have been done without? First, the idea of repression opens the door for a systematic exploration of processes that before were unexplainable. Slips of the tongue, dreams, and symptoms can be accounted for without having to postulate witches or demons. It then invites further explorations of the dynamics of the mind. And in effect, repression became one of the cornerstones of the whole psychoanalytical theory. *Second,* on the empirical side, the notion of repression offers a way for action. For, if some ideas are repressed after affects have been detached, these initial ideas can be unlocked—at that time, through hypnosis, but later on through what will become the analytical treatment. Psychoanalysis as a therapy uses the technique of "free association": The patient is asked to say everything that comes to mind. Listening with "floating attention" to the flow of discourse, with its recurrent themes, avoided points, changes in tone, contradictions, and so on, the analyst can then make hypotheses about possible underpinnings and active "repressed" ideas. Identifying these repressed ideas and bringing the patient to understand them consciously has a major impact on the disappearance of the patient's symptoms.

More systematically, from a pragmatic stance, psychoanalysis is relevant because it deeply changed not only Freud and his disciples, but also, shortly thereafter, the general public's representations of what is mind and how much of our life is unconscious. Freud's awareness of the ways analysis was changing people's relationship to reality appears perhaps too proudly, in the statement he reportedly made to Carl G. Jung as they were approaching America in 1909: "They don't realize that we are bringing them the plague."[3] And in effect, psychoanalysis deeply changed the way in which people understand themselves and others, in many parts of the world. Psychoanalytical ideas penetrated all spheres of society—doctors', psychologists', educationalists', and social workers' practices were shaped by psychoanalytical ideas—but also cinema and arts, and lay people. Hence Moscovici (2008) showed how terms from Freud's work became part of daily discussions in France in the 1960s—as when people speak of someone's "inferiority complex" or "denial" or "repressed anger." Artists and film directors have often deliberately used psychoanalytical ideas to touch their audience, or have represented people dealing with violent drives and their repressions, or psychoanalysts and their patients (e.g., Kaplan, 1990; Lebeau, 2001)—without speaking of commercials, literature, and so on, targeted to touch upon audiences' basic drives. Occidental societies have been shown to be deeply shaken in their basic beliefs that people might be self-determined and have free will; Freud's work, together with Marx and Nietzsche, has indeed brought a deep suspicion—people appear greatly determined by forces far beyond control, be they unconscious or social, in a godless world. Such analysis, identified as "hermeneutics of suspicion" (Ricoeur, 1965), has deeply transformed social sciences and humanities (bringing postmodernism, etc.).

Third, Freud saw the pragmatic effect of psychoanalysis in its power to heal patients, or more modestly, to bring them to more self-knowledge and inner freedom (for instance, Freud, 1938/2001). One might still question the outdated nature of the "hydraulic" nature of Freud's economic model, but if the model is actionable enough to guide the therapist's interventions and durably change people's lives, is it such a problem? Yet Freud himself suggested that his models were open to revision and some more efficient and economic way to better patients' lives was still to come—perhaps even medication (Freud, 1938/2001).

This leads me to pragmatism as a "genetic theory of truth" based on a dynamic movement of abduction. Although Freud does not use the term, the movement by which his theories develop corresponds to the characteristics highlighted by James: he develops new notions or generalization every time new facts contradict the existing state of knowledge. The example above perfectly illustrates that principle—in Freud's words, the new explanation "is provisionally justified by its utility in coordinating and explaining a great variety of psychical states" (1894/2001, p. 61). More generally, on the one hand, Freud works by assembling, over years, large numbers of examples and occurrences of a phenomenon—his own, friends', and family's dreams for his *Interpretation of Dreams* (1900/2001), thousands of jokes for his *Jokes and Their Relation to the Unconscious* (1905/2001)—and clinical cases in his other books. Thus, his main theoretical contributions are based on case studies then considered as exemplum—*Studies on Hysteria* (with Breuer, 1895/2001), *Two Case Studies:* 'Little Hans' *and* 'the Rat Man' (1905/2001), etc. On the other hand, each of Freud's major theoretical revisions is, on the contrary, triggered by confrontation to cases or an accumulation of facts that could not be accounted for with the previous state of his theory. This is what let him expand his first model of the mind by a second one (Freud, 1923/2001), or to make the hypothesis of a death instinct (Freud, 1920/2001)—still controversial ideas among analysts—to account for some of his patients' tendencies to systematically repeat past mistakes, refuse any health progress, or more generally, systematically put themselves in harmful and dangerous situations, and perhaps also to account for Europe's two major self-destructive attempts in less than forty years.

The third acceptation of James' pragmatism might appear less relevant here. However, although Freud was a self-declared atheist who even analyzed religion as a collective illusion (*The Future of an Illusion*, 1927/2001), his position seems precisely to consist in identifying what good such metaphysic ideas have for people—similarly as he would tolerate his patients maintaining their beliefs or idiosyncrasies as long as they do not suffer from them, and that these enable them to attain a certain health, that is, not preventing them from being able to love and to work.

. . . AND LATER ON

During Freud's life and after his death, psychoanalysis evolved into an institution. Doing so, it activated concurrences, fights for power, dissensions, and many unhappy scissions and creations of parallel or concurrent schools. If institutions were necessary to maintain the experience accumulated by analysts and develop a training curriculum to protect patients from self-declared therapists, they also had the negative effect of rigidifying psychoanalysis as theory, research method, and practice. However, it is also comforting to see that, thanks to these institutions, a few generations after Freud, the theory continued to develop very pragmatically in Europe and Britain. Theoretical innovations were made to account for pathologies that escaped Freud or that are due to the evolution of society (such as psychosis border-lines, or new forms of addictions; see for instance Anzieu, 1995; Bion, 1977; Green, 1999, 2005; Tisseron, 2005). Clinical techniques were also diversified for curing these new complaints—adjusting the psychoanalytical setting, including play, psychodrama, tales reading, "packing," and so on (Anzieu, 1995; Winnicott, 2001), or to deal with cultural diversities and migration, sometimes resulting in therapeutic bricolage—expanded setting with translators, delegates from various ethnic groups, quasi-magical injunctions and rituals—mainly acceptable because "they work" (Nathan, 1991, 2001). Analysts also remained in principle nonjudgmental regarding their patients' religious beliefs as long as they were nondetrimental "for other vital benefits" (such as for instance Masud Khan's therapy of a young person then going to an ashram, Khan, 1983). Finally, psychoanalysis was expanded and integrated in other fields of social practice: it changed the understanding of the dynamics of teaching-learning and is at times still used to overcome learning difficulties (Alvarez, 1992; Boimare, 2004; Hatchuel, 2007; Pontecorvo & Pontecorvo, 1986; Rochex, 1998); it is used to analyze group and institutional functioning (Anzieu, 1999; Bion, 1968; Kaës, 2012); it was actualized to account for political violence (Puget, 1989) and developed to reflect on the role of cinema, videogames, and new media in people's thinking and maturation (Tisseron, 2005), and so on. It is also still developing to maintain a dialogue with advances in neurosciences (Ansermet & Magistretti, 2004; Solms, 1997), cultural psychology (Salvatore & Zittoun, 2011), or early developmental psychology (Fonagy, Target, Gergely, & Jurist, 2002).

Freud's psychoanalysis remains controversial—yet seen as a pragmatist endeavor, it sets very clear methodological and epistemological standards for the assessment of its validity—namely, an ideographic science with a focus on psychological processes, with the requirement of a strong consistency between generalized theory and observations through abduction, and with actual clinical care for the efficiency of the hypotheses as therapeutic means. During Freud's lifetime, psychoanalysis as a theory, a practice, and a method was constantly updated and a few times deeply revised. Freud wished to see his work pursued, revised, and expanded after his death—with basic assumptions about unconscious dynamics being respected. Psychoanalysis actually had in some institutional and national contexts the vitality to develop and adjust to new historical and social challenges, advances in sciences, and new needs. In other situations, psychoanalysis has been regularly and strongly opposed by science and laypeople, and psychology professionals have been deeply divided internally. Unfortunately, most of the controversies have been ideological—refusing this or that aspect because it hurts people's common sense or positivist credo, and thus too-often cutting short the otherwise endless innovation and courage that pragmatism entails.

NOTES

1. John Stuart Mill's Gesammelte Werke. Autorisierte Uebersetzung unter der Redaction von Professor Dr. Theodor Gomperz. Zwelfter Band. Vermischte Schriften III. Plato. Arbeiterfrage. Socialismus. Uebersetzt von Siegmund Freud (Leipzig).
2. Unverified source: apparently his family is friend with family Mill. http://www.trincoll.edu/depts/phil/philo/phils/wjames.html
3. Lacan apparently reported that Jung told him this anecdote in 1954 (Stadlen, 2009).

REFERENCES

Adams, J. E. (1992). Philosophical forgetfulness: John Stuart Mill's "Nature". *Journal of the History of Ideas, 53*(3), 437–454. doi:10.2307/2709886

Alvarez, A. (1992). *Live company: Psychoanalytic psychotherapy with autistic, borderline, deprived and abused children* (1st ed.). London, UK: Routledge.

Ansermet, F., & Magistretti, P. (2004). *A chacun son cerveau. Plasticité neuronale et inconscient.* Paris, France: Odile Jacob.

Anzieu, D. (1995). *Le Moi-peau* (2nd ed.). Paris, France: Dunod.

Anzieu, D. (1999). *Le groupe et l'inconscient* (3e ed.). Paris, France: Dunod.

Bion, W. R. (1968). *Experiences in groups and other papers.* London, UK: Routledge.

Bion, W. R. (1977). *Seven servants: Four works.* New York, NY: Jason Aronson.

Boimare, S. (2004). *L'enfant et la peur d'apprendre* (2nd ed.). Paris, France: Dunod.

Brentano, F. (1995). *Psychology from an empirical standpoint* (2nd ed.). New York, NY: Routledge. (Original German edition published 1874)

Breuer, J., & Freud, S. (2001). On the psychical mechanisms of hysterical phenomena: Preliminary communication. In J. Strachey (Trans. and Ed.), *The standard edition of the complete psychological works of Sigmund Freud* (Vol. 2, pp. 1–19). London, UK: Vintage. (Original German edition published 1893)

Breuer, J., & Freud, S. (2001). Studies on hysteria. In J. Strachey (Trans. and Ed.), *The standard edition of the complete psychological works of Sigmund Freud* (Vol. 2, Chap. I–IV). London, UK: Vintage. (Original German edition published 1895)

Dadoun, R. (1992). *Freud.* (revised and expanded). Paris, France: P. Belfond.

Delrieu, A. (2008). *Sigmund Freud: Index Thématique.* Collection "Psychanalyse" (3rd ed.). Paris, France: Economica : Anthropos.

Evans, R. B., & Koelsh, W. A. (1985). Psychoanalysis arrives in America: The 1909 Psychology Conference at Clark University. *American Psychologist, 40*(8), 942–948.

Fancher, R. E. (1977). Brentano's psychology from an empirical standpoint and Freud's early metapsychology. *Journal of the History of the Behavioral Sciences, 13*(3), 207–227. doi:10.1002/1520-6696(197707)13:3<207::AID-JHBS2300130302>3.0.CO;2-#

Fonagy, P., Target, M., Gergely, G., & Jurist, E. L. (2002). *Affect regulation, mentalization, and the development of self.* New York, NY: Other Press.

Freud, S. (1953). *On Aphasia.* New York, NY: International University Press. (Original German edition published 1891)

Freud, S. (2001). An outline of psychoanalysis. In J. Strachey (Trans. and Ed.), *The standard edition of the complete psychological works of Sigmund Freud* (Vol. 23, pp. 139–207). London, UK: Vintage. (Original German edition published 1938, English version 1940)

Freud, S. (2001). Analysis terminable and interminable. In J. Strachey (Trans. and Ed.), *The standard edition of the complete psychological works of Sigmund Freud* (Vol. 23, pp. 210–253). London, UK: Vintage. (Original German edition published 1937, English version 1937)

Freud, S. (2001). Beyond the pleasure principle. In J. Strachey (Trans. and Ed.), *The standard edition of the complete psychological works of Sigmund Freud* (New Ed., Vol. 18, pp. 7–64). London, UK: Vintage. (Original German edition published 1920)

Freud, S. (2001). Two encyclopedia articles. A psycho-analysis. In J. Strachey (Trans. and Ed.), *The standard edition of the complete psychological works of Sigmund Freud* (Vol. 13, pp. 235–254). London, UK: Vintage. (Original German edition published 1922)

Freud, S. (2001). The ego and the id. In J. Strachey (Trans. and Ed.), *The standard edition of the complete psychological works of Sigmund Freud* (Vol. 19, pp. 3–66). London, UK: Vintage. (Original German publication 1923)

Freud, S. (2001). The future of an illusion. In J. Strachey (Trans. and Ed.), *The standard edition of the complete psychological works of Sigmund Freud* (Vol. 21, pp. 3–56). London, UK: Vintage. (Original German edition published 1927)

Freud, S. (2001). The interpretation of dreams. In J. Strachey (Trans. and Ed.), *The standard edition of the complete psychological works of Sigmund Freud* (Vol. 4-5). London, UK: Vintage. (Original German edition published 1900)

Freud, S. (2001). Totem and taboo. In J. Strachey (Trans. and Ed.), *The standard edition of the complete psychological works of Sigmund Freud* (Vol. 13, pp. 1–161). London, UK: Vintage. (Original German edition published 1913)

Freud, S. (2001). Two case studies: 'Little Hans' and 'the Rat man'. In J. Strachey (Trans. and Ed.), *The standard edition of the complete psychological works of Sigmund Freud* (Vol. 10). London, UK: Vintage. (Original German edition published 1909)

Freud, S. (2001). Jokes and their relation to the unconscious. In J. Strachey (Trans. and Ed.), *The standard edition of the complete psychological works of Sigmund Freud* (Vol. 8). London, UK: Vintage. (Original German edition published 1905)

Freud, S. (2001). The neuro-psychoses of defense. (An attempt at a psychological theory of acquired hysteria, of many phobias and obsessions and of certain hallucinatory psychoses). In J. Strachey (Trans. and Ed.), *The standard edition of the complete psychological works of Sigmund Freud* (Vol. 3, pp. 41–61). London, UK: Vintage. (Original German edition published 1894)

Freud. S. (2001). Group psychology and the analysis of the ego. In J. Strachey (Trans. and Ed.), *The standard edition of the complete psychological works of Sigmund Freud* (Vol. 18, pp. 67–137). London, UK: Vintage. (Original German edition published 1921)

Gay, P. (1988). *Freud. A life of our time.* London: J. M. Dent & Sons Ltd.

Goodman, R. (2009). William James. In E. N. Zalta (Ed.), *The Stanford encyclopedia of philosophy.* Retrieved from http://plato.stanford.edu/archives/win2009/entries/james/

Govrin, A. (2004). Some utilitarian influences in Freud's early writings. *Psychoanalysis and History, 6*, 5–21.

Green, A. (1999). *The fabric of affect in the psychoanalytic discourse.* New York, NY: Routledge.

Green, A. (2005). *Key ideas for a contemporary psychoanalysis. Misrecognition and recognition of the unconscious.* London, UK: Routledge.

Hatchuel, F. (2007). *Savoir, apprendre, transmettre. Une approche psychanalytique du rapport au savoir.* Paris, France: La Découverte.

James, W. (1904). *What is pragmatism? A new name for some old ways of thinking* (writings 1902–1920). Des Moines, IA: The Library of America. Retrieved from http://www.marxists.org/reference/subject/philosophy/works/us/james.htm

James, W. (1975). *Pragmatism. A new name for some old ways of thinking* (Original publication 1907). Cambridge, MA: Harrvard University Press.

James, W. (1981). *The principles of psychology.* Cambridge, MA: Harvard University Press. (Original work published 1890)

James, W. (2004). *The varieties of religious experience: A study in human nature.* New York, NY: Barnes & Noble Classics. (Original work published 1902)

Kaës, R. (Ed.). (2012). *L'institution et les institutions : Études psychanalytiques.* Paris, France: Dunod.

Kaplan, E. A. (1990). *Psychoanalysis & cinema.* London, UK: Routledge.

Kersten, F. (1969). Franz Brentano and William James. *Journal of the History of Philosophy, 7*(2), 177–191.

Khan, M. M. R. (1983). *Hidden selves: Between theory and practice in psychoanalysis.* Richmond, VA: The Hogarth Press.

Lebeau, V. (2001). *Psychoanalysis and cinema.* London, UK: Wallflower Press.

Madelrieux, S. (2007). Préface. In W. James (Ed.), *Le pragmatisme* (pp. 7–68). Paris, France: Flammarion.

Marková, I. (2005). *Dialogicality and social representations: The dynamics of mind.* Cambridge, UK: Cambridge University Press.

Merlan, P. (1945). Brentano and Freud. *Journal of the History of Ideas, 6*(3), 375–377. doi:10.2307/2707299

Merlan, P. (1949). Brentano and Freud—A Sequel. *Journal of the History of Ideas, 10*(3), 451. doi:10.2307/2707048

Mitchell, J. (2000). *Mad men and Medusas: Reclaiming hysteria.* London, UK: Penguin.

Molnar, M. (1999). John Stuart Mill translated by Sigmund Freud. *Psychoanalytical History, 1,* 195–205.

Moscovici, S. (2008). *Psychoanalysis: Its image and its public* (D. Macey, Trans.). Cambridge, UK: Polity Press.

Nathan, T. (1991). Fier de n'avoir si pays ni amis, quelle sottise c'était... *Psychologie Française, 36*(4), 295–306.

Nathan, T. (2001). *L'influence qui guérit.* Paris, France: Odile Jacob.

Perret-Clermont, A.-N. (2008). Piaget, his elders and his peers. In A. N. Perret-Clermont & J.-M. Barrelet (Eds.), *Jean Piaget and Neuchâtel: The learner and the scholar* (pp. 202–231). New York, NY: Routledge.

Pontecorvo, C., & Pontecorvo, M. (1986). *Psicologia dell'educazione, conoscere a scuola.* Bologna, Italy: Il Mulino.

Puget, J. (Ed.). (1989). *Violence d'Etat et psychanalyse.* Paris, France: Dunod.

Ricoeur, P. (1965). *De l'interprétation. Essai sur Sigmund Freud.* Paris, France: Seuil.

Rochex, J.-Y. (1998). *Le sens de l'expérience scolaire.* Paris, France: Presses universitaires de France.

Salvatore, S., & Zittoun, T. (2011). *Cultural psychology and psychoanalysis: Pathways to synthesis.* Charlotte, NC: Information Age Publishing.

Solms, M. (1997). *The neuropsychology of dreams: A clinico-anatomical study.* Hove, UK: Psychology Press.

Stadlen, A. (2009, September). Existential psychotherapy and inner circle seminars: "Bringing them the Plague": Freud in USA (1909). Inner Circle Seminar 142. *Existential Psychotherapy & Inner Circle Seminars.* Retrieved from http://anthonystadlen.blogspot.com/2010/01/bringing-them-plague-centenary.html

Sulloway, F. J. (1992). *Freud, biologist of the mind: Beyond the psychoanalytic legend* (Original publication 1979). Cambridge, MA: Harvard University Press.

Taylor, E. (1999). William James and Sigmund Freud: "The future of psychology belongs to your work." *Psychological Science, 10*(6), 465–469.

Throntveit, T. (2011). William James's Ethical Republic. *Journal of the History of Ideas, 72*(2), 255–277. doi:10.1353/jhi.2011.0009

Tisseron, S. (2005). *Psychanalyse de l'Image : Des premiers traits au virtuel* (3rd ed.). Paris, France: Dunod.

Valsiner, J. (2000). *Culture and human development.* Thousand Oaks, CA: Sage.

Winnicott, D. W. (2001). *Playing and reality.* Philadelphia/Sussex: Routledge. (original work published 1971)

Zittoun, T., Perret-Clermont, A.-N., & Barrelet, J.-M. (2008). The socio-intellectual genealogy of Jean Piaget. In A. N. Perret-Clermont & J.-M. Barrelet (Eds.), *Jean Piaget and Neuchâtel: The Learner and the Scholar* (pp. 109–118). New York, NY: Routledge.

CHAPTER 2

SELF AS A SIGN

Locating Peirce's Semiotics in Sullivan's Self-System

Philip J. Rosenbaum
Haverford College

INTRODUCTION

The theory of interpersonal psychoanalysis as developed by Harry Stack Sullivan (1892–1949) (1950, 1953a, 1953b, 1953c, 1938/1995) has profoundly shaped the contours of contemporary psychoanalysis. Specifically, his focus on understanding how real interpersonal events generate "difficulties in living" is a cornerstone of both interpersonal and relational theories (Greenberg & Mitchell, 1983; Harris, 2011; Mitchell, 1986, 1988; Ortmeyer, 1995). Influenced by the intellectual climate of his time, Sullivan added insights from pragmatism, anthropology, and linguistic theory to his own training in psychiatry to explain how interpersonal relationships shape the development of individual personality and pathology (Green, 1962; Lincourt & Olczak, 1974, 1979; Mitchell & Harris, 2004; Ortmeyer, 1995; Percy, 1972; Perry, 1987). His ideas laid the foundation for and anticipated many recent developments in psychoanalysis, such as the consideration of language as a form

Making Our Ideas Clear, pages 43–71
Copyright © 2015 by Information Age Publishing
All rights of reproduction in any form reserved.

of action (Levenson, 1979/2005; 1983/2005), the importance of dissociation (Bromberg, 1998; Stern, 2003), the role of early interpersonal trauma (Putnam, 1990), ideas about the multiplicity of self-states (Bromberg, 1998; Stern, 2004), and working in the here-and-now (Ehrenberg, 1992).

At the same time, he often is criticized for his view of a private and unique self as being an "illusion" (Sullivan, 1950; 1938/1995). Alternatively labeled a behaviorist and social psychologist (Greenberg & Mitchell, 1983), he gets treated as dismissing the self entirely. Critiques of the latter argue that Sullivan's self simply responds to environmental stimuli, while those of the former conceptualize Sullivan's self as totally composed of social influences and thus lacking individual agency and the capacity for an inner world of private thinking, fantasy, dreaming, and so on. Recently, Sullivan has even been linked with the growing movement of Buddhist psychoanalysts who consider the self an illusion (Engler, 2003). However, in this chapter I will argue that these views ignore Sullivan's grounding in American pragmatism, which posits the necessity of an agentic self that is both private and public. Following the pragmatists, especially Charles Sanders Peirce's construction of the self as semiotic or sign-based, I will explicate the role of signs in Sullivan's self-system, demonstrating its social origins and private functioning (Phillips, 2000; Wiley, 1994).

With this goal in mind, I begin by introducing the reader to the semiotic thinking of Charles Sanders Peirce, considered the founder of American pragmatism and an innovator of semiotic theory. Interestingly, while psychoanalysts have developed the ideas of Peirce's contemporary Saussure—notably Lacan and other French psychoanalysts—Peirce's ideas, likely because of their complexity, jargon, and never being laid out in systematic fashion, have only recently begun to be incorporated into psychoanalysis (i.e., Muller, 1996, 2000). Despite this, they are often considered some of the most original and innovative in American philosophy, anticipating many of Sullivan's ideas (Green, 1962), making them well worth investigation. Given their complexity, I present them entirely rather than organizing the paper around themes shared by each of them.

Peirce's conception of the sign leads to unique ideas about the self and its working. Specifically, I highlight how the self serves as a sign for Peirce and is thus intrinsically relational, dialogical, and grounded in social practice (codes). Peirce considers self as emergent from continuous social interactions and best understood as a series of processes. These ideas are important for how Sullivan also conceived of the self. Although Sullivan discusses the role of signs in the self (1953b, pp. 75–79, 87–89, 186–187; 1962, pp. 83–92), his focus is less on developing a semiotic or sign system than on its practical application. As I will demonstrate, his ideas overlap considerably with those of Peirce.

Considering Sullivan's self as semiotic and more than an illusion has ramifications for understanding his theory. First, it calls into question readings of his work denying an active subject. While his self may be highly idiosyncratic, divergent, sensitive to context, ambiguous, and changing; it also acts as an agent, consistent and durable throughout time. One of the benefits of explicating semiotics is its ability to make sense of the apparent complexities of self (Wiley, 1994).

Second, this view has implications for learning about the self. Since we can only know ourselves indirectly—as a sign—self-knowledge develops out of interactions (both with ourselves and with others) and subsequent feedback. As demonstrating the manner in which we learn about the self directly relates to the question of its existence, much of the chapter is devoted to this topic.

SETTING THE STAGE: WHY STUDY SEMIOTICS?

Theories of semiotics or signs are, as Sebeok (2001) reminds us, not new. Hippocrates studied signs trying to understand how symptoms (rashes, bruises, coughs, etc.) stood for other bodily and medical phenomena (allergies, broken bones, a cold, etc.)—the insight here being that something represents something else.

Since these beginnings, the field of semiotics has developed and grown to encompass the study of signs. These include signs naturally occurring in the world as well as those conventionally created by man, such as language, both written and spoken (Sebeok, 2001). Signs are seen as representing objective reality, requiring interpretation in order to be understood. From this perspective, reality can never be known *a priori* but rather is understood as codes and texts, or ongoing strings of successive signs (Sebeok, 2001). Groups of signs, which can be thought of as codes, follow certain rules structuring and organizing them (such as the way language has grammar). Codes contain and communicate information (Eco, 1984) between a source who generates the message and a receiver who interprets it. Since codes can be interpreted and understood, they can also be analyzed and both their message (content) and rules (structure) explicated. In this sense, semiotics provides the basis of not just structuralism, or the studying of codes, but also deconstructionism—the taking apart of codes (Chandler, 2007).

Broadly, semiotics can be thought of as studying "the exchange of any messages whatever and of the system of signs which underlie them" (Sebeok, 2001, p. 128). Semiotics has been applied to a number of fields, such as biosemiotics (von Uexküll, 1957) and globalized society (Douglas, 1971). In psychology, an emphasis has been placed on understanding how signs are constructed, made sense of, and used. This process, by which signs and their meanings develop and are constructed, is known as semiosis (Sebeok, 2001). In other words, while semiotics interests itself in the study of exchange, semiosis focuses more specifically on the generation and active use of signs.

As Gedo (2000) observed, since the decoding of and understanding of human communication and conduct (conscious or unconscious) are some of the main goals of psychoanalysis, studying processes of communication is a worthwhile project. This would seem particularly true for interpersonal psychoanalysis, with its emphasis on understanding the impact of real interactions, where continuous communication (verbal and nonverbal alike) and interaction are the dominant mode of exchange. Interestingly, despite the acknowledged historical influence of pragmatism on Sullivan, very little has been done comparing the systems between the two.[1] With this in mind, I turn my attention to the view of signs, sign types, and semiosis described by the pragmatist, Charles Sanders Peirce. This provides the context for more fully understanding Sullivan's writing on self.

PRAGMATISM: HOW WE COME TO KNOW THE WORLD THROUGH SIGNS

Charles Sanders Peirce—Considerations of Signs

Charles Sanders Peirce and Ferdinand Saussure independently and nearly simultaneously reinvigorated the study of semiotics in the late 19th and early 20th century (Chandler, 2007). There are at least three main distinctions between them. First, Saussure described the sign in dyadic terms (signifier/signified; word/concept), while Peirce described the sign as involving an irreducibly triadic relationship (Lincourt, 1976). Second, Saussure considered the relationship between signifier and signified as completely arbitrary. In other words there is no mandated relationship between a specific sign and its meaning. As we will see, Peirce by contrast felt that signs might be connected in real ways to their meanings. Third, Saussure's theory on language distinguishes between *langue*, the abstract system and logic of language; and *parole*, the phenomenological and actual usage of language by the individual. He felt that *langue* could be studied systematically and scientifically, whereas since *parole* is subjective it could not be. Saussure considered the goal of psychology the study of *parole* (Colapietro, 1989; Rosa, 2007). Peirce, who intended to develop an abstract theory of logic, offers a more phenomenologically based account of the development and usage of signs. In this regard, he's seen by some (Rosa, 2007) as providing a scientific and logical account of *parole* that Saussure did not. Peirce's work on semiotics closely dovetails with his writings on pragmatism providing the basis of understanding his thinking about the experiential self (Brent, 2000; Uslucan, 2010).

Peirce's Triadic Definition of the Sign

With regards to the study of psychology,[2] Peirce considered all thought—both conscious and unconscious—as sign-based, and thus semiotic (Sebeok, 2001). His view of the sign developed throughout his lifetime, but he was consistent in thinking of it as involving a triadic relationship between the *representamen* (sign vehicle), *object,* and *interpretant.* For Peirce, a sign must contain these three elements, though somewhat confusingly, he also often refers to the sign as the *representamen.*[3]

To begin Peirce, stated, "A sign, or *representamen,* is something which stands to somebody for something in some respect or capacity. It addresses somebody, that is creates in the mind of that person an equivalent sign, or perhaps a more developed one" (quoted in Chandler, 2007, p. 29).

For Peirce, the representamen (that which does the representing) is the form a sign takes, such as the sound of a voice, a pointing finger, a photograph, the printing of words on a page, and so on. The representamen stands for the immediate object, something such as a word, abstract idea, landscape, or object. The representamen itself does not communicate knowledge but requires interpretation (decoding, unpacking, etc.) by a receiving other—an interpreter as it were—to construct meaning (Goetzmann & Schwegler, 2004; Uslucan, 2010). This demonstrates the relational component of the sign. In order for something to be counted as a sign, it has to have an effect such as generating a type of action (physical, mental, etc.) on something else. This effect becomes a new sign, as Peirce directly continues: "That sign which it creates I call the *interpretant* of the first sign. The sign stands for something, its *object.* It stands for that object not in all respects but in reference to a sort of idea, which I have sometimes called the *ground* of the representamen" (quoted in Chandler, 2007, p. 29).

There is progression and development of the sign. The relationship between the original sign and the receiving "somebody" develops as the *interpretant.* Itself a sign, the interpretant can be thought of as the effect or the meaning and understanding of the original sign. In the ongoing process of signification, the interpretant becomes a new representamen standing in relation to an object and generating another interpretant. As the representamen stands only for part of the object, the entire object never is fully signified. The impossibility of fully grasping the object generates tension within the signification process ensuring its dynamic continuance (see the chapters by Salvatore and White, this volume).

Meaning making thus involves an ongoing process of interpretation and signification. Notably, "Peirce's emphasis on sense-making involves a rejection of the equation of 'content' and meaning; the meaning of a sign is not contained within it, but arises in its interpretation" (Chandler, 2007, p. 32). Meaning making thus involves a constant active process of interpretation and construction of signs, which Peirce termed semiosis. Considered the core of his semiotic theory semiosis will be described in detail following the next section.

Sign Types (Relations)

Peirce articulated a number of sign classifications (typologies) building off the different possible relationships between the elements of a sign (typologies) (Rosa, 2007; Sebeok, 2001). A convenient way of thinking of these sign types are as entailing a relationship between the *representamen* and the object (Phillips, 2000). However, it should be remembered that for Peirce the interpretant is always the necessary condition of the relationship actually constituting a sign. Of these classifications the most durable has been his articulation of *icon, index,* and *symbol* (Rosa, 2007).

Iconic signs are those where the *representamen* shares a likeness with the *object.* Examples include images, how a photograph or painting resembles scenes or people (Chandler, 2007); metaphor, and the ways apes act as icons of humans (Phillips, 2000); and also diagrams, which share similarities with their object (Sebeok, 2001). Icons are among the most fundamental of signs existing in both nature and conventional sign systems (Sebeok, 2001). As icons exist in both sign systems they are ubiquitous in codes. According to Muller, icons are psychologically experienced by the individual as diffuse and immediate feelings.

Indexical signs also exist in both nature and conventional systems. Unlike iconic signs, which share a likeness with their *object,* indexical signs denote a physical connection to the object (Brent, 2000; Chandler, 2007; Sebeok, 2001). Indices help designate types of relationship, making them factual as they are physically connected. For instance, smoke indicates fire, and a mold of a bullet hole provides an index of a bullet having been shot from a gun. From a psychological perspective, indices provide greater boundaries around experience, concretizing it in some way (Muller, 2000).

Symbols constitute the final class of signs to be discussed. Unlike the previous two classes, symbols designate a relationship entirely based upon convention (Chandler, 2007). A rose symbolizes love not out of any natural relationship, but one solely based upon conventional culture (Phillips, 2000). Language is almost entirely comprised of symbols or words that represent objects in standard and agreed-upon ways. As a result, in order to become significant, symbols are learned through habit and generalization (Sebeok, 2001).

Symbols were particularly important to Peirce and, as will be seen, Sullivan (Lincourt & Olczak, 1974, 1979; Lincourt, 1976). Through symbolic thinking, individuals are able to link together past experiences in anticipation of future ones (Green, 1962; Valsiner, 2007). Moreover, symbolic constructions such as language, which are learned by convention and maintained through habit, provide constancy and unity to mental life. At the same time they are flexible and provide the ability to explain experiences in different ways and different contexts. Symbolic communications are distinctly human, offering general and potentially self-reflective ways of interpreting objects and experience (Sebeok, 2001; Wiley, 1994).

Semiosis

While Peirce's typology of signs can be understood as a relationship between *representamen* and *object*, recall that there necessarily is an *interpretant* of this interaction (Phillips, 2000). Peirce (1907/1998) defines the action or the understanding of the sign relationship as semiosis, stating, "But by 'semiosis' I mean, on the contrary, an action, or influence, which is, or involves a cooperation of *three* subjects, such as a sign [representamen], its object, and its interpretant, this tri-relative influence not being in any way resolvable into actions between pairs" (p. 411).

As indicated earlier, the signification process does not stop with the interpretant. Indeed, in order to complete the signification process, the interpretant becomes a representamen. In other words, the meaning of the sign is embedded in its effects on the interpreter. Signs can only be understood through the process of interpretation of the successive sign, which can be an equivalent or more developed sign. Peirce described different types of interpretants, including affective, energetic, and logical. He strongly emphasized the affective component or the sense impression of the sign that he considered forming the basis of emotions (Goetzmann & Schwegler, 2004). In a similar manner, the energetic interpretant leads to actions and logical interpretants to thoughts, each furthering the chain of meaning making.

Semiosis is orientated towards the future, intended on explaining how the present moment develops into future ones (Colapietro, 1989; Green, 1962; Valsiner, 2007; Wiley, 1994). This ensures that Peirce's unit of analysis is the action and the interaction between sign users. For instance:

> A person points (index) up at the sky and his companion looks up (interpretant) to see the object of the sign. Someone else may call out, "What do you see up there?" which is also an interpretant of the original sign. For Peirce any appropriate response to a sign is acting as another sign of the originally signified. A sunflower following the sun across the sky with its face is also an interpretant. (Brent, 2000, p. 12)

The pointing action is a sign (an index) directing the attention of his companion. The object may be the target of the pointing in the sky, the finger, or alternatively the will of the person pointing, directing his companions' gaze. The *representamen* conveys a number of possible aspects of the object requiring further elaboration by the interpretant. The companion's reaction completes the different possible acts of signification. Looking up offers an energetic interpretation completing the idea that looking follows pointing, while asking a question is a logical interpretation completing a different idea. Remarking how beautiful the sky is would be still yet another interpretation. These actions are appropriate interpretations geared towards understanding or decoding the action and can only be understood as part of an interactional whole.

Since we can never have unmediated or full access to the object of signification, knowledge requires the gradual development of ideas. For Peirce, the signification of the *object* via the *representamen* leads to its *interpretant* (understanding), which then comprises another sign-object relationship and its understanding, continuing semiosis (Lincourt & Olczak, 1974; and see White, this volume, for some considerations of this). The following is a lengthy description of this process:

> The three elements that make up a sign function like a label on an opaque box that contains an object. At first the mere fact that there is a box with a label on it suggests that it contains something, and then when we read the label we discover what that something is. The process of semiosis, or decoding the sign is as follows. The first thing that is noticed (the *representamen*) is the box and label; this prompts the realization that something is inside the box (the *object*). This realization, as well as the knowledge of what the box contains, is provided by the *interpretant*. "Reading the label" is actually just a metaphor for the process of decoding the sign. The important part to be aware of here is that object of a sign is always hidden. We cannot actually open the box and inspect it directly. The reason for this is simple: if the object could be known directly, there would be no need of a sign to represent it. We only know about the object from noticing the label and the box and then "reading the label" and forming a mental picture of the object in our mind. Therefore the hidden object of a sign is only brought to realization through the interaction of the representamen, the object and the interpretant. (Chandler, 2007, p. 31)

Semiosis, and the process of "reading the label," move us continually closer (but never all the way) to knowledge about the object inside the box. The goal of semiosis is that something of the sign-object relationship becomes known. In Peirce's words, "ultimately some sign of itself, containing its own explanation, is reached" (Quoted from Lincourt & Olczak, 1974, p. 82). Semiosis provides the basis for Peirce's understanding of communication. Each interpretant becomes a sign in a chain of interpretants. The individual reception and understanding determines the effects of the original sign. This becomes known through the following actions, feelings, thoughts, and so on.

The Role of the Ground and Context

Within the process of signification, the ground refers to the manner in which the *representamen* stands for its *object* (Colapietro, 1989). The process of signification is guided by the context of the event, which mitigates some of the uncertainty of the hidden object. Peirce considers the context: "the environment—physical, psychological, and social—in which a sign or text is used or occurs" (Sebeok, 2001, p. 8), ensuring that the signification process is intelligible. Moreover, the ground highlights processes of constraint by limiting the respect that the sign stands for the object, occurring continuously during semiosis. Peirce considers the process of signification during semiosis as constitutive but not causal. In this regard, signification is neither determined nor random but generated by the different relationships amongst the semiotic triad. These are seen as limiting the possible meanings created by the interpretant.

For example, the *object* restrains what can be signified by the *representamen*. Whether a natural relationship, such as the likeness of a photograph or the direction of an index, the shape of the box in the example above, or a conventional one, objects establish a range of what can be represented. The ground ensures some connection with the real world of objects (Peirce felt one existed; see Ograv & Neuman, this volume), preventing endless pluralism and relativism (Colapietro, 1989).

Context provides the necessary conditions for understanding conduct through the establishing of basic semiotic codes.

> [These] can be defined as systems of signs that are held together by paradigmatic [conditions by which signs are differentiated, i.e., the sound between cat–hat] and syntagmatic [how signs can be combined in an intelligible way] relations. Cartesian geometry, for instance, is a *code* because it has specific structural properties.... Language too is a code because it has paradigmatic (pin *vs.* bin) and syntagmatic (plan but not pfan) properties. (Sebeok, 2001, pp. 7–8)

Our developed familiarity with codes and their contexts enables them to slip away, such that it feels as if we do not mediate our experience, a form of semiotic transparency (Phillips, 2000), which is necessary to action. Experience often feels much like after we've learned to drive a car—we do not hesitate to stop at red and go at green; however, this is a result of a complex semiotic process. Similarly, we can lose ourselves in a movie or good book, taking semiotic mediation for granted and only experiencing the meaning of the film or text. However, a cell phone going off in the theatre, violating the code, reminds us of our mediated experience.

Learning of Codes and Knowledge

Knowledge about the world develops through semiosis, the complicated progression of signification within a particular context. Children are born into highly complicated social environments without the benefit of having fully developed cognitive capacities. However, as is becoming increasingly clear, they do possess the capabilities to interact and begin learning the rules (Beebe & Lachmann, 2003). One of their goals is to learn the rules and develop the skills to successfully move within various social situations, each with their own code of conduct. Clearly reliant upon adults—in particular, parents—children are taught to navigate the complexities of their environment. For Peirce, children learn about themselves and the necessary social skills to successfully adapt through comments and feedback provided by the "Other."

Here, culture, implicit communication, and the symbolic world of language play a central role. For instance, Muller (1996, 2000) has explored literature on infant development demonstrating the centrality of cultural signs. He argues that adults initially mediate the relationship between the infant and their world, while at the same time teaching them how to navigate it themselves. Focusing on the transactional quality of semiosis, he observes how infant and mother mutually regulate each other through their gaze. Muller (1996) considers this as developing through a type of initial resemblance (iconicity) where the infant's gaze corresponds to the mother:

> The infant's gaze appears to enact iconically what the infant has come to expect from the mother, implying the use of a rudimentary icon of the mother's gaze. The infant's own act of gazing aims at the mother's corresponding gaze, and when it is not found in the withdrawn face of the mother, visible and corresponding withdrawal on the part of the infant occurs; the mother's gaze and vocalizing, moreover, through emotional induction or "contagion," creates its icon in the mirroring response of the infant. (p. 35)

The mother's response regulates the infant and vice versa. As the mother has greater semiotic knowledge, not only does she respond but she also helps the infant to develop his own understanding of the rules (Beebe & Lachmann, 1998, 2003). This involves increasing semiotic awareness, such that the child learns to connect experiences. Muller envisions a progression from direct signs to more abstract ones and eventually towards symbols.

Peirce's View of Self

Through interaction with the other and the gradual acquisition of cultural codes, including language, behaviors, mannerisms, and so on, the child discovers her own activity and desire in the world. For Peirce, communication is particularly important to this process, enabling children to experience conflict between their impressions of the world and an "Other's" (typically a parent's) impressions of the world. Conflict is both verbal and experiential. For example, the parent says to the child that "the stove is hot," and the child retorts, "no, it's not." The child then touches the stove and learns both experientially that it is hot and that testimony of an adult may be more accurate than her own (Colapietro, 1989).[4]

Having learned that the reporting of his parents may be more accurate than his own inclinations, the child begins to recognize his own ignorance. In turn, the child hypothesizes the presence of a self where the ignorance takes place and occurs (Lincourt & Olczak, 1979). In other words, the child's experience of herself as a conscious and unique self who is different from her parents begins, as a postulate intended on explaining the irregularities and contradictions between her view of the world and how other people view the world (Colapietro, 1989). Consciousness serves to make sense of error in the world.

Peirce considers self-consciousness developing from the elaboration of the experience of error. In this case, the child comes to recognize that other selves, like adults, each have what amounts to their own private experiences and wishes, which are different than not only the child's, but also other adults'. Mother may not want the child to move the chair, but father may want the child to. Learning of individual difference furthers the child's own sense of error—that is, the sense that his feelings are different than other people's and part of his own private experience. The child considers private as synonymous with erroneous and develops a sense of self-conscious experiencing of error. This leads to the idea that the child's self, like other people's, is fallible, necessitating that the child continuously look towards the Other for feedback (Colapietro, 1989).

Since self emerges through a comparison with Other, Peirce contends that it remains in relationship as distinguishable but not separable from the Other (Colapeitro, 1989). Peirce's self as experiential and historical ensures the uniqueness of self. For instance, the experience of being burned while similar to how a child's parents may have been burned is also uniquely constrained by the child's biology, history and experience. In this matter Peirce preserves private and unique experience, while arguing that the core of the self's identity involves continual communication and relationships. Communication involves both silent dialogue with our selves as well as the more traditional spoken dialogue (Wiley, 1994). Notably, even in spoken dialogue, private dialogue remains through the function of hearing ourselves speak, which Bahktin referred to as "double directionality" (Salgado & Gonçalves, 2007).

This leads to Peirce's consideration of all conscious thought as dialogue and sign-based and, in turn, his belief that the self is a sign.[5] He further advances the idea that the self is the semiotic total of the signs available to oneself. In order to coordinate the various ideas of the self within space and time (context), Peirce hypothesizes a *personality*. One's *personality* organizes the different ideas and dialogues about one's self, by remaining in continuous communication with self and Other. This process involves ongoing interaction acting as an interpreter and also being interpreted. As we will see, when this ability becomes interfered with, the self loses its ability to actualize and construct new meaning.

Personality more broadly becomes the sense of continuity or consistency, which provides the experience of habit. Often, the process of signification fades to the background as described earlier, and we may not experience our conscious actions and decisions in the world. However, the possibilities of error, fallibility, and ignorance, as well as reflective thinking, pave the way for self-conscious experiencing. These may occur when our habits are interfered with (ruptures). Peirce also stresses the importance of learning to exert control over our experience, such as by committing to certain ideas, values, and beliefs (Colapeitro, 1989; Uslucan, 2010). Indeed, habits may often reflect implicit beliefs and values (Stern, 2012). Through the elaboration of personal codes and beliefs, the individual influences her future experience. In this manner, self-organization is hierarchical. Immediate experience is more connected with the here-and-now as icons, gradually becoming increasingly conventional and abstract as indices and symbols, up until it recursively becomes private again as beliefs and codes (Wiley, 1994).

Peirce in Summary

Peirce described the sign in triadic terms, where the sign represents something about an object to an interpretant. This provides the basis of typologies of sign relationships, of which three (icon, index, symbol) were described. These typologies describe the varying ways we can, through signs, come to know the world. Icons offer likeness, indices physical connections, and symbols conventional knowledge. Symbols are particularly important for studies of language and communication, given their ability to convey condensed information about conventional knowledge. Peirce considers the signification process as ongoing, known as semiosis, which occurs in particular contexts. Understandable as codes, context provides the social feedback through which self comes inferentially to be known. Self emerges as a dialogical sign intended on making sense of error. The self is unique, maintaining a sense of embodied history of sign usage and possessing the agency of self-conscious choice, but is never fully private, always being in relationship to something or someone else.

HARRY STACK SULLIVAN: SEMIOTICS IN PRAXIS

Peirce, as indicated, was not interested in human pathology but rather in developing systems of logic and epistemology (Lincourt & Olczak, 1974).

Highly abstract and complicated, Peirce was nonetheless consistent with pragmatic thinking. He paid close attention to the way self emerges out of relationships and actions. In following Peirce's consideration of the self as a sign, "The investigative focus shifts from a mechanical, linear, causal model to an interactive, probabilistic one in which codes play a central role. There is more to a system than its semiotic code, but without taking the code into account the system's behavior is not intelligible" (Muller, 2000, p. 54).

Sullivan's insight and genius was his recognition of the need to study these codes and relationships in order to understand difficulties in living. Moreover, he was adept at translating the language of pragmatism and semiotics into a systematic and sophisticated praxis,[6] intended on unraveling, interpreting, and most of all understanding these codes. In this sense, his development of an "experience near" method of treatment focused on the analytic dyad and each individual's two-person field of relating shares considerably with the work of pragmatism (Fiscalini, 1995, 2007).

He was as interested in working with pathology as Peirce was not. Building off the emphasis on the role of communication and information—or broadly the social structure of self—prevalent in American thinking at the turn of the century, Sullivan developed sophisticated ideas about how the self functions and malfunctions within interpersonal situations. His "theory of living to problems in living was intentionally seamless, because of his belief that the psychosocial processes underlying the 'normality' and 'pathology' of interpersonal relationships were much more similar than otherwise" (Evans, 1996, p. 134). In other words, problems stem from general processes of interaction, "which vary [in patients] from so-called normals not in the kind, but in the degree of pervasiveness, of difficulty" (Evans, 1996, p. 134). As we will see, his focus on the self-system, distortion, anxiety, and selective inattention hinges on the potential problems that self can experience within interpersonal situations, which are in turn mediated by cultural signs. Not only is Sullivan's self, like Peirce's, semiotic, but the ways in which it gets into trouble are also semiotic.

While Sullivan does not mention having read Peirce he does credit George Herbert Mead's theory of self as strongly influencing his own (Sullivan, 1953b, pp. 16–17; Greenberg & Mitchell, 1983 pp. 96–97). Although, the relationship between Peirce and Mead is unclear, they are generally considered amongst the forefathers of pragmatism and their ideas have been compared fruitfully in the literature (i.e., Gillespie, 2003, 2005; Usluscan, 2010; Wiley, 1994). Some scholars consider Mead's thinking of self as having been preceded in significant fashion by Peirce's amongst other early 20th century American philosophers, noting that while different it remains within the same philosophical tradition (Lincourt & Olczak, 1974; Usluscan, 2010).

Conception of Reality and Mediation

A more direct influence on Sullivan was Adolph Meyer, who was familiar with and influenced by the work of James and Peirce, among other influential figures (Lincourt & Olcak, 1979; Meyer, 1958). Not surprisingly, Meyer's influence on Sullivan is apparent in Sullivan's consideration of reality, which maintains a central pragmatic—and Peircean—idea of mediation. For instance, Sullivan considers how Meyer freed psychology from its biologically reductive roots. Sullivan, quotes from Meyer's biography, states, "Meyer recognizes the hierarchies of organization and proceeds from a consideration of organismic integrating factors.... To bridge the gap between biology and psychiatry by the concept of *mentation*, a peculiarly effective integrating activity by the use of symbols and meanings" (p. 9).

The influence of Meyer's thinking can be seen on Sullivan's development of a psychobiology and descriptions of dynamisms to understand not only problematic patterns of interpersonal relationships but also the interplay between physiology on experiences of satisfaction and anxiety (Evans, 1996; Sullivan 1938/1995, p. 15 for a description of this interplay; Sullivan, 1953a, 1962). Indeed, Meyer's and Sullivan's focus on signs of biological communication in addition to interpersonal share interesting similarity with those of Jakob Von Uexküll (Von Uexküll, 1934/1957; Wagoner & Rosenbaum, 2009).

Clearly, Sullivan was aware of the role that signs and semiotics play not only in the representation of reality but also in the generation of problems. These are distinctly interpersonal problems. Sullivan (1938/1995) defined the field of psychiatry broadly "as a science concerned with the thinkings and doings of persons, real and illusory" (p. 7). More specifically, psychiatry worked "to discover and formulate the laws of human personality.... [I]ts peculiar field is the study of *interpersonal phenomena*. Personality is made manifest in interpersonal situations and not otherwise" (Sullivan, 1938/1995, p. 8).

Sullivan's Theory of Signs

Sullivan does not articulate a comprehensive theory of signs similar to Peirce's, however they feature extensively in his writing (Lincourt & Olczak, 1974, 1979). For example, the role of symbols in thinking is prominent in his early theorizing about self and schizophrenia. Sullivan (1962) states:

> Thought, for our purposes, is organisimic activity by the implicit functioning of symbols themselves abstracts from the 'material' of life-events. In the ontogenesis of a personality, we can see cadres of these symbols, the fundamental differentia among the individual members of which reside in the order of their abstraction from the experiential basis. (p. 83)

Working to develop a theory to understand and treat schizophrenics, for whom at the time assistance was considered outside the realm of psychiatry, Sullivan focused on the meanings conveyed by symbols (Greenberg & Mitchell, 1983). His thinking highlights the difficulties schizophrenics face in elaborating (abstracting) symbols to represent their experiences when compared to non-schizophrenic members of society. He endorsed the then radical idea that schizophrenics are capable of and in fact do use symbols to communicate; however, "many such primitive symbols escape elaboration into higher order symbols in awareness" (Sullivan, 1962, p. 87). This impedes their ability to communicate and in Peirce's terms means that schizophrenics are not able to abstract to and maintain a self-symbol in the world, which can accommodate changing social habits and contexts.

Sullivan considered the poorly symbolized self of a schizophrenic as an adaptation necessary to protect the patient from interpersonal situations that would otherwise lead to the full disintegration of self. He describes this process "as a whole, a peculiarly inadequate adaptation of the cognitive processes to the necessities of adult life" (Sullivan, 1962, p. 92). Considering schizophrenia an interpersonal process enabled Sullivan to focus on trying to understand the context of the schizophrenic's language usage (and not just the content) as central for determining the patient's prognosis (Sullivan, 1962; Greenberg & Mitchell, 1983).

Sullivan's Three Modes of Experience

Aware of the power of language to mediate reality (Greenberg & Mitchell, 1983; Lincourt & Olczak, 1974), Sullivan's later work further developed his theory of signs into a central component of his self-system. He delineates three modes, *prototaxic, parataxic,* and *syntaxic* (1953b), that characterize an individual's semiotic abilities as well as cognitive experience and development. Notably, these modes are closely related to his considerations of personality, the self, and the self-system. However, as they characterize both his thinking on cognition as well as development, they are presented prior to the more specific applications in his self-system.

Prototaxic Experience

Sullivan considers babies as born into a prototaxic mode of experience. Perhaps the simplest and most abundant form of experience, Sullivan suggests that infants do not experience temporality. They also do not differentiate between themselves and the world. Their experience is precognitive, mostly affective, and unanalyzed. Prototaxic experience "may be regarded as the discrete series of momentary states of the sensitive organism, with special reference to the zones of interaction with the environment"

(Sullivan, 1953b, p. 29). The zones of interaction that localize an exchange between the child and her environment characterize prototaxic experiencing. These zones are seen as leading to the satisfaction of basic needs for intimacy, closeness, and tenderness. Notably, "the primary function of the zones of interaction, however, is to provide a channel to the other, to facilitate the interpersonal integrations necessary for the satisfaction of needs, operating as integrating tendencies" (Greenberg & Mitchell, 1983, pp. 92–93). One way to understand these zones during prototaxic experience are as icons[7] calling forth responses from the caregiver similar to the need represented by the zone.

For example, Sullivan (1953a) notes the way that crying for the baby represents his needs in the mind of the mother (Lincourt & Olczak, 1974 p. 78). In this case, the meaning of the babies crying resides not in the baby's mind, but rather in the mind of the mother who actively cares for the baby. Problematically, the mother does not necessarily know the needs of the baby that need caring for (is the baby hungry? sick? tired?) and has to respond in a way that addresses this unknown. For Sullivan, the mother's response has to address both the need and the affect, in a sense serving an iconic function. Similar to Peirce's considerations, the babies crying likely generates similar affect within the mother, who has the capacity to symbolize in order to care for the child. The mother's interpretation of the baby's needs (the unknown object as it were) in turn shapes the baby's own understanding of his needs (this process can be compared to Bion's process of metabolizing as discussed by White, this volume, and as a precursor to infant development and communication studies; i.e., Beebe & Lachmann, 2003).

The uncertainty throughout this process makes childrearing anxiety provoking for both mother and child. Problematically, the child has relatively few ways of protecting herself from the harmful effects of anxiety. The methods available include apathy and somnolent detachment—a type of avoidance and trying to ignore the anxiety-provoking circumstance. For Sullivan, anxiety threatens the child's developing self-system. He considers it a contagion, which the child catches from the parent, whose anxiety may not even be about the child (Evans, 1996). What makes the anxiety so threatening is that it cannot, like other experiences, be controlled or resolved by the child. Much like anxiety prevents adults from eating, playing, or sometimes even thinking, it is similar for the child, who has only minimal capabilities to escape it (Greenberg & Mitchell, 1983).

Parataxic Experiencing

Sullivan describes a second mode of experience as parataxic. Here, the wholeness of experience becomes broken up into parts that are not yet related to each other. Experiences are not logically connected and not linked to previous or future experiences. However, in parataxic experiencing, children attend to their environment in greater detail. They are able to discriminate between self and the external world of objects and other people (Lincourt & Olczak, 1979). Sullivan (1953b) considered infants as having prehensions rather than fully developed perceptions of their environment. Prehensions are related directly to early images and sensations—experienced primarily through sound and vision—that allow children to make these distinctions.

As part of parataxic experiencing, the infant learns to distinguish the mood of the "Other" in such a way as to "prehend" distress or anxiety within a particular context. The "infant first learns to discriminate 'signs' connected with the anxious as opposed to nonanxious mother—wrinkled brow, postural tensions, and so on. These earliest prehensions are registered because they are *useful.* The infant learns to anticipate whether anxious or nonanxious mother will appear" (Greenberg & Mitchell, 1983, p. 96). Here, the infant's ability is expanded to include indices, which connect the world in physical ways (sound, sight, etc.).

The physical contingency between signs and their objects also includes early language acquisition. Sullivan notes that language during parataxic experience is highly private, or autistic. Meaning is not yet conventional or subjected to influence resulting from interpersonal interaction. The qualities of parataxic experiencing are important for Sullivan's consideration of pathology. He notes that parataxic distorting "refers to any attitude toward another person which is based on a phantasied or distorted evaluation of that person or on an identification of that person with other figures from past life" (Lincourt & Olczak, 1979, p. 13). In other words, the baby's view of the mother may suffer from parataxic distortion, influenced by his need for security, and thus become warped so that it does not represent how the mother is at all. Not surprisingly, parataxic experience and distortion also characterizes schizophrenia due to the experience of bizarre communication, disorganization, private meaning, and frequent interruptions.

Syntaxic Mode of Experience

Finally, Sullivan was interested in the syntaxic experiencing of children, where the acquisition of language helps them to group together and integrate their experiences. Whereas the prior modes are outside of temporal experience, syntaxic experience enables children to develop a sense of before and after producing logical order, better communication, and object permanence. Here, the child becomes able to recognize that "good mother" and "bad mother" are in fact the same person and correct the distortion of parataxic experiencing (Greenberg & Mitchell, 1983).

An important function of symbolic thought for Sullivan is its ability to generate symbolic consciousness that holds together multiple and conflicting ideas. Symbols mediate the relationship between other signs helping the individual distance themselves from their here-now sign relationships. This occurs since "a word [a symbol] is a condensation of human experience, the intensity and clarity is raised when consciousness is directed to symbols of experience" (Lincourt & Olczak, 1974, p. 80). In addition to recognizing that good and bad mother is the same, the child also "begins to anticipate and to link his behaviors with the mother's affective state" (Greenberg & Mitchell, 1983, p. 97). Accordingly, the behaviors that mother approves of are those that keep her anxiety down, maintaining empathic linkage become labeled "good me," while the behaviors and experiences that make the mother more anxious and distant become "bad me." Finally, are those experiences that cause mother to become intensely anxious— practically not present. These experiences are terrifying to the infant and become labeled "not me" (Evans, 1996; Greenberg & Mitchell, 1983).

As we see, the infant's achievement of symbolic functioning remains closely attuned with her sense of self. Self-consciousness emerges as the ability to condense and reflect on conscious experiencing. Indeed, the central function of the syntaxic mode of experience is to help the child deal with the potential for anxiety that would upset the rest of self-experiencing. Failure to develop or maintain syntaxic experience can lead to mental disorders or movement back into a more sustained state of parataxic distortion. Notably, as these modes characterize cognitive styles, in addition to developmental milestones, people move between them throughout their lives.

Sullivan's Consideration of the Self-System

The syntaxic mode of experience develops along with more complex interpersonal processes, including symbolic consciousness or the ability to take the perspective of the "Other" (Lincourt & Olczak, 1974). This capacity emerges along with ones sense of self. Here, Sullivan (1953b) explicitly acknowledges and builds off (p. 16–17) George Herbert Mead's (1934) thinking about self. Mead's theory[8] maintains the distinction between a "me" that is social and the knowing "I," which develops in response to the "me." Here, the "I" grows and learns in coordination and dialogue with the "me." The "me" develops through the way the individual is seen by the "Other," or imagines themselves as being seen in the eyes of the "Other."[9] Much like with Peirce and James', the self for Mead is dialogical (Gillespie, 2005 p. 33). Self emerges from ongoing dialogical relationship where the "I" as knower develops via interactions with the "me" as known. Developmentally, the "me" exists prior to the emergence of the "I," such that symbolic consciousness develops out of prior social relationships and not before them (see Bellehsen, this volume for elaborations of these ideas).[10]

Sullivan (1953b) distinguished between *personality*, which he considers the sum total of who one is, including social appraisal and the parts of oneself that other people acknowledge but are not recognized by the self (they may be dissociated, not acknowledged, split off and so forth), and *self*, which is an individual's conscious understanding of these appraisals, or an individual's understanding of their self at a given point in time (Greenberg & Mitchell, 1983). In other words, *personality* is the observable "I and Me" while the *self* is the person's subjective awareness of the "I and me." Much as with Peirce's self, ones *personality* emerges through the reflected appraisals of the "Other." The role of *personality* is to coordinate these different appraisals. However, unlike Peirce, who felt that self emerges as a hypothesis intended to mediate the experience of error and ignorance, for Sullivan, *self* is concerned with obtaining satisfaction and security through the minimization of anxiety. He termed these functional and organizing aspects of the self the "self-system" (Sullivan, 1938/1995, 1950).

Self-System as a Semiotic Process

Sullivan's self-system is tasked with preserving security. Like Peirce's self, it emerges within a dialogical two-person field emphasizing the reflected appraisal of the "Other," which Sullivan termed *consensual validation.* In order to exist within a social matrix, children use symbols to integrate diverse experiences in such a way to ensure effective communication. This requires that they become proficient symbol users in ways that approximate how they are used in their cultural environment. Sullivan (1950) states that "social organization, such things as language, formulated ideas, and so on, are indispensible and equally absolutely necessary part of the environment of the human being, of the person" (p. 324). In other words, children learn to become competent code users and creators.

From this idea, develops perhaps Sullivan's most controversial and perhaps most misunderstood idea—though one most pragmatists were in agreement with—the self as an illusion (1938/1995, 1950). Sullivan (1950), who focused on the importance of the social world in which the child develops, wants to know how *personality* and *self* develop out of syntaxic experience. Focusing on communication as the means of feedback (appraisals), he asks:

> How can the thing be made to communicate? How can I tell somebody about this? And we finally, if we are fairly clever, get the answer. Once we have got that, the unique individuality of the experience begins to shrink, it becomes part of the general structure of life, we forget how strikingly novel the experience was and how peculiarly it had fringes which apply only to us—we lose that in the process of validation. (p. 326)

The answer to the question of how we are able to discuss our experience, make sense of it, and eventually develop a self-narrative is that the uniqueness around the fringes disappears. Or, in other words, much like with Peirce's description of habit, experience begins as unique and idiosyncratic and becomes more commonplace with experience. Here, Sullivan is again highlighting the mediated aspect of our experience. We can only communicate through signs, which we acquire socially through interaction and validation. In this he agrees with Peirce's earlier declaration that the self is both a sign and the semiotic process by which we access the world (Phillips, 2000).

The system of signs and signification that Sullivan put forth seems to highlight the importance of transparency. Phillips (2000) notes, "As we see *through* signs to the world, we do not take note of the signs" (p. 17, original emphasis). In other words, when we learn to communicate, much of the uniqueness and novelty of experience is forgotten. In this sense, we are often unaware of the mediating effect that culture has on experience. Indeed, we can imagine the difficulties that would (and sadly do) ensue if we tried to explain each experience's unique texture to the fullest in all circumstances (though deconstruction, poetry, music sometimes work by creating purposeful ruptures in the semiotic process). This of course does not mean this does not happen, but rather for smooth functioning in the world, it happens less frequently.

Sullivan's background working with schizophrenics would have made him aware of the difficulties that occur when semiotic processes are disturbed. His work understanding these processes anticipates current literature on schizophrenia and even trauma. For example, Phillips (2000) discusses schizophrenia as a breakdown in the everyday transparency of semiotic processes. He notes the way schizophrenics become "engulfed by" (p. 19) the external world of signs, literally almost becoming that which is being signified. Similarly, Muller (1996) describes "the breakdown of normal language use in schizophrenia as a failure to use language in its mediating role between the subject and the unarticulated unsymbolized world" (Phillips, 2000, p. 20).

From this observation follows Sullivan's disputing the possibility of their being a true, essential, *a priori* self so to speak. Sullivan argued against the isolated self that existed prior to growth and interpersonal relationships, in favor of a self that is engaged in process of relating, whether to a past self or a real dialogical other. His emphasis on process does not mean that he was uninterested in unique experience and in studying individuals. He remarked, "Anything of value in our work . . . comes from the intimate and detailed study of particular individuals" (Greenberg & Mitchell, 1983, p. 84). However, the mediated quality of self ensures that an individual can only be studied and understood within the context of their relationship to an "Other." Again, similar to Peirce, the private self only becomes known in relationship to other parts of itself, constituting an interpersonal relationship. The illusion for Sullivan and Peirce is of a fully private and insular self, which remains untouched by the influence of an "Other." To be clear, Sullivan does not consider internal experience (i.e., dreams, fantasy, inner thought, and so forth) or the idea of a self an illusion, but rather the idea of a *fully* internal and *completely* private self is the illusion. That something is internal already calls into mind the idea of external, pointing to a relationship between self and other.

Me–You Patterns

That the self does not exist outside of relationships does not mean it is not enduring, stable, and agentic. Rather, the self-system works continuously to anticipate anxiety and achieve satisfaction in its relationships. Like for Peirce, the self as a sign actively locates itself spatially and temporarily among other relationships.

> We symbolize and formulate the present—and by symbolize we mean we relate it to things, thought forms, words, and so on, which will stand for it.... And as I said before, we project the future by juggling with past symbolizations, understandings, and present formulations in terms of probable future events. To the extent that we project well—that is we are careful in decided probabilities of certain course of events—we sometimes exercise foresight and are prepared for what happens. (Sullivan, 1950, p. 319)

The self works through semiosis to relate current experience to past experience and understandings with the intent of stabilizing the uncertain future (Sullivan, 1953b; Valsiner, 2007). Like Peirce, whose semiotic system was directed towards the future, Sullivan's concern was with an individual's ability to preadapt in new circumstances by anticipating anxiety learned from previous experiences. These lead to the development of "me–you" interpersonal configurations or dynamisms (Evans, 1996). Often the attempt to foresee the future leads to the application of distorted "me–you" configurations as a way of stabilizing potential anxiety. These parataxic distortions not only apply experiences from the past to the present but can also call out the complementary responses in the interlocutor. Thus, these patterns become "a way of being-in-the-world which is idiosyncratic, highly creative, and powerfully redundant; that is capable of provoking the other people in the patient's world to react in predictable and controllable ways—not, one notes, necessarily gratifying or rewarding ways" (Levenson, 1989, p. 541).

In this sense, "me–you" patterns function similarly to how Peirce indicated symbolic communication does. Signs exist for both parties in real ways. Sullivan's description of this process reflects considerable subtlety as he attends to the various verbal and nonverbal (implicit and explicit) semiotic processes at work. Indeed, as not all experiences are parataxic but are syntaxic as well, the individual can flexibly and purposefully "juggle" understandings and meanings as they work to achieve satisfying experiences.

Within "me–you" patterns, these satisfying experiences are considered integrating tendencies allowing for greater growth and flexibility. However, as Sullivan was more interested in pathology, or the degree to which processes went amok, he focused more on how anxiety-provoking experiences lead to a lack of security and the disintegration of the self. In other words, these experiences prevent the self from actively making meaning, instead causing it to freeze up and not respond flexibly to the environment. As described earlier, for Sullivan anxiety was particularly threatening due to its contagious and rather amorphous nature. "The self-system thus is an organization of educative experience called into being by the necessity to avoid or to minimize incidents of anxiety" (Sullivan, 1953b, p. 165). The organization used to minimize anxiety he termed *security operations* (Evans, 1996).

Security Operations

Security operations are the methods the self uses to avoid anxiety. Due to their function, they are largely habitual and not conscious. Notably, security operations, when functioning appropriately, also aid the self in its aims of integration. When functioning poorly, they hamper interpersonal learning and growth by the development of maladaptive "me–you" patterns (Evans, 1996).

Sullivan described a number of security operations, including selective inattention, dissociation, sublimation, verbalisms, "as if" performances, and malevolent transformation (Evans, 1996). As processes they can be thought of as influencing the process of semiosis, disturbing how meaning is made. For example, *selective inattention* helps to guard against uncertainty and disintegrating experiences and preserve a sense of oneself as good, knowing, and in control. Here, there is a "process of shifting awareness away from anxiety-laden interpersonal situations" (Evans, 1996, p. 144). Selective inattention usefully helps us forget anxiety-inducing experiences, but it can also problematically exclude information that would be helpful in learning more effective interpersonal patterns. Alternatively, with *dissociation* an individual inhibits the motivation required to satisfy certain needs by making associations or connections. As a result they not only do not satisfy the need, but they do not recognize the experience of having a need to be satisfied at all. This is similar to a type of splitting of the personality considered threatening away from the self (Evans, 1996). In order to protect itself from overwhelming experiencing, the self becomes unaware of its impact on self and on the "Other."

Considering these processes from the view of self as semiotic, we see how semiosis or the process of signification is impacted. In selective inattention the dialogical loop of the I–you–me interaction is overtly constrained such that contextual cues and interpersonal processes, which if noticed would produce anxiety are ignored. In a more extreme fashion, dissociation appears to switch off the social act, preventing the self from experiencing feedback from the "Other." In both cases, experience is no longer an open and integrated system but rather becomes a closed discrete loop. In these moments, individuals do not experience error or ignorance required to actively make meaning. Instead, their agency cannot be recognized likely generating experiences of anxiety, helplessness, and depression. In other words, the self becomes "a sign cut off from its future interpretants… a sign denied the possibility of realizing its essence; that is the possibility of being a sign" (Colapietro, 1989, p. 77).

It is worth recalling that Sullivan did not consider these processes innately pathological, but rather normative and varying in degree but not type. Considered in this fashion, security operations are intended to protect the individual's agency, the ability to juggle different understandings, meanings, desires, wishes, options, and so forth in the pursuit of satisfying experiences. The self, as a semiotic construct and not an essentially private entity, in fact possibly offers a greater degree of agency through being able to imaginatively and creatively take the perspective of the other as well as that of the self. A pluralistic self provides increased opportunities for novelty than a closed off and isolated monological one.

Sullivan in Summary

Interested in understanding pathological developments of otherwise normative processes, Sullivan applied insights from pragmatism towards his study of psychiatry. He paid particular attention to the importance of symbolic thinking and the role of consensual validation in the development of the self and the functional systems used by the self to minimize anxiety and achieve satisfaction as well as security. These systems are distinctly interpersonal leading to the establishment of habitual and enduring ways of interacting with the "Other." As a result, Sullivan came to consider the idea of a private self an illusion, instead emphasizing the mediated and social nature of the self. From this develops a view of the results of mild, moderate, and severe disturbances in the self-systems processes generating a host of maladaptive ways of being in the world. These are contrasted with less maladaptive ways of protecting the self and preserving its creative and agentic functions.

CONCLUSIONS: IMPLICATIONS OF COMPARING SULLIVAN'S AND PEIRCE'S SELF

Explicating the influence of Peirce's thinking about semiotics on Sullivan's theory and clinical practice has several useful implications. Peirce's semiotics provides a description of the self that, while based in social practice, retains agency, the ability to make choices and act willfully in the world. Individuals develop personal codes of values and beliefs, which, while based upon conventional and culturally guided forms of meaning, are nonetheless idiosyncratic and unique. For Peirce, self-consciousness develops from considering the self a sign, open to and capable of interpretation. Semiosis ensures that meanings are made along different levels (hierarchies) of abstraction. These levels move from the most immediate and private (icons) to the consensual and intangible (indices and symbols) and then recursively feed into the private as personal beliefs and codes. In turn, beliefs influence future experiences and are modified by them and so on. Of course, the construction of private personal beliefs need not always be explicit and chosen, but are also implicit, unconscious, and nonreflective.

Semiosis can be seen as influencing Sullivan's thinking of how normal processes of living can develop into "problems in living." Since anxiety for Sullivan is unavoidable and necessary, the self grows within a potentially compromised and ambiguous context. Meaning making allows the self to develop processes or security operations that minimize anxiety within interpersonal situations. Semiosis also leads to the construction of private beliefs related to these security operations. The meanings an individual makes can be understood as a blending of syntaxic and parataxic experiencing. Much like Peirce's development of conscious and self-conscious experience, these beliefs come about during the socialization process of learning cultural codes. They become personally meaningful in ways that are recursive and not always self-conscious. As security operations, they guide social behavior in repetitive ways, maintaining a sense of homeostasis, though not necessarily of satisfaction by influencing interpersonal conduct.

"Problems in living" develop along the continuum of these semiotic processes. For instance, the open self-system can develop into a closed one, where semiotic loops prevent new meanings from developing. Here, the self remains stuck within pre-existing meanings and as a result cannot interpret and integrate new experiences. In other words, the self continually (re)interprets experience based upon an implicit belief or code of meaning. The condensation of experiencing of the code is unique to the individual and may prevent new potentially threatening meanings from developing. In order to keep anxiety minimal, selective inattention can be employed so that semiosis ignores important contextual and interpersonal stimuli. A feedback system evolves where selective inattention leads to the articulation of beliefs that feed into future experiencing. Within a closed system of meaning making, feelings of anxiety and depression are likely symptoms highlighting the difficulties self faces in generating new meanings and remaining open to new experiences.

Of course, the opposite is also possible, where the self-system remains too open,[11] unable to constrain the production of new meanings. In other words, the self generates an overabundance of interpretations and cannot put a halt to the interpretive process. The lack of a semiotic stop sign paralyzes the individual and prevents her from acting willfully in the world. Here, meanings may be generated in ways that are not fixed within a particular context or become detached from a specific object. In these cases, it is possible to imagine that mania, psychosis, or obsessive thinking ensues.

From a semiotic perspective, the treatment situation provides the possibility of a unique experience with an interlocutor similar enough to communicate and engage the patient, but different enough to create a potential space for the development of new meanings (Mitchell, 1988). Within this situation, the implicit and recursive system becomes explicit, elaborated upon, and open to change. The therapist, by holding specific theories, having adapted different codes of meanings, expressing a willingness to emphasize, being interested in different parts of the patient, and so on, can be thought of as providing an opportunity to restart or realign the semiotic process. Treating the patient and his story as a sign capable of further signification enables the therapist to further symbolize with the patient.

One hypothesis of how the therapeutic process works involves the analyst and patient constructing a shared understanding of the patient's more private language. Perhaps in this model, first a picture (icon) of the patient's life and problems emerges. Next, patient and analyst construct a more concrete idea (index) of what causes the patient's suffering. Then, a space is created for new meanings and play to take place and become symbolized, which of course influences the picture of the patient's life. Through this process, the patient's capacity to experience the playful and creative side of meaning making emerges. Whether verbal and logical, leading to generating more nuanced stories; or affective helping the patient to recognize and articulate emotions; or even behavioral, attempting to initiate new behavioral responses, therapy serves as a catalyst reinvigorating semiosis and enabling the patient greater access to his or her own semiotic agency.

NOTES

1. From a philosophical tradition, see Lincourt & Olczak (1974) for a comparison of Sullivan and Peirce; Lincourt & Olczak (1979) for a study of Sullivan's phenomenology; Lincourt (1976) for Peirce's importance to psychiatry; and Green (1962) for the most extensive discussion on pragmatisms influence on Sullivan's theory from a psychoanalytic perspective I can find; and Levenson

(1983/2005) notes the importance of semiotics and of Peirce's influence but does not develop the system.

2. Peirce intended to develop his view of signs as a form of abstract logic, which would not have to refer to human thought, and thus be independent of psychology, anthropology, sociology, etc. (Brent, 2000; Phillips, 2000; Sebeok, 2001).
3. To limit this confusion, others have referred to the *representamen* as the sign vehicle. However, in order to limit conceptual problems with this, I work to keep *representamen* as part of the semiotic process and use *sign* to refer to the relationship between all three components.
4. It's worth remarking that for Peirce the body was central to the experience of the emerging self. The child's earliest experiences are all organized through their body and their bodily experience (see Colapietro, 1989, pp. 69–72).
5. I'm indebted to Carl Auerbach for offering his helpful and clarifying thoughts about this idea.
6. I'm indebted to Phil Blumberg for helping with this connection.
7. Lincourt & Olczaz (1979) relate Sullivan's modes of experience to Peirce's thinking Peirce's phenomenological approach towards understanding cognition. This system also is structured as a triad (firstness, secondness, thirdness) and maps well onto Sullivan's system. In a similar light, Muller (1996) has considered the ways that Peirce's phenomenological system maps onto his semiotic triad (firstness being similar to icon; secondnes to index; thirdness to symbol). He has also discussed how this triad fits into Lacan's system of the real, imaginary, and symbolic (Muller, DATE). I consider Sullivan's cognitive modes along the lines of the semiotic triad because I feel that these ideas have greater accessibility and perhaps application to clinical work.
8. Mead's theory is based on William James's (1890/1950) distinction of the "I" and "me."
9. For Mead, the social act (Gillespie, 2005) sets the conditions for the development of self through the significant symbol. This symbol "is genuinely intersubjective and dialogic for it is, even it its most minimal form, the integration of at least two different perspectives" (Gillespie, 2005, p. 33). It allows for an account of an ongoing dialogical relationship where the "I" as knower develops through interactions with the "me" (the generalized other as it were) as known.
10. Notably, this does not deny reflective self-conscious experience but localizes it within ongoing relationships. Experience can be "private," in the sense it is not shared or even known by an individual—but that when it becomes conscious and self-conscious it emerges through some form of relationship (self–other; self–self). Experience develops within the context of continuing relational events.
11. The idea of open and closed systems is a bit more complicated. Here, the meaning-making process is considered open or lacking the contextual constraint required for making decisions and choices. Meanings in other words are generated in abundance but not organized or put a stop to. As a result, the self may be experienced as being closed similar to what was described earlier, however it is closed not because of an over generalized meaning, but the inability to stop meanings from being generated.

REFERENCES

Beebe, B., & Lachmann, F. (1998). Co-constructing inner and relational process: Self and mutual regulation in infant research and adult treatment. *Psychoanalytic Psychology, 15*(4), 480–516.

Beebe, B., & Lachmann, F. (2003). The relational turn in psychoanalysis: A dyadic systems view from infant research. *Contemporary Psychoanalysis, 39*, 379–409.

Brent, J. (2000). A brief introduction to the life and thought of Charles Sanders Peirce. In J. Muller & J. Brent (Eds.), *Peirce, semiotics, and psychoanalysis* (pp. 1–15). Baltimore, MD: Johns Hopkins University Press.

Bromberg, P. (1998). *Standing in the spaces.* Hillsdale, NJ: The Analytic Press.

Chandler, D. C. (2007). *Semiotics: The basics* (2nd ed.). New York, NY: Routledge.

Colapietro, V. M. (1989). *Peirce's approach to the self.* Albany, NY: State University of New York Press.

Douglas, M. (1971). *Deciphering a meal.* In C. Geetz (Ed.), *Myth, symbol and culture* (pp. 61–82). New York, NY: Norton.

Eco, U. (1984). *Semiotics and the philosophy of language.* Bloomington, IN: Indiana University Press.

Ehrenberg, D. (1992). *The intimate edge: Extending the reach of psychoanalytic interaction.* New York, NY: Norton.

Evans, F. B. (1996). *Harry Stack Sullivan: Interpersonal theory and psychotherapy.* New York, NY: Routledge.

Engler, J. (2003). Being somebody and being nobody: A reexamination of the understanding of self in psychoanalysis and Buddhism. In J. D. Safran (Ed.), *Psychoanalysis and Buddhism: An unfolding dialogue* (pp. 35–80). Somerville, MA: Wisdom Publications.

Fiscalini, J. (1995). *Introduction.* In D. B. Stern, C. H. Mann, S. Kantor, & G. Schlesinger (Eds.), *The pioneers of interpersonal psychoanalysis* (pp. 1–7). New York, NY: Routledge.

Fiscalini, J. (2007). The coparticipant field: Commentary on a paper by Juan Tubert-Oklander. *Psychoanalytic Dialogues, 17*, 133–141.

Gedo, J. E. (2000). Protolinguistic phenomena in psychoanalysis. In J. Muller & J. Brent (Eds.), *Peirce, semiotics, and psychoanalysis* (pp. 37–49). Baltimore, MD: Johns Hopkins University Press.

Gillespie, A. (2003). Supplementarity and surplus: Moving between the dimensions of otherness. *Culture & Psychology, 9*, 209–220.

Gillespie, A. (2005). G. H. Mead: Theorist of the social act. *Journal for the Theory of Social Behaviour, 35*, 19–39.

Goetzmann, L., & Schwegler, K. (2004). Semiotic aspects of the countertransference: Some observations of the 'immediate object' and the 'interpretant' in the work of Charles S. Peirce. *The International Journal of Psychoanalysis, 85*, 1423–1438.

Green, M. R. (1962). The roots of Sullivan's concept of self. *Psychoanalytic Quarterly; 36*, 271–282.

Greenberg, J. R., & Mitchell, S. A. (1983). *Object relations in psychoanalytic theory.* Cambridge, MA: Harvard University Press.

Harris, A. E. (2011). The relational tradition: Landscape and cannon. *Journal of the American Psychoanalytic Association, 59,* 701–735.

James, W. (1950). *The principles of psychology* (Authorized ed.). New York, NY: Dover Publications (original publication 1890).

Levenson, E. A. (2005). *The fallacy of understanding.* New York, NY: Routledge. (Original work published 1979)

Levenson, E. A. (2005). *The ambiguity of change.* New York, NY: Routledge. (Original work published 1983)

Lincourt, J. M. (1976). Charles S. Peirce and psychiatry. *Transactions of the Charles S. Peirce Society, 12,* 33–45.

Lincourt, J. M., & Olczak, P. V. (1974). C. S. Peirce and H. S. Sullivan on the human self. *Psychiatry, 37,* 78–84.

Lincourt, J. M., & Olczak, P. V. (1979). H. S. Sullivan and the phenomenology of human cognition. *International Journal of Social Psychiatry, 25,* 10–16.

Mead, G., & Morris, C. (1934/1967). *Mind, self & society from the standpoint of a social behaviorist.* Chicago, IL: University of Chicago Press.

Meyer, E. (1958). Psychobiology: A science of man. *Psychoanalytic Quarterly, 27,* 273–275.

Mitchell, S. A. (1986). Roots and status. *Contemporary Psychoanalysis, 22,* 458–466.

Mitchell, S. (1988). *Relational concepts in psychoanalysis.* Cambridge, MA: Harvard University Press.

Mitchell, S. A., & Harris, A. (2004). What's American about American psychoanalysis. *Psychoanalytic Dialogues; 14,* 165–191.

Muller, J. P. (1996). *Beyond the psychoanalytic dyad: Developmental semiotics in Freud, Peirce and Lacan.* London, UK: Routledge Publications.

Muller, J. (2000). Hierarchical models in semiotics and psychoanalysis. In J. Muller & J. Brent (Eds.), *Peirce, semiotics, and psychoanalysis* (pp. 49–68). Baltimore, MD: Johns Hopkins University Press.

Ortmeyer, D. (1995). History of the founders of interpersonal psychoanalysis. In M. Lionells, J. Fiscalini, C. H. Mann, & D. B. Stern (Eds.), *Handbook of interpersonal psychoanalysis* (pp. 11–27). Hillsdale, NJ: Analytic Press.

Peirce, C. S. (1998). *The essential Peirce: Selected philosophical writings* (Peirce Edition Project, Eds., Vol. 2). Bloomington, IN: Indiana University Press. (Original work published 1907)

Percy, W. (1972). Towards a triadic theory of meaning. *Psychiatry, 35,* 1–19.

Perry, H. S. (1987). *Psychiatrist of America: The life of Henry Stack Sullivan.* Cambridge, MA: Belknap Press.

Phillips, J. (2000). Peircean reflections on psychotic discourse. In J. Muller & J. Brent (Eds.), *Peirce, semiotics, and psychoanalysis* (pp. 16–37). Baltimore, MD: Johns Hopkins University Press.

Putnam, F. W. (1990). Disturbances of "self" in victims of childhood sexual abuse. In R. P. Kluft (Ed.), *Incest related syndromes of adult psychopathology* (pp. 113–133). Arlington, VA: American Psychiatric Institute.

Rosa, A. (2007). Acts of Psyche: Actuations as synthesis of semiosis and action. In J. Valsiner & A. Rosa (Eds.), *The Cambridge handbook of sociocultural psychology* (pp. 205–237). Cambridge, UK: Cambridge University Press.

Salgado, J., & Gonçalves, M. (2007). The dialogical self: Social, personal and (un) conscious). In J. Valsiner & A. Rosa (Eds), *The Cambridge handbook of sociocultural psychology* (pp. 608–621). Cambridge, UK: Cambridge University Press.

Sebeok, T. A. (2001). *Signs: An introduction to semiotics.* Toronto, ON: University of Toronto Press.

Stern, D. B. (2003). The fusions of horizons: Dissociation, enactment, and understanding. *Psychoanalytic Dialogues, 13,* 843–873.

Stern, D. B. (2004). The eye sees itself: Dissociation enactment and the achievement of conflict. *Contemporary Psychoanalysis, 40,* 197–237.

Stern, D. B. (2012). Implicit theories of technique and the values that inspire them. *Psychoanalytic Inquiry, 32,* 33–49. doi: 10.1080/07351690.2011.553163.

Sullivan, H. S. S. (1995). Data of psychiatry. In D. B. Stern, C. H. Mann, S. Kantor, & G. Schlesinger (Eds.), *The pioneers of interpersonal psychoanalysis.* New York, NY: Routledge. (Original work published 1938)

Sullivan, H. S. S. (1950). The illusion of individual personality. *Psychiatry, 13,* 317–332.

Sullivan, H. S. S. (1953a). *Conceptions of modern psychiatry.* New York, NY: W.W. Norton.

Sullivan, H. S. S. (1953b). *The Interpersonal theory of psychiatry.* New York, NY: W.W. Norton.

Sullivan, H. S. S. (1953c). *The psychiatric interview.* New York, NY: W.W. Norton.

Sullivan, H. S. S. (1962). *Schizophrenia as a human process.* New York, NY: W.W. Norton.

Uexküll, J. von. (1957). A stroll through the world of animals and men: A picture book of invisible worlds. In C. Schiller (Ed.), *Instinctive behavior: The development of a modern concept* (pp. 5–80). New York, NY: International University Press.

Uslucan, H-H. (2010). Charles Sanders Peirce and the semiotic foundation of self and reason. *Mind, Culture & Activity, 11,* 96–108.

Valsiner, J. (2007). *Culture in minds and societies: Foundations of cultural psychology.* Thousand Oaks, CA: Sage Publications.

Wagoner, B., & Rosenbaum, P. J. (2009). From cellular to human worlds. In R. I. Sokol (Ed.), *Relating to environments: A new look at Umwelt* (pp. 3–23). Charlotte, NC: Information Age.

Wiley, N. W. (1994). *The semiotic self.* Chicago, IL: The University of Chicago Press.

CHAPTER 3

WILFRED BION

A Piercean Semiotic Reading

Robert White
Private Practice

INTRODUCTION

Wilfred Bion was a British psychoanalyst in the Kleinian object relations tradition who has become quite influential in recent years for his innovative use of projective identification and his theory of nonverbal psychic development. His writings are dense, often aphoristic, and lend themselves to multiple interpretations. I will suggest that a semiotic reading of Bion will help us clear up some inconsistencies. In particular, I will focus on Bion's theory of thinking, which develops out of a primeval formlessness through a series of steps toward symbolic thinking. Piece's triad of index, icon, and symbol will help us to order this progression. What is the nature of our most primitive thoughts? How do these primitive forms of thinking influence later behavior? Bion, in turn, will give a developmental theory to Peirce's semiotic theory. Interestingly, both men struggled with the question of how to conceive of a mind that understands finite sequences when semiotic series have no potential starting and ending points. This is the question of

Making Our Ideas Clear, pages 73–90
Copyright © 2015 by Information Age Publishing
All rights of reproduction in any form reserved.

pragmatics. How do we practically fit in a world of infinite possibilities and make finite choices? Peirce's discussion of infinite series of semiotics will help us to unpack Bion's concept of the infinite. I would emphasize that Bion and Peirce are writing in totally different domains. Bion is applying psychoanalytic theory to understand clinical phenomena and is loosely using theory from philosophy and theology as metaphors to illustrate his clinical points. Peirce is a philosopher of science and logic who developed a semiotic theory of signs and symbols as a means of communication. Communication, then, is the bridge between the two theorists, as Bion is trying to explain how the ability to communicate develops.

WILFRED BION

Bion (1897–1979) is, arguably, one of the most innovative psychoanalysts in the twentieth century. He was born in India but lived most of his life in England. Much like Charles Peirce, he was a true polymath, having extensive interests in mathematics, philosophy, logic, and theology. Like Charles Peirce, he tended to develop his own unique professional vocabulary, and his writings are dense and difficult. There is no evidence in his writing that Bion had any reading of Pierce or any of the other European semioticians.

His early training was in the British object relations of Melanie Klein. Projective identification was first formulated by Klein (1946) as a complex defense, where the infant fantasizes projecting a hated part of the self into another person and then fantasizes that the hated self-part, now embodied in the other person, is attacking and forcing itself back into the self. This preserves the internal feeling of goodness, while isolating badness outside in the other. The unconscious aim of the infant is to preserve itself from feared destruction. However, the infant is continuously threatened by potential attack from the hated external object, leading to a paranoid position.

The container–contained is a further development of projective identification. Bion thought that the projected self-part is actually felt by the recipient object, causing a reaction in the recipient. It moves the concept of projective identification from a one-person fantasy to a two-person interaction in the container–contained and serves as a model for unconscious communication. Projective identification in this sense is a normal aspect of the mother–infant relationship. The good enough mother can contain the hated projections, modify them to make them less toxic, and then feed them back to the infant at appropriate moments. Here Bion is adding to the Kleinian emphasis on internal fantasy with the actual interaction between infant and mother. There is also a pathological form of projective identification in which the infant must eject terrifying elements because they cannot be contained and transformed. Projective identification is not, for Bion, a ubiquitous defense of early development but a defense triggered by failure to achieve language and thought. Language at this level is unavailable because the primitive elements are not transformable. He thinks of the Kleinian positions, the movement from the paranoid-schizoid position to the depressive position, not as fixed developmental stages, but as poles that continually oscillate throughout life. Bion sees an ongoing process of dividing and uniting in the oscillation between paranoid-schizoid and depressive positions.

This also serves as a model of therapeutic action in psychoanalysis. The analyst receives the projections as counter-transference (a form of communication), contains the projections, and uses them to make appropriate interpretations. These ideas have all been absorbed into the mainstream Kleinian theory. Greenberg and Mitchell (1983) argue, rightly in my opinion, that Klein makes a transition from the Freudian emphasis on drives to an emphasis on objects. For Klein, desire is always for something. What is important clinically are unconscious fantasies about our objects.

Bion's Theory of Thinking and Terminology

Bion (1962a, 1963, 1965, 1970) is offering a radical shift in Freudian metapsychology. He wants to move away from a motivational system based on pleasure and pain and toward a motivational system based on the desire for truth and growth. It is growth in the ability to think. The acceptance of suffering does not involve a delay in the pleasure principle. Emotional growth has taken the place of the pleasure–pain principle. Freud believed that thinking served to reduce psychic tension, while Bion believed thinking was useful in managing tension (Symington & Symington, 1996). It is the ability to manage tensions through manipulation of symbols that is ultimately motivating and more useful than tension discharge. In the ability to think, we can form symbolic internal fantasy about our objects and thus are freed from concrete object ties.

> Thoughts then, or these primitive elements that are proto-thoughts, are bad, needed objects and to be got rid of because they are bad. They can be got rid of either by evasion or modification. The problem is solved by evacuation if the personality is dominated by the impulse to evade frustration and by thinking the objects if the personality is dominated by the impulse to modify the frustration. (Bion, 1962a, p. 84)

Mental growth is dependent on whether frustration is evaded or faced. Bad objects are those events or persons perceived as frustrating, causing displeasure. The idea of primary and secondary process is replaced by beta (β) and alpha (α) elements. Growth is called alpha function, the development of the ability to think, replacing the move from the pleasure principle to the reality principle. Instincts are replaced by linkages, love (L), hate (H) and knowledge (K). The unconscious is now seen as formless (the infinite) and consciousness as what is formed and linked (the finite) (Symington & Symington, 1996).

The Beta Space

The theory of alpha function and beta and alpha elements is first outlined in *Living from Experience* (Bion, 1962a). Bion postulates a different unconscious from that of Freud and Klein. Both Freud and Klein think of the unconscious as populated with formed objects while for Bion, the unconscious processes unformed emotional data into formed objects that the mind can use as the basis for thinking. This unconscious is composed of the most primitive mental elements which Bion calls beta (β) elements. This second unconscious is what the infant is born with. It has no structure and no links. You can think of it as an empty space that starts to be filled up with sensory elements. Bion describes β-elements as "things in themselves . . . objects of sense" (Bion, 1962a, p. 6). Bion thinks of the β-elements as unstable. They either need to be processed via α-function into α-elements or they will be evacuated outside the self, leading to projective identification, "to rid the psyche of accretions of stimuli" (Bion, 1962a, p. 7). "If there are only beta-elements, which cannot be made unconscious [through α-function], there can be no repression, suppression, or learning" (Bion, 1962a, p. 8). All defenses are based on a management of excessive β-elements, by splitting, hyper-control, or phobicizing (Ferro, 2005).

Bion is unclear about the nature of β-elements. On the one hand, he appears to equate β-elements with pure sense impressions, calling them "undigested facts" (p. 7). Grotstein (2007) seems to take this first meaning of sense impressions; β-elements are "the impersonalness of Fate" (p. 61). In this sense, β-elements are physical sense impressions as opposed to mental events. On the other hand, β-elements can have an emotional valance. Bion goes onto say that β-elements can produce acting out or can be used in thinking that manipulates things in themselves. This seems to suggest that β-elements do have an emotional valance. Ferro (2006) describes β-elements as "emotional or sensory-perceptual proto-tensions" (p. 46). He goes onto postulate balpha-elements, which are a mixture of partly digested β-elements stored in lumps (Ferro, 2005).

Alpha Function

In normal development, β elements are transformed by alpha (α) function into α-elements. α-function is a description of the transformation of unformed mental elements into more organized mental elements. These organized mental elements, α-elements, start to take on symbolization. "alpha-elements . . . resemble(s), and may in fact be identical with, the visual images with which we are familiar in dreams" (Bion, 1962a, p. 7). They may consist of visual images, auditory patterns, or olfactory patterns. Ferro (2006) describes α-elements as visual pictograms. If α-elements cannot be formed, the person is unable to dream. α- elements are storable and available for further processing in thinking, memory and learning. α-elements can only be known consciously in two narrow channels, a visual flash or through reverie (Ferro, 2006). Normally, α-elements go on to form narrative derivatives, dreams, unconscious fantasy, memories and conscious narrative structures (Ferro, 2006). Bion uses the labels α and β for two reasons: He wants to avoid any connotations with previous theory and he does not know the mechanism of these functions.

Regression of α-elements back into β-elements can be caused by attacks on α-function. For Bion, envy of the loved object and envy of third objects are ubiquitous. Envy aroused by the breast causes destruction of α-function. This destruction can attack the mental ability to symbolize or attack the symbols themselves. The visual pictograms can be de-linked and regress back into β-elements. In either case, the mind is left with an excess of β-elements. This obstruction then causes the infant guilt and fear of aggression. The fear of starvation causes a split between maternal and psychical satisfaction.

> This split, enforced by starvation and fear of death through starvation on the one hand, and by love and the fear of associated murderous envy and hate on the other, produces a mental state in which the patient greedily pursues every form of material comfort; he is at once insatiable and implacable in his pursuit of satiation. (Bion, 1962a, p. 11)

There is a search for a lost object and increased dependence on the mother. The universe is felt to be full of inanimate objects. Here is another model of β-elements. The regressed α-elements retain their charge and are now elements of terror and violence. Grotstein (2007) thinks that degraded α-elements exist from the beginning and constitute the terrifying aspects of this unformed space.

The Contact Barrier

Another aspect of α-function is to form a contact barrier. The contact barrier forms the separation of conscious and unconscious processes. If there is a failure of α function, then a β-screen develops. The β-screen leads to confusion between conscious and unconscious. There is no capacity for linkages and there is no resistance of passage of elements from different zones. The normal semipermeable barrier does not exist. Since there is free discharge of β-elements, the analyst is burdened with a heavy countertransference, as the patient tries to manipulate the analyst via the evacuation of β-elements. Another aspect of the destruction of α-function is the formation of bizarre objects. These are composed of β-elements infused with ego and superego traces, making them appear even more dangerous.

Reverie

The infant's α-function develops in reverie. Bion (1962a) states:

> [R]everie is that state of mind which is open to the reception of any "objects" from the loved object and is therefore capable of reception of the infant's projective identifications whether they are felt by the infant to be good or bad. In short, reverie is a factor of the mother's alpha-function. (p. 36)

Later, he goes on to say:

> In the situation where the β-element, say the fear that it is dying, is projected by the infant and received by the container in such a way that it is "detoxicated," that is, modified by the container so that the infant may take it back into its own personality in a tolerable form. The operation is analogous to that performed by α-function. The infant depends on the Mother to act as its α-function. (Bion, 1963, p. 24)

The infant's hateful and terrified β-elements are evacuated and placed in the feeding mother. If she, in her reverie, can tolerate and contain the infant's β-elements, she will use her own α-function to transform these elements and, at an appropriate time, feed them back to the infant as α-elements. Over time, the infant is able to gradually develop his or her own α-function. This forms a bidirectional unconscious communication system between infant and mother. This is called container/contained (♀♂). Bion would regard this as a normal or regular use of projective identification and as the primitive basis for thinking. Failure of reverie results in increased frustration in the infant and possible breakdown.

Ferro (2006) defines reverie as the analyst's ability "to enter into contact with his waking dream thought and its compositional subunits—the α-elements—and to narrate these in words" (p. 100). In reverie, the analyst's mind must be semipermeable. If there are no cracks that allow β-elements to be projected, the analysis remains sterile and at an impasse. If the cracks are too wide, then the analyst is overwhelmed by psychotic transferences (Ferro, 2005). Container/contained, in the therapeutic situation, can become an important area of unconscious communication between analyst and patient. The analyst can contain what his patient has projected into him, often experienced as a pressure toward action, and "read" it as an indication of the patient's unconscious mental state (Ogden, 1997).

Bion's Infinite Series

In a set of later works, Bion (1962) develops an alternative way to understand the growth of thought. It is one of several attempts that Bion makes to explain the growth of thought. He classifies thoughts as preconceptions, conceptions, and concepts. He characterizes preconception as an "empty thought" that exists as an inborn disposition. The conception is realized by a conjunction of a preconception with a realization. Thus, a priori knowledge meets up with experience to produce a thought. "Conceptions therefore will be expected to be constantly conjoined with an emotional experience of satisfaction" (1962b, pp. 306–307). The linkage of the expectation with the experience produces a more organized idea. The concept is a named and fixed thought. The preconception can also be understood as unsaturated (Bion, 1963). Unsaturated elements are states of expectation that, when supplied with a constant, become saturated. The saturated elements are enlarged and become unsaturated elements in more complex formations. This can also be understood as a container ♀ searching for a realization ♂. The result of the mating of ♀ and ♂ is a conception. When this mating occurs at any level, the conception becomes a preconception at the next level of thinking. This leads to an infinite series of the formation of conceptions and preconceptions, much as in Hegel's dialectic in the *Phenomenology of Spirit* (1977). We can see this as a general model of development. Thoughts, by grasping experience, become more complex and open to larger experiences, leading to a progressive series. This is a second model of the growth of thinking (Symington & Symington, 1996).

CHARLES SANDERS PEIRCE

Charles Sanders Peirce (1839–1914) was the son of Benjamin Peirce, a Harvard professor and the foremost mathematician of his day. Charles Peirce was a polymath, making original contributions in mathematical logic, the logic of relations, phenomenology, the philosophy of pragmatics, the philosophy of science, and the theory of signs. He was a true original, yet he never developed any systematic unity, was endlessly revising his ideas, and published many papers but never a philosophical book. He had a strong influence on William James' and John Dewey's development of pragmatism. His writings are digressive and filled with invented terms, making them difficult and inaccessible. In his personal life, he tended to get into fights and couldn't hold onto academic positions. He was probably manic-depressive, suffered from painful trigeminal neuralgia, and addicted to various drugs (Brent, 2000). He was divorced and lived with his second wife before they were married, a scandal at the time. He ended his life impoverished and isolated.

Peirce's Development of Semiotics

The term "semiotic" (he spells it "semeiotics") is probably taken from Locke (1959), who proclaimed in his essay a "new doctrine of signs." Among signs, Locke included both words and ideas. The concept of signs goes back to pre-Socratic philosophy. Both Plato and Aristotle spoke of thoughts as an internal language. Aristotle made the point that words symbolize thoughts. Augustine was the first to incorporate both natural events (i.e., where there is smoke, there is fire) and words under signs. Peirce's theory of signs came more directly from Kant's theory of knowledge. Ideas (*Vorstellung*) or presentations are a general term for any mental content. Semiotics for Peirce developed out of Kant's doctrine that objects not constituted by thought are unknowable. Peirce developed the idea that all thinking is done via signs, mostly words but other images as well. If thought is essentially verbal and words are signs, then thoughts are signs. Thought depends on words having meaning. All thinking is dialogic and inherently communicational. Thinking is not a succession of individual thoughts, as Locke thought, but a development of external and internal signs. Cognition consists of the manipulation of signs (Skagestead, 2004). Peirce understood that sense experience is continuous, in opposition to Kant, who held that separate impressions must be combined in synthesis. It is through thinking that the whole is broken up into parts, as analysis or explanation (Short, 2007).

Peirce in America was roughly contemporary with Ferdinand de Saussure in France, but there is no evidence that either of them was aware of the other. Peirce's theory of signs and Saussure's theory of signs are actually quite different. Saussure's concept of signifier and signified is largely synchronic and privileges verbal symbols (*language*) and their interconnectedness through convention. Saussure does not account for how language is about the world. De Saussure had a strong influence on European philosophy and can be found in Lacan's theory of psychoanalysis. Peirce enlarges the concept of sign to include natural signs, images, feelings, and actions. The Peircean account is diachronic and emphasizes process over time. The Peircean account also includes natural signs, thus extending it beyond the human context (Short, 2007).

The Theory of Signs

In his early writings, Peirce thought of ideas as representations or signs. Peirce defined a sign as "anything which determines something else (its *interpretant*) to refer to an object to which itself refers (its *object*) in the same way, the interpretant becoming in turn a sign, and so on *ad infinitum*" (Peirce, 1991, p. 239). The sign or representamen is the form that the sign takes. It can be physical or not. It is roughly similar to Saussure's signifier. The object is what the sign stands for. It too can be physical or not. The object determines the sign by the placing of constraints or conditions on successful signification by the object, rather than the object causing or generating the sign. Peirce thought that the sign–object relationship was not able to sustain an account of representation. It needed a third component, interpretation. An interpretant is the sense made of the sign, similar to Saussure's signified. The pragmatic use of symbols is the effect caused in the interpreter's mind. Its consequences can be thought or action. In this sense, interpretants are dynamic. There is no agreement about the relationship among the triad's components. The sign's meaning may be the object, emphasizing the sign's semantic properties relating signified and signifier. Or the sign's meaning may be the interpretant, stressing the sign's pragmatic properties linking sign-object to its interpretive effect. It is quite possible to see both positions in a fluid and shifting relationship (Moorjani, 2000). "The entire intellectual purport of any symbol consists in the total of all general modes of rational conduct which, conditionally upon all the possible different circumstances and desires, would ensue upon the acceptance of the symbol" (Peirce, quoted in Misak, 2004, p. 9).

In actual use, the subject may be the sign, the object, or an interpretant. In a dyad, each subject will communicate signs that refer to the other person, but at the same time, refer to himself as an object or provide interpretation. Any of these roles can reverse or change at any time (Phillips, 2000). As an example, take a stop sign. We have a sign and an action in response to the sign (the object), stopping. Between the sign and the action, there are numerous interpretants. I may ignore or misread the sign and not stop. The sign points to where I should stop. I can think there is danger in not stopping, I could hit a pedestrian or by another car. I can decide to slow down or completely stop. And so on.

Indexes, Icons, and Symbols

Peirce had a number of logical typologies of signs. One of his basic classifications has been widely accepted. He regarded it as the most fundamental division of signs. This is the division of signs into symbol, icon, and index.

As an *icon,* the representamen resembles or imitates the object physically, possesses some of its qualities. The icon represents its object mainly by similarity or likeness. Every picture and diagram is an icon. There is no dynamic connection with the object. A pure icon is independent of any purpose. Icons can be used as examples, likenesses, and samples. Most semioticians agree that there are no pure icons; there is always an element of cultural convention involved. They are seen as more natural, a monadic relationship either by resemblance or by exemplification.

As an *index,* the representamen is physically or causally connected to the object, either observed or inferred. Indexes are also called semes and are least conventional. It indicates something. Index and object are connected as a matter of fact, a real connection, like a fragment torn away from the object. There is a dynamic connection between object and sign. They are not based on resemblances but focus the attention. Metonymic relationships, contiguity or closeness are indexes. Indexes can be thought of as dyadic, with minimal interpretation. The role of the index is to set us in a certain direction.

As a *symbol,* the representamen is fundamentally arbitrary and conventional. There is no physical relationship between the representamen and the object. Symbols are also called tokens and are most conventional. A sign refers to the object by an association of ideas. They are constituted as such merely by understanding. All words and sentences are symbols. A symbol is a sign of an object that is assigned to it by a rule of interpretation. Symbols can only signify types, not individuals. Symbols are always a triadic relationship.

We can use a map as a sign system. The map as a sign could have a number of objects. An object might be a particular place or feature of the landscape depicted on the map. The interpretant is locating a particular position; that is, *X.* Then *X* becomes a sign for another interpretant. An object might be me traveling in the landscape depicted by the map. I see I am here or I need to go there. An object might be a certain feeling I have about a town located on the map. I had a bad meal in *X.* An object might be my inability to communicate with the inhabitants of the landscape of the map. I do not speak the language of this place. A sign can be a symbol, icon, index, or any combination. A map is indexical in pointing to locations, iconic in its scaling directions and distances, and symbolic in its use of conventional symbols and names. None is mutually exclusive. It is often thought that the three modes will coexist in a hierarchy in which one mode will dominate, to be determined by context. Which mode is dominant will depend on how the sign is used. Signs may shift over time.

Infinite Semiosis

However, an interpretant is itself a sign in the mind, equivalent or more developed. It is best thought of as the understanding that we have of the sign/object relation. An interpretant can be a feeling, a thought, or an action. This makes the interpretant central to the content of the sign, in that the meaning of a sign is manifest in the interpretation that it generates in sign users. The interpretant may be a different person, may be a communication, may be an internal dialogue, or need not involve minds at all: a formal logic. The interpretant is a second signifier of the object, now mental. Since any sign must determine an interpretant in order to count as a sign, and interpretants are themselves signs, infinite chains of signs seem to become conceptually necessary. This is called infinite semiosis.

In 1868–1869, Peirce attacked Cartesian objective certainty,[1] where we have truth in what we can introspect. Rather, if thoughts are signs and every thought produces another thought, then we have an infinite progress toward meaning and regress toward reference. Every thought is both a sign and an interpretant. There is no such thing as an intuition, a foundational object thought, a thing-in-itself. All thinking is inductive and signs are always arbitrary. It implies that meaning is only an endless substitution of one symbol for another. This does not allow for individual thoughts. How does one account for one thinker to approach a truth but never completely? The task was to identify how signs could signify individual objects. By 1885, Peirce found the answer in indexical reference. Indexical is always a particular connection to a particular object at a particular time and space. "The index asserts nothing: it only says 'There!' It takes hold of our eyes, as it were, and forcibly directs them to a particular object, and there it stops. Demonstrative and relative pronouns are nearly pure indices, because they denote things without describing them" (Peirce, quoted in Short, 2007, p. 49).

This is later described as a "perceptual judgment," a hypothesis, subject to later correction. Anything that compels attention in a particular direction is an index. This leads to the inclusion of natural signs as indexes. Icons were recognized as something that signifies by resemblance. Peirce added both actions and emotions as possible interpretants. By 1903, Pierce suggested that an interpretant, which he had always maintained was another sign, could also be potential. "It is not necessary that the Interpretant should actually exist. A being *in futuro* will suffice" (Peirce, quoted in Short, 2007, p. 54). Signs may be interpreted infinitely but their actually being interpreted is not necessary for their having significance. Finally, in 1907, he came to the view that there must be final interpretants. While explanation and meaning are inexhaustible, it is the practical aspect of purposeful action, understood to its fullest, that counts.

Development of Signs

Although Peirce did not elaborate much in this area, one can construct a developmental theory of signs. Indexes would be the most primitive and concrete of signs. Out of indexes develop icons, which are not part of the object but depict it transparently. Most developed and abstract would be symbols and verbal thinking. Pierce generally prioritized symbolic thinking and thought that sign-systems evolved toward the symbolic. Iconicity is the default mode of signification. In the evolution of languages, there is a tendency to evolve from indexical and iconic forms toward the symbolic. Many of the early Western languages were pictographs, ideographs, and hieroglyphs.

Peirce's Theory of Perception

Perception is not something just there but involves an interpretive creativity by the perceiver (Rosenthal, 2000). The percept is a sensory element presented in sensory awareness. The percept instigates the formation of a perceptual judgment, a creative interpretation of what the content is. The percept as interpreted is what we are immediately aware of. A perception is already a sign of something else[2] (Moorjani, 2000). What Peirce calls the "percipuum" in the wider sense is the flow of experience and in the narrow sense as interpreted. Sensory content is grasped as repeated content. It is a possibility of repetition, that activates a habit. As Peirce says: "the percipuum is a recognition of the character of what is past" (Peirce, quoted in Rosenthal, 2004, p. 196). It contains no reference to future experience. Appearance always incorporates meaning, the percept as a recognized content. What is "given" is in fact a "taken." Experience then is a unity of interaction between human understanding and the facticity of the external world. The external world is real and independent from mind, yet is partially dependent on the noetic act of grasping. A "this" is an object selected by a subject from a continuum of possibility. Truth, for Peirce, is a convergence theory, what is workable, what conforms with what we ask, what is perspectival.

Peirce too has a theory of the unconscious (Moorjani, 2000). The unconscious is composed of habits of mind, unconscious social beliefs, and can be brought into consciousness by need and desire. Logical interpretants mediate between the unconscious and conscious aspects of mind and work through association of index and icon. Peirce states: "belief is . . . a habit of mind essentially enduring for some time, and mostly (at least) unconscious" (quoted in Moorjani, 2000, p. 105).

DISCUSSION

A Peircean Reading of Perception

Bion shares Peirce's view that thoughts must be symbolized to be knowable. In Bion's view, the mind is originally composed of β-elements. β-elements are never knowable in themselves. It is unclear if β-elements represent a passive representation of sensory elements or it already contains emotional valances. When Bion refers to β-elements as "undigested facts" or "things-in-themselves," he seems to imply pure sensory experience. In Peircean language, β-elements are objects. Later commentators of Bion have tried to account for an emotional valance by postulating a mixture of β and α-elements, such as balpha-elements or degraded α-elements. Yet we know from Peirce that objects do not exist in the mind by themselves; they are always accompanied by signs and interpretants. Perception is not a passive affair but always involves signs in the mind and an interpretation. The percipuum is always grasped as a repetition of the past. I believe β-elements are best thought of as indexes. They are signs that directly point to objects in an interpretation that is based on past experience. There is a dynamic connection between object and sign. β-elements, then, are directly connected to what is perceived but involves an interpretation of that perception. For Bion, early experience is always conditioned by the defense of splitting. Thus, β-elements are either felt as bad and terrifying experiences or as idealized experiences. If β-elements cannot be transformed, they maintain an indexical relationship to real terrifying events, which must be gotten rid of by projection or evacuation. We can see how Peirce's triad is much more useful to psychoanalysis that de Saussure's dyad of signified and signifier. β-elements can only be accounted for if there are a relationship between object and sign. Moreover, β-elements involve use of natural signs, emotions and actions.

A Peircean Reading of Development

The α-function, then, can be understood as a symbolization process. It is the transformation of an index into an icon. At the index level, there is no emotional distance; what is pointed to is here-and-now. If α-elements are visual pictograms and dream thoughts, then the resulting sign is iconic. Remember that the icon represents its object mainly by similarity or likeness. The icon is less physically connected to its objects and has a higher degree of organization. It is not immediately present. We have moved from a pointing operation to a representing operation. There is also a move from more highly charged to less highly charged emotions. Reverie is an interpersonal form of α-function, where the β-elements reside in one person while the transforming function resides in another person. α-elements can now be stored in the mind in their iconic forms but are not yet suitable for thinking. The Freudian theory of primary process or latent dream thoughts would roughly correspond to Bion's α space. There is a further transformation of iconic thinking into symbolic thinking, primarily in words, in narratives, in fantasy. These transformations are subject to repressive defensive functions and result in the manifest dream and the dynamic unconscious.

Clinical Example

A patient reports that he has been very anxious, like a crazy man. The hour centers on his mixed feelings about my "help." He has seen me for many years and I haven't helped him. Yet I have pushed "too deep" and it will "tear him apart." He thinks of seeing someone else who is more "supportive" but he can't imagine not seeing me. He likes to hear my opinions, but it came out that he doesn't really listen to the content but much more to the emotional tone. He likes that I am honest, that I have stuck with him, and that I take him seriously. He cannot believe that I could like him. He would prefer to keep the relationship intellectual. When I draw his attention to depending on me, he switches to an angry rejection and the feeling that I am no good. Then in another spontaneous switch, his voices changes and he sounds childlike. He is no good. His wife and son would be better off without him. He is a failure. Work was his life and then he was fired. He will kill himself if he can't work. His wife and son are bonded and he is left out. Now he is full of sadness. I point out that he may be reacting to my being away in the next week. He says it is like going from full speed to nothing. He returns to the need of something more supportive. When I say we have to stop, he immediately becomes angry and brings up the idea of suing me because I didn't call him back the other night.

Here is a patient who is largely residing in a β space. When he becomes emotionally involved with me, he is terrified. He perceives me as either tearing him apart or abandoning him. He is the little child, unprotected and vulnerable to rejection and abandonment. He is connected to me as the bad object. Yet he can quickly switch into an idealizing mode, in which I provide great understanding and support. Let us see how this could be understood as a semiotic series. In the first sequence, he takes me (in the transference) as the object. He interprets me as pushing too deep and represents the interpretation as the feeling of being torn apart. Now he is the torn apart person. He now interprets me as unsupportive and sees himself as alone and unsupported. But in his alone state, he can interpret me as sticking with him. Now he is supported. Then I introduce the interpretation of his depending on me. Now I am the object again and he is not supported, hated, a failure. The series continues.

What I do in actuality, end the session or not call him back, takes on an indexical function. It immediately points to attack, hate, and action. He believes that I hate him and want to get rid of him. Action on my part can only be met with a counteraction on his part. There is an absence of any higher symbolizing functions. His β-elements of hate and abandonment are evacuated into me. I feel that I must be the worst therapist in the world to not call him back or to fail to help him feel better. It is also hard to me at this point to symbolize, to gain some emotional distance, to remember other points of view. So I too feel pulled into an indexical relationship with him. There is a notable absence of iconic or symbolic functioning. We are tied together by indexing. There is no emotional distance provided by symbolizing work and whatever I feel is read by him as terrifyingly real.

A Bionian Reading of Development

Bion fills in a theory of development of thinking that Peirce only alludes to. Bion's theory is one of identification. When the infant is born, she has no symbolizing function. Following the Kleinian position, all "bad" perceptions are ejected and all "good" perceptions are accumulated inside the mind. The mother has the capability to sooth the child by containing and keeping whatever "bad" projections she feels, uses her own α-function to detoxify them and gives them back to the infant in a formula she can digest, as α-elements. The infant gradually can internalize her own α-function and take over its function. The infant bit by bit learns to symbolize. Bion is silent on a concurring inner maturation of inherent functioning, but this would easily fit into his schema. Under stress, α-function can always be lost, so that the individual is always gaining and losing her capacity to symbolize.

Nachträglichkeit

Neither Bion nor Peirce use Freud's concept of *nachträglichkeit*, yet it is a concept embedded in both their theories. In a letter to Fliess, Freud (1896) writes: "I am working on the assumption that our psychical mechanism has come into being by a process of stratification: the material present in the form of memory-traces being subjected from time to time to a *re-arrangement* in accordance with fresh circumstances—to a *re-transcription*" (p. 233).

Strachey, in the *Standard Edition*, translates *nachträglichkeit* as deferred action. The term appears infrequently in Freud's earlier works. For example, in the case of the Wolfman, the primal scene witnessed at age one is reinterpreted retrospectively at age 4 through oedipal eyes (Freud, 1918). The French translate *nachträglichkeit* as *après-coup*.[3] We see two steps. There is something already there but excluded, which has a meaning. We anticipate a meaning that is not quite there. In the second step, separated in time, a retrospective meaning is assigned to what is already there. Faimberg (2007) proposed an enlarged meaning to *après-coup* that is closer to what I propose here. She suggests that a meaning is given for the first time to something already there but which has nonaccessible traces, something that has no original meaning because it is unformed. Only in the après-coup can the something there take on meaning.

This is, in essence, a description of a sign theory of psychic meaning. The retranscription is the use of new interpretants of a sign–object relationship. In development, we see a complex movement of gradual accruing meaning and symbolization in α-function. In the analytic process, what we experience can be more discontinuous, when a series of mysterious mental states suddenly take on meaning and can be spoken of.

Infinite Series

As we have seen, Peirce struggled with the intellectual question of an infinite series of semiotics, one triad becoming the foundation for the next triad, and so on. Bion, too, has a concept of the infinite and a similar series. To start with the Freudian unconscious, Freud spoke of primary process as timeless and not ordered temporally or spatially. Contents are only ordered by their strength of pleasure and pain (Freud, 1915). Bion postulated a different kind of unconscious. He was fond of quoting Milton (*Paradise Lost*, Book III):

> The rising world of waters dark and deep
> won from the void and formless infinite.

Rather than stressing conscious and unconscious, he had a dichotomy between finite and infinite. By infinite, he meant unformed, unknowable, undifferentiated, uncountable. The unformed also lacks the ordering of time and space, and contains emotional valances (the β-elements). To make finite means "to become," to take on form. "Confronted with the unknown, 'the void and formless infinite,' the personality of whatever age fills the void (saturates the element), provides a form (names and binds a constant conjunction) and gives boundaries to the infinite (number and position)" (Bion, 1965, p. 171). In Bion's terms, objects become saturated—that is, take on specific meanings.

Bion also has a triad of the development of thinking: preconception, conception, and realization. This, too, has the potential for an infinite series. Like Peirce, the realization, the product of the mating of a preconception with a conception, serves as a preconception for the next series of the triad. Theoretically, *nachträglichkeit* is an infinite process. We can think of an infinite chain of associations within the mind. Freud thought of psychoanalysis as interminable (Freud, 1937). Both Peirce and Bion faced the same intellectual puzzle. If an infinite series of thoughts is theoretically possible, how does one find a beginning and an ending? How does such a series become temporal and finite? Bion, too, finds a pragmatic solution. Thinking begins with innate elements, inborn preconceptions. This solution is not without controversy. For example, Bion states that the knowledge of the oedipal situation is inborn, an assertion most psychoanalysts could not accept. However, it does seem possible to postulate inborn personality tendencies or instinctual strengths that could serve as basic building blocks of thinking. Similar to Peirce, the most basic beta elements are indexical, the most physical and concrete of signs. Bion does not directly address how this series can be terminated. I think he would be quite comfortable with Peirce's solution that while an infinite series is possible, there are pragmatic and finite limits to thinking. Ultimate truths can be approached but never reached. We face these issues everyday in our analytic work. Is the interpretation good enough? If I interpret one conflict, I am inevitably missing another conflict. I am inherently limited by my own subjectivity and am blind to certain aspects in my patients. Have we done enough work to terminate the analysis? Both Peirce and Bion see a progression from unformed to formed thinking. What Bion develops is a theory of development, something Peirce alludes to but does not develop.

CONCLUSIONS

Bion has developed a theory of thinking in psychoanalytic terms. Applying Pierce's semiotic series to Bion's theory clears up some inconsistencies in his work. Perception, what Bion calls β-elements, from the beginning, is a synthesis of sensory input and mental anticipation. What we see and hear already has an emotional valance. Due to primitive emotions of hate and envy, β-elements are often filled with terror and have to be expelled. Yet because they function as indexical, they remain tied to the self, even when expelled. This is the concept of projective identification. In the growth from the indexical function to fully symbolized, how can we conceive of the movement from the infinite unconscious to the finite conscious? Pierce points to pragmatic solutions. We start with a concrete point of index: this points to that. We continue to have infinite possibilities, but we pragmatically find a good-enough ending point, a best fit. This becomes a model for psychoanalytic interpretation. There is no final truth, just what best fits the evidence now.

NOTES

1. See "Questions Concerning Certain Faculties Claimed for Man," "Some Consequences of Four Incapacities," and "Grounds of Validity of the Laws of Logic" (Peirce, 1991).
2. Similar to the forms of judgment of Kant
3. Lacan first drew attention to the importance of *aprés-coup* in the Wolfman and then in Laplanche and Pontalis (1983).

REFERENCES

Bion, W. R. (1962a). *Learning from experience.* London, UK: Karnac.

Bion, W. R. (1962b). The psycho-analytic study of thinking. *International Journal of Psychoanalysis, 43,* 306–310.

Bion, W. R. (1963). *Elements of psycho-analysis.* London, UK: Karnac.

Bion, W. R. (1965). *Transformations, change from learning to growth.* London, UK: Karnac.

Bion, W. R. (1970). *Attention and interpretation.* London, UK: Karnac.

Brent, B. (2000). A brief introduction to the life and thought of Charles Sanders Peirce. In J. Muller & J. Brent (Eds.), *Pierce, semiotics, and psychoanalysis* (pp. 1–15). Baltimore, MD: John Hopkins University Press.

Faimberg, H. (2007). A plea for a broader concept of Nachtraglichkeit. *Psychoanalytic Quarterly, 76,* 1221–1240.

Ferro, A. (2005). *Seeds of illness, seeds of recovery* (P. Slotkin, trans.). New York, NY: Brunner-Routledge.

Ferro, A. (2006). *Psychoanalysis as therapy and storytelling* (P. Slotkin, trans.). London, UK: Routledge.

Freud, S. (1896). Letter 52. *Standard Edition, 1,* 233–234.

Freud, S. (1915). The unconscious. *Standard Edition, 14,* 161–215.

Freud, S. (1918). From the history of an infantile neurosis. *Standard Edition, 17,* 7–122.

Freud, S. (1937). Analysis terminable and interminable. *Standard Edition, 23,* 216–253.

Greenberg, J., & Mitchell, S. (1983). *Object relations in psychoanalytic theory.* Cambridge, MA: Harvard University Press.

Grotstein, J. (2007). *A beam of intense darkness.* London, UK: Karnac Books.

Hegel, G. W. F. (1977). *Phenomenology of spirit.* (A. V. Miller, Trans.). Oxford, UK: Oxford University Press.

Klein, M. (1946). Notes on some schizoid mechanisms. In *Envy and gratitude and other works.* England: Delacorte Press.

Laplanche, J., & Pontalis, J.-B. (1983). *The language of psycho-analysis* (D. Smith, Trans.). London, UK: Hogarth Press.

Locke, J. (1959). *An essay concerning human understanding.* Mineola, NY: Dover Publications

Misak, C. (2004). Charles Sanders Peirce. In C. Misak (Ed.), *The Cambridge companion to Peirce* (pp. 1–26). New York, NY: Cambridge University Press.

Moorjani, A. (2000). Peirce and psychopragmatics. In J. Muller & J. Brent (Ed.), *Peirce, semiotics and psychoanalysis* (pp. 102–121). Baltimore, MD: John Hopkins University Press.

Ogden, T. (1997). *Reverie and interpretation: Sensing something human.* Northvale, NJ: Jason Aronson.

Peirce, C. (1991). *Peirce on signs* (J. Hoopes, Ed.). Chapel Hill, NC: University of North Carolina Press.

Phillips, J. (2000). Peircean reflections on psychotic discourse. In J. Muller & J. Brent (Eds.), *Peirce, semiotics and psychoanalysis* (pp. 16–36). Baltimore, MD: John Hopkins University Press.

Rosenthal, S. (2004). peirce's pragmatic account of perception: Issues and implications. In C. Misak (Ed.), *The Cambridge companion to Peirce* (pp. 193–213). New York, NY: Cambridge University Press.

Short, T. (2007). *Peirce's theory of signs.* Cambridge, UK: Cambridge University Press.

Skagestad, P. (2004). Peirce's semeiotic model of the mind. In C. Misak (Ed.), *The Cambridge companion to Peirce* (pp. 241–256). New York, NY: Cambridge University Press.

Symington, J., & Symington, N. (1996). *The clinical thinking of Wilfred Bion.* New York, NY: Brunner-Routledge.

COMMENTARY ON PRAGMATISM AND PSYCHOANALYSIS

Katharina Rothe
William Alanson White Institute

PRAGMATIC THEORIZING AND THE HUMAN CONDITION

I read the two chapters linking pragmatism and psychoanalysis by Tania Zittoun and Philip Rosenbaum with great interest. As a European psychologist and researcher, I am not familiar with the founding theorists of pragmatism, William James and Charles Sanders Peirce. Yet, as I was soon to discover, pragmatic theorizing is as much concerned with the major questions of the human condition—how we become social and individual beings, how we make meaning, how the mind works—as is psychoanalysis; and what is more, the former addresses them in a similar way.

As Tania Zittoun shows brilliantly, pragmatism developed a very similar stance to Freudian psychoanalysis with regard to those questions. Not only did Sigmund Freud and William James share a common zeitgeist, have knowledge of the same debates, and share references such as J. S. Mill; they both shared basic conceptualizations of the human mind. Specifically, Zittoun identifies mind as a flow of consciousness, of which large parts tend

Making Our Ideas Clear, pages 91–95
Copyright © 2015 by Information Age Publishing
All rights of reproduction in any form reserved.

to become unconscious, the idea that embodied emotional experience precedes thinking and that the latter evolves from the former. Also, they shared a stance against a positivistic psychology, dominant since the 1920s.

Zittoun explores clearly and convincingly how in Freud's work we can find the major pragmatist ideas of method and epistemology. James characterized pragmatism by three points regarding method, epistemology and metaphysics, all of which Zittoun rediscovers in Freud's oeuvre. Methodologically, pragmatism relies on the utility of a notion; a theory is regarded as an instrument to grasp certain aspects of reality, as opposed to an absolute truth. Pragmatism poses the question, "what difference would it practically make . . . if this notion rather than that notion were true?" (James 1904, p. 2, quoted in Zittoun, this volume). Freud's notions, such as the concept of repression, can indeed be understood as a theorem at a given historic time that enabled us to grasp an aspect of the human mind that would otherwise have remained obscure: dreams, symptoms, or slips of the tongue. As Zittoun quotes Freud, the notion of repression was "provisionally justified by its utility in coordinating and explaining a great variety of psychical states" (Freud, 1894/2001, p. 61).

Furthermore, the most pragmatic juncture of theory and praxis lies in the fact that Freud grounded his theorizing of the human mind in his attempts to ameliorate problems in people's lives. In this light, I would like to mention Freud's famous "Junktim von Heilen und Forschen" (Freud, 1927a, p. 293), the linkage between healing and research. This refers to the idea that psychoanalytic praxis is a juncture of meaning-making of and ameliorating mental phenomena that people at a given historic time struggle with. Moreover, this is also the route of research on those phenomena. Freud's theorizing emerged from the experience with his patients and the phenomena he encountered in them as well as in himself. The idea also speaks to the phenomena that psychoanalysis can and should research that exceed individual symptoms. Given that what people suffer from is always embedded in a certain historic time and specific societal structures, the way we think as psychoanalysts and researchers is informed by our "Unbehagen in der Kultur" (Freud 1930; or, in English, "Civilization and its Discontents," Freud, 1989).

One of the major misunderstandings of Freud by U.S.-American ego-psychologists has been their usage of Freudian theor*izing* as a fixed *theory* that they would then impose on clinical data. This mistake is ever more peculiar, as Freud's theorizing, for the very reasons brought to light in Zittoun's chapter, was emerging from the clinical data and therefore much more grounded in experience or empirical in the original meaning of the term. Of course, once formulated, a particular theorem, such as the Oedipus complex, in turn informs our experience of clinical and societal data. However, if we take the junction of healing and research seriously, we should constantly make the effort to remain affected—touched, moved, shaken, irritated, and changed—by (our/somebody's) experience in our re-thinking and re-searching.

Zittoun spells out in the terms of pragmatic epistemology how psychoanalysis can thereby discover something formerly unformulated: The pragmatic truth is to be found in a "dynamic of abduction," as Zittoun says, citing Valsiner (2000). Interestingly, but not surprisingly, from several unrelated perspectives, the psychoanalytic method has also been identified as abductive, for instance by the interpersonalist Stern (1990) as well as the psychoanalysts Hegener and Möller (1999) and Warsitz (2006). As Peirce spoke of abduction in contrast to both the logics of deduction and of induction, all these authors stress the unforeseeable element of psychoanalytic conclusions.

Stern posits that "in a careful analytic inquiry, what is learned must come unbidden" (Stern, 1990, p. 467). Citing Peirce, Hegener, and Möller suggest that psychoanalytic conclusions originate in surprising moments, after the analyst—like a detective—holds in her hand complex elements of a hypothesis that she has not found yet. In an instant, when those elements coalesce in a so far unfathomable way, she then makes a guess (Hegener & Möller, 1999). Warsitz argues that the epistemology of psychoanalysis is to be found between the scientific paradigm of explanation, on the one hand, and the hermeneutic paradigm of interpretation on the other. In similar reasoning, Zittoun posits that Freud's theorizing is in fact abductive and thereby pragmatist. According to James, "the pragmatist clings to facts and concreteness, observes truth at its work in particular cases, and generalizes" (1904, p. 8, quoted by Zittoun, this volume)—"until new facts create some trouble again. Knowledge development is in that sense a never-ending story" (Zittoun, this volume). Freud coined the idea of the "analysis interminable," which can not only be said with regard to treatment but also with regard to his theorizing of the mind. Therefore, whenever the state of his theorizing did not anymore bring to light processes that Freud studied, he would reformulate his theory or even develop a whole new model, as he did in 1905 (with his first drive theory) (Freud, 1905), in 1920 (with his second drive theory) (Freud, 1920), and in 1923 (introducing the structural model of the mind) (Freud, 1923).

The third characteristic of pragmatism, however, its view of metaphysics, seems to be Zittoun's weakest point in relation to Freud. Although she quotes Freud's critical essay (Freud, 1927b), she tries to make the link to Freud's clinical work, in that Freud would "tolerate his patients maintaining their beliefs... as long as they do not suffer from them." That this clinical nonjudgmental position would be equivalent to accepting metaphysical (e.g., religious) ideas as truth if they "have a value for concrete life" (James, 1904, p. 10, quoted by Zittoun, this volume) is highly questionable. Freud's critical analysis of the function of religion as a defense against the basic human experience of powerlessness and helplessness leave me doubt.

So far, the marriage of pragmatism and psychoanalysis has been most illuminating for me and leaves me with the impression that a lot of theoretical argument between schools of thought stems from lack of knowledge of culturally specific literature and the lack of adequate translations rather than from more interesting, fundamentally different ontologies. It is in that same light that I have studied Rosenbaum's chapter on discovering Peirce's semiotics in Harry Stack Sullivan's theorizing of the self-system. European psychoanalysts read Freud, and if they are interested in semiotics and symbolization they might study Lacan, who heavily relies on de Saussure.

SULLIVAN AND PEIRCE: A QUESTION OF SELF

However, as I was soon to discover, the pragmatic semiotics of Peirce prove more complex and rich compared to the dyadic theory of de Saussure. How rich to my ears seem the triadic semiotics of Peirce as introduced by Philip Rosenbaum! He provides a brilliant introduction to Peirce's work for anybody who has not read it, but probably also for all of those who did study Peirce. Rosenbaum gives the most clear and concise account of Peirce's triadic conception of the sign without reducing its complexity. The chapter is also very useful in order to grasp Sullivan's work, as his writings are highly idiosyncratic. By linking Sullivan's model of the mind with pragmatism, however, Rosenbaum elevates the epistemological basis of interpersonal theory and praxis. Furthermore, he demonstrates how fruitful theorizing can be as opposed to the antitheoretical stance of some interpersonalists.

Rosenbaum compares the clinical writings of the interpersonalist Sullivan with Peirce's ideas about the "self as sign" and finds, indeed, that Sullivan's thinking was deeply grounded in American pragmatism. By making this argument, Rosenbaum opposes one of the major criticisms of Sullivan, that he negated individuality by calling its idea an "illusion" and positing that there is "no such thing as the durable, unique, individual personality," but that "every human being has as many personalities as he has interpersonal relations" (Sullivan, 1964, p. 143). Rosenbaum shows how Sullivan's notion of the self is more "semiotic" than otherwise and "more than an illusion" (Rosenbaum, this volume). As "Peirce's self serves as a sign . . . and is thus intrinsically relational, dialogical, and grounded in social practice" (Rosenbaum, this volume), Sullivan's conception of the "self may be highly idiosyncratic, divergent, sensitive to context, ambiguous, and changing; it also acts as an agent, consistent and durable throughout time" (ibid.).

Yet I do not quite understand what Rosenbaum means by "an active subject" and an "agentic self." Does this only refer to the continuous experience of a self? According to Freud, this self is also deeply rooted in the corporeal and unconscious desires. So would this be a fundamental contradiction to Freud's insight, that basically the agentic ego as master of the drives is an illusion, that "the Ego is not master in its own house" (Freud, 1917, p. 143)? These questions remain to be discussed.

REFERENCES

Freud, S. (1905). Drei Abhandlungen zur Sexualtheorie. *Studienausgabe, 5,* 37–134.

Freud, S. (1917). A difficulty in the path of psycho-analysis. *Standard Edition, 17.*

Freud, S. (1920). Jenseits des Lustprinzips. *Studienausgabe, 3,* 213–272

Freud, S. (1923). Das Ich und das Es. *Studienausgabe, 3,* 273–330

Freud, S. (1927a). Nachwort zur Laienanalyse. *Gesammelte Werke, 14,* 287–296

Freud, S. (1927b). Die Zukunft einer Illusion, *Studienausgabe, 9,* 135–189.

Freud, S. (1930). Das Unbehagen in der Kultur. *Studienausgabe, 9,* 191–270.

Freud S. (1989). *Civilization and its discontents.* New York, NY: Norton.

Hegener, W., & Möller, H. (1999). Zu schön, um wahr zu sein? Psychoanalyse zwischen Kunst und Wissenschaft. In: *Texte aus dem Colloquium Psychoanalyse, 4,* 4–18.

James, W. (1904). *What is pragmatism? A new name for some old ways of thinking* (writings 1902–1920). Des Moines, IA: The Library of America. Retrieved from http://www.marxists.org/reference/subject/philosophy/works/us/james.htm

Stern, D. (1990). Courting surprise—Unbidden perceptions in clinical practice. *Contemporary Psychoanalysis, 26,* 452–478.

Sullivan, H. S. (1964). A theory of interpersonal relations: The illusion of personal individuality. In H. M. Ruitenbeek (Ed.), *Varieties of personality theory* (pp. 145–166). New York, NY: Dutton.

Valsiner, J. (2000). *Culture and human development.* Thousand Oaks, CA: Sage.

Warsitz, R.-P. (2006). "Ein Zeichen sind wir deutungslos": Die psychoanalytische Erfahrung zwischen den Methodologien der Wissenschaften. In E. Löchel & I. Härtel (Ed.), *Verwicklungen* (pp. 30–63). Göttingen, Germany: Vandenhoeck & Ruprecht.

SECTION II

APPLYING PRAGMATIC THEORY TO CONTEMPORARY QUESTIONS

CHAPTER 4

DIALOGUE BETWEEN MULTIPLE SELF MODELS

Moving Towards Integration

Mayer Bellehsen
North Shore Long Island Jewish Health System, Zucker Hillside Hospital

INTRODUCTION

The lineage of pragmatism extends to various domains of current scientific and intellectual thought (Menand, 1997), but to our detriment it is rarely explicated. This is too often the case in theories of the self and psychopathology, where the early pragmatists often made significant contributions that are less visible in contemporary theory. Though Harry Stack Sullivan's theory of interpersonal psychoanalysis was rooted in George Herbert Mead's thought (Evans, 1996), it can be argued that its contemporary iteration is perhaps even closer to his thought than realized.

Over the past two decades, psychoanalytic, narrative, and other theorists have posited that the individual should not be viewed as constituted by a unitary self, but rather as comprised of multiple selves that come into interaction with one another and that rely on social processes for their

Making Our Ideas Clear, pages 99–125
Copyright © 2015 by Information Age Publishing
All rights of reproduction in any form reserved.

development (Bromberg, 1998; Hermans, Kempen, & van Loon, 1992; see Howell, 2005 for a review of some clinical models). Though many of these models were derived from clinical observations—particularly regarding the impact of trauma on the self and the splitting apart of consciousness as first noted by Pierre Janet (Howell, 2005)—one can observe a convergence between the line of thinking of early pragmatist thinkers like William James and Mead with contemporary clinical thought (Harris, 2011). Greater attention to the pragmatic roots of a multiple, social self can enhance our understanding of contemporary multiple self-state models and also point to new directions for exploring clinical process.

It is the goal of this chapter to demonstrate that within the tradition of pragmatism there are tools for mapping the development and functioning of relational, multiple selves on conscious and unconscious levels and that this can be of benefit to current relational theory. This will be explored in stages throughout the chapter. First, I will offer an explication of a relational, multiple self model and how it can be grounded in a qualitative analysis. I will do so by reviewing the model of the dialogical self (Hermans et al., 1992), which is explicitly linked to William James, and then anchoring this model in a previously conducted empirical study (Bellehsen, 2011) regarding the traumatic impact of cancer and the use of the other in coping with trauma. As discussed elsewhere (Bellehsen, 2011; Valsiner, 2005), difficulties with the model will then be identified. To address these difficulties and to add to contemporary clinical thought, I will subsequently turn to an exploration of George Herbert Mead's (1934) theory regarding the self and mind to offer another starting point for developing a relational, multiple self model that can look similar to the dialogical self.

In the pragmatic tradition of putting ideas to work, the importance of turning to Mead will be illuminated by elucidating some of the practical extensions of his theory, such as his emphasis on the conversation of gestures. In particular, it will be argued that incorporating an emphasis on the mediation of symbols in contemporary relational theory, like that of the multiple self-state work of Bromberg (1998), can reinforce the relational, multiple self model and open it to new avenues of study.

The Dialogical Self

The dialogical self (DS) is a narrative model of how the self works, developed by Hermans et al. (1992). It is based on previous research into the self and dialogue by William James (1890) and the Russian literary critic Mikhail Bakhtain (1984). Hermans et al. (1992) construct a model of the self that is constituted of multiple narrative selves. These selves are developed at different points in time through different relationships with others.

They are thus temporal and spatial, as well as socially constructed. As the individual moves through time, these selves come into interaction with one another, as will be made clearer below.

William James and the Self

James' (1890) distinction within the self between an "I" that is the knower and the "Me" that is the known is the foundation for Hermans et al.'s (1992) thinking. The "Me" is an aggregate of constituent selves that are in the field of the "I." James included in the "Me" a "spiritual self," a "material self, " and the "social self." In creating these classes of selves that are all circumscribed by the "Me," James allowed for an extension of the concept of the individual into his or her environment—the self overcomes the dualities of mind/body and individual/community by internalizing these "known" aspects of the self. Accordingly, one's body, social relations, and property, all of which may have previously been thought of as external, become a part of the self.

Of particular note to this model is James' (1890) description of the social self, which he describes as the recognition the individual receives from his or her peers. He explains that "a man has as many social selves as there are individuals who recognize him" (p. 294). A man can thus have a "famous self" or an "honorable self" as well as a "doctor self" or "layman self." He argues that each of these selves can guide a person's actions as when a "layman self" might abandon a city infected with cholera, but the "doctor self" stays behind and treats the sick.

The second component of the self is the "I," or "self as knower." As Hermans summarizes (Hermans, 2001), it can be considered the author of one's life due to three features: continuity, distinctness, and volition (James, 1890). Through thought and memory, the "I" of the self maintains a sense of sameness throughout the course of life, stands distinct from others, and actively possesses experience by appropriating and rejecting thoughts.

The individual is thus divided into a self that is the author of one's life and the multiple selves that are the object of this author. The self extends beyond the individual organism into the environment. James (1890) explains, "*In its widest possible sense,* however, *a man's Self is the sum of all that he* CAN *call his,* not only his body, but his clothes, and his house, his wife and children" (p. 291, emphasis in original). Yet, as Hermans (2001) highlights, the divided and multiple self is not comprised of equitable parts, it is still dominated by the "I" that is a knower.

The Polyphonic Novel

In his literary analysis of Fyodor Dostoevsky's writing, Mikhail Bakhtain (1984) proposed that Dostoevsky created characters that represented independent voices within the author's consciousness. He noted that

Dostoevsky's own voice receded into the background and each character came to embody a separate voice that was both an author and object, as opposed to objects in the field of Dostoevsky's consciousness. The interaction of these characters arose through dialogue, which created a differentiated inner world that resembled the differentiated interpersonal world. Each character was placed in relation to one another both spatially (one compared with the other) and temporally (across time as in a child and adult version of a character). Bakthtain called this model of a novel the "polyphonic novel."

Bakhtain saw that the dialogue of multiple heterogeneous voices allowed for the development of greater complexity and dynamism in exploring themes like love, and he extended the concept of plurality of consciousness to characterize personality in general (Hermans et al., 1992). Hermans (2001) argues that this emphasis on multivoicedness in dialogue generates a concept of mind that is less centralized than James' version, which is dominated by the "I" as knower.

Dialogical Relationships

The root of the differentiation seen in Bakhtain's model is the notion of dialogical relationships. Valsiner (2002) explains that dialogicality is "the general property of systems to entail relations between their parts as definitive for the system" (p. 251). In other words, in a general system, it is the relations between parts of the system that maintain the system. Salgado and Hermans (2005) explain that in psychology it is through the relations of parts that human meaning is created.

Hermans et al. (1992) illustrate how the generation of meaning can occur through dialogical relationships by highlighting the relationship of two people uttering the phrases "life is good" and then "life is good." Dialogically speaking, the utterances arise from two spatially separated people at different points in time. Thus, the first makes a statement and the second indicates confirmation; they are relating to one another through a relationship of agreement. Other examples of dialogical relationship may include dominance, disagreements, and modification. For example, if the second person stated, "Actually, most people agree that life is *not* good," there would be both disagreement as well as dominance if the second person ceded. On the other hand, if the second person said, "Life is great," she would be adding to original statement.

The Dialogical Self as a Model of the Individual

The model of the dialogical self (Hermans, 1996, 2001, 2003, 2004; Hermans et al. 1992) integrates the above theories such that James' distinction of I–Me—author and subject—is expanded in terms of Bakhtain's emphasis on multivoicedness. That is to say that there are multiple "author–subject" configurations in the self. This is captured in the construct of "I-positions," which are dynamic, autonomous selves that are in dialogical relationships with each other. The individual is an imaginal landscape within which I-positions from across space and time come into dialogue with one another to maintain the integrity of the system.

I-Positions

The "I-positions" of the dialogical self represent different voices and stories about the self that arise from different spatial and temporal contexts. These I-positions are assumed imaginatively and come into dialogue within the individual to generate a differentiated intrapersonal world, much like two or more people would in the interpersonal world. For example, an individual may be comprised of an I-position of "Parent" and "Child" at the same time. This would represent the spatial relation of being a parent to one's child as well as the historically developed position of being a child to one's parents. Through dialogue between these I-positions, dialogical relations (e.g., agreement and dominance) arise that maintain the general dialogical self system (Hermans, 2001, 2004; Hermans et al., 1992). There are two classes of I-positions: external I-positions and internal I-positions. Both types of I-positions are considered part of the self, and an individual may embody any of these positions at any point in time. However, the external I-positions are those that are felt to come from the environment, such as an I-position of daughter, while the internal I-positions are those that are felt as a part of the self, like an I-position as a parent. One can imaginatively embody either of these positions when negotiating the environment, such as purchasing a toy (feeling and considering the competing desires and demands as one moves from the daughter to parent I-positions). These I-positions may also be evoked when dealing with actual others in various contexts (e.g., as a therapist with patients, but husband when returning home to one's wife). Additionally, the collective voices of culture may also be internalized as I-positions (e.g., I-position of American) (Hermans, 2003, 2004).

Organization of the Dialogical Self

To understand the individual's experience, one must take into account not only the content, but also the organization of a person's I-position repertoire. Regarding the organization, one must consider the hierarchy that prevents over-fragmentation, the accessibility of I-positions, the flexibility of movement between positions as circumstances vary, the affective quality of the I-positions, and the presence of a meta-position from which the individual may observe other positions and generate linkage between them (Hermans, 2004). It is posited that psychopatholgy may develop when there is either a problem in the organization of the I-position repertoire or there is a lack of I-positions to manage events. To this end, Hermans (1997) discussed an experience with a patient who suffered from dissociation. It was found that she struggled with integrating two strongly affectively laden I-positions ("I-position of Witch" and "I-position of herself") into a larger narrative, such that the dominance of these two positions switched with little understanding or awareness as to why. Therapy focused on fostering dialogue between these positions.

The Multivoiced and Social Nature of the Dialogical Self

The framework of the dialogical self continues the tradition of James in extending the individual into the environment; I-positions are embodiments of others (external I-positions) and experiences of the self (internal I-positions) that arise from interactions with the environment, thereby reflecting the social nature of the self. The dialogical self also conceives the individual as multiple rather than unitary, which allows for an understanding of the differentiated complexity of the individual as he or she reacts differently in different circumstances.

In the tradition of Bakhtain, this multiplicity is conceived of as multivoicedness, which implies autonomy for each I-position and greater decentralization in the self. Instead of one dominant "I" that is consistent across time, there are multiple I-positions that dynamically organize (i.e., form hierarchies, come into dominance, recede) depending on the context. This is crucial, because it allows for the establishment of dialogical relations between parts (the I-positions) of the system (the dialogical self) as a central process in the development of meaning. Thus, the individual is a social being in two ways: (a) He or she is extended into the environment through the construction of I-positions, and (b) the intrapersonal world comes to resemble the social environment. This is because I-positions interact via dialogical relations to maintain the system like interpersonal dialogical relations maintain the social world. These insights provide a lens for understanding how psychopathology and clinical work are socially embedded and what processes may ameliorate distress. In particular, even while focusing on the individual, conceptualizing the person as a system of selves (I-Positions) guides our thinking and intervention in the direction of understanding relational and systemic processes. To this end, the next section will focus on illustrating the model of the dialogical self within the context of a trauma.

The Traumatic Experience of Cancer From the Dialogical Self Perspective

In past work (Bellehsen, 2011), I sought to explore the phenomenological experience of an individual and a couple who had recently undergone the traumatic impact of a cancer diagnosis and treatment through a grounded theory approach. Using semi-structured interviews of 14 couples (see Bellehsen, 2011 for further details on study design and sample), I examined how each individual of the relationship (patient and partner) were affected, how this in turn influenced the couple dyad, and how this influence reciprocally impacted the individual. In so doing, it was possible to look at how the interpersonal context of the individual influences the individual and vice versa. This allowed for the opportunity to evaluate the theory of the dialogical self in a grounded fashion, while also opening the door to modifications of the theory. Lastly, I was evaluating the usefulness of integrating the theory of semiotic mediation in this sample, which will be turned to later in this chapter.

Simultaneous examination of the individual and one of his or her interpersonal environments (i.e., the couple dyad) was chosen to help illuminate the social nature of the dialogical self, detailed above. Additionally, the study of a traumatic experience, like cancer, was decided upon in part because of past insights into the ability of trauma and dissociation to highlight the multiplicity of selves (Howell, 2005).

For the purposes of this chapter, I would like to highlight three findings that will be relevant to further analysis of the pragmatic roots of the social, multiple self and to opening up new avenues of thought: First, the trauma of the diagnosis resulted in a destabilization of the dialogical self as seen through the disorganization of the I-position repertoire and/or inadequacy of I-positions. Second, individuals relied on I-positions to regulate their affective experience following trauma. Third, the interpersonal context of the couple dyad facilitated the development and usage of I-positions for achieving this regulation.

Destabilization of the Dialogical Self

Chief among the study's findings was that cancer created a rupture in the dialogical self system because the future uncertainty of cancer challenged the resilience of the dialogical self in various ways. Two of these challenges entailed the recognition that the dialogical self repertoire was either inadequately organized or lacked the I-positions to handle the threat of cancer.

As an example of inadequate organization we can begin by looking at husband 3 (H#3) of couple 3 (C#3; H = Husband, W = wife, and C = couple). His spouse described him as "very even keeled, very, like, his nature is just very calm. And you know he just doesn't really get anxious about stuff." He was further characterized by her as "being kinda like *a rock.*" As a couple, they had commented that during other crises, his "rock" I-position would dominate H#3's experience. This allowed him to stay calm, which helped W#3 and the overall couple dyad to remain calm. This I-position organized his other I-positions in a coalition to manage obstacles. Yet, when he heard about his diagnosis, he initially had an atypical reaction:

> Well, the hardest part was when the doctor called me in and he said, it's a tumor until proven otherwise, we have to remove your testicle. That's when I, *I completely lost it in the doctor's office.* I'm *not a person who cries, at all*! And I was crying and he couldn't even talk to me, he told me to come back later in the week when I was a little more calm.

In this instance, H#3 moved out of his "rock" I-position and into an "emotionally vulnerable" I-position. He describes this experience as having "completely lost it" because of its unfamiliar organization of his self and his wish to resume his "rock" I-position. However, he did not completely lose his memory of himself in a dissociated experience as much as he lost the stability that was found in the typical organization of his multivoiced, dialogical self repertoire as dominated by his "rock" I-position.

Subsequently, he restored balance by finding a way to reintegrate this experience under a coalition in which his "rock" I-position could dominate again. He shared that soon after this experience, "I didn't really feel like upset anymore. I was, I mean I did at first, but then once I accepted it, I just kinda had the attitude like, alright, what, being negative is not gonna make this any easier." By "accepting" the diagnosis he was able to reassume his "rock" I-position and could fit the cancer into a narrative of facing adversity.[1]

On the other hand, there were individuals and couples for whom the challenge of cancer was that there were no immediately available I-positions to embody, rather than the disruption to the organization of their dialogical self repertoire. The young, newly married individuals in C#11 highlighted this when they shared, "We were just adults.... It was like, we don't know what to do with ourselves because there's this huge thing that just happened." These two were just developing their I-positions of being adults and spouses; they had no idea of what I-position they could embody to manage this event.

The preceding examples demonstrate instances of trauma that have been previously understood as threatening to an individual's daily assumptions or "absolutisms" in living (e.g., Janoff-Bullman, 1992; Stolorow, 2007). Yet they highlight that the experience of the individual is more nuanced than the breakdown of some hard-and-fast rules or the "shattering" of a unitary self. Rather, there is a multiplicity of selves that the individual may come to embody, and the threat of trauma is that it challenges the overall system to adapt in ways that force a reorganization of the dialogical self system or demand the development of new selves in that system. It is the dialogical relations between I-positions that become strained. Dominant I-positions or hierarchies may become dislodged such that the individual feels in unfamiliar territory. Yet, as will be seen below, the resilience of the individual lies in the ability of the dialogical self system to recruit other or new I-positions, as well as establish new dialogical relations between I-positions. This is possible because of the multiplicity in the system.

Regulation Through the Assumption of I-positions

In response to the disruption of the dialogical self, individuals utilized I-positions to restore balance in various ways. One instance of this was the manner in which the negative affect of the trauma was managed by different I-positions. In response to the anxiety of cancer, individuals often came to embody or develop I-positions that were more accustomed to managing the emotions of the experience. This was seen when H#3 found a way to return to his "rock" I-position. This restored calm for both him and his partner. Thus, it stabilized not only his dialogical self system, but also the system of the couple dyad.

Similarly, in C#9, each member found an I-position from within their repertoires that enabled them to reduce anxiety. W#9 was an oncologist and came to embody this position when thinking of her husband's diagnosis. She felt "scared a little bit, but also knowing that it was something that was truly beatable. I think that I have a sense of cancer treatment that is a little less frightened than some others. For several reasons, one is that I have given it to people and I have seen people." Her ability to embody the "oncologist" I-position helped her moderate her feeling of being scared by shaping her expectations of the future. She did not always assume this position, especially not when regularly interacting with her husband, but in the context of his cancer, it was embodied.

Meanwhile, her husband, the patient, was a psychologist who shared, "I don't get that disorganized that easily. So part of that is my training and part of that is my own capacity for self-awareness." In general, his ability to embody his "therapist" I-position allowed him to process negative feelings and avoid disorganization. He embodied this position when experiencing the trauma of a cancer diagnosis: "I had both eyes wide open to what this meant.... that's sort of how I handle things in general."

Notably, the use of these I-positions when managing cancer was not limited to regulating emotions. Some subjects came to embody I-positions to determine how to deal with the unique daily challenges of dealing with cancer or to manage other aspects of their lives. For instance, H#5 talked about adopting the I-position of "good patient" when considering how to interact with his doctors. He thought about "how to be a *good patient.* How to ask the right questions? How to assess whether this doctor with whom I was meeting was a good person to go with? . . . How much to honor timeliness and pursue the surgery quickly versus go through a really methodical set of consultations?"

Meanwhile, others acknowledged that circumstances simply demanded a shift from embodying one I-position or another. W#12 related that she was able to pull out of the "paralysis" of dealing with her husband's diagnosis because, "I had to do—I had no choice. *I had kids, I have John, I have an office, I've got to function, I have clients, and I just went back into it.*" Her relation to each of these others in her life catalyzed a transition from being paralyzed to embodying various I-positions in her dialogical self repertoire (e.g., parent, spouse, employer, businesswoman).

Notably, while the preceding analysis focused on examples of individuals successfully using I-positions to regulate their experience, there were instances in which attempts were made to embody an I-position, but fell short. For instance, W#1 noted that her husband was unable to use his "physician" I-position to help her manage her medical obstacles: He "became very frightened and very panicky, understandably. And couldn't really take part in helping to look for doctors and you know, what am I gonna do and stuff like that, which is unlike the physician that usually can do that." H#1 acted more like a "frightened husband" than "calm physician." He had both I-positions, but the one that dominated in this instance was that of "husband," which was too terrified to be fully supportive. Yet, even though he did not manage his emotions very well through the embodiment of this position, note that he still engaged in an available "I-position" to navigate the experience.

The use of I-positions to adapt, as seen above, once again highlights that trauma affects individuals who are constituted of multiple selves and that the resilience of the system comes in the ability to creatively engage other I-positions and/or form new I-positions. In addition, recall that the model of the dialogical self is one that is not only multiple, but also socially constituted. In the above delineation of adaptive I-positions, one sees this social constitution through the adoption of positions like therapist, oncologist, husband, physician, parent, employer, and so on. The individual has developed these I-positions through interactions with others. Additionally, they are social in that they carry cultural representations that guide the actions and feelings of the individual. This was prominently seen with those who identified I-positions with their profession as well as W#1's expectation that her husband would have embodied a medically helpful "physician" I-position.

The Couple Dyad and I-Positions

The emphasis on the use of socially constituted I-positions to manage the trauma of cancer begins to highlight how a trauma comes to be regulated through others. However, at this point it is through the development of mostly internal I-positions that are embodied when relating to others. By interviewing the individuals in the couple dyad together, it was also possible to demonstrate that individuals came to adopt the I-positions of their partners to regulate their own experience.

For example, W#2 had served in the "caretaker" I-position for her husband for a long time after he suffered from a stroke. When she was diagnosed with cancer, the I-positions became reversed such that the husband adopted her I-position of "caregiver" in relation towards her: "*I was the caregiver for him for a long time.* . . . So the difference was, here is somebody in there, kind of helping me out."

This process of adopting the other's I-position highlights an externalizing-internalizing-externalizing dynamic in which one individual embodies an I-position for the partner, the partner finds a way to internalize it, and the partner can then embody it for the other.[2] This was seen with C#5 who discussed their process of soothing one another when scared. W#5 shared:

> I always felt like *we had this up-down thing, there would be times where I would feel I was falling apart* and I would say to you, I'm so scared, I can't even see straight, and you would say something like, *it's okay, we're gonna get through this . . . or vice versa,* there were times where you would cry. . . . *I felt like we found this balance* that you know, helped get us through really difficult, really challenging moments throughout that period.

The members of this couple took turns in embodying an "optimistic" I-position to comfort the other when fearful of the future.

This process of embodying the external I-position of one's partner is also seen quite vividly with C4. The wife had noted that in general she saw herself as more of a "risk taker," while her husband was more of a sober "anchor." She noted that this led to a "good balance" in the relationship. She further highlighted ways in which each partner found ways to embody the other person's I-position when approaching certain actions. She reflected, "I think because he's so anchored, my risk taking helps him because he would never take those risks if I wasn't."

Meanwhile, with respect to her cancer, she explained that his more conservative "anchor" position helped her confront her cancer head on: "Well, I think in nonverbal ways, he made me accept that I actually did have cancer. I think I could've gone on and said, 'Oh, I had a wart.' I think that I didn't want to accept that I had gotten cancer." Had she embodied her usual I-positions, she seems to feel that she would not have accepted her diagnosis. However, by embodying her husband's more grounded "anchor" I-position, she could appreciate the severity of her diagnosis and the need to treat it.

From the above two examples, we see the reciprocal process of embodying an I-position and then having the other embody the position. We have seen that individuals not only develop and embody internal I-positions through their interactions with others, but that they also find ways to imaginatively embody the external I-positions that they normally associate with their partners. These I-positions are considered external I-positions, as they are more associated with the individual's partner, but they do become part of the landscape of the self and promote internal dialogue as individuals can use these I-positions to sustain their own dialogical self and that of their partner. This offers further support for the dialogical self model in general, and particularly for its social constitution.

Limitations of the Dialogical Self Model

Despite the robustness of this model for explaining and mapping the social nature of the self, its explication of the mechanisms by which the dialogical self works is limited. Specifically, for all the delineation of the manners in which I-positions may organize, establish dialogical relationships, and arise in the self, as Valsiner (2005) notes, there is no developmental framework to explain the processes of how these transitions occur over time. In other words, what accounts for transformations and movement in the dialogical self? To address these developmental concerns, Valsiner (2005) argues for the need to integrate a system in which signs and symbols are regulated interpersonally and intrapersonally (semiotic mediation) with the dialogical self.

The next section will show that in the writing of George Herbert Mead (1934) there is a starting point for a developmental model of the self that is social and multiple, like the dialogical self. Additionally, within his model there is the answer to the developmental problems that Valsiner raises with the dialogical self. Particularly, Mead's focus on the conversation of gestures emphasizes the need to consider signs and symbols in regulating the self. This focus on the use of signs is most relevant for current clinical thinking in that it offers a point of entry for investigating and intervening with clients when working from a relational, multiple self frame.

MEAD AND THE BASIS FOR A RELATIONAL, MULTIPLE SELF MODEL

As seen up to now, the model of the dialogical self offers a framework to understand the complexity of an individual's experience and regulation of trauma in a manner that highlights multiplicity in the self and the social nature of the self. This model was built in part off of the research of William James into the self, which began to highlight the presence of multiplicity as well as the relevance of social processes in understanding the self. However, for James, these selves maintained a distinction between author/object, between the "I" and multiple "Me's." Accordingly, by integrating Bakhtain's notion of polyphony, Hermans et al. (1992) were able to posit a model of the self in which these multiple selves can occupy a position of both author and object as "I-positions." However, to explain the developmental mechanisms for the dialogical self, it was necessary to integrate a model of semiotic mediation to describe the origination and movement of I-positions. This integrated model stresses both the social development and functioning of the self, along with the role of communication (in particular language) in explaining the functioning of the self.

The remainder of this chapter will argue that in considering both the social nature of the self and the importance of signs, George Herbert Mead (1934)[3] offers a more compelling account of the social self that circumvents the developmental problems of the dialogical self through his emphasis on the conversation of gestures. His account offers an alternative starting point for the dialogical self that both allows for the development of multiple, social selves and resolves the developmental difficulties of how I-positions form and are regulated, which adds to contemporary clinical thinking, particularly from a relational psychoanalytic perspective.

The Social Origins of the Individual

Mead (1934) argues that the fundamental difficulty with understanding the self is that if one starts from the position that the self exists and then comes into relations with others in the social world, it is not possible to account for how the self arises in the first place. Instead, he posits that one should begin from a perspective of assuming social processes, which are already present and analyzable in the social environment, and develop an account of the mind and self from there. He explains that:

> Our contention is that mind can never find expression and could never have come into existence at all, except in terms of a social environment; *that an organized set or pattern of social relations and interactions (especially those of communication by means of gestures functioning as significant symbols and thus creating a universe of discourse) is necessarily presupposed by it and involved in nature.* (p. 223, italics added)

For Mead, the starting point of understanding the self and mind is the social environment: An individual's behavior impacts the larger social group and therefore must be analyzed in the context of his interpersonal environment. As he explains, "we are starting out with a given social whole of complex group activity, into which we analyze (as elements) the behavior of each of the separate individuals composing it" (p. 7).

Furthermore, the entirety of the social act must be considered, which means also taking into account the organism's anticipation of the impact of her behavior on others. This allows Mead to move his behavioral analysis beyond the focus on an organism's immediately observable response to a stimulus. Instead he highlights the need to consider internal experience as well the future consequences of behavior that may impact one's present conduct.

The Conversation of Gestures and the Significant Symbol

To this end, Mead highlights the "conversation of gestures" that takes place in any interaction. This conversation entails a cooperative process in which organisms act in response to one another. This does not have to be verbal or include conscious processes; it is simply the action on the part of one organism that acts as a stimulus to call forth a response by the other organism, which in turn serves as a new stimulus for the first organism to respond. As an example, he describes the instinctive acts of one boxer in response to the movements of the other boxer. One can also consider the mother–child relationship and the responses that the infant's cry calls forth in the mother, such as holding or feeding gestures, which then result in a pleased response from the infant. This represents a basic exchange or communication between organisms. The conversation of gestures is thus the interplay of stimulus-response-stimulus between organisms.

Mead argues that meaning arises from this conversation when there is recognition that one stimulus will lead to a certain set of responses. Although not necessarily done consciously, the first gesture can serve as a symbol to indicate the resultant responses that will emerge out of the cooperative process—leading to meaning. He goes on to argue that among human beings, there is the capacity to recognize the meaning of an action in terms of its final results and to indicate this meaning with symbols to both the other and oneself. He labels a symbol that has this capacity for reflectiveness of meaning by both members the *significant symbol.*

The meaning of an act can serve as a stimulus to current actions as the expected results serve to guide current behavior. Again, in the example of the boxer, Mead notes that a boxer's initial move to throw a punch calls out in him the guarding reaction that is anticipated by the other individual, which serves as a stimulus to the first boxer to look for an opening for a subsequent blow. Thus, for Mead, when the individual can knowingly call out the response of the other in herself, she has used symbols to achieve thought:

> That is the general mechanism of what we term "thought," for in order that thought may exist there must be symbols, vocal gestures generally, which arouse in the individual himself the response which he is calling out in the other, and such that from the point of view of his response he is able to direct later conduct. (p. 73)

The above paragraph highlights three important points. First is the capacity for humans to use symbols to guide their conduct by anticipating responses, which can be used as further stimuli to guide current action. Essentially, thought through symbols evokes potential futures and prepares the individual for those futures by guiding present action.

Second is Mead's reference to vocal gestures. As he later explains, language is not a symbol that denotes an inherent conscious state, but rather it is another form of gestures that are part of the cooperative process of organisms adjusting to one another. As such, language is comprised of verbal gestures that are arbitrarily determined by the group of individuals (e.g., culture) in which they occur. These groups also set the expected responses that the gesture will yield.

Third is the organism's ability to take the other's response into account. Accordingly, in thoughtful conduct, the individual is affecting himself as he is affecting others, which is why he can respond to that impact even before the other has responded—as in the case of rewording what one is about to say or has said based on hearing oneself and anticipating a misunderstanding. Language thus mediates a social process of cooperation. This is a social process that yields meaning in conventional terms—the gesture is related to the expected resultant in the group. When it is not symbolized it is not made conscious, but it is still present. Through significant symbols like language, it can be made conscious and the individual essentially assumes the position of the other in his or her response.

The Generalized Other

It is through the capacity for the individual to take all the attitudes of others towards himself and then generalize all of these attitudes into a single attitude towards the self that yields what Mead terms the "generalized other" (p. 90). In carrying the attitudes ot the generalized other, the individual also takes the attitudes of the social group towards the set of activities that the group is engaged in. This attitude then guides his activity. As an example, Mead talks about an individual on a baseball team. The individual carries the attitudes of the other members in order to know what play is expected of him at the next moment (e.g., the pitcher will pitch and the ball may be hit to me). He also carries the goals of the team, such that he contributes in the effort to win as a team. The conduct of the individual in this process is guided by the contributions that he is expected to make to the whole.

Against this backdrop of the generalized other, the reflective self can emerge. Through significant symbols, the conversation of gestures is carried over into the individual who carries the responses of the other in the form of the generalized other and also offers her own responses towards achieving the attitude of the community. Upon taking this position in social relations, and with the capacity for significant symbolization (i.e., reflectiveness through symbols), the individual can become a reflective object to herself. The individual thus achieves reflective self-consciousness through her relations to the social whole.

The "I" and the "Me"

Mead takes this a step further to account for two phases in the experience of the self. Like James, he makes a distinction between the "I" and the "me." However, this is a very different "I" and "me." In Mead's account, the "me" stands in for the generalized other—that is, the general attitudes of others that the self has internalized. The "I" stands in relation to this "me" as the part of the individual's experience that responds to, or talks to, the general attitudes of the "me." As Mead states, "The 'I' is the response of the organism to the attitudes of the others.... The attitudes of the others constitute the organized 'me,' and then one reacts towards that as an 'I'" (p. 175).

This "I" is only one phase in the experience of the organism in relation to the social environment. Importantly, Mead stresses that the reactions of this "I" are always uncertain—even to the organism itself—and can therefore introduce novelty. He notes that particular situations may evoke a set of responses associated with the generalized other that will influence the response of the "I," but the particular response of the "I" is never guaranteed. Returning to the example of the baseball player: When the ball is hit to the individual, she may know what to do based on the organization of the attitudes of others (i.e., the "me" demands for the ball to be caught), but she may not react accordingly. For instance, she may catch the ball, but she may also make an error.

The Generalized Other and the Social Self

From the above account, one can better understand how self-consciousness is socially developed. The self cannot arise without others to stand in relation to. These others are captured in the "me." It is conventional in that it represents what the community expects. However, two important features may lead to novelty. Firstly, each individual's "me" may be organized differently due to his or her different positions vis-à-vis the social whole. Secondly, the responses of the "I" are uncertain and can therefore represent the uniqueness of each organism. Consequently, as each individual's "I" adjusts to his "me" in unique ways, the "me" becomes newly organized, which may be externalized back into the general community (e.g., as when a baseball player makes an acrobatic catch that others now try to copy). According to Mead, the resultant of the conversation between the "me" and "I" in response to the social environment constitutes what we term personality.

Mead's account of the self thus far highlights the social nature of the self along two dimensions: First, both the "I" and "me" are phases of the self in the larger social act that the organism finds itself in (e.g., a play in a baseball game). Second, there is a dialogue between the "I" and "me" that can generate novelty in the experience and that allows the individual to take on the attitudes of others so as to plan its own conduct. This give and take is essentially an internalization of the conversation of gestures seen between organisms—even nonreflective animals that are not capable of generating a significant symbolic to introduce the "generalized other." Mead explains, "Mind is nothing but the importation of this external process [cooperative activity through gestures] into the conduct of the individual so as to meet the problems that arise" (p. 188). Thus, the self both arises through interactions with others and is in some respects like a microcosm of the social environment in that a similar process of the conversation of gestures is at work between the "I" and "me."

This is a very similar finding to what was discussed above with respect to the dialogical self. Like the I-positions in the dialogical self, Mead's self is social in that it develops through relations with others and comprises one part that represents others (the "me" of the generalized other) and a position that relates to those others (the "I"). Also, just as the dialogical self mimics the social world through ongoing dialogical exchanges, there are exchanges between Mead's "I" and "me." However, Mead highlights the importance of the conversation of gestures in these exchanges—particularly the significant symbol, which in essence is a semiotic process that guides the development of Mead's self.

Multiplicity in the Self

Turning towards the issue of multiplicity in the self, Mead does not address this as explicitly as the model of the dialogical self, but similar foundations can be found in his writing. Firstly, as Hermans et al. (1992) do with James, one can view Mead's differentiation of the self into the "I" and "me" along with the equating of the "me" with different aspects of the environment, as introducing some degree of division, and hence multiplicity, in the self.

Mead explains that he primarily considers these two phases of the self as coming together coherently to comprise one social self, however he does point in a direction for considering the possibility of *multiple* social selves that break down into separate units of "I" and "Me": "Normally, within the sort of community as a whole to which we belong there is a unified self, but that may be broken up" (p.143).

He explains that in the case of multiple personalities or with someone who is

> nervously unstable and [in] whom there is a line of cleavage, certain activities become impossible, and that set of activities may separate and evolve another

> self. Two separate "me's" and "I's," two different selves, result, and that is the condition under which there is a tendency to break up the personality. (p. 143)

These lines of cleavage are based upon the separation of memories that may have been associated with some form of pain (psychic or physical) such that different contents of experience are dissociated. Memories that are relevant to the genesis of particular selves become cut off from other memories. Thus, in one context a particular "generalized other" along with its associated sets of responses and reactions of the "I" may exist in contrast to other contexts where a different set of "I's" and "me's" may arise. As the patterns of interaction between these phases of self constitute a personality, multiple, separated "I–Me" patterns would constitute multiple personalities in the whole individual, or multiple selves.

Mead's account of the self thus sounds quite modern in its depiction of multiplicity and the role of trauma and dissociation in highlighting the fissures in the self. He thus presages Bromberg (1998), Hermans, Rijks, and Kempen (1993), and others who argue that the self is fundamentally multiple and social. For Mead, a "multiple personality is in a certain sense normal" (p. 142). However, in a healthy individual he argues that the person unifies these different selves into a whole. Mead explains that dissociations mark the

> breaking up of the complete, unitary self into the component selves of which it is composed, and which respectively correspond to different aspects of the social process in which the person is involved, and within which his complete or unitary self has arisen; these aspects being the different social groups to which he belongs within that process. (p. 144)

MEAD AND THE DIALOGICAL SELF

Similarities to the Dialogical Self

The preceding review of Mead's description of the self fits comfortably with the framework of the dialogical self. Each I-position can be understood as both a "me," or "generalized other," and the "I" that responds to the "me." Movement between I-positions represents movement between the constituent "I–me's" that Mead argues make up the unitary self.

Similar to the "generalized other," I-positions are constructed from one's internalization of the set of attitudes and responses of others. External I-positions (e.g., that of my wife) most obviously represent internalization of others' attitudes. Yet internal I-positions can also be viewed as a "generalized other" in that they too represent a set of attitudes and beliefs of culture, but as a self-conscious reflection of this self in relation to others. In other words, one's experience as a husband represents the internalization of the set of culture's attitudes and responses as a husband along with adjustments of the experience and expectations of engaging one's particular wife.

Furthermore, Hermans et al. (1992) claimed that James placed too great an emphasis on the role of the "I" in defining the self, which constrained the polyphony of the self. They therefore turned to Bakhtain's notion of the polyphonic novel to endow each I-position with a more authoritative voice or "I." Mead places equal emphasis on both phases of the self: "Both aspects of the 'I' and 'me' are essential to the self in its full expression" (p. 199). As seen above, there is a constant movement between the "I" and "me," which can generate novelty and uniqueness. Thus, Mead's vision of the self would allow for different component selves that—like I-positions—carry both the attitudes of subsets of generalized others as well as the different voices or "I's" that respond to and help form these component selves. Additionally, given Mead's acknowledgment of the self as constructed of multiple selves and his emphasis on mind as the importation of the conversation of gestures, one could have also used Mead's language to describe dialogical relations between the different component selves, similar to how Hermans et al. (1993) describe dialogical relations in the dialogical self.

Taken together, the empirical data presented above could have been explained via an extrapolation of Mead's theory of the self and mind. The impact of the trauma of cancer to the self could have been viewed as an impact to particular sub-selves of "I–me" configurations. For instance, the destabilizing impact of cancer on H#3's "rock" identity would constitute an inability for that person to engage that "I–me" sub-self that is normally prominent in his awareness. Additionally, the ability to respond to the trauma could have been highlighted as the capacity of the individual to engage other "I–me" configurations of the larger self. Lastly, the demonstration of I-positions as emerging through the internalization and externalization dynamic as the two individuals attempt to help the other deal with the trauma can also be presented as evidence for the development of a "generalized other" out of the experience of the other and its adjustment through the internalization into the organism and the responses of the "I."

Contrast With the Dialogical Self

However, there are differences that emerge from using one theory over and above the other. It is hoped that highlighting these differences can give direction for further adaptation of the theory of the dialogical self and subsequently for understanding relational models of multiplicity. First, the model of the dialogical self as narrative and I-positions offers a more coherent lens for capturing the interplay of multiple, social selves from a phenomenological position. By casting the set of attitudes, beliefs, and emotions as abstracted wholes called I-positions, one can represent them as if talking about actual selves and use the more appropriate language of dialogical relations in describing the interactions between these I-positions. To describe these positions in Mead's language of multiple "I" and "me" configurations that come together from different contexts would not only be more awkward, but also removed from the experience of the individual. Mead's language may, however, offer a more useful frame for analyzing the construction of an I-position, as it can be evaluated through the development of associated sets of social stimuli and anticipated responses.

Another important distinction is that Mead actually viewed the healthy individual as a "unitary" self. While there is room to talk about multiple social selves, this was not his focus. By contrast, through incorporating Bakhtain, the dialogical self normalizes the experience of multiplicity in the self. For Mead, looking at component selves is reserved for instances of psychopathology—particularly dissociation and multiple personality disorder. For Hermans et al. (1993), the individual is an imaginal landscape within which different selves (i.e., I-positions) interact. The unitary self is considered to be more of an illusion. Accordingly, while Mead provides language that can explain the construction of multiple selves, Hermans et al. (1993) make the notion of multiple selves central to the experience of the individual.

Placing this emphasis on multiplicity then allows one to analyze the dialogical relations between parts as an experience of the self is fashioned. It also permits focus on the different factors that influence these relations and trigger movements between these parts, including affect, relevant stimuli, and the interpersonal context.

Yet the manner in which the dialogical self model may have benefitted from incorporating Mead's language is in his emphasis of the conversation of gestures, symbols, and the significant symbol. Recall from earlier that Valsiner (2005) highlighted the need for a developmental framework to account for changes in the dialogical self. To accomplish this, it was necessary to turn to semiotic mediation to explain how new I-positions develop and transform. It is here that Mead can become particularly relevant.

From Mead to Semiotic Mediation in the Dialogical Self

As in the model of the dialogical self, Mead's theory stresses communication. However, he frames this in the language of symbols and the social act. As previously explained, he notes that all social acts require an adjustment of one organism to the other through the interplay of stimulus-response-stimulus that is the conversation of gestures. Mead (1934) explains that when a stimulus like a gesture can be interpreted to represent an ensuing set of responses, it is termed a symbol. If it is a symbol that the individual is consciously aware will lead to a particular response, then it is a significant symbol (e.g., if someone calls out "fire," the word carries with it a set of responses like run or call emergency services that both that caller and those who hear him are aware of). This usage of symbols in constructing his concept of mind and the self opens the thought of Mead up to the field of semiotics.

In general, semiotics (Sebeok, 2001) is the scientific study of how living things make and understand signs to communicate.[4] With respect to humans, it is the ways in which signs allow people to make knowledge of their world. As Valsiner (2007) explains, signs "are made by minds, and minds operate through signs" (p. 40). Signs are reacted to both knowingly and unknowingly, and can be nonverbal as well as verbal. Language is a complex, largely conventional system of particular types of signs to communicate messages that are called symbols. An individual can generate them, but they are made sense of in an interpersonal environment. Signs are both individually internalized to represent experience, but they are also externalized back into the interpersonal space in a new form (Valsiner, 2001, 2007). They are a shared product of the interpersonal and intrapersonal world that guides the meaning making of an individual in the present as he or she moves towards the future (Valsiner, 2007).

Mead's Relevance to the Dialogical Self

Mead's emphasis on the conversations between organisms as mediated by stimuli that are symbols for further responses is a semiotic account of how organisms construct their world both interpersonally as well as intrapersonally (between the "I" and "me"). His distinction between symbol and significant symbol is similar to the distinction between signs that are differentiated as symbols like words and those that may simply be reacted to on a lower, unconscious level. This emphasis on symbols adds significantly to the model of the dialogical self by offering mechanisms for the development of I-positions and the formation of dialogical relations between I-positions. Contained in Mead's self is both a model for construing the self as social and multiple and the semiotic mechanisms for understanding how this self is constructed. Thus, by integrating Mead—perhaps even in place of James—with the narrative model of the dialogical self, one can supply the semiotic mechanisms for transformation in the I-positions of the dialogical self through emphasis on the conversation of gestures. Some of the benefits of doing this will now be discussed with regards to what it may add for contemporary clinical thinking.

THE RELATIONAL SELF AND THE SEMIOTICALLY MEDIATED DIALOGICAL SELF MODEL

Self States

In relational psychoanalytic theory there has been much emphasis on the generation and application of models of the self that are constructed of multiple, relational selves (Howell, 2005; Mitchell, 2000). Of particular note is Bromberg's account of self states (1998). He explains that the self should be construed as consisting of multiple, affective self states that arise out of the various relational configurations (me–other) that the individual is engaged in through development and that become internalized in the self. The self is viewed as socially developed and embedded, as well as multiple in its constitution. Bromberg posits that these self states are dissociated from one another in that they are originally developed separately. However, over time the individual is able to bring these self states into communication with one another to create the illusion of unity in the self. His view of the healthy self is an individual who can "stand in the spaces" between these self states so that she can see her various self states. In instances of psychopathology, dissociations connected to significant anxiety like that of trauma inhibit the integration of these self states because the anxiety associated with those self states is defensively warded off in order to prevent a disintegration of the illusion of self.

Bromberg (1998) explains that his perspective is rooted primarily in the interpersonal theory of Sullivan—which was heavily influenced by Mead—but with the addition of theory from the British school of object relations to better account for the subjective experience of the individual. He explains that Sullivan's theory remained too cognitive and externalized by focusing on achieving consensual validation of experience. Meanwhile, object relations opened the door to accessing the felt, inner experience of the individual. Additionally, Bromberg notes that his theory is more an account of observed clinical process than an extension of any particular theoretical model.

Dialogue Between Multiple Self Models

In many ways, what Bromberg depicts is similar to the model of dialogical self. This model shares with Bromberg the emphasis on multiplicity in the self, the importance of relatedness, and the importance of access to the subjective experience of the individual. Traumas like cancer are seen to impede the communication between I-positions and the organization of I-positions in the dialogical self repertoire. When severe enough, the experience of particular I-positions may be completely blocked off, as in dissociative experiences, to protect the stability of the overall dialogical self (Bellehsen, 2011). This is similar to how Bromberg views traumatic dissociation as a lack of integration of self states to preserve the illusion of a cohesive self.

Additionally, the dialogical self model in general is narrative, which allows for an approach to the subjective and phenomenological experience of the individual. As shown in previous sections, much of what the dialogical self offers is also found in the pragmatic tradition of Mead and would approximate what Bromberg describes. However, Bromberg's point of the need to move away from the cognitive and external in order to access the internal may still stand.

The Relevance of Mead

Yet the building blocks for linking the external environment with the internal world (cognitively and affectively) are inherent to Mead's theory. Mead's (1934) construction of the self and mind as an importation of social processes based on the conversation of gestures, symbols, significant symbols, and the generalized other enables signs like words or behaviors to link the intrapersonal world and interpersonal field. A systemic model of semiotic mediation that explores the connection between affect and signs for regulating experience provides a theoretical bridge to move back and forth between these two worlds. These tools can be easily introduced into the dialogical self (Bellehsen, 2011) but can also be applied to the self state model of Bromberg, explaining the dynamics of the clinical process he highlights. Accordingly, as will be briefly explored in the next section, one could more readily trace the development of self states from the interpersonal field in which the person is located, as well as the signs that trigger movements into these self states.

Such a model also comes closer to the interpersonal tradition of locating the self in the social world because I-positions are constructed out of the perceptions of others, similar to the generalized other. This slightly alters Bromberg's conception of self states that arise from interactions with others, as self states bring the focus more on a self that is experiencing others, rather than selves that are also others. However, it does allow for a discussion and mapping of the internal world of the self.

Lastly, Bromberg (1998) briefly notes that in doing clinical work with self states, it can approach the experience of doing couples counseling because one is addressing parts in relation to an overall unit. In fact, a semiotically mediated multiple self model as based on the dialogical self or an extension of Mead's thought would suggest that this is precisely what is being done, and it offers a landscape and map for doing so; while maintaining sensitivity to the felt experience of the whole individual, it allows for addressing the nuances of experience through the parts of the self and the organization of these parts into dialogical relations as guided by signs.

Semiotic Mediation of Affect

To illustrate some of how it may look to incorporate semiotics in a relational, multiple self model, it is necessary to first review one model of semiotic mediation. Valsiner (2005, 2007) outlines a framework for applying semiotics to the affective experience of the individual. He articulates the manner in which signs can move through levels in a hierarchy of greater and greater abstraction, such that more generalized signs can represent and regulate classes of signs underneath them. For instance, the experience of enjoying an ice cream cone may become abstracted into a word like happy or even a smiley face. It may be further abstracted into a word like good. Note that as the sign becomes more generalized it also becomes less differentiated.

Valsiner (2005, 2007) goes on to explain that in a similar vein, human affective experience proceeds from one level to the next with greater abstraction and generalization, and with an associated semiotic device. At the bottom of the hierarchy is a diffuse experience—as when the child starts to feel positively aroused when she anticipates ice cream. As the experience is made further sense of, it becomes generalized into signs like happy and good, which link it with other experiences that were happy and good. Note that the bottom level of experience carries some features of a sign, but it is not yet symbolized in language, while some higher levels are. Nevertheless, all levels can come under the influence of the symbols of higher or equal levels. Accordingly, if the child is feeling good about ice cream, she may relish the experience and stay in the store so that she continues to experience that positive arousal. Alternatively, if she is allergic to milk, she may move through a different line of generalizations and signs (such as ice cream is "poison" → "bad") that guide the child to remove herself from the experience.

Semiotic Mediation of the Dialogical Self[5]

The above cursory review captures some of the features of what Valsiner (2007) describes as semiotic mediation of affect. Importantly, he argues that this model of affect regulation can be adapted to the dialogical self model to explain the movements between I-positions (Valsiner, 2005). In particular, there are signs that guide the individual towards embodying an I-position and its relation to another I-position. To this end, in past writings

(Bellehsen, 2011) I adapted semiotic mediation to help trace the movements of individuals into and out of particular I-positions in response to the trauma of cancer along with the usage of words by partners to mediate the development of I-positions.

For instance, the meaning of cancer as captured in words by the physician, as well as other signs, was seen to serve as a catalyst for moving the individual into and out of his or her accustomed I-positions. This was seen in the data above when H#3 "completely lost it" and moved out of his "rock" I-position in response to his physician's statement that he had a tumor that required removal of a testicle. Subsequently, individuals regained old I-positions or adopted new I-positions with their associated signs to regulate their experience (affectively, behaviorally, and cognitively).

Importantly, many of the signs to regulate one's dialogical self were seen to emerge in part from the exchanges between individuals in a relationship. As seen above, W#4 shared that she was able to embody her husband's "anchor" I-position through their engagement: "Well, I think in nonverbal ways, he made me accept that I actually did have cancer."

Thus, I was able to describe the phenomenology of the overall traumatic experience in terms of I-positions, but highlight that signs mediated the development of I-positions and the movement between them. Importantly, because of the nature for some signs to be differentiated in the form of words and others to be reacted to affectively without awareness, experience could be depicted in terms of conscious and unconscious processes.

CONCLUSION

The current emphasis on the use of a relational, multiple self model in understanding the experience of the self was born out of clinical observations in working with trauma and through the integration of the interpersonal and object relations schools of thought. However, the seeds of such a model were sown long ago in the work of James and even more so of Mead. Additionally, while it may have seemed that the pragmatists and Sullivan were more exclusively focused on the external behaviors of the interpersonal environment, they also laid a solid foundation for understanding the intrapersonal world. In particular, an emphasis on signs, as seen with Mead's emphasis on the conversation of gestures and the significant symbol, enables a rich, detailed analysis of the conscious and unconscious intrapersonal world of the individual. This can be seen in the empirical application of the dialogical self and semiotic mediation to the experience of couples with the trauma of cancer. As the dialogical self model bears significant resemblance to Bromberg's multiple self-state model, similarly applying the science of signs and conversation among signs should also offer new tools for understanding and researching Bromberg's clinically anchored model.

NOTES

1. From his words, it might be inferred that he found a way to have his "rock" and "emotionally vulnerable" I-positions come into dialogue such that they were integrated. However, this cannot be stated with certainty given the retrospective account. It could have also been that he found a way to return to his "rock" I-position and avoid returning to the "emotionally vulnerable" I-position. In fact, this would be more consistent with other parts of the interview that highlighted his desire not to discuss emotional content, which dissatisfied his partner.
2. See Bellehsen (2011) for a more detailed discussion of this dynamic labeled as *Holding the Other and Balancing the Other*, including more examples and the importance of dialogical forms of communication as a mechanism in this process.
3. For the remainder of this chapter, any references to Mead, including page numbers, come from Mead (1934).
4. Notably, Charles Sanders Pierce was one of the founders of semiotics and was also credited by William James for his influence on the development of pragmatism.
5. A fuller account of the application of semiotic mediation in this data can be seen in Bellehsen (2011).

REFERENCES

Bakhtain, M. M. (1984). *Problems of Dostoevsky's Poetics.* (C. Emerson, Trans.) Minneapolis, MN: University of Minnesota Press.

Bellehsen, M. (2011). *Negotiating the traumatic impact of cancer.* Doctoral Dissertation, Yeshiva University, 2011. *Dissertations Abstract International, 73,* 3256.

Bromberg, P. (1998). *Standing in the spaces: Essays on clinical process, trauma, and dissociation.* Hillsdale, NJ: The Analytic Press.

Evans III, F. B. (1996). *Harry Stack Sullivan: Interpersonal theory and psychotherapy.* London, UK: Routledge.

Harris, A. E. (2011). The relational tradition: Landscape and canon. *Journal of the American Psychoanalytic Association,* 59, 701–734.

Hermans, H. (2001). The dialogical self: Toward a theory of personal and cultural positioning. *Culture Psychology,* 7, 243–281.

Hermans, H. (2004). The dialogical self: between exchange and power. In H. Hermans & C. Dimagio (Eds.), *The dialogical self in psychotherapy* (pp. 13–28). New York, NY: Brunner Routledge.

Hermans, H. J. M. (1996). Voicing the self: From information processing to dialogical interchange. *Psychological Bulletin, 119,* 31–50.

Hermans, H. J. M. (1997). Dissociation as disorganized self narrative: Tension between splitting and integration. *Journal of Psychotherapy Integration,* 7, 213–223.

Hermans, H. J. M. (2003). The construction and reconstruction of a dialogical self. *Journal of Constructivist Psychology, 16,* 89–130.
Hermans, H. J. M., Kempen, H. J. G., & van Loon, R. J. P. (1992). The dialogical self: Beyond individualism and rationalism. *American Psychologist, 47*(1), 23–33.
Hermans, H. J. M., Rijks, T. I., Kempen, H. J. G. (1993). Imaginal dialogues in the self: Theory and method. *Journal of Personality, 61,* 207–236.
Howell, E. (2005). *The dissociative mind.* Hillsdale, NJ: The Analytic Press.
James, W. (1890). *The principles of psychology* (Vol 1). Mineola, NY: Dover.
Janoff-Bulman, R. (1992). *Shattered assumptions: Towards a new psychology of trauma.* New York, NY: The Free Press.
Mead, G. H. (1934). *Mind, self, and society from the standpoint of a social behaviorist* (C. W. Morris, Ed.). Chicago, IL: The University of Chicago Press.
Menand, L. (1997). An Introduction to pragmatism. In L. Menand (Ed.), *Pragmatism: A reader* (pp. xi–xxxiv). New York, NY: Vintage Books
Mitchell, S. A. (2000). *Relationality: From attachment to intersubjectivity.* Hillsdale, NJ: The Analytic Press.
Salgado, J., & Hermans, H. J. M. (2005). The return of subjectivity: From a multiplicity of selves to the dialogical self. *E-Journal of Applied Psychology: Clinical Section, 1,* 3–13.
Sebeok, T. A. (2001). *Signs: An introduction to semiotics* (2nd ed). Toronto, ON: Toronto University Press.
Stolorow, R. D. (2007). *Trauma and human existence: Autobiographical, psychoanalytic, and philosophical reflections.* Hillsdale, NJ: The Analytic Press.
Valsiner, J. (2001). Process structure of semiotic mediation in human development. *Human Development, 44,* 84–97.
Valsiner, J. (2002). Forms of dialogical relations and semiotic autoregulation within the self. *Theory and Psychology, 12,* 251–265.
Valsiner, J. (2005). Scaffolding within the structure of dialogical self. Hierarchical dynamics of semiotic mediation. *New Ideas in Psychology, 23,* 197–206.
Valsiner, J. (2007). *Culture in minds and societies: Foundations of cultural psychology.* London, UK: Sage Publications.

CHAPTER 5

ACHIEVING PURPOSE IN AN OPEN COSMOS

The Continuing Relevance of William James for Relational and Interpersonal Theory

Jon Weidenbaum
Berkeley College–New York City

INTRODUCTION

In "The Illusion of Personal Identity," Harry Stack Sullivan expresses a strong appreciation for the word *nexus* (1950a).[1] Latin for "bind" or "connection," and not of Greek origin as he suggests, the term nexus is employed by Sullivan in order to depict how prior experiences gel to form our view of things.[2] Informing us that the word was also favored by Alfred North Whitehead, Sullivan undoubtedly borrowed it directly from the great British philosopher. This should come as no surprise. Just as Whitehead outlines an organic and interrelated picture of the cosmos in which individual events are fashioned largely (but not completely) out of other events, so Sullivan retools psychoanalysis, "Freud's epoch-making invention" (1950b, p. 93), to establish a

Making Our Ideas Clear, pages 127–152
Copyright © 2015 by Information Age Publishing
All rights of reproduction in any form reserved.

vision of the psyche as constituted by living relationships to others past and present. "It pleased Whitehead also," states Sullivan of his adopted term, "so at least I am in good company for the moment" (1950a, p. 319).

Sullivan's understanding of the psyche as a product of social relations not only sits at the very foundation of interpersonal theory, but it has anticipated many contemporary views of human nature and personal identity. The independent and self-transparent ego of our Cartesian and Western intellectual heritage—whose contemporary incarnation is pejoratively labeled by Roger Frie as "the Marlboro Man" (2011)—is now deemed untenable and unrealistic, even socially and culturally arrogant.[3] The rational and atomic "I" is equated by Frie with an imperialist posture toward other cultures, a dangerous triumphalism of science and technology over the environment, and an obliviousness to the relevant differences between race, gender, and social class. If psychoanalysis "has played a major role in the development of a complex, decentered, contextualized understanding of what it means to be a person," as Stephen Mitchell and Margaret Black aptly point out (1995, p. 84), then philosophical postmodernism has taken this up a notch by denying personal agency and even embracing an outright antihumanism. Ensconced within an intellectual and academic environment in which persons are seen as expressions of language and culture, the more orthodox followers of Harry Stack Sullivan are in good company. The author of *The Interpersonal Theory of Psychiatry* notoriously denies the existence of both the individual self and the volitional will (Sullivan, 1953; Fiscalini, 2008).[4]

Even for those sympathetic to interpersonal and relational theories of the psyche, the specter of postmodernism, along with the more controversial ideas of Sullivan, has generated more than a few questions. In *Understanding Experience*, Frie provides a number of these:

> If there is no person for whom experience takes place, then who can be said to experience anything at all? How do we explain individual change, innovation, or creativity if the person is subverted? And how do we account for the determination of meaning or the ability to choose one course of action over another without a concept of personal agency? (2003, p. 3)

These questions are particularly relevant for psychotherapists, social workers, and professionals in any field who seek to assist others in achieving more positive and constructive forms of behavior. Of course, they are just as applicable to the therapist who must innovate in order to enact such a transformation in his or her clients.

One means of steering between the classical Cartesian self on the one hand and the postmodern denial of the individual person on the other is to draw upon a different stream coursing through European intellectual history: the existential-phenomenological tradition. This is the path taken by Frie and numerous others, and it involves the incorporation of insights from philosophers such as Martin Heidegger, Martin Buber, Emmanuel Levinas, Jean-Paul Sartre, and Maurice Merleau-Ponty, as well as the use of an earlier wave of psychotherapists who have already fertilized psychoanalytic theory with the aforementioned figures, including Erich Fromm, Ludwig Binswanger, Medard Boss, Victor Frankl, and Rollo May. In a nutshell, this inheritance paints a fundamentally embodied and situated portrait of the human animal—one in which we exist inseparably from larger cultural contexts. Yet, as this same tradition also holds, we are not *reducible* to these contexts, for our existence is also somewhat uprooted, anticipatory, and (incompletely) severed from the complacency and comfort of the present. Unlike trees and coffee cups, to be human is to face a range of possibilities, to make decisions that shape who we are. My refusal to participate in a violent political conflict, for instance, assists me in crafting a personality unsullied by hatred and resentment. We may not choose the place and time we are born, but we are endowed with a facility, however limited, for self-creation. In short, we are a "situated freedom" (Burston & Frie, 2006).[5] Another important strand of this tradition explores the manner in which our experience is enriched, or disrupted, by our encounters with other human beings.

It is far from the mission of the present author to suggest that the use of the existential-phenomenological tradition has not been fruitful. It is to argue for the importance of yet another figure, one whose impact is present to some degree in the work of all the thinkers mentioned above. William James's pioneering study of the mind in his monumental *Principles of Psychology* is not only a landmark in the history of psychology as a whole; his exquisite observations of our perceptual and experiential life were admired by Edmund Husserl, the very founder of phenomenology (Wilshire, 1968). James was a major influence on Sullivan by way of George Herbert Mead and Adolf Meyer (Perry, 1982).[6] Whitehead's ontology of process, another inspiration for Sullivan, is highly indebted to James (Weber, 2011).[7] Clearly, existentialists, phenomenologists, and interpersonal theorists who peruse the writings of James are in good company indeed.[8]

But the task of the pages which follow is not to simply report the historical relevance of James for interpersonal and relational theory; it is to argue for his *continuing* relevance. I proceed through the following stages:

1. I argue that James offers a unique angle on the question of the self, particularly as it is compatible with a wider context or field of relations. James here joins the existential-phenomenological tradition in challenging the autonomous and unchanging ego of Descartes while retaining the personal and volitional character of our existence. That James deflates the assumptions of Cartesianism without col-

lapsing into the antihumanism of so much postmodern theory lends further credence to his title, along with Whitehead and other giants in American philosophy, of being a *constructive* postmodernist (Ford, 1993).[9] The next two sections examine the phenomenological and ethical implications of this position respectively.

2. I unpack those facets of experience, illuminated by James, that serve as the conditions for individual selfhood and invest it with significance. James's penchant for outlining and sympathizing with a varied range of experience is well noted, and parallels are often drawn between James and the existentialists on this topic alone.
3. In the penultimate section I show how James's doctrine of an unfinished universe allows for what is arguably his core theme to make its appearance—one of particular value for human flourishing. This is our sense of being contributors to the outcome of things, active players rather than passive recipients to the cosmos.
4. Finally, I conclude by briefly drawing out the concrete applications of James's philosophy by discussing its relevance for psychotherapy and personal development.

A few disclaimers are necessary before I proceed. As with Wittgenstein, Nietzsche, and Kierkegaard, figures with which he is often compared, James is too often pinned as an antisystematic thinker. Although James did voice a profound distrust of closed and totalizing philosophical systems (partly in rebellion against the neo-Hegelian and idealist metaphysics in vogue during his time), there is certainly a continuity of themes that surface time and again in his work. Nonetheless, James is not always consistent, and his thinking on any issue, even the topics closest to him, were as tentative and open as his picture of the universe. I suggest that the relevance of James is found more in what can be mined from the rich and protean nature of his work than any finished and final statement on his part.[10] For example, many of his most path-breaking insights are further elaborated and refined in the later ideas of Whitehead, a fact I accentuate throughout.[11] There is also an occasional tone of "been there, done that" heard among some champions of American philosophy when addressing Continental thought, as if everything in phenomenology and existentialism is prefigured within Peirce, James, or Dewey.[12] This, however, is not the case. In her comparison of Emmanuel Levinas and William James, Megan Craig astutely affirms: "Despite similarities, there is of course no one-to-one correspondence between Levinas and James, or between phenomenology and pragmatism" (2010, p. 101). If there is any larger agenda to this study it is to engender the spirit of James's own eclecticism. Alternatively stated, we should seek to wean truth from wherever it can be found, whether home or abroad.

THE SELF AND ITS FIELD

Sullivan and the Self-System

In her biography of Sullivan, Helen Swick Perry explains that his article "The Illusion of Personal Identity" was so disturbing to his colleagues that it was not published until after his death. "In a society that prides itself on the uniqueness of each person," she states, "this cross-section view of humanity was revolutionary" (1982, p. 226). By a cross-section view, Perry refers to the network of social relations within which the psyche is developed. For Sullivan, the personality is not a plaything of instincts and buried conflicts, nor an aggregate of well-defined if occasionally clashing entities (as the id, ego, and superego of Freud's structural model can seem), but "the relatively enduring pattern of recurrent interpersonal situations which characterize a human life" (1953, pp. 110–111). What shocks those versed in classical psychoanalytic theory in this definition are the very same things that strike scholars of American philosophy as familiar: the avoidance of rigid and essentialized structures, the preference for the temporal over the static, and the stress on a mesh of forces rather than an upsurge of biologically preexisting drives.

In place of the invisible and unchanging core of our being, the *res cogito* of Descartes, or the "soul" of traditional religious faith, Sullivan writes of a "self-system" (1953). The "self-system"—note the sheer impersonality of the term—is but a number of strategies erected by the personality during its formative period, a sort of mechanism designed to increase satisfaction and boost security. In particular, it is the means by which the personality seeks to evade anxiety, that troublesome emotion which first arises in our relationship to the mother figure of our earliest childhood. Anxiety, in this context, is a sense of severe apprehension which arises through our more problematic encounters with others. Sullivan, not usually renowned for the accessibility of his writing, succinctly tags the self-system as "the tree that all too frequently reflects the way the twig was bent in the developmental years" (1950, p. 115). In other words, our behavioral, cognitive, and emotional styles of being are shadows of the relational vectors of our past. Thus, it is not only the unique and abiding ego which is an illusion according to Sullivan, but also the volitional will (1953).[13] To expound the details of Sullivan's complex account of personal development is not necessary here. The point is that for Sullivan, the isolated, volitional, and active self disappears into tissue of relations, a *field*.[14]

James and the "I"

Understood as a broader network of connections underlying and shaping our more explicit acts of cognition, the idea of a field is found throughout

James's authorship. There is a crucial difference, however, between his earlier and later use of this concept. In *The Principles of Psychology* and *Psychology: Briefer Course* (published in 1890 and 1892, respectively), the field is primarily found as a structure of our mental life. Hence it is understood as "the halo of felt relations" surrounding our thoughts, the dimly perceived periphery or *fringe* into which our focus of awareness gradually shades off. "When very fresh," James states in Chapter 9 of *The Principles,* "our minds carry an immense horizon with them" (1890/1950a, p. 256). Beginning with his 1895–1896 seminar on "The Feelings," and then crystallizing into his philosophy of "radical empiricism," the field is then transformed into the one complex substance from which the mind *and* the external world are constituted (Lamberth, 1999), an ontological development I will describe below.[15] Between these two phases of his thinking—his works in psychology and his later metaphysics—James shows how a field theory of meaning and experience can be affirmed without denying the existence of an active and individualized self.

James's most exhaustive investigation into personal identity is found in Chapter 10 of *The Principles of Psychology*, "The Consciousness of Self." Here James first describes the ways in which we *appear* to ourselves, what he calls the "empirical self" or "me." These include the material, social, and spiritual selves. While the first is composed of our possessions and the second the recognition we receive from others, James's search for the spiritual self, our "inner and subjective being," leads to nothing but movements felt in the eyeballs, the glottis, the palate, the brow, and the eyelids.[16] James concludes: "*the 'Self of all selves', when carefully examined, is found to consist mainly of the collection of these peculiar motions in the head or between the head and throat*" (1890/1950a, p. 301, emphasis in original).

But if the "me" is an object *for* consciousness, what of the subject to whom the "me" appears? After all, *some* part of our awareness is registering the phenomenon called "me." This facet of our subjectivity is labeled by James as the "I." But what is this "I"? Its status up to this point remains a mystery, and James calls it "the most puzzling puzzle with which psychology has to deal" (1890/1950a, p. 330). Indeed, James even toys with the idea that consciousness in its purest form may be *entirely* impersonal, a bare awareness bereft of an individualized self. Immediate experience, before the distinction between "Self" and "not-Self," is at one point labeled by James as *sciousness* as opposed to consciousness—a field devoid of any "me" or "I" whatsoever (1890/1950a, p. 304).[17] But James does not remain with this position. Seeking to capture the personalized feel of our conscious experience, he proceeds to delve more deeply into the question of personal identity.

The only "I" James can find in the flow of conscious experience is a succession of momentary thoughts, each of which appropriates the one before. These acts of appropriation are based upon a shared "warmth and intimacy" found between the different thoughts, which, in turn, are derived from their association with "the whole cubic mass of our body" (1890/1950a, p. 333). For instance, the "I" who types this sentence onto the page identifies itself with the "I" of two moments ago, since both seem to radiate from the same physical posture and position. In this sense, the previous "I" that is claimed by the current one is the bodily *me.*[18]

James's vivid and memorable analogy for the whole process is that of a herdsman who, in recognizing his brand on his cattle, gathers them together as his own. The herdsman is that portion of consciousness known as the "I," and the brand found on the cattle is the "warmth and intimacy" upon which the connection between the different thoughts is made. As each passing thought is recognized and absorbed by the one before, James asks us to imagine a continually perishing but constant sequence of herdsmen, each of which inherits the title of "owner" from the previous one. "May not the 'title' of a collective self," asks James, "be passed from one Thought to another in some analogous way?" (1890/1950a, p. 339). Thus, the self is not an abiding and unalterable substance, but a plurality of cognitions, each linked to the other in a contingent rather than necessary manner. James here offers a scheme that can speak to our sense of continuity over time, all the while avoiding both the skepticism of Hume's empiricism (in which no self can be found among disparate and isolated sense data) as well as the need to posit a soul or "transcendental ego" submerged beneath our everyday experience (1890/1950a).

As with every area explored in *The Principles,* James does not pretend to have exhausted or settled the queries introduced at the beginning of the chapter. Scholars such as Richard Gale (1999) and Gerald Myers (1986) go to great pains to point out how James did not so much deny the existence of a spiritual and metaphysical self as neglect to find experiential evidence for one; that he never settled on a definition of the self even within the *Principles*; and that the scarcity of James's writings on the issue toward the end of his career demonstrates his final preference for a kind of silence on the topic.[19]

Pure Experience

In chapter ten of *The Principles,* the "I" is a component of consciousness, a fragment perpetually recreating itself within the stream of thought. In James's "radical empiricism," the inner core of his later philosophy, consciousness is itself carved out of a larger field. Labeled by James as "pure experience" (1912/1996b), this field is a primordial whole that precedes the divisions between mind and body, subject and object.

At the present moment, an essay is being typed. Taken strictly as an experience, and received without metaphysical commitments and assumptions, there is the arising and combining of thoughts, the movement of fingers and buttons, and the appearance of characters on a screen. Observed from one direction, it is correct to say that the experience is that of a person organizing and crystallizing his ideas. Seen from another angle, however, the experience can be understood as a piece of technology registering letters and words while plugged into a café wall. The two approaches are equally valid, since they highlight different cross-sections of significance from a single reality. Pure experience "is only virtually or potentially either object or subject as yet. For the time being, it is plain, unqualified actuality, or existence, a simple *that*" (1912/1996b, pp. 23–24). As a simple *that*, experience for James is the basic substratum of the cosmos, with the mental and the physical as two of its modes.[20]

If Sullivan articulated a field of interpersonal and social relations in order to account for human development and the phenomenon of psychiatric illness, James created his concept of pure experience in order to resolve a few seemingly intractable problems in philosophy. One classic issue in epistemology is how we can be sure that our mental representations match up with the world outside of us. The skeptic doubts that we can be assured of such a connection: Existence may be entirely different than how we conceive it. But if pure experience is a seamless unity out of which subject and object are aspects, then the gap between our psyche and the environment is overcome. Since the cleavage between subject and object is finally bridged, we are therefore no longer haunted by questions such as how we can *know* that the chair we are sitting on actually exists, or how two or more minds can be sure they are seeing the same thing. Furthermore, because consciousness is not understood as some ghostly and mysterious entity independent from the rest of the universe, but as simply another organization of pure experience (a set of purposeful activities that James calls a *function*), the mind–body problem vanishes as well. We are no longer burdened with explaining how the mind, previously conceived as a kind of substance with no mass, can interact with the rest of nature.[21]

The implications of pure experience for the topic of personal identity are also clear: As with James's account of the self in chapter ten of the *Principles,* we are not unchanging essences, minds in a vacuum, but a series of operations occurring within a broader medium.

Bud Theory

Concerning the relationship between the self and its field, what *precisely* does James provide in order to prevent the "I" from being a passive recipient of external influences, a mere puppet whose strings are pulled by the surrounding context of meaning? Returning to Chapter 10 of the *Principles,* it cannot be the selectivity exercised by each thought in claiming the one before—since this is a result of the "warmth and intimacy" it *already* finds there. Largely an unconscious activity, the recognition between current and prior thoughts is based upon a discovery rather than a choice (namely that the different thoughts share the same body), and is therefore more a product of the underlying field than our own initiative.[22]

The answer is a concept that, though introduced in the *Principles*, plays a cardinal role in James's later metaphysics. This is the idea that experience (whether in our minds or generalized to reality at large) is comprised of individualized buds or pulsations. While Chapter 9 of the *The Principles* famously speaks of a "stream of consciousness," we have already seen how James proposes a string of discrete thoughts in his analysis of the self (1890/1950).[23] Likewise, his radical empiricism depicts the cosmos as a ceaseless wave of experiences that, though occasionally including and informing each other, are ultimately distinct. "On the discontinuity-theory," James states in his final and unfinished book, "time, change, etc., would grow by finite buds or drops, either nothing coming at all, or certain units of amount bursting into being 'at a stroke'" (1911/1996c, p. 154).[24]

The picture of spontaneously arising pulses of experience (rather than a monochrome flow without discernable transitions) is what introduces both freshness and individuality into the Jamesian universe. It is what prevents a cosmos of interrelated events from otherwise lapsing into one of mere homogeneity and conformity. While the "warmth and intimacy" discovered by buds in previous ones may be testimony to the influence of the past, it is the initial *freedom* of each bud from earlier ones, the eruption of the new and the unprecedented between pulsations, that initiates the grasping for such warmth and intimacy to begin with.

It can be argued that James's bud theory, particularly as it develops in his later thought, contains a few resources to combat determinism. Nonetheless, it should be recognized that throughout his authorship, James approaches the age-old controversy of free will versus determinism through a number of angles, and he employs a variety of phenomenological and ethical arguments. The topic was of major philosophical and personal importance to James, and we will return to it again in the section after next.

While James hereby avoids the dissolving of all particularity and novelty into a uniform flow or flat monism, what prevents him from collapsing into the opposite danger of a hard and fragmented atomism (i.e., that of classical empiricism)? This is the manner of the *relations* subsisting between pulsations. As we have seen in Chapter 10 of the *Principles*, the causal connections between pulsations are *internal* in nature. Each experience subsumes the legacy of earlier ones directly into itself and is in turn appropriated by others. It is this doctrine of internal relations between drops of experience that permits James to label his ontology a "concatenated world" (1912/1996b, p. 108) as much as a pluralism, a makeshift and complex whole in which the ingredient parts are retained rather than homogenized. The idea of felt relations binding droplets of experience together along with the (relative) freedom possessed by each is a heavy influence on the process ontology of Whitehead (Weber, 2011).[25]

To summarize: For Sullivan, the self is merely a "self-system," a construct formed in order to protect the human organism from anxiety. But personal individuality for Sullivan is, finally, an illusion; there is no true "I" over and above the fabric of social relations, the *field*. James accounts for the personal character of our awareness without succumbing to the idea of a soul-substance existing above or beneath the flux of experience or train of thoughts. In one of his more celebrated statements (no small accolade for a writer of his ability) James proclaims that "thought is itself the thinker" (1890/1950a, p. 401). In contrast with Sullivan, however, the Jamesian self is informed by the continual introduction of novelty into the cosmos. The individual and volitional self, for James, is therefore no mirage.

EXPERIENCE AND MEANING

A Thick Universe

From *The Principles of Psychology* to his radical empiricism, the "I" is preserved rather than nullified in the thought of James and yet freed of Cartesian assumptions of a static and self-contained thinking substance. But where is the full-blooded nature of our personal experience? Taken in isolation, the above analyses (a succession of thoughts or a function within experience) yields a rather pallid and thin picture of who we are and nothing like the man of "flesh and bone"—to borrow a phrase from Miguel de Unamuno (1954, p. 1). What is needed, according to many contemporary philosophers and psychotherapists, is an account of what Frie describes as "the affective, embodied, and relational processing of human experience" (2008, p. 371). European thinkers, particularly from the existential and phenomenological traditions, certainly contribute to this effort. But James affords a treasure-trove of resources for this very same end. Radical empiricism is, first and foremost, the endeavor to register experience in all of its dimensions (conversely, to include nothing that is *not* found within experience).[26] The result is what James calls a "thick" universe (1909/1996a) as opposed to the pale abstractions of the more systematic philosophers of his era. Chief of these is the Absolute of the neo-Hegelians and the idealists—what James rather picturesquely dismisses as "too buttoned up and white-chokered and clean-shaven a thing to speak for the vast slow-breathing unconscious Kosmos with its dread abysses and its unknown tides" (1912/1996b, pp. 277–278).

Experience, for James, is no well-lit closet but a pool that, however clear on the surface, turns increasingly opaque as it descends. The purpose of this section is to show how this opacity, "the darker, blinder strata" of our being (1902/1958, p. 379), both serves as the condition for our existence and suffuses it with meaning. Among these strata are our embodiment, our finitude, our encounters with others, and spiritual experiences. I will briefly examine each of these in turn.

Embodiment

The place of our insertion within reality and the primary locus of our perception is, of course, the body. We have already seen the role of corporeality in the constitution of the self, but James elaborates on the relationship of the body to experience in an extraordinary footnote to his "The Experience of Activity." Our perception of the world, we are told, "comes at all times with our body as its centre, centre of vision, centre of action, centre of interest" (1912/1996b, p. 170). The objects and relations of our environment are in fact granted their relevance through our embodiment. Because things and events are converted into "this," "then," or "there" in approximation to our physical presence, "no developed or active experience exists for us at all except in that ordered form" (1912/1996b, p. 170).[27] James's view that corporeality is the "storm-centre" of consciousness, both in "The Experience of Activity" and elsewhere, stands in sharp contrast to Descartes's identification of the self as a purely thinking substance (1912/1996b, p. 170).[28]

Finitude

With embodiment comes finitude, and James waxes elegantly, if morbidly, on "the worm at the core of all our usual springs of delight" in the chapter on "The Sick Soul" in *The Varieties of Religious Experience* (1902/1958, p. 121). The awareness of death, for James, is a shadow cast over our sunniest moments. And death is not the only form of finitude discussed in this chapter: A macabre description of an encounter with a sickly patient in an insane asylum (a boy with green complexion and resembling an "Egyptian cat or Peruvian mummy") turns into a reflection on the terrifying reality of psychological fragility (1902/1958, pp. 135–136).[29] Finally, our finitude is also found in the process of self-realization, as outlined in "The Consciousness of Self" chapter of *The Principles.* Here James argues that over the course of our lives we are all forced to choose among a variety of potential selves while watching the others pass us by (1890/1950a, pp. 309–310). In dedicating years to earning a PhD in philosophy, for instance, I have jettisoned my earlier dream of becoming a filmmaker. To be an active, volitional, and existing self is to face our finitude at every juncture. Appreciating this fact is a necessary condition for assessing what is at stake in our actions and decisions, including what trajectory we are to take in forming our character.

One of James's most persistent themes is our intellectual finitude. James is one of the great anti-totalizers in the history of philosophy, and he never tires of stressing our inability to close off a final (or even adequate) picture of reality. As James states in *A Pluralistic Universe*, the "each-forms" in which the cosmos discloses itself to us can never gather itself into an "all-form," and there will always be an element of things that evades our conceptual and rational categories (1909/1996a, p. 34). James's passion for psychical research and the paranormal, along with his hunger for experiences typically marginalized by the scientific and academic community (i.e., his experimentation with nitrous oxide) were at least partly motivated to establish just this fact.[30]

Encounters With Others

Among James's most beautiful descriptions is the manner in which the subjective life of another human being breaks through our barriers of self-preoccupation and complacency. Whatever it is that jolts us out of our previously indifferent relationship to the person facing us, the consequences for our experience are momentous: "Then the whole scheme of our customary values gets confounded, then our self is riven and its narrow interests fly to pieces, then a new centre and a new perspective must be found" (1899/1962, p. 118).[31] In the *Varieties*, James speaks of the contemplative and the converted as the "twice-born" self as opposed to the pagan immediacy of the natural person (1902/1958). Although not labeled as such by James, a similar rebirth occurs in our full receptivity to others.

James occasionally enlarges these acts of intuition beyond the faces of human beings. "As a single stroke," he states of the perspective of the person who embraces theism, "it changes the dead blank *it* of the world into a living *thou*, with whom the man may have dealings" (1956, p. 127).[32] In sympathy with poets like Whitman and Wordsworth, James writes of the astonishment one can find in the sheer ineffability of things, the uncanny beauty of the ordinary when glimpsed by artists and saints alike. Insights such as these, he suggests, are spontaneous rather than a result of effort, gifts instead of achievements (1899/1962, p. 125). To extend our earlier analogy: the pool of experience, however murky, bubbles with epiphanies.

What may serve to demystify these kinds of intuitions is a closer inspection of James's bud theory. We have seen how, for James, buds or pulses of experience continually interpenetrate. In "A World of Pure Experience," he further explains that while experiences enter and inform one another, they rarely do so in an even and predictable manner (1912/1996b). Moreover, droplets do not give themselves over completely, and the gaps and disconnections between buds are as real as the connections. In this sense, an ontology of mutual immanence is synthesized with one of partial transcendence: Buds both contain *and* elude one another.[33] It is evident that James allows this kind of dynamic to reverberate throughout every level of being, including the relations between human beings. This ontology may be said to provide a metaphysical scaffolding and support on which to rest the dialogic philosophy and radical ethics of Buber and Levinas—for an activity similar to their account of interpersonal relations is here read by James into the very material of the universe.[34]

Spiritual Experiences

No less than Freud, James sees human beings as having limited self-transparency. The darker strata descending beneath our conscious awareness contains, among other things, alternative personalities: multiple and hidden ego-identities awaiting the opportunity to surface in rare cases of psychological abnormality (1890/1950a). But in James's mature thought, what is perhaps the most expansive of all selves is reached through religious ecstasy: for the "more" into which the periphery of our awareness shades off is the divine mother-sea consciousness in which our individualized egos are a part (1902/1958). The range of spirituality offered in the *Varieties of Religious Experience*, however, is not exhausted by the mystical sense of transparency to God. In the chapter on "The Divided Self," James writes of the grinding tension between our ideal and lower selves; the "battle-ground" between the morally stainless person towards which we aspire and the tainted and flawed being we currently are (1902/1958, p. 143). Our inability to integrate this agonizing disparity leads to a cathartic, sudden, and involuntary resolution after which we become new creatures entirely. Breaking down before its limitations, and rendered helpless by its own efforts, the self is now open to a spiritual influence.[35] James here speaks for a venerable and longstanding religious sentiment running from Augustine to Kierkegaard, and beyond his own time to the neo-orthodox theologians of the twentieth century (Browning, 1980).[36]

The above are but a sample of the array of experiences disclosed in the writings of James. They demonstrate our boundaries and our vulnerability, our cognitive and corporeal limitations, our potential for surprise. Radical empiricism yields a world whose details far exceed our grasp, and which is even somewhat precarious. For James, the proper reaction of all this is no lapse into pessimism, for acknowledging the ambiguities and difficulties of existence, along with our vital connections to others, is precisely what fuels the morally vigorous form of life.[37]

An Open Cosmos

Tensions That Cause War

Just after the Second World War, Sullivan contributed to a volume of essays put together by UNESCO in order to prevent future conflicts. Sullivan's lengthy piece, one of the last things he wrote before he died, employs his theory of interpersonal relations to both account and offer solutions for the violence, hatred, and demonization occurring between nations. Another contributor to the same collection, the critical theorist Max Horkeimer (1950), offers a few criticisms of Sullivan's essay. One of these is aimed at Sullivan's theory of the individual. "It may very well be that the de-subjectification of modern man," states Horkheimer, "his transformation into a mere center of conditioned reflexes, his readiness to compromise with almost any powerful social reality, is exactly what is highly responsible for authoritarian pliability and hence for the acceptance of social and national divisions as they explode into wars and persecutions" (1950, p. 138). Another of Horkeimer's objections concerns the use of psychiatry for social and political ills. Whereas Sullivan perceives the main issue to be the reality-warping tendencies of the self-system, Horkheimer admonishes us to concentrate instead upon "the removal of the objective causes for such anxieties, which are far from purely psychogenic in nature" (1950, p. 138).

We have seen how James not only preserves (albeit redefines) the individual self for a post-Cartesian era, but in contrast to what Horkheimer sees as the modern condition, he re-subjectifies it entirely. The Jamesean self arrives replete with a body, an environment, a sense of finitude, a volitional will, full and transformative relations to others, and a diverse and multifaceted spiritual life. He or she is contextualized and intimately social, yet not dissolvable within a whole of any kind. The Jamesian simply cannot approach human beings as blank slates to be filled or cogs to be manipulated.

To be fair, Sullivan's theory of the human being is larger than the defense mechanisms of the self-system, as Jay Greenberg and Stephen Mitchell point out. A serious misunderstanding arises from conflating Sullivan's ideas of the self with the entire personality, and the latter "contains many constructive, unique, and authentic features" (Greenberg & Mitchell, 1983, p. 113). Too many critics overlook the dialectic between the negative and inhibiting activities of the self-system and those factors of the personality which, articulated by Sullivan, strive toward expanded forms of well-being and integration. The real problem with Sullivan, Greenberg and Mitchell argue, is the absence of a model for optimal and healthy forms of functioning, along with his "deterministic approach to the issue of the will" (1983, p. 115). Sullivan, it should be remembered, spent a deeply formative part of his career working with serious psychiatric illnesses like schizophrenia. It therefore makes perfect sense that he focuses on the means of alleviating a patient's disturbed relations to others and restoring a state of equilibrium between the individual and the social. But the great bulk of human beings, including neurotic ones, are not schizophrenics, and individuals yearn for fulfillment at least as often as they desire to "fit in" with their family and society.

Exertion

Sullivan's strategy for defusing international tension is to relieve the buildup of anxiety in the collective self-systems of nations and ethnic groups. If anxiety is the most negative of all emotions for Sullivan, the catalyst for the rising of the self-system, his cure is the healthy adjustment of personalities to the larger realities and relationships in which they inhere. In the thought of James, by contrast, the true and authentic life is not that of adjustment but *exertion*. Life is in fact meaningless for James without an unfinished and even hazardous cosmos in which to exercise our efforts for the good. We have now arrived at the innermost center of James's philosophical oeuvre, for it is in facing an open universe—one dangerous but somewhat amenable to our individual and collective contribution—wherein we achieve real and abiding purpose. The essential point of "The Sentiment of Rationality" for instance, is that the only cosmos in which we can call home is one ripe for our active participation, yet one resistant enough to provide hurdles for us to surmount (1897/1956). Even James's god is a finite being in perpetual struggle with other forces in the universe (including, possibly, other deities) and requiring of human assistance (1909/1996a).[38]

Free Will

That even our *convictions* can add to the cosmos is one of James's most controversial themes. The much commented-on ending of "The Will to Believe," at its most audacious, argues that our very belief in certain truths can actually assist in their creation (James, 1897/1956).[39] Likewise, *A Pluralistic Universe* suggests that our devotion to the idea of a plastic and evolving cosmos just might help to bring this kind of world into being (James, 1909/1996a). Perhaps the most riveting treatment of this idea in James's entire authorship is his earliest, a result of his youthful wrestling with the issue of free will verses determinism.

Like many of the topics closest to him, James arrived at this issue from out of his own personal and existential struggles. The prospect of a cosmos without freedom, one in which we are little more than automatons, horrified the young James. Nearly incapacitated by depression and anxiety, he reached a watershed moment while reading Charles Renouvier on the subject. In his diary is found the following well-known revelation:

> I finished the first part of Renouvier's second *Essais* and see no reason why his definition of free will—"the sustaining of a thought *because I choose to* when I might have other thoughts"—need be the definition of an illusion. At any rate, I will assume for the present—until next year—that it is no illusion. My first act of free will shall be to believe in free will...
>
> Hitherto, when I have felt like taking a free initiative, like daring to act originally without carefully waiting for contemplation of the external world to determine all for me, Suicide seemed the most manly form to put my daring into; Now, I will go a step further with my will, not only act with it, but believe as well; believe in my individual reality and creative power. (Myers, 1986, pp. 388–389)

It is understandable that critics and scholars of James compare these passages to the stress on commitment and resolve so typical among the existentialists. These elements are unquestionably present. It is the last two words, however, that should draw our attention; for affirming one's *creative power* assumes our ability to contribute something that was not there previously.

Arnold Modell (2008) has recently argued that free will, along with the self, is a chimera created by our nervous system. Nonetheless, he explains that our sense of freedom is a *necessary* illusion, without which our lives would be intolerable. Modell even attempts to enlist the support of James in his conclusion that "our sense of agency feels real because we need it to be so" (2008, p. 47). But James incessantly advocates the belief that our actions have a genuine, and not merely apparent, influence on things. While Modell possesses more than a century on *The Principles* in regards to a science of the brain, the issue for James is to be decided upon experiential and ethical grounds (1890/1950b). James, the founder of the first laboratory in experimental psychology in the United States, certainly does not advocate a disdain for the sciences. As we have seen in the previous section, he simply asks us to take seriously a range of experience stretching beyond the more empirically verifiable facets of our cognition. Moreover, to accept determinism is to encourage an attitude of resignation in the face of external circumstances, and not the morally vigorous life (1897/1956).[40] Hence, what is gained through a conformity to the sciences, at least in their stricter and narrower forms, is at the cost of our more practical and meaningful dealings with the world.[41]

As James states in his chapter on "The Will" in *The Principles,* there will be continual stacking of evidence and arguments on both sides of the contest between free will and determinism (1890/1950b). Nevertheless it is our betting on the reality of our "creative power," along with a cosmos that responds to our efforts, that makes our lives truly significant.

The Moral Equivalent of War

The idea of an open cosmos as introducing purpose into human experience can also address Horkheimer's second major critique of Sullivan. To unpack this further, it is useful to turn to a popular work of James's, one seemingly custom-tailored for precisely this issue.[42]

Concerning "The Moral Equivalent of War," John Dewey once exclaimed that "an immense debt is due William James for the mere title of his essay" (Richardson, 2006, p. 515). Published the year of James's death, this piece seeks to recognize the desirable character traits and innate tendencies traditionally built for armed conflict, and to provide the means by which to cultivate these same virtues for peaceful and constructive endeavors. While James lambastes the "mawkish and dishwatery" flavor of the pacifist ideals of his day, what he sees as a naïve and tepid worldview which seems to favor a life of never-ending complacency and consumer comforts

("Fie upon such a cattleyard of a planet!"), he also criticizes the military-minded camp for their lack of imagination (1910/2010, p. 305). War is not only the way of instilling discipline, sacrifice, and the love of community, he suggests. Acknowledging that the world is already a dangerous and unfair place, James argues for a kind of civic army or domestic peace corps through which generations of youth may devote their energies toward the correcting and healing of environmental, economic, and societal problems. James here directs us toward the shortcomings and calamities of both the social and natural worlds in which we live, a move which not only addresses "the objective causes" of our anxieties, but feeds our yearning for real and nonfrivolous meaning.

If James's call for his proposed civic army to join in the "immemorial human warfare against nature" (1910/2010, p. 311) sounds a bit harsh for today's ecologically sensitive culture, it is because of our failure to place these words against the context of his later philosophy. *A Pluralistic Universe*, James's most mature theological and metaphysical statement, chooses among ontological frameworks based upon the criterion of our *intimacy* with the cosmos (James, 1990/1996a). We are to understand ourselves, according to this standard, as organically continuous with the universe, as partners rather than subordinates or superiors. James's later thought, complete with it nonatomized pluralism and concatenated unities, its de-centered and relational selves, its defiance of all totalizations, its rejection of a monarchical form of theism, its stress on spiritual and other marginalized experiences, and its use of intimacy as a standard for choosing among ontologies, can be employed to support environmental and even feminist-type philosophies far more than is ordinarily supposed.[43] Here, we have come as far from the rugged, autonomous, and domineering Marlboro Man conception of the self as we can.

It may be useful to review what James has to offer an orthodox Sullivanian in regards to ethical and political matters. We have seen that understanding human beings as mere receptacles of the social (our "de-subjectification" according to Horkheimer) encourages the kind of mass movements that lead to war, hatred, and oppression. We have also seen that treating political and social problems as symptoms of psychological malaise may serve to distract us from their *real* and external causes (class struggle, competition over resources, etc.). The thought of James can assist by providing two fundamental insights: First, restoring an appreciation for the volitional and individual person offers some resistance to the conformist pressures of society. Second, affirming a pliant and even unstable cosmos not only propels us toward fixing concrete social and natural evils, but makes life *meaningful*.

Finally, James suggests that our commitment to both free will and a malleable universe can assist in making them true. Of course, the idea that our very convictions can alter reality may strain our common sense as well as our reason. And yet this might be the strongest expression of the heart of James's philosophy of existence: namely the obligation to take up our role as co-creators rather than spectators in the nature of things.

CONCLUSION: PSYCHOTHERAPY AND THE CREATIVE ADVANCE

In *The Interpersonal Theory of Psychiatry*, Sullivan (1953) cites Whitehead as a philosopher who perceives the universe as a giant organism in which all living entities are a part. As outlined in the pages preceding, we are participants in a field, occurrences within a web of forces. Although constituted in part by prior events, each and every entity for Whitehead possesses a measure of self-determination as well as the ability to pass on its content to the next wave of events. Increasing the harmony and aesthetic intensity of the cosmos, each may contribute to what Whitehead (1979) calls "the creative advance." Of course, a human being is a *nexus* or synthesis of such events, and thus expresses the same inner dynamic and the same role in the scheme of things. While Sullivan concentrates on addressing the unhealthy patterns of the "self-system," thus aiming at a proper reintegration of the subject into society, there is a more forward-seeking and even metaphysical end to be achieved for the Whiteheadian self—a meaningful direction beyond the relieving of individual anxiety and the restoration of personal security.[44] Of course, Whitehead's depiction of all things as a succession of experiences, the nature of the relations subsisting between them, and the efficacy of our efforts upon a plastic and ever-evolving universe bears the strong influence of William James (Weber, 2011).[45]

In a recent study of Jamesian–Whiteheadian thought and its application to a variety of practical and speculative domains, Michel Weber points out the relevance of a process ontology for psychotherapy. Focusing upon the continual introduction of novelty into reality—the bud theory created by James and further articulated by Whitehead—Weber explains how those stuck within maladaptive patterns of existing are granted the possibility of radical re-creation. In *Process and Reality*, Whitehead (1978) argues for a deity who sends suggestions into the cosmos, intimations on how to best actualize our potential both for ourselves as well as the collective good. Weber would have the therapist assume this role. Thus, if conventional psychotherapies spend an inordinate amount of time seeking to unearth the underlying *reasons* for our unhappiness, the Jamesian or Whiteheadian therapist is to concentrate upon the transformative capacity of the present. Although mindful and sympathetic to our personal history, and thoroughly acquainted with how we perceive the world, he or she is to exploit the force of discontinuity informing every instant. The point is not an endless rumination over incidents which (presumably) made us who we are, but to encourage an active break from the past, a sudden recalibration of the self in light of a future pregnant with possibilities (Weber, 2011).[46]

At the end of *The Varieties of Religious Experience*, James instructs us in the benefit of accepting a universe with only "the *chance* of salvation." Eloquently paraphrasing Edward Gurney, he suggests that accepting real contingency in the universe makes the difference between "a life of which the keynote is resignation and a life of which the keynote is hope" (1902/1958, p. 397). As we have seen, James's philosophical vision is motivated primarily by moral as well as experiential concerns. True to the more personal and existential character of his thinking, James goes as far as to affirm an element of real danger in the universe, a means by which he seeks to tear us out of our complacency and cultivate within us a desire for the ethically vigorous life. The potential for failure is unnerving indeed, but with the absence of certainty comes the necessity of effort and a renewed rationale for living. For James, as for Whitehead, slavishness to the past simply has no place in a world perpetually in the making.

The Jamesian self exists within a larger experiential and perceptual field. Though a strand within this larger texture it may, animated by the thrust toward novelty coursing through nature, lift itself above the fray just enough to both define itself and push out the boundaries of the whole pattern. In this way, through the marriage of self-realization and social/environmental progress, we achieve our life's purpose in an open cosmos.

NOTES

1. Page 319.
2. Originally accepting Sullivan's translation, I thank Michel Weber for the correction.
3. The Marlboro Man also makes its appearance in Frie's earlier essay "Fundamentally Embodied."
4. As Fiscalini (2008) explains: "The primary architect of interpersonal psychoanalytic theory and its most influential theorist, Sullivan (1940) explicitly repudiated the notion of personal agency and the will" (p. 156).
5. Burston and Frie (2006) state: "We are always more than our contexts. There is inevitably a surfeit of meaning that cannot be reduced to the contexts or constructs we use to explain experience" (*Psychotherapy as a Human Science*, p. 260).
6. See Perry (1982), *Psychiatrist of America*, p. 237 for a brief summary of this influence. For the importance of Adolf Meyer, see pp. 232–240. Perry quotes Sullivan on the ranking his influences (in terms of importance) on page 226–227.
7. In *Modes of Thought*, Whitehead places James on the same level as Plato, Aristotle, and Leibniz in terms of philosophical importance. For the explicit connections between the ideas of James and Whitehead, a handy source is Michel Weber's (2001) *Whitehead's Pancreativism: Jamesian Applications*, Chapter 1.

8. Even the methods used by today's most probing theoretical psychoanalysts read like an echo of James, even if this has not come about by direct influence. In regards to the problem of personal identity in systems and relational theory, William Coburn (2011) argues for the confluence of both phenomenological and scientific approaches (see his concluding essay from *Selves in Context*). Likewise, Don Browning affirms "that the heart of James's creativity was his attempt to hold together a descriptive *and* an explanatory approach to the study of human nature" (1980, p. 32).
9. See Marcus Ford's essay "William James" in *Founders of Constructive Postmodernism* (1993). A postmodernist, for the authors of this book, is one who breaks from the modern Western assumptions in the fields of epistemology (i.e., the primacy of reason and/or sense experience, the split between subject and object, the search for an indubitable truth) and metaphysics (i.e., mind/body dualism, a substance ontology wherein the material universe is understood as permanent and bare extension). While the "negative postmodernism" found among so many contemporary Continental philosophers rejects these factors, no positive doctrines are put in their place. Thus, we are left with either a relativism wherein no positive statements can be made about anything, or a perpetual dismantling of theories without the offering of any content. Constructive postmodernism only begins with the rejection of modernist philosophical assumptions, and then proceeds to offer novel ideas concerning the nature of knowledge and reality.
10. Gale's thesis in *The Divided Self of William James* (1999) is the presence of a major disparity and tension within the philosophy of James, namely that between the mystical and ethical or "promethean" dimensions of his thought. The fullest and most intractable factor of this split (or "aporia") is between the tentative knowledge claims of the promethean self and the absolute ones of the mystic. For Gale, however, these tensions, however unresolved, add rather than detract from James's richness as a thinker.
11. In *Founders of Constructive Postmodernism*, John Cobb (1993) states: "Whitehead believes that philosophical movements typically have two key moments. There is the genius who inaugurates the movement, and the systematizer who follows. He seems to depict himself in the latter role in relation to James. He accepts and adopts many of James' key insights, and then goes on to develop them in rich and rigorous detail" (p. 166).
12. Robert Macleod states that "Heidegger and Sartre have made no contributions to the understanding of human experience that were not anticipated in James" (Quoted in Browning, 1980, p. 30). Charles Hartshorne expresses a bit of this as well: "To survey the resources of philosophy generally, one scarcely needs, any longer to look across the Atlantic" (1984, p. 4). But to be fair, Hartshorne also warns that we should not "fall into mere provincialism ourselves" (Ibid, p. 7).
13. In *The Interpersonal Theory of Psychiatry*, Sullivan (1953) states that "there seems to be very little profit in psychiatry from dependence on any such idea as the mysterious power of the will" (p. 301).
14. There is considerable controversy in what Sullivan really meant in his denial of the individual self. In "Sullivan's Concept of Unique Individuality," an in-

fluential article on Sullivan, Ralph Crowley (1973) explains that Sullivan did not so much deny the existence of an individual self as perceive to be outside the boundaries of psychiatry. This interpretation of Sullivan is hotly contested by Donnel Stern (1997). "But he *did* mean to exlude the unique, individual self," states Stern, "he meant just what he said." And: "We are nothing more, [Sullivan] says, than agglomerations of interpersonal relations, although many of those relations may go on privately (that is, with a symbolic or fantasized other) after an origin in the external world" (1997, p. 149).

15. See Lamberth (1999), *William James and the Metaphysics of Experience*, pp. 83–91.
16. James's passages on the social self share a kinship with the possibility raised by Sullivan that "for all I know every human being has as many personalities as he has interpersonal relations" (1890/1950a, p. 329).
17. Ibid, p. 304. For a fuller exploration of James's notion of "sciousness," including its relationship to Buddhist and non-Western thought, see Jonathan Bricklin's (2006) edited volume *Sciousness*. Of particular value is his chapter: "Sciousness and Con-sciousness: William James and the Prime Reality of Non-Dual Experience."
18. It is perhaps worthwhile mentioning that one of the few places in *The Principles* where James explicitly mentions the field is in his discussion of our corporeality—particularly in its importance for the structure of the self. Concerning the importance our bodies in the stream of experience, James states, "they too are percepts in our objective field—they are simply the most interesting percepts there. What happens to them excites in us emotions and tendencies to action more energetic and habitual than any which are excited by other portions of the 'field'" (1890/1950a, p. 320).
19. See Richard Gale's appendix to his *The Divided Self of William James*. Also see Gerald Myers's chapter on "The Self" from *William James: His Life and Thought* (1986). Myers explains that James "seems to have concluded that a philosophical account of the self gives way to a mystical one and that useful words on the subject are rapidly exhausted" (p. 344).
20. Those unsympathetic with the idealist tendencies in James's ontology of pure experience may appreciate the influence of radical empiricism upon the more naturalistic work of James Gibson. A good account of James's influence upon Gibson, along with what the latter has to offer the philosophy of James, is found in Harry Heft: *Ecological Psychology in Context* (2001).
21. Yet another principle of James's radical empiricism, its very "statement of fact" (*The Meaning of Truth*, 1909/1975, pp. 6–7), is that the connections and transitions between things in our experience are to counted as intrinsic to reality—and not super-imposed either by habits formed by previous experiences (as argued by David Hume) or by the transcendental parts of the mind (as argued by rationalists). Thus, the problem of accounting for causality, the main assumption of the empirical sciences, is safely avoided.
22. The "process psychology" of Jon Mills, though indebted to Hegel above all, bears a strong influence of Whitehead—particularly on the concept of an unconscious relationship between experiences. For Mills, this is an essential condition for our conscious life. See his "Whitehead's Unconscious Ontology" (n.d.). Of course, this is a concept Whitehead borrowed from James.

23. See Marcus Ford's (1993) essay on James in *The Founders of Constructive Postmodernism,* p. 103.
24. The reasons for James's bud theory is, first, to provide a more accurate description of our experience (as in Chapter 10 of the *Principles*), and second, to overcome a few philosophical conundrums. One of these is Zeno's paradoxes. If space and time is composed of an infinite number of points, then we are stuck with the classic picture of Achilles always catching up to the tortoise, but never arriving (since a line of infinite points can be halved indefinitely). But if time and space go by irreducible drops, buds that cannot be broken down into smaller components, then Zeno's paradox is safely avoided.
25. Michel Weber states: "*Process and Reality* is entirely built upon the adoption of ontological percolation. From the perspective of the postmodern significance of Whitehead's thought, the atomization of the act of experience is of tremendous importance. It seals a mutual requirement between epochality, liberty and novelty, thereby allowing a complete reformation of the old-fashioned philosophical substantialism and of its heir, scientific materialism" (2011, p. 20).
26. The most concise statement of the principles behind radical empiricism is found in the preface to *The Meaning of Truth* (1909/1975, pp. 6–7).
27. James here describes the meaning of our embodiment forty-one years before Maurice Merleau-Ponty (1962) wrote of the *body-subject* and ninety years before neuroscientist Antonio Damasio (1994) labels the body as the "ground-reference" of our consciousness.
28. It can be claimed that James's account of our embodiment, while never revoked, sits uneasily with his other doctrines. This is particularly the case with the idealistic tendencies of his later thought wherein all of reality, including our bodies, are composed of pure experience. See Myers (1986) on this issue: *William James: His Life and Thought,* chapter 12.
29. Knowledge of James's life-long struggle with depression and anxiety increases the significance of the latter (much discussed) passage, which is suspiciously disguised by him as the writing of a French correspondent.
30. In a footnote to "On Some Hegelians," James takes nitrous oxide in order to finally understand the idealism of Hegel (1897/1956a, pp. 294–298).
31. The quote is from "On a Certain Blindness in Human Beings." Similar passages are found in "What Makes Life Significant?" from the same book, and a brief discussion toward the end of *Human Immortality; Two Supposed Objections to the Doctrine* (1898/1956). In the last of these, James reminds those racist to foreign ethnicities that despised and ignored peoples are "animated by an inner joy of living as hot or hotter than that which you feel beating in your private breast" (p. 39).
32. In his chapter on James and mysticism from *The Divided Self,* Richard Gale (1999) makes frequent comparisons between James and Martin Buber.
33. For a rather colorful analogy of this dynamic between experiences, see James's description of a shrunken head: *Essays In Radical Empiricism* (1912/1996b, pp. 46–47).
34. Gerald Myers explains: "It is a common judgment that James's *Anschauung* was excessively individualistic and ignored the role of community; on the contrary, he sought notions of self and reality that permit communality of the profound-

est sort—in the depths of the most intimate personal experience. He hoped that the metaphysics of radical empiricism and pluralistic universe would indicate that a genuine overlap of many individuals' experiences might occur at levels of consciousness we do not yet understand" (1986, p. 350). For an illuminating and eloquent comparison of James with Emmanuel Levinas, see Megan Craig's *Levinas and James: Toward a Pragmatic Phenomenology* (20100.

35. That many forms of religious experience seem to issue from beyond the self, particularly when the latter is at its most impotent, is what leads James to affirm that the divine mother-sea consciousness is personal and volitional. This is in contrast to the impersonal *oversoul* of Emersonian Transcendentalism. See James (1902/1958, p. 389, note 32).
36. In regards to this topic Browning (1980) claims that "the Niebuhrs, Tillichs, and Bultmanns of the neo-orthodox period could have turned to James as easily as to Kierkegaard or Heidegger. And had they done so, they would not have separated themselves from a modern world view so profoundly as they did" (p. 249).
37. In his contribution to the *Blackwell Guide to American Philosophy*, William Gavin (2004) wisely employs the concept of "vagueness" as a useful angle into the thought of James. In one shot, Gavin is able to point to the richly textured character of our experience as James portrays it, as well as a universe which, being indeterminate, calls for our active participation. These are the phenomenological and ethical concerns underlying practically all of James's authorship (pp. 101–116).
38. James's doctrine of a finite god evolves over his entire career. See "The Dilemma of Determinism" and "Is Life Worth Living?," James's "over-beliefs" at the end of *The Varieties of Religious Experience* (1902/1958), *Pragmatism* (1907/1975), and *A Pluralistic Universe* (1909/1996a). The last of these contains his final statement on the topic.
39. There is much ambiguity at the end of this essay between the idea that our commitment places us in a position to *recognize* certain truths that are already there (meeting them half-way as it were), and the idea that our belief actually *creates* them. Both concepts seem to be present side by side.
40. Modell suggests that through recontextualizing our memories, the brain can strengthen the illusion of agency and thereby make our lives more satisfying. But this is no improvement for James, who in "The Dilemma of Determinism" explicitly argues against accepting the idea—a sort of compromise popular in James's time—that what matters is our *view* of reality, and not our ability to influence reality itself. James asserts that, among other things, this position "fosters the fatalistic mood of mind" (1897/1956, p. 171).
41. Marcus Ford (1993) offers an informative discussion of James's dissatisfaction with the science of his day, and his attempts to amend this situation through two strategies: that of supplementing the sciences with the truths generated through other disciplines (aesthetics, religion, ethics, etc.), and his mission to broaden science by freeing it from a reliance upon an inadequate metaphysics and a shallow account of experience. See Ford (1993) pp. 104–112.
42. Gale (1999) criticizes the thought of James in precisely the same manner that Horkheimer critiques Sullivan: namely that James overlooks the social and eco-

nomic conditions that make a rich inner life possible. But Gale ignores the relevance of James's "The Moral Equivalent of War," among other things (p. 249).

43. Along these same lines, Myers states of James's "Great Men and Their Environment": "James's contribution was not simply a defense of the common belief that great persons influence history or that the origins of great persons defy the explanations of social scientists borrowing from Darwin; he was in effect questioning the picture of the great person verses the environment, replacing it with the transactionist theory that both person and environment are mutually transformed by their transaction with each other" (1986, p. 412).
44. In his comparison of the two thinkers, Thomas Regan explains that while Sullivan approaches the needs of the psyche as propelled by a yearning for security, "Whitehead discusses the same dynamic by placing an emphasis on the realization of aesthetic value to be achieved by the given nexus" (1990, p. 9).
45. For a careful and thorough account of what Whitehead explicitly borrowed from James, see the first chapter of Michel Weber's *Whitehead's Pancreativism: Jamesian Applications* (2011).
46. See "The Art of Epochal Change," in *Whitehead's Pancreativism: Jamesian Applications* (Weber, 2011). Weber goes to great length to demonstrate the parallels between Whitehead's metaphysics of process and the "brief therapy" of Paul Watzlawick.

REFERENCES

Bricklin, J. (2006). Sciousness and con-sciousness: William James and the prime reality of non-dual experience. In J. Bricklin (Ed.), *Sciousness* (pp. 19–85). Guilford, CT: Eirini Press.

Browning, D. S. (1980). *Pluralism and personality: William James and some contemporary cultures of psychology.* Toronto, ON: Associated University Presses.

Burston, D., & Frie, R. (2006). *Psychotherapy as a human science.* Pittsburgh, PA: Duquesne University Press.

Cobb Jr., J. B. (1993). William James. In D. R. Griffin, J. B. Cobb Jr., M. P. Ford, P. A. Y. Gunter, & P. Ochs (Eds.), *Founders of constructive postmodern philosophy: Peirce, James, Bergson, Whitehead, and Hartshorne* (pp. 165–195). Albany: State University of New York Press.

Coburn, W. (2011). Recontextualizing individuality and therapeutic action in psychoanalysis and psychotherapy. In R. Frie & W. J. Coburn (Eds.), *Persons in context: The challenge of individuality in theory and practice* (pp. 121–146). New York, NY: Routledge.

Craig, M. (2010). *Levinas and James; Toward a pragmatic phenomenology.* Bloomington, IN: Indiana University Press.

Crowley, R. (1973). Sullivan's concept of unique individuality. *Contemporary Psychoanalysis, 9,* 130–133.

Damasio, A. (1994). *Descartes' error: Emotion, reason, and the human brain.* New York, NY: G.P. Putnam's Sons.

Fiscalini, J. (2008). Dimensions of agency and the process of coparticipant inquiry. In R. Frie (Ed.), *Psychological agency: Theory, practice, and culture* (pp. 155–174). Cambridge, MA: MIT Press.

Ford, M. P. (1993). William James. In D. R. Griffin, J. B. Cobb Jr., M. P. Ford, P. A. Y. Gunter, & P. Ochs (Eds.), *Founders of constructive postmodern philosophy: Peirce, James, Bergson, Whitehead, and Hartshorne* (pp. 89–132). Albany: State University of New York Press.

Frie, R. (2003). Between modernism and postmodernism: Rethinking psychological agency. In R. Frie (Ed.), *Understanding experience; Psychotherapy and postmodernism* (pp. 1–26). New York, NY: Routledge.

Frie, R. (2008). Fundamentally embodied: The experience of psychological agency. *Contemporary Psychoanalysis, 44*, 367–376.

Frie, R. (2011). Culture and context: From individualism to situated experience. In R. Frie & W. J. Coburn (Eds.), *Persons in context: The challenge of individuality in theory and practice* (pp. 3–19). New York, NY: Routledge.

Gale, R. M. (1999). *The divided self of William James.* Cambridge, UK: Cambridge University.

Gavin, W. J. (2004). William James, 1842–1910. In A. T. Marsoobian & J. Ryder (Eds.), *The Blackwell guide to American philosophy* (pp. 101–116). Malden, UK: Blackwell Publishing.

Greenberg, J. R. & Mitchell, S. A. (1983). *Object relations in psychoanalytic theory.* Cambridge, MA: Harvard University Press.

Hartshorne, C. (1984). *Creativity in American philosophy.* Albany, NY: State University of New York Press.

Heft, H. (2001). *Ecological psychology in context: James Gibson, Roger Barker, and the legacy of William James's radical empiricism.* Mahwah, NJ: Lawrence Erlbaum.

Horkheimer, M. (1950). Comments to Harry Stack Sullivan's "Tensions Interpersonal and International: A Psychiatrist's View." In H. Cantril (Ed.), *Tensions that cause wars* (pp. 136–138). Urbana: University of Illinois Press.

James, W. (1950a). *The principles of psychology: Volume one.* Mineola, NY: Dover. (Original work published 1890, Henry Holt & Co.)

James, W. (1950b). *The principles of psychology: Volume two.* Mineola, NY: Dover. (Original work published 1890, Henry Holt & Co.)

James, W. (1956). *The Will to believe and other essays in popular philosophy,* and *Human immortality: Two supposed objections to the doctrine.* Mineola, NY: Dover. (Original works published 1897, Longmans, Green & Co; and 1898, Houghton Mifflin & Co., respectively)

James, W. (1958). *The varieties of religious experience.* New York, NY: Mentor Books. (Original work published 1902, Longmans, Green & Co.)

James, W. (1962). *Talks to teachers on psychology and to students on some of life's ideals.* Mineola, NY: Dover. (Original work published 1899, Henry Holt & Co.)

James, W. (1975). *Pragmatism* and *The meaning of truth.* Cambridge, MA: Harvard University Press. (Original works published 1907 and 1909, Longmans, Green and Co.)

James, W. (1996a). *A pluralistic universe.* Lincoln: University of Nebraska Press. (Original work published 1909, Longmans, Green, and Co.)

James, W. (1996b). *Essays in radical empiricism.* Lincoln: University of Nebraska Press. (Original work published 1912, Longmans, Green and Co.)

James, W. (1996c). *Some problems of philosophy: A beginning of an introduction to philosophy.* Lincoln: University of Nebraska Press. (Original work published 1911, Longmans, Green and Co.)

James, W. (2010). The moral equivalent of war. In R. Richardson (Ed.), *The heart of William James* (pp. 301–313). Cambridge, MA: Harvard University Press. (Original work published 1910, International Conciliation no. 27.)

Lamberth, D. C. (1999). *William James and the metaphysics of experience.* Cambridge, MA: Cambridge University Press.

Merleau-Ponty, M. (1962). *The phenomenology of perception.* (Colin Smith, Trans.) New York, NY: Routledge & Kegan Paul.

Mills, J. (n.d.). Whitehead's unconscious ontology. Retrieved from http://www.processpsychology.com/new-articles/Whitehead.htm

Mitchell, S. A. & Black, M. J. (1995). *Freud and beyond: A history of modern psychoanalytic thought.* New York, NY: BasicBooks.

Modell, A. (2008). The agency of the self and the brain's illusions. In R. Frie (Ed.), *Psychological agency: Theory, practice, and culture* (pp. 35–49). Cambridge, MA: The MIT Press.

Myers, G. E. (1986). *William James: His life and thought.* New Haven, CT: Yale University Press.

Perry, H. S. (1982). *Psychiatrist of America: The life of Harry Stack Sullivan.* Cambridge, MA: Belknap Press.

Regan, T. J. (1990). The matrix of personality: A Whiteheadian corroboration of Harry Stack Sullivan's interpersonal theory of psychiatry. *Process Studies, 19*(3), 189–198.

Richardson, R. D. (2006). *William James. In the maelstrom of American modernism.* New York, NY: Houghton Mifflin.

Stern, D. B. (1997). *Unformulated experience: From dissociation to imagination in psychoanalysis.* Hillsdale, NJ: The Analytic Press.

Sullivan, H. S. (1950a). The illusion of personal individuality. *Psychiatry, 13*(3), 317–332.

Sullivan, H. S. (1950b). Tensions interpersonal and international: A psychiatrist's view. In H. Cantril (Ed.), *Tensions that cause wars* (pp. 79–138). Urbana: University of Illinois Press.

Sullivan, H. S. (1953). *The interpersonal theory of psychiatry* (H. Swick Perry & M. Ladd Gawel, Eds.) New York, NY: W.W. Norton & Company.

Unamuno, M. de. (1954). *Tragic sense of life.* (J. E. Crawford Flitch, trans.) Mineola, NY: Dover.

Weber, M. (2011). *Whitehead's pancreativism: Jamesian applications.* New Brunswick, NJ: Ontos Verlag.

Whitehead, A. N. (1968). *Modes of thought.* New York, NY: The Free Press. (1938, Macmillan Company).

Whitehead, A. N. (1979). *Process and reality* (corrected version; D. R. Griffin & D. W. Sherburne, Eds.) New York NY: The Free Press.

Wilshire, B. (1968). *William James and phenomenology: A study of "The Principles of Psychology."* Bloomington, IN: Indiana University Press.

CHAPTER 6

FROM MEANING TO SENSEMAKING

Implications of a Semiotic and Dynamic Model of Mind for Psychoanalysis

Sergio Salvatore
University of Salento, Italy

INTRODUCTION

The notion of meaning plays a central role in psychoanalytic theory and theory of the technique. Concepts like representation, object, affects, fantasy, interpersonal schemata, just to take a few examples, entail the basic idea of the mind as a system working through and/or on meanings.

Despite this, it is only recently that psychoanalysts have expressed some commitment to developing the theory of meaning that grounds psychoanalytic thought (Barclay & Kee, 2001; Muller, 1996; Muller & Brent, 2000; Neuman, 2009, 2010; Olds, 2000; Saporta, 2011). As a result, contemporary psychoanalysis is still based on a conception of meaning that has a glorious past (Bühler, 1934/1990; De Saussure, 1916/1977; Frege, 1892/1980; see also Eco, 1975) but that needs to be radically updated.

Making Our Ideas Clear, pages 153–176
Copyright © 2015 by Information Age Publishing
All rights of reproduction in any form reserved.

The traditional conception assumes that meaning is an autonomous entity, pre-existing its private and/or public representation. According to this assumption, individuals have a given content in their mind (a concept, an image, a representation—a significance) and this is why they can express it (Salvatore, 2012). However, the idea of the autonomy of meaning has been subjected to a major revision in the last three decades as a result of the increasing interest in the work of authors like Wittgenstein, Peirce, and Bakhtin, accompanying the linguistic and semiotic turnaround in psychology (Gergen, 1999; Harre & Gillet, 1994; Kirshner, 2010; Lepper, in press; Linell, 2009). What has emerged as a result of these innovations is a pragmatic, contextual, dialogical, dynamic conception of meaning and sensemaking that has played a major role in the growth of several areas of psychology (Salvatore, Forges Davanzati, Potì, & Ruggiero, 2009; Salvatore & Freda, 2011; Valsiner, 2009).

The same has not happened in the psychoanalytic domain, where so far the new vision of meaning has had a more limited impact (Leiman, 2000). This has prevented the development of a fruitful dialogue with the most innovative frontiers of psychology—in the final analysis, impoverishing the heuristic potentiality of psychoanalytic theory (Salvatore et al., 2003; Salvatore & Zittoun, 2011a).

In this chapter I intend to highlight some theoretical, methodological, and technical implications for psychoanalysis stemming from the semiotic, pragmatist, and dynamic view of meaning. The work is divided into three parts. In the first, I briefly discuss the traditional conception of meaning, highlighting its role in psychoanalytic theory. In the second, I outline an alternative view, focusing on a specific semiotic and pragmatist model of the microdynamics of sensemaking. Finally, I highlight some implications of such a view for psychoanalytic theory and theory of the technique.

THE TRADITIONAL IDEA OF MEANING

Consider this brief description a person makes of a particular moment of her life.

> I am sitting in front of my notebook, thinking of the best way of expressing my idea on meaning, how to put it into words. I have already written several versions of the text, but I am not satisfied with them—I do not consider these versions to fully convey the idea I believe I have in mind.

For the sake of our discussion, three aspects of this sketch are worth pointing out. First, the person assumes that the idea (i.e., the meaning) is something that exists within her head, before she expresses it in text.

Second, she can have the intention of expressing her idea just because she thinks she has an idea in her mind that can be/needs to be expressed. Thus, it is the meaning that motivates its expression: there can be a text representing the meaning insofar as there is something that can be—and pushes to be—conveyed. Third, she may have tried various forms of expressing of her idea, writing and rewriting her text, simply because she assumes that such an activity of expressing does not affect her idea. Rather, it is the implicit representation of her idea that works as the normative criterion for defining whether—to what extent—the expression of it actually represents it (consider statements like: "I did not mean that"; "do *You* really believe what *You* said?").

These three aspects are the elements that characterize what I have referred to above as the traditional conception of meaning—namely, the idea of meaning as an autonomous entity existing beforehand and being essentially independent from its expression.

THE AUTONOMY OF MEANING IN PSYCHOANALYSIS

The idea of the autonomy of meaning has played a major role in psychoanalytic theory and practice. It has provided a general framework for connecting the inner and outer world, often delineated as constructs and observables—the former have been considered the significance of the latter, the latter have been considered the significance of the former. In this way, psychoanalysis has become a hermeneutic theory and practice (Neuman, 2010; Ricoeur, 1981; Salvatore & Zittoun, 2011a), focused on semiotic connections between ostensible events—acts, narratives, speech, perceivable objects—and states of mind, assumed as sustaining the (inter)subjective sense of the experience. In de Saussure's terminology, overt behavior *X* is seen as the significant of the inner state of mind *Y*; conversely, the interpretation of *X* enables us to capture *Y*.

Psychoanalytic theories vary as concerns what is assumed to be *Y*. Ego psychology identifies drives and defence mechanisms as preferential *Y*, whereas the objects relations theory sees the inner affective representation of objects as elective *Y*. In this perspective, it is worth referring to the Kleinian psychoanalyst Franco Fornari (1979, 1981; see also Giannakoulas, 1984), who describes the unconscious as a semiotic device feeding the striving of the subject to signify itself and the world in terms of very basic affects (*coinems* in Fornari's terminology). Such basic affects are considered to be fundamental, emotional, preconceptual meanings consisting of the basic vital forms of experience (life, death, parental relationship, parts of the body). According to Fornari, individuals reveal two coextensive ways of signifying: one working under the socially shared rules of formal thinking—the "diurnal" side of operative categorization—and the other working according to the primary process—the "onirical" side of affective symbolization, which works through the mobilization of *coinems*. In brief, affective symbolization is the process of projecting every object of experience onto the symbolic space of *coinems*. In so doing, the individual makes every element of experience become charged with affective meaning (e.g., the student projects the teacher onto the affective category of "mother-ness," consequently feeling and interacting with him/her as if he/she were a mother, namely someone having a function of holding, feeding, and taking care of him/her). According to Fornari, there are very few *coinems*—he speaks of the *coinems* as "the few things oniric symbolism is about" (p. 73, my translation from the Italian original); they therefore work as generalized classes, homogenizing experience: Patterns of experience that have no semantic linkage can be made identical by being projected onto the same coinemic category.

Stolorow, Orange, and Atwood (2001) provide an intersubjective version of *Y*. According to them, the classes of affective meanings sustaining the inner world are made of patterns of interpersonal experiences, rather than of universal *a priori* categories (as coinems are).

> In place of Freud's topographical and structural theories of mind we envision an organized totality of lived personal experience, more or less conscious and more or less contoured according to those emotional and relational experiences. Instead of a container we picture an experiential system of expectations, interpretative patterns and meanings.... Within such a system or world, one can feel and know certain things often repetitively and with unshakable certainty. (Stolorow et al., 2001, p. 675)

In sum, psychoanalytic theories define the target process (*Y*) in different ways, according to a plurality of frameworks (Pine, 1988; Tuckett, 2008). Nevertheless, they share the basic syntax grounding the way the target process is connected to the ostensible phenomenon (*X*). This syntax is the classical semiological logic in accordance to which the ostensible phenomenon expresses and conveys the target process which comes before and is independent of the latter.

THE LIMITS OF THE TRADITIONAL VIEW OF MEANING

The idea of the autonomy of meaning is seductive, since it is consistent with common sense. Nevertheless, it raises many problems, highlighted by a vast literature (e.g., Gergen, 1999; Gillespie, 2010; Harré & Gillet, 1994; Salvatore, 2012). Below I focus on just one issue: the transformation of what has to be explained (*explanandum*) with what explains (*explanans*).

The assumption of meaning as *a priori* transforms such a construct into an entity—a piece of the world with the capacity to produce an effect on the world (e.g., on the brain's functioning, on the actor's actions). Such entification of meaning entails an inversion between *explanans* and *explanandum*: what has to be understood (i.e., the meaning produced by and at the same time regulating sensemaking) is transformed into what allows understanding. In other words—given an (inter)subjective event E (e.g., a thought, a sentence, an act), it is explained as being motivated—as the effect, the reaction, the regulated output, the defense from, and the like—by the meaning M. Therefore, M is the source of the explanation, rather than the target phenomenon to be explained; namely, $E = f(M)$, rather than $M = f(E)$: "X has acted thus (E) because she has an inner representation of herself as a nourishing mother (M)."

The *explanans–explanandum* inversion raises a number of issues. I will confine myself to pointing out two main points. First, it leads to a kind of explanation that can hardly avoid the classical problem of the homunculus. Say that meaning M motivated the (inter)subjective event E; now, this raises the question of how M performed this. And the answer to this question cannot but bring into the discussion an inner interpreter (the homunculus) of M, having the function of representing the meaning of M and transforming this representation (M') into a decision/action. Yet, in turn, this raises the question of how such an interpreter works. And the answer to this question cannot but bring into the discussion an inner interpreter within the inner interpreter, having the function of representing the meaning of the inner interpreter (M') and transforming such representation (M'') into a decision/action according to which the inner interpreter produces its decision/action. And in turn, this entails an inner interpreter within the inner interpreter within the inner interpreter, and so forth *ad infinitum*. Second, it entails the *post hoc ergo propter hoc* (after this, so because of this) fallacy: M is considered to be the cause of E just because it is alleged to occur beforehand. This fallacy consists of confusing a necessary condition with a sufficient condition—M has to come before E for it to be considered a cause of E. Yet, the fact that M comes before E is not a sufficient reason to consider M the cause of E—for instance, the fact that I am going out my house with an umbrella after hearing the weather forecast for the day does not mean that if it rains in the next hour this depends on the fact that I have taken an umbrella. On the other hand, the very fact that meaning comes before its manifest expression is a hotly debated topic. Though controversial, the classical experiment by Libet (1999) has provided evidence in favor of the fact that the action comes before the representation of the inner state that is assumed to be the agentive factor motivating the action at stake.

Thus, it seems to be less problematic to consider the notion of meaning as a *post hoc* description enabling us to order the data of experience, rather than the causative source of such data. This shift is clearly expressed in relation to the role of rules (Salvatore et al., 2009; see also Croom, 2012). From the classical point of view, the mind's functioning (e.g., the way of using language, the way of reasoning) is the consequence of the application of rules; therefore, according to this point of view, rules have a causative role. Yet this assumption is clearly contrasted by the experience of daily life: People first learn to act (to reason, to speak a language, to perform in accordance to given scripts) in a certain way—they acquire habits, in Peirce's terminology—and then interpret such a way as a manner of following a given rule.

THE PRAGMATIST AND DYNAMIC VIEW OF SEMIOSIS: FROM MEANING TO SENSEMAKING

The problems raised by the traditional idea of meaning lead us to embrace a different approach, rooted in the teaching of Wittgenstein and Peirce. Wittgenstein (1958) stated that the meaning of a sign is the way it is used. This definition provides the basis for a radical revision of the traditional idea of meaning, grounding a pragmatic, contextual, dialogical semiotics—namely a semiotics which no longer considers meaning as existing before sensemaking (i.e., the use of the sign; language-games, in Wittgenstein's terminology), but as emerging from it. In other words, after Wittgenstein one can look at meaning as the product, rather than the cause, of sensemaking.

Peirce (1897/1932)'s vision of semiosis as an infinite flow of interpretations provides an insightful way of understanding meaning as the product of sensemaking. A sign

> ...or *representamen*, is something which stands to somebody for something in some respect or capacity. It addresses somebody, that is, creates in the mind of that person an equivalent sign, or perhaps a more developed sign. The sign stands for something, its object. It stands for that object, not in all respects, but in reference to a sort of idea which I have sometimes called the ground of the representamen. (Peirce, 1897/1932, p. 228)

A sign (*representamen*) stands for the object through the mediation of another sign (the equivalent sign) aroused "in the mind of that person." The equivalent sign qualifies in which "respect or capacity" the representamen sign represents the object (i.e., the ground of the representation). Hence, the sign performs its semiotic function (i.e., standing for something else) through the relation with another sign (the equivalent sign, also defined *interpretant* by Peirce), which in turn will be interpreted by another sign. Semiosis is the infinite process of the interpretation of signs by means of other signs elicited in the mind of the interpreter. Sensemaking consists of that *recursive, asymptotic stream of interpreting signs.* It is permanently stretched out toward its ungraspable object (De Leo, 2009), and this permanent tension makes it *an inexhaustible generative dynamic.* We can and must always interpret because no interpretation is conclusive: Each triggers a further one, just as any step towards the horizon moves the horizon itself ahead. *Sensemaking is the incessant tension of filling the emptiness between language and the world.*

This dynamic and relational idea of meaning reflects the pragmatist view of semiotics, namely the idea of meaning as the *effect* the sign produces on the addressee (Linell, 2009). This effect has to be conceptualized as a further sign: an equivalent sign—be it a reaction, a refusal, or an affective appraisal of the addresser's sign, the addressee's response works as the interpretant of the former, and in so doing develops the chain of signs, keeping the meaning active and at the same time transforming it through time.

This leads us to conclude that meaning is the way signs combine with each other in the recursive movement of interpreting the object they stand for. Meaning is given by the capability of semiosis to keep signs in (some kind of) correspondence with the reality they refer to *by means of their connection with other interpreting signs,* in turn in correspondence with reality by means of other interpreting signs, and so on in an infinite semiotic flow. Every new interpretant somehow rewrites the relationship of equivalence that the previous sign has with the object; at the same time, in the very fact of doing so, it keeps this relationship active, opening to further potentiality of signification.

In sum, meaning can be seen as the *trajectory of the chain of interpreting signs.* In the final analysis, the sign in itself has no content; rather, it has to be conceived of as a *space of potential relationality* (Visetti & Cadiot, 2002), namely the distribution of probability associated with the set of transitions to signs that can follow it. Complementarily, meaning is the reproduction through time of the equivalence between a sign and the following one, as such assumed to be equivalent to—therefore standing for—the original relation between the sign and its object. Meaning is the sign that follows.

SIGNIFICANCE IN PRAESENTIA (SIP) AND SIGNIFICANCE IN ABSENTIA (SIA)

The considerations made above lead meaning to be viewed as consisting of two components. On the one hand, as we have already said, meaning is the sign that follows, namely the equivalence that the sequence reproduces through time—rewriting it to a certain extent as well. This component is the one that common sense experiences and treats as *the* meaning—it constitutes the core content of consciousness. Accordingly, henceforth I refer to this component as *Significance In Praesentia* (SIP).

On the other hand, the equivalence between two signs—more in general between two elements—is always with respect to a particular standpoint—what

Peirce calls the ground of the representamen; two elements are in a relation of equivalence as concerns a property, a criterion, a certain state of the art. The equivalence may be more or less broad, but it never fully saturates the infinite dimensions with which two elements can be placed in relation. If it were so, the equivalence would be *sameness* (Frege, 1892/1980; see also Sovran, 1992). In contrast, equivalence always entails *pertinence*, namely the specific standpoint governing how the relation of equivalence is defined. Therefore, in the final analysis, establishing equivalence between two or more elements means setting a boundary distinguishing between a region of the relationship seen to be pertinent and all the other infinite dimensions pushed into the background, as not pertinent. For example, the semiotic relation of equivalence between the photo of a cake and the piece of cake concerns the dimensions of color and form, but not smell, taste, substance, and so forth—usually we do not eat photos of cakes.

This border of pertinences is the second component of meaning. It defines the *field of pertinent following signs*—namely, the pertinent signs' subset of the infinite set of signs that are virtually available in the world. Pertinent following signs are the ones that *may* follow the representamen as valid interpretants of the relation of equivalence in question. Faced with a photo of a cake, people usually speak and act in a way that is different from how they might act if the cake were present. For instance, one does not pick up a fork or say, "Please put the rest of the cake in the refrigerator after cutting your slice." Accordingly, I refer to this component of meaning as the *Significance in Absentia* (SIA) in order to highlight its character of potentiality.

In sum, the SIA is the set of signs that may potentially follow the current sign. The bivalence of meaning (Abbey & Valsiner, 2005; Carli, 2007; Ribeiro, Gonçalves, & Santos, 2012; Valsiner, 2007) lies in the fact that meaning does not consist of the SIP only; the phenomenical component of meaning—the SIP—is not enough to produce meaning. Meaning *is the effect of the cooperative tension between SIP and SIA through time.* Take the lottery: the prize associated with a given number—and therefore the meaning of the selected number—depends neither on its content (whether it is 1 or 1,000 is irrelevant) nor on the very fact of having been selected in itself. Rather, what defines the prize is the relationship between the number and all the others that may be selected. The number would have a different value if extracted from a set of 100 numbers or from a set of 10,000 numbers. In the same way, meaning is *a matter of positioning within a field of possibilities.*

The Variable Boundaries of the SIA

Actually, the example of the lottery is valid only as an initial approximation. In the case of the lottery, in fact, the numbers all have the same probability of being selected; consequently, all the cases have the same value, the same meaning. And this condition does not vary through time. It is not so in the case of the transition between signs. The field of pertinent signs in which the SIA consists of is not homogeneous and invariant; rather, its boundaries are contingent to the circumstances of sensemaking. Boundaries change through and as a result of the semiotic flow that, on the other hand, they trigger. Which dimensions govern the defining of a given semiotic relationship of pertinence depends on the communicational circumstances. Take the previous example of the photo of a cake. Actually, we can image a situation in which the utterance "please, put the rest of the cake in the refrigerator after cutting *your* slice" is uttered in a meaningful way—for instance, in the context of a game between a child and her parent. The chips used in the casino are in a relation of equivalence with money in the casino in which they are distributed; in that circumstance, and only there, they stand for money and can be used in place of money.

In the final analysis, the *meaning depends on the shape of the SIA's boundaries*—namely the boundaries governing whether a certain sign acquires the status of being a pertinent following sign (say: S_2). Thus, sensemaking consists of a kind of cooperative tension between SIP and SIA—the SIP defines the constraints that trigger/force the interpreter to shape the boundaries of SIA in a certain way, so that the transition to such a SIP is made possible. Consider a person saying to an interlocutor: "I am quite hungry" (S_1). One can imagine very many utterances—and actions—as SIP, namely as the sign (S_2) following S_1: "Do *you* want to go to a restaurant before going home?"; "and what about *your* sleep?"; "Shall we have a break?" Each of these SIPs is the fittest following sign in terms of a given scenario. Therefore, to understand (to interpret) the SIP means defining the scenario in which the S1–S2 transition makes sense. Thus, for example, if the SIP were "Do *you* want to go to a restaurant before going home?", then the interpreter would imagine a scenario of two people negotiating where to have dinner, in order to make sense of the transition; instead, if the SIP were "and what about *your* sleep?", the scenario involved might be something like a medical visit, with a doctor collecting data on the patient; if the SIP were "Shall we have a break?", one might imagine something like two colleagues that have to decide together when to stop working. Needless to say, one can imagine many other scenarios as well. However, whatever scenario is involved, S_2 acquires "*senseness*"—namely, it enters the semiotic flow as a sign allowing/demanding to be interpreted—only because of the scenario. In sum, sensemaking consists of the cooperative tension between SIP and SIA—the SIP defines the constraints that trigger/force the interpreter to shape the boundaries of SIA in a certain way, so that the transition to such a SIP is made possible. In other words, *meaning is the boundary of the potentially infinite SIA under the condition of a certain SIP; and sensemaking is the process of making such boundaries.*

THE ABDUCTIVE NATURE OF SENSEMAKING

The way of viewing the relation between SIA and SIP proposed above entails a counterintuitive shift. According to this view, the pertinentization of the SIA comes *after*, rather than before, the S_1–S_2 transition. This shift is a way of avoiding some of the conceptual problems raised by the traditional vision of meaning. It is consistent with the pragmatic standpoint claiming that *it is the movements of signs that produce meaning, not the meaning that moves signs.* According to this standpoint, it is not true that the pertinentized SIA is expressed/conveyed by the sign that it motivates; rather, the interpreter operates the pertinentization of the SIA with the constraint of assuming S_2 as a sign, namely in order to make it *senseful*—namely interpretable: something standing for something else.

Miming provides a fine example of the backward production of SIA. The mime produces some movements that work as a sign (SIP). The spectator sees these movements as a "senseful" action, a sign having the meaning M. For the spectator, the SIP stands for M. Yet it would be misleading to consider M the content conveyed by the SIP. M is not contained in the SIP; rather, it is the spectator who presentifies M as the interpretation of the SIP. Moreover, the spectator performs this interpretative activity by adding a set of further data from the imagination (i.e., scenarios sourced from memory) that work as the SIA of the SIP; in so doing, she defines the gestalt totality providing the *condition of interpretability* of the SIP. The mime moves his arms and hands in a certain way; Yet the interpretation of these movements, like "pulling a rope," requires the spectator to complete the gestalt with a scenario concerning a long thin object being grasped, connected at the opposite end with something that resists his efforts. In sum, the meaning of the mime consists of the cooperative tension between what is seen and what is added to make what is seen interpretable. It is only on this condition that the mime's movements can be interpreted as "pulling a rope." The interpretation starts, is constrained by and has the SIP as its target, Yet, strictly speaking, *it does not concern it.* Rather, the SIP is the catalytic trigger for the interpreter's hermeneutic activity of shaping an SIA that has to be added to the field of experience in order to make the latter a meaningful gestalt. *The interpretation of a sign does not specify something that is "within" the interpretant—it adds something further to it.* In sum, when the spectators give meaning to the mime's movement, their interpretative work is not limited to the representation of what they perceive. Rather, they provide something else, complementing the gestalt. It is the pertinentization of the SIA that allows the closure of the gestalt that makes interpretation possible. Abduction is not one of the possible modalities of sensemaking—it is the inherent logic of its functioning.

THE BOOTSTRAPPING MECHANISM OF SENSEMAKING

The backward mechanism entailed in the abductive dynamics of the bordering of the SIA cannot lend itself to being conceived of in terms of ready-to-use meanings selectively triggered by the SIP. Such a view would contrast with the pragmatist vision of meaning as produced by the signs' use—it would entail the idea of meanings as fixed entities available before their use (i.e., sensemaking).

As an alternative view, I propose to consider abductive dynamics in terms of what I would define a *bootstrapping mechanism* (Salvatore, Tebaldi, & Potì, 2009; Salvatore, 2012; see also Tronick & Beeghly, 2011). This mechanism works through two stages—a stage of *propagation* and a stage of *reduction*. Below we provide some details on how such a two-stage bootstrapping mechanism might work.

Take the S_1–S_2 transition. According to my argument, S_2 triggers the propagation stage—namely *all connections between signs are activated*. This process of propagation can be understood in the light of Matte Blanco's bi-logic theory (Matte Blanco, 1975; see also Rayner, 1995). Accordingly, the propagation works in terms of the principle of symmetry: Any relation of contiguity among signs is transformed into identity; consequently, a homogeneous totality of connection is activated, tendentially encompassing the infinite set of signs the interpreter has stored in memory. One can consider this global state of activation as a potential absolute SIA (see Figure 6.1).

The propagation is antagonized by the opposite movement, which characterizes the second stage: the *fading off of the nonpertinent connections*. This movement of reduction consists of a process of differentiation of the absolute SIA. It does not work randomly; rather, it is channelled by the gradient of association among the signs, as experienced by the subject. Thus, a sign tends to fade off, unless the subject has experienced it in the same circumstances where the S_1– S_2 transition occurs.

For instance, say that S_1 is "apple" and S_2 is "orange"; then the sign "sugar" might be kept pertinent, because a circumstance like GOING SHOPPING holding the triggering transition "apple"–"orange" holds "sugar" as well; conversely, the sign "logistic regression" would probably fade off because it rarely co-occurs with the signs "apple" and "orange." Thus, many connections, those that share few or no circumstances with the S_1–S_2 transition, fall into the background, while the surviving signs keep themselves in the foreground. In so doing, they emerge as the SIA, namely the domain of

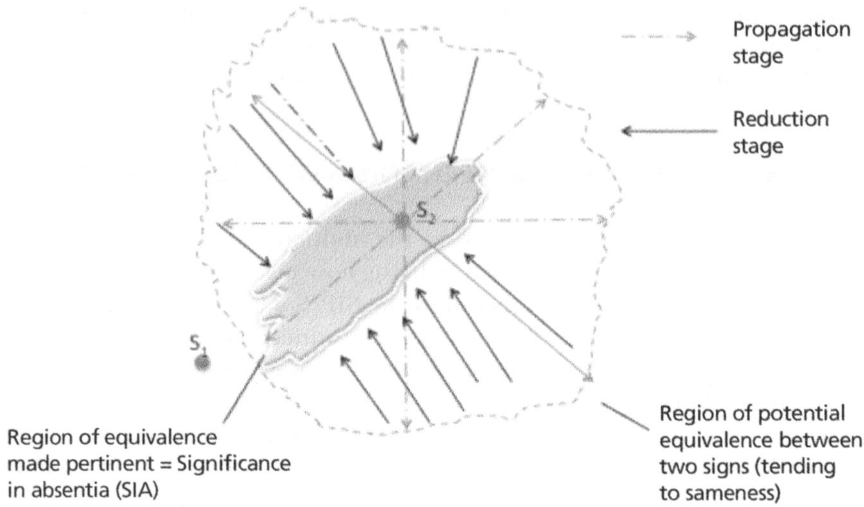

Figure 6.1 The two-stage mechanism of sense making.

equivalence between S_2 and S_1. This is what has to be considered the semiotic value of the sign—its meaning.

In sum, the two-stage model proposed above depicts the SIA as the output of a process of sculpture, rather than of painting, as distinguished by the classical student of art, Giorgio Vasari. Painting is a way of representing in terms of adding onto emptiness (i.e., putting chromatic pigments on the white canvas), while sculpture is a matter of taking off from the whole (i.e., eliminating something from the block, so to extract a form).

IMPLICATIONS FOR THEORY AND THEORY OF TECHNIQUE

Primary Process, Affects and Sensemaking: Rediscovering Metapsychology

The bootstrapping model has implications for psychoanalytic theory. It entails the reference to the basic psychoanalytic concepts of primary and secondary process. Though several cognitive models have proposed computational mechanisms resembling the bootstrapping one (e.g., Kintsch, 1988; Landauer & Dumais, 1997), in the final analysis the latter makes full sense in the light of the dialectic between primary and secondary process. As a matter of fact, the way the propagation stage works clearly reflects the logic of the primary process—in the propagation stage any relationship among signs is treated as identity (Matte Blanco, 1975), and in so doing transforms the experience of the present moment into a whole where perception and memory are merged in an unique infinite totality/sameness (Matte Blanco, 1975; Singer & Conway, 2011; Stern, 2004).

From a complementary standpoint, the reduction stage can be interpreted as the result of the contrasting action of the secondary process, placing constraints on the primary process—namely, the action of introducing distinctions within the totality of the basic experience.

Reading the bootstrapping mechanisms in terms of the dialectics between primary and secondary process can be represented in the terms of the Freudian energetic model (Freud, 1895/1950). In the propagation stage, operating in the domain of the primary process, the libidinal charges are free to fluctuate and spread themselves over the whole memory, namely on the network of signs stored. Thus, the network is activated in a global and homogeneous way, with each zone having an equivalent, low rate of charge. Then, as the secondary process comes into play, a progressive asymmetrization emerges in the distribution of the charges. Thus, some regions of the network prove to be competitively activated—and therefore come to the foreground—compared to others that prove to be not activated—that is, pushed into the background.

The bootstrapping model provides a specific way of considering the notion of affects in sensemaking, too. Psychoanalysis sees the affects as bodily states of activation endowed with hedonic basic values (positive vs. negative, exciting vs. relaxing) (Salvatore & Zittoun, 2011b; Stein, 1991). Accordingly, affects' hedonic value represents the basic form of differentiation of the field of experience and affects can be considered as basic classes of meaning (Matte Blanco, 1975: Smith, 2000; Salvatore & Venuleo, 2008; Salvatore & Zittoun, 2011b; Tronick, 2010)—highly abstract and generalized, internally homogeneous sets of embodied meanings working as the fundamental forms of interpretation of the world (Salvatore & Venuleo, 2010; from a neuroscientific standpoint, see Panksepp, 1998). Human experience takes its basic and primary shape in terms of the hedonic value sustaining affects (Salvatore & Venuleo, 2008). Affects are *highly abstracted*, in the sense that they are defined and differentiated from each other in terms of polarized hedonic values (e.g., pleasant vs. unpleasant). They are *internally homogeneous*, because all contents of experience within the same hedonic class are defined precisely in terms of the shared hedonic value defining the class—which means that intra-class contents are made identical with each other. Finally, affects are highly *generalized* classes of meaning, because they cover any content of experience, assimilating it to the polarized hedonic value.

The semiotic interpretation of affects proposed above paves the way for highlighting the role that they play in the bootstrapping mechanism. The hedonic values sustaining the affective categories lend themselves to be considered the first form of reduction of the SIA, the embodied constraints channelling the process of shaping the SIA's boundaries. Accordingly, the very basic differentiation of the absolute SIA is that which produces the opposition between two global scenarios—the infinite set of signs belonging to the class GOODNESS as opposed to the infinite class of signs belonging to the class BADNESS (Klein, 1967; see also Carli & Giovagnoli, 2011; Carli & Paniccia, 2003). In this way a basic semiotic distinction of the undifferentiated field of experience is made, and at the same time, the foundations are laid for, on the one hand, a hypergeneralized assimilation of experience (i.e., the experience-as-a-whole understood as GOODNESS or BADNESS) and, on the other hand, the recursive process of further semiotic differentiation of the field of experience.

In sum, affects can be interpreted as the first form of bordering of the SIA, emerging as the initial output of the second stage of the bootstrapping mechanism (the stage of reduction). As such, they are to be considered the ground of sensemaking—affects work as the first semiotic environment governing the way the transition between signs is carried out (for a model developing this semiotic interpretation of affects, see Salvatore & Freda, 2011; Salvatore & Zittoun, 2011).

Before concluding this section, is worth highlighting that the connections I have made between the bootstrapping mechanism and the psychoanalytic notions of primary/secondary process and affects are more than a speculative exercise. As underlined above, the reference to psychoanalytic notions paves the way for an understanding of sensemaking that avoids the pitfalls of assuming a reified idea of meaning—namely, the view of meaning as something existing before sensemaking and as such regulating/grounding the transition between signs. This represents a step ahead in psychological theory as well as a way of integrating psychoanalytic theory into more general psychological science. In so doing, psychoanalysis rediscovers its original status of general theory—the Freudian metapsychology—whose concepts are essential for modeling the mind's functioning.

Clinical Theory in a Semiotic Key: Rethinking Projective Identification

From a complementary standpoint, the semiotic-pragmatic view of sensemaking provides a way towards a deeper understanding of basic concepts of the psychoanalytic clinical theory and theory of technique. Below we focus on one of them—the notion of projective identification (Klein, 1946)—in order to highlight the richness of clinical implications entailed in the semiotic-pragmatic view.

As we all know, projective identification is the process of a person projecting onto another person feelings and, more in general, parts of his/her own self, which, as a result, are assumed and felt to be his/her own by the recipient. This concept has gained a major place in the psychoanalytic literature (e.g., Casement, 1985; Laplanche & Pontalis, 1973; Ogden, 1979; Rosenfeld, 1983), as a way of depicting the unconscious dimension of human communication and psychological development. Thanks to this concept, in fact, it is possible to understand how persons regulate with each other through the exchange of unconscious contents—person *A* projects feeling *X* (anxiety, anger, affiliation) onto person *B* in such a way that the latter identifies with this feeling; namely, person *B* experiences feeling *X* as something belonging to herself. In this way, person *A* constructs the image of the other, using what she rejects/expels of herself, and at the same time she constructs her own self through positioning in front to this projected other.

What makes the concept of projective identification one of the most powerful notions elaborated by psychoanalysis is the fact that it combines in a whole dynamics intra-psychic and interpersonal dimensions, showing the reciprocal implication of such dimensions—projection is the way the projecter constructs and regulates the relationship with the other person and at the same time regulates her own inner world. The other person acquires the theoretical value of a dynamic component of the self; complementarily, the inner organization of the self acquires the value of a dynamic component of the relationship.

On the other hand, while the concept of projective identification is largely used for understanding clinical (e.g., the transference-counter-transference dynamics) and relational phenomena (e.g., the mother–child relationship, the couple's dynamics), its own dynamics remain largely unexplained. We recognize the *effect* of projective identification, but how this effect is brought about is not clear—in which way and through which micromechanism is person *A's* feeling retrieved by person *B* and, above all, considered by the latter as her own feeling, a part of her own self? Psychoanalytic theory has provided no definitive answer to this issue, being more interested in using the notion as an explanans, rather than an explanandum.

The semiotic model of sensemaking proposed in the first part of this chapter provides a way of answering this question. The central point at stake is the bivalence of meaning and the abductive nature of sensemaking. As observed above (see the analogy of miming), the interpreter has to add something to make the sign "senseful." The representamen does not convey any meaning—its meaning is the gestalt that the interpreter has to develop in order to construct the condition of interpretability of the representamen itself. Above, I have conceptualized this gestalt in terms of SIA: a constrained field of potentiality of connection among signs. I have also underlined that the affects represent a generalized form of SIA. These conceptualizations allow us to put forward an interpretation of the microdynamics of projective identification. According to my view, projective identification consists of *the* *induction performed by person A's representamen (SIP_A) on person B's construction of the affective, generalized SIA defining the condition of interpretability of SIP_A.*

Thus, person *A* induces an affective state in the person *B* not through a direct communication/transmission of it, but by triggering and somehow constraining person *B's* process of regulation of her own mental states performed in order to assimilate person *A's* sign. In other words, the subject (person *A*) transforms the other (person *B*) by creating the semiotic conditions in terms of which the other (person *B*) performs the transformation of her own other (person *A*) (for a similar mechanism, though not focused on projective identification, see Valsiner, 1999).

An example can help to show how such a mechanism works in more detail. Imagine a couple. The husband is grasped by a generalized, latent feeling of anger. He feels this feeling by dwelling on of the image of the other—his wife—being upset with him: |I feel I am the recipient of my wife's anger|. Incidentally, note that at the level of the mind's functioning where such a process works—namely, a level where the primary process prevails—the distinction between self and other has no relevance (Matte Blanco, 1975; Salvatore & Freda, 2011; Salvatore & Zittoun, 2011b). The image of the wife is, however, a component of the husband's self; this makes it possible for the source of the anger to be inverted.

The mechanism of projection consists of this inversion. Now, as a result and complement of this inversion, the husband will react to the image of the wife's anger in the same way he usually deals with such a relational circumstance—that is, with a sarcastic attitude and at the same time withdrawing from his wife. In turn, the pattern of signs produced by the husband will compellingly trigger the wife's construction of an affective scenario (i.e., an SIA), the one that the wife has to shape as the condition of interpretability of the pattern itself. And due to the fact that, as it were, in the history of the couple the most efficient way of interpreting a pattern of this kind is to place it in a scenario of anger, the wife will develop such latent scenario as the gestalt grounding her semiotization of the relational event (i.e., of the husband pattern of signs)—a process that from a metaphorical point of view can be depicted as the introjection and identification with the projected content of the husband's mind. Also in this case, the fact that the SIA serves to make senseful the other's sign—rather than one's own sign—is irrelevant (at the level of sensemaking involved), because the mechanism of projective identification entails a level of mind where the inner and outer world—self and other—are not distinguished (Carvalho, Ginzburg, Lombardi, & Sanchez-Cardenas, 2009; Freud, 1900/1953; Matte Blanco, 1975; Sanchez-Cardenas, 2011).

In sum, according to the model proposed above, projective identification does not entail any exchange of content between minds. Rather, it is a matter of reciprocal adjustment between subjects, triggered and constrained by the other's movement of adjustment to her own other.

Considerations of Theory of Technique: A New Look at the Psychoanalytic Interpretation

Interpretation is a central topic of the psychoanalytic theory of technique (e.g., Etchegoyen, 1991; Hoffman, 1998; Neuman, 2010; Strachey, 1934). The semiotic standpoint grounds a particular attitude to such a concept both at a methodological and a technical level.

The different psychoanalytic theories of techniques have proposed a plurality of ways of defining the target object of the interpretation (cf. Etchegoyen, 1991). According to the theoretical framework assumed, the interpretation has been conceived of as a way of revealing/expressing unconscious or at any rate implicit mental contents (ideas, feelings, fantasies), of highlighting the action of defense mechanisms or other patterns of mental functioning, of recognizing the affective inner and/or interpersonal scenarios. At the same time, the interpretative work has been considered as being aimed at a plurality of clinical functions—to understand the subject, to regulate the clinical exchange, to explain behaviors, to enable the patient to express herself and get a deeper linkage with her subjectivity, to mentalize components of the self, to empower the regulation of the inner emotional dynamics, to reduce the intensity of inner conflicts, and so forth. With respect to all these options, the semiotic standpoint presented above offers its own particular way of defining the *what* and the *why* of psychoanalytic interpretation: *interpretation concerns the representation of the SIA, in particular in its generalized, affective dimension.*

The idea that interpretation has the SIA as its object means that ultimately psychoanalytic hermeneutics does not finish its task in addressing specific discrete contents (affects and ideas seen as being held in the patient's mind or in the interpersonal field). Rather, it addresses the semiotic gestalt working as the ground, the matrix shaping the discrete mental object and endowing them with the quality of being senseful. This is so because, as discussed above, the SIA is the ground of the interpreter's hermeneutic activity—namely the foundation of the condition of interpretability of the sign. In other words, psychoanalysis does not settle for understanding the output of mental processes—the SIP; rather, it goes to the root of such mental processes and maps the field semiotic conditions (i.e., the SIA) in their form and content. Thus, the interest of the analysis is not only or mainly how the subject feels and what fantasies she experiences—rather, it is the generalized SIA (i.e., the generalized affective scenario) working as the mental field generating those feelings, ideative contents, and fantasies. In this sense, the interpretation is always *genetic*—not in the historical sense, but in the sense of aiming systematically to understand the condition of thinkability governing whether a certain pattern of mental content comes to be involved.

An example might illustrate this point. Consider a patient who arrives at a session over forty minutes late, close to the time the session usually ends. This enactment could be read in different ways, according to the clinical framework. The therapist might hypothesize, for example, that the patient has tried to avoid the encounter so as to remove herself from a source of anxiety; or that she is enacting the fantasy of attacking a persecutory object; or that in so doing she is experiencing a form of grandiosity of her own Self, through the devaluation of the therapist; or that such an enacting is a marker of the patient's weak capacity to place a limit on impulses. These, as well as other possible interpretations, despite their being framed in different clinical standpoints, share a fundamental methodological assumption: All of them consider the delay as the target of the interpretation; in other words, they focus on the SIP, interpreted according to the culture of a given social context (one understands that arriving at a certain time is being late not because she has been attended psychoanalytic training, but simply because it is part of a cultural context). The focus on the SIA as the condition of thinkability changes the methodological frame. In this case, the interpretation does not concern the explication of the event as already having a meaning in itself; rather, the focus is on its construction as an event—namely, the assumptions according to which the act of arriving at that time, close to the end of the session, acquires *sensefulness* for the clinical dyad. From this point of view, one could hypothesise that, for example, the patient has to assume that the therapist is waiting for her; that there is a boundary within which the therapist and the patient relate, regardless of what the patient does; that the patient is with the therapist during that hour, regardless of her material presence. Other possible hypotheses are of course possible. What characterizes such hypotheses is the fact that they do not concern the interpretation of the fact in itself—namely the arrival close to the end of the session—but the system of assumptions making this event a sign. It is in this sense that such hypotheses are genetic interpretations—*they generate the clinical datum*, where the latter is seen as the SIA grounding the sensefulness of the event. In the final analysis, while the former interpretation is a *second-order interpretation*—the interpretation of the commonsensical interpretation of the fact—the latter interpretation is focused on the construction of the reality as a taken-for-granted datum of experience (i.e., being late).

Several theoretical and methodological implications can be drawn from the situation presented above. Here I will simply point out just one basic theoretical aspect.

The interpretative focus on the condition of thinkableness/sensefulness—rather than on the sign made senseful—means restoring the centrality of the role of the primary process in the clinical setting. For the sake of dialoguing with other clinical theories and with the empiricist paradigm dominating contemporary psychological science, current psychoanalysis seems to have somehow put into the background the revolutionary and counterintuitive idea of a dimension of the mind working in terms of creating a relation of identity, as such following a systematic mode of functioning, *Y*et different from and irreducible to the classical logic of rationality, as commonly understood (Freud, 1900/1953). In so doing, psychoanalytic clinical thought has lost its force of innovation and specificity—Freud considered his basic discovery to be the primary process and not the existence of an unconscious part of the mind (Freud, 1940/1964). Yet in the contemporary psychoanalytic dictionary, "unconscious" is no longer psychic reality working according to its own rules; rather, it has become a synonym of "unaware": a descriptive attribute of the cognitive life (Salvatore & Freda, 2011).

Now, the focus on discrete mental contents is consistent with the secondarization of contemporary psychoanalysis (Malone & Roberts, 2010). This is so because discrete mental contents are already a product of the process of differentiation and extraction of relationships within the unrelated wholeness of the unconscious, carried out by the secondary process (on this point Matte Blanco's notion of lateral insertion of the instinct is illuminating; Matte Blanco, 1975 p. 131; see also Salvatore & Zittoun, 2011b). According to secondarization, psychoanalytic interpretation ends up being seen as an exercise of making explicit/retrieving specific feelings, ideas, and fantasies of which the subject is supposed to be unaware. In the final analysis, this means that the psychodynamic value of the interpretation lies not in the translation between two different logics of mental functioning (Aristotelian logic versus the oniric logic of the unconscious)—as Freud stated in *the Interpretation of Dreams* (and Matte Blanco modelled in formal terms; cfr. Matte Blanco, 1975)—but in the merely descriptive difference between what is aware and what is not. In sum, the *represented–not represented* dichotomy—seen as two alternative characteristics that the same mental content can assume due to its position in terms of the focus of the subject's consciousness, replaces the dialectics between *representable-unrepresentable*—namely, the dialectics between symbolic processes elaborated according to the rules of the secondary process, and thus transformed into specific representations and symbolic processes working under the power of the primary process, as such unsuitable to be brought into language.

CONCLUSIONS

Psychoanalysis, like any other domain of knowledge, is grounded on generalized conceptions framing the way of addressing the theoretical and clinical issues, as well as providing analogies and ontologies. As is recognized, the extraordinary Freudian conceptual architecture is founded on the vision of the world of that time, qualified by Victorian moral feeling as well as the discoveries of electromagnetic dynamics. Theories are, however, the product of human beings. As such, they are grounded, motivated, shaped, and constrained by more general canonical views—the un-thought allowing the thinking—representing the horizon of sense within which the vision moves.

This chapter is a contribution added to the others that, in recent Years, have been trying to push this horizon forward. Psychoanalytic theory and practice are grounded on a vision of the mind and meaning that needs to be updated. This is so neither for aesthetic reasons, nor for the pleasure of novelty for its own sake. The recognition of the dynamicity and contextuality of sensemaking, of the processual nature of meaning, allows psychoanalysis to rethink some basic assumptions on which it has based its enhancement for decades, but at the same time has limited its possibility of development. In the final analysis, psychoanalysis can apply its own basic tenet to itself—development is a matter of recognizing the constraining power produced by the assumptions that allow us to think.

ACKNOWLEDGMENT

The content of this paper was presented at the London Bi-Logic Group Spring 2011 Meeting (London, 2nd of April, 2011), with the title "Rereading Matte Blanco through the Lens of Pierce's Semiotic Triangle: Bags of Symmetry as Affective Semiosis." I am grateful to the participants of the seminar for their thoughtful comments, which enable me to develop the ideas of the paper. I also want to thank Michel Sanchez-Cardenas, with whom I have discussed several of the ideas proposed in the paper. He read and insightfully commented on a previous version of the paper.

REFERENCES

Abbey, E., & Valsiner, J. (2005). Emergence of meanings through ambivalence. *Forum Qualitative Sozialforschung /Forum: Qualitative Social Research, 6*(1), 58.

Barclay, M. W., & Kee, M. (2001). Towards a semiotic psychotherapy: Semiotic objects and semiotic selves. *Theory and Psychology, 11*(5), 671–686.

Bühler, K. (1990). *Theory of language: The representational function of language.* Amsterdam, The Netherlands: John Benjamins Publishing Company. (Original work published 1934)

Carli, R. (2007). Pulcinello or "on ambiguity." *Rivista di psicologia clinica/Journal of Clinical Psychology, 3.* Retrieved from http://www.rivistadipsicologiaclinica.it/english/number3_07/Carli.htm

Carli R., & Giovagnoli F. (2011). A Cultural approach to clinical psychology. Psychoanalysis and analysis of the demand. In S. Salvatore, & T. Zittoun (Eds.), *Cultural psychology and psychoanalysis. Pathways to synthesis* (pp. 117–150). Charlotte, NC: Information Age.

Carli., R., & Paniccia, R. M. (2003). *Analisi della domanda: Teoria e tecnica dell'intervento in psicologia clinica [Analysis of demand. Theory and technique of the intervention in clinical psychology].* Bologna, IT: Il Mulino.

Carvalho R., Ginzburg A., Lombardi R., & Sanchez-Cardenas M. (2009). *Matte Blanco: une autre pensée psychanalytique. L'inconscient (a)logique.* [Matte Blanco. A different psychoanalytic thought. The (un)logic unconscious.] Paris, France: L'Harmattan.

Casement, P. (1985). *On learning from the patient.* London, UK: Routledge.

Croom, A. M. (in press). Aesthetic concepts, perceptual learning, and linguistic enculturation: Considerations from Wittgenstein, language, and music. *Integrative Psychological and Behavioral Science, 6*(1), 90–117. doi: 10.1007/s12124-011-9184-5.

De Leo, D. (2009). intersubjectivity as co-phenomenology: from the holism of meaning to the being-in-the-world-with-others. *Integrative Psychological & Behavioral Science, 43*(1), 78–83.

Eco, U. (1975). *A theory of semiotic.* Bloomington, IN: Indiana University Press.

Etchegoyen, R. H. (1991). *The fundamentals of psychoanalytic technique.* London, UK: Karnac Books (Original work published 1986)

Fornari, F. (1979). *I fondamenti di una teoria psicoanalitica del linguaggio [Foundations for a psychoanalytic theory of the language].* Torino, IT: Boringhieri.

Fornari, F. (1981). *Il codice vivente [The living code].* Torino, IT: Bollati Boringhieri.

Frege, G. (1980). On sense and reference (M. Black, Trans.). In P. Geach & M. Black (Eds. and Trans.), *Translations from the philosophical writings of Gottlob Frege* (3rd ed., pp. 56–78). Oxford, UK: Blackwell. (Original work published 1892)

Freud, S. (1950). Project for a scientific psychology. In J. Strachey (Ed. and Trans.), *The standard edition of the complete psychological works of Sigmund Freud* (Vol. 1, pp. 281–391). London, UK: The Hogarth Press and the Institute of Psycho-analysis. (Original work published 1895).

Freud, S. (1953). The interpretation of dreams. In J. Strachey (Ed. and Trans.), *The standard edition of the complete psychological works of Sigmund Freud* (Vol. 4–5). London, UK: The Hogarth Press and the Institute of Psycho-analysis. (Original work published 1900).

Freud, S. (1964). An outline of psycho-analysis. In J. Strachey (Ed. and Trans.), *The standard edition of the complete psychological works of Sigmund Freud* (Vol. 23, pp. 139–207). London, UK: The Hogarth Press and the Institute of Psycho-analysis. (Original work published 1940)

Gergen, K. J. (1999). *An invitation to social construction.* London, UK: Sage.

Giannakoulas, A. (1984). *I Fondamenti di una Teoria Psicoanalitica del linguaggio.* Turin, Italy: Boringhieri.

Harré, R., & Gillett, G. (1994). *The discursive mind.* London, UK: Sage.

Hoffman, I. Z. (1998). *Ritual and spontaneity in the psychoanalytic process: A dialectical-constructivist view.* Hillsdale, NJ: The Analytic Press

Kintsch, W. (1988). The use of knowledge in discourse processing: A construction–integration model. *Psychological Review, 95,* 163–182.

Kirshner, L., A. (2010). Between Winnicott and Lacan: Reclaiming the subject of psychoanalysis. *American Imago, 67,* 331–351

Klein, M. (1946). Notes on some schizoid mechanisms. *International Journal of Psycho-Analysis, 27,* 99–110.

Klein, M. (1967). *Contribution to Psychoanalysis, 1921–1945.* New York: Mac Graw-Hill.

Landauer, T. K., & Dumais, S. (1997). A solution to Plato's problem: The latent semantic analysis theory of acquisition, induction and representation of knowledge. *Psychological Review, 104,* 211–240.

Laplanche J., & Pontalis J. B. (1973). *The language of psycho-analysis.* London, UK: Hogarth.

Leiman, M. (2000). Ogden's matrix of transference and the concept of sign. *British Journal of Medical Psychology, 73,* 385–397.

Lepper, G. (in press). Taking a pragmatic approach to dialogical science. *International Journal of Dialogical Science.*

Libet, B. (1999). Do we have free will? *Journal of Consciousness Studies, 6*(8-9), 47–57.

Linell, P. (2009). *Rethinking language, mind and world dialogically: Interactional and contextual theories of sense-making.* Charlotte, NC: Information Age Publishing.

Matte Blanco, I. (1975). *The unconscious as infinite sets. An essays in bi-logic.* London, UK: Gerald Duckworth and Company Ltd.

Malone, K. R., & Roberts. J. L. (2010). In the world of language but not of it: Lacanian inquiry into the subject of discourse psychology. *Theory & Psychology, 20*(6), 835–854.

Muller, J. P. (1996). *Beyond the psychoanalytic dyad. Developmental semiotics in Freud, Peirce and Lacan.* London, UK: Routledge.

Muller, J., & Brent, J. (Eds.). (2000). *Peirce, semiotics, and psychoanalysis.* Baltimore, MD: The Johns Hopkins University Press.

Neuman, Y. (2009). On love, hate and knowledge. *The International Journal of Psychoanalysis, 90,* 697–712.

Neuman, Y. (2010). Penultimate interpretation. *The International Journal of Psychoanalysis, 91,* 1043–1054.

Ogden, T. H. (1979). On projective identification. *International Journal of Psycho-Analysis, 60,* 357–373.

Olds, D. D. (2000). A semiotic model of mind. *Journal of American Psychoanalysis Association, 48,* 497–529.

Panksepp, J. (1998). *Affective neuroscience: The foundations of human and animal emotion.* Oxford, UK: Oxford University Press.

Peirce, C. S. (1932). *Collected papers of Charles Sanders Peirce* (C. Hartshorne & P. Weiss, Eds., vol. 2). Cambridge, MA: Harvard University Press. (Original version published 1897)

Pine, F. (1988). The four psychologies of psychoanalysis and their place in clinical work. *The Journal of the American Psychoanalytic Association, 36,* 571–596.

Rayner, E. (1995). *Unconscious logic. An introduction to Matte Blanco's bi-logic and its uses.* New York, NY: Brunner-Routledge Taylor and Francis Group.

Ribeiro, A., Gonçalves, M., & Santos, A. (2012). Innovative moments in psychotherapy: From the narrative outputs to the semiotic-dialogical processes. In S. Salvatore, A. Gennaro, & J. Valsiner (Eds.). *Making sense of infinite uniqueness: The emerging system of idiographic science. Yearbook of Idiographic Science, Volume 4* (pp. 149–176). Charlotte, NC: Information Age.

Ricoeur, P. (1981). *Hermeneutics and human sciences* (J. B. Thompson, Ed. and Trans.). Cambridge, UK: Cambridge University Press.

Rosenfeld, H. (1983): Primitive object relations and mechanisms. *International Journal of Psycho-Analysis, 64,* 261–267.

Salvatore S. (2012). Social life of the sign: Sensemaking in society. In J. Valsiner (Ed.), *The Oxford handbook of culture and psychology* (pp. 241–254). Oxford, UK: Oxford University Press.

Salvatore, S., Forges Davanzati, G., Potì, S., & Ruggeri, R. (2009), Mainstream economics and sensemaking. *Integrative Psychological and Behavioral Science, 43*(2), 158–177.

Salvatore, S., & Freda, M. F. (2011). Affect, unconscious and sensemaking. A psychodynamic semiotic and dialogic model. *New Ideas in Psychology, 29,* 119–135.

Salvatore, S., Freda M. F., Ligorio B., Iannaccone A., Rubino F., Scotto di Carlo M., Bastianoni P., & Gentile, M. (2003). Socioconstructivism and theory of the unconscious: A gaze over a research horizon. *European Journal of School Psychology, 1*(1), 9–36.

Salvatore, S., Tebaldi, C., & Poti, S. (2009). The discursive dynamics of sensemaking. In S. Salvatore, J. Valsiner, S. Strout, & J. Clegg (Eds.), *YIS: Yearbook of Idiographic Science 2008–Volume 1* (pp. 39–72). Rome, IT: Firera Publishing.

Salvatore, S., & Valsiner, J. (2010). Between the general and the unique: Overcoming the nomothetic *versus* idiographic opposition. *Theory and Psychology, 20*(6), 817–833.

Salvatore, S., & Venuleo C. (2008). Understanding the role of emotion in sensemaking: A semiotic psychoanalytic oriented. *Integrative Psychological and Behavioral Science, 42*(1), 32–46.

Salvatore, S., & Venuleo, C. (2010). The unconscious as source of sense: A psychodynamic approach to meaning. In B. Wagoner (Ed.), *Symbolic transformation: The mind in movement through culture and society* (pp. 59–74). London, UK: Routledge.

Salvatore, S., & Zittoun, T. (Eds). (2011a). *Cultural psychology and psychoanalysis in dialogue: Issues for constructive theoretical and methodological synergies.* Charlotte, NC: Information Age.

Salvatore, S., & Zittoun, T. (Eds). (2011b). Outlines of a psychoanalytically informed cultural psychology. In S. Salvatore & T. Zittoun (Eds.), *Cultural psychology and psychoanalysis in dialogue: Issues for constructive theoretical and methodological synergies* (pp. 3–46). Charlotte, NC: Information Age.

Saporta, S. (2011, June). *A semiotic and socio-cultural perspective on mentalizing.* Paper presented at McLean Hospital, McLean Borderline Center Conference, Belmont, MA.

Sanchez-Cardenas, M. (2011). Matte Blanco's thought and epistemological pluralism in psychoanalysis. *The International Journal of Psycho-analysis, 92*(4), 811–831. doi:10.1111/j.1745-8315.2011.00381.x

Saussure, F. d. (1977) *Course in general linguistics* (W. Baskin, Trans.). Glasgow, UK: Fontana/Collins. (Original work published 1916)

Singer, J. A., & Conway, M. A. (2011). Reconsidering therapeutic action: Loewald, cognitive neuroscience and the integration of memory's duality. *International Journal of Psycho-Analysis, 92,* 1183–1207.

Smith, J. H. (2000). Feeling and firstness in Freud and Peirce. In J. Muller & J. Brent (Eds.), *Peirce, semiotics, and psychoanalysis* (pp. 68–83). Baltimore, MD: The Johns Hopkins University Press.

Sovran, T. (1992). Between similarity and sameness. *Journal of Pragmatics, 18,* 329–344.

Stein, R. (1991). *Psychoanalytic theories of affect.* London, UK: Karnac Books.

Stern, D. N. (2004). *The Present moment in psychotherapy and everyday life.* New York, NY: W. W. Norton.

Stolorow, R. D., Orange, D. M., & Atwood, G. E. (2001). World horizons. A Post-Cartesian alternative to the Freudian unconscious. *Contemporary Psychoanalysis, 37*(1), 43–61. In A. M. Cooper (Eds.), *Contemporary psychoanalysis in America. Leading analysts present their work* (pp. 671–699) .Washington, DC: American Psychiatric Publishing.

Strachey, J. (1934). The nature of therapeutic action of psychoanalysis. *International Journal of Psycho-Analysis, 15,* 127–159.

Tronick, E. (2010). Multilevel meaning making and dyadic expansion of consciousness theory: The emotional and the polymorphic polysemic flow of meaning. In D. Fosha, D. J. Siegel, & M. Solomon (Eds.), *The healing power of emotion* (pp. 86–111). New York, NY: W. W. Norton.

Tronick, E., & Beeghly, M. (2011). Infants' meaning-making and the development of mental health problems. *American Psychologist, 6*(2), 107–119.

Tuckett, D. (Ed). (2008). *Psychoanalysis comparable & incomparable: The evolution of a method to describe and compare psychoanalytic approaches.* London, UK: Routledge.

Valsiner, J. (1999). I create You to control me: a glimpse into basic processes of semiotic mediation. *Human Development, 42,* 26–30.

Valsiner, J. (2007). *Culture in minds and societies: Foundations of cultural psychology.* New Delhi, India: Sage.

Valsiner, J. (2009). Integrating psychology within the globalizing world: A requiem to the post-modernist experiment with Wissenschaft. *Integrative Psychological and Behavioral Science, 43*(1), 1–21.

Visetti, Y. M., & Cadiot, P. (2002). Instability and theory of semantic forms: Starting from the case of prepositions. In S. Feigenbaum & D. Kurzon (Eds.), *Prepositions in their syntactic, semantic and pragmatic context* (pp. 9–39). Amsterdam, The Netherlands: John Benjamins.

Wittgenstein, L. (1958). *Philosophical investigations.* Oxford, UK: Basil Blackwell.

CHAPTER 7

THE AMERICAN IDEA IN SIBLINGHOOD—INTERPERSONAL PSYCHOANALYSIS AND PRAGMATISM

Knowing and the Problem of the Unconscious

Michael Mance
NYU Post Doc

INTRODUCTION

It would seem fair to say that during the course of any treatment there comes a point at which a clinician must ask himself,[1] "What is it that I truly know about this patient?" The answer to this question may be vastly different depending on the orientation of the analyst. The question itself reflects the natural tension between an intersubjective perspective and a more objectivist one-person psychology. Presumably a patient comes to treatment

Making Our Ideas Clear, pages 177–194
Copyright © 2015 by Information Age Publishing
All rights of reproduction in any form reserved.

of his own accord in order to reduce his experience of day-to-day suffering. In doing so, it is probable that the patient acquires knowledge of one sort or another in moving towards greater psychological health. Certainly clinicians acquire what is justly termed knowledge of the patient, whether it be after only a few minutes of speaking on the phone (Ogden, 1992) or engagement with a patient over many years (McWilliams, 2004). This knowledge may be closer or farther from the patient's self experience, be more or less well connected to reality, and have varying degrees of usefulness.

Yet, as far as treatment goes, it would be unfair to state from a contemporary perspective that there exists no information that the clinician is aware of that lies outside the bounds of the treatment frame. In other words, there is nothing a clinician can know about a patient that the patient herself hasn't provided. However, this knowledge may be at odds with the purpose with which a patient presents or is perhaps beyond the patient's self-awareness. Without being unfairly reductive here, let us say that for many people knowledge is defined as applicable to something that exists in the real world. In this understanding, knowing something has some connection to day-to-day activity. Further, reality is known because it is observable and measurable.

Depending on one's treatment approach and the accompanying philosophical underpinnings, we might consider certain facts, specifically phenomena that appear to be outside of the patient's immediate awareness, to be highly relevant, worthy of conversation, and perhaps even in need of action. Indeed, this is not unlike what Komprides (2006) describes as second-order disclosure. This is not a new discussion: known and unknown, what is agreed upon, what each party privately believes, how knowledge informs experience to alter and broaden day to day experience of the self-in-the-world. The validity of these compelling questions has been explored elsewhere, and their importance need not be belabored (Mitchell & Harris, 2004). What is perhaps a more fresh discussion is one exploring the nuances of how the analytic community has, in a continuing way, engaged with the question of knowledge. While at present the schools of psychoanalysis have never been more in lock-step, they were each born, like the Greek gods, in fierce embrasure and contest. Psychoanalysis has ever been in the cross-current of culture, time, space, and personality. All of these have molded the various approaches in such a way that they stand in conflicted harmony with the each other, like a minor chord.

Of particular interest is interpersonal psychoanalysis, historically at odds with the many other branches of psychoanalysis. In part this was due to the fact that it was an extension of the American ideal, based on the philosophy of pragmatism, and separate from European intellectual traditions. As an "independent" school of psychoanalysis (if there can be such a thing) in its formation, the philosophical structure that supports it is vastly different from the same components of the Freudian/post-Freudian European practice. The aegis of this chapter is to examine the relationship between the philosophy of pragmatism and interpersonal psychoanalysis. It may be best for the purposes of this examination, and in doing so we may eliminate some confusion by focusing on the concept of knowledge as defined within the pragmatism. My best effort will be made to avoid the various interplaying concepts that reach out for consideration including being, self, and other like concepts.

One significant discrepancy between interpersonal psychoanalysis and other psychoanalytic theories is the way in which interpersonal psychoanalysis answers questions about knowledge. Interpersonal psychoanalysis, in its most classic form, owes a particularly great deal to the philosophy of pragmatism. As interpersonal psychoanalysis is the only purely American psychoanalysis (with the possible exception of the sardonically named "American middle school" of object relations), so too is pragmatism the only purely American philosophy. This mutual connection in and of itself makes the two schools blood-brothers, of a sort, despite being in separate fields. However, this is not the limit of their connection. Interpersonal psychoanalysis was influenced both in its very inception and in its historical growth and development by the philosophy of pragmatism. At its root interpersonal psychoanalysis follows the dictates of classical pragmatism. Consequently, in order to understand how Interpersonal psychoanalysis answers questions about knowing, we must understand the combined history of both it and pragmatism. Armed with such an understanding, we can then turn our attention to the discussion of knowledge (epistemology, as it is known) and spend the rest of the chapter exploring the contemporary presence of both.

I think it is fair to take a moment at this point to acknowledge some of the demands that this kind of text makes on the writer–reader dyad. Unavoidably, in writing about either psychoanalysis or philosophy, the writer is confronted with three difficulties. In the first, the writing risks becoming belabored with a recounting of historical context rather that an examination of fresh questions. Second, any discussion will run afoul of the fact that in almost any domain, a close examination of major theorists, conceptualizations, and structures will yield a welter of confusion. The danger here is that the lion's share of time will be spent working through the minutia of one particular position versus another, with hardly anything to recommend the discussion beyond compulsive regurgitation of facts. This accomplishes nothing but adding greatly to confusion and detracting substantially from forming new understanding. Third, any statement of a theoretical position, especially within philosophy, necessitates an encyclopedic knowledge of all the philosophy that came before. I write this with an eye towards this danger's counterbalance: that a little knowledge is worse than none. The wary writer will then learn to avoid the trap of stagnation, finding what is fresh and relevant in a discussion in a way that will inform the reader. What then, can be written about either pragmatism or interpersonal psychoanalysis that is not discursive or replete with uninteresting asides?

With these difficulties clearly laid out, let us turn our attention to the way in which the roots of interpersonal psychoanalysis in American pragmatism shapes their answers to these questions of knowing.

A BRIEF HISTORY OF TWO AMERICAN ORIGINALS, PRAGMATISM AND INTERPERSONAL PSYCHOANALYSIS

In 1909, during his only visit to the United States, Freud, along with his then protégé Carl Jung and, lest we forget, Sandor Ferenczi, met with a number of luminaries of the relatively nascent American Psychology Association. This meeting included both William James and G. Stanley Hall. James, a core member of the pragmatic school of thought, and founding member of the Metaphysical Club, was reputedly much taken with Freud, saying that "the future of psychology lay with him [Freud]" (Jones, 1955, p. 15 as cited in Taylor, 1999, p. 469). It is difficult to know how to interpret this comment, beyond flattery, as it is well known that James felt that Freud was somewhat obsessional about his metapsychological formulations (Simon, 1967). Those familiar with Freud (Jones, 1961) will most likely admit that Freud was likely attempting to make a convert in James. Sadly, perhaps, James could not help him there for long, as he would be dead within the year of the meeting. History does not record what, if any, compliments James paid to either Sandor Ferenczi or Carl Jung.

It would not be unjust to point out that some blame is to be cast at the foot of the philosophy of pragmatism as a culprit in the split between continental psychoanalysis and American made psychoanalysis.[2] It would be fair to summarize the commonly accepted narrative of European origin as the following: prior to Freud, America was something of a wilderness, untutored in psychoanalysis until, as Freud himself put it, America was "brought the plague" (Lacan, 1977, p. 116). Over the course of the next thirty years Psychoanalysis made steady inroads, and all was well, until the psychoanalytic Diaspora triggered by World War II. Upon landing on these bucolic shores of America, figures like Heinz Hartmann,[3] Heinz Kohut, Margret Mahler, Erik Ericson, and Theodore Reik brought orthodoxy with them, causing or perhaps revealing innumerable rifts amongst American analysts of various sorts (Galdi, 2007; Quinn, 1987). This phenomenon was abetted by the ongoing animosity between the Kleinians, the ideological ego psychologists, and the adherents English Middle School. More than anything, the adherents to Freud and the newly forged school of ego psychology disapproved of the interpersonalist's objection to the existence of the unconscious (Chodorow, 2004; White, 2001). Without the unconscious, there was no place for drives, no purchase for the structural model, and no safe harbor for unresolved sexual conflict. The New York Psychoanalytic Society and the American Psychoanalytic community as a whole responded to the influx of European practitioners with their own retreat into orthodoxy, rigidity, and a descent into a hermetic position. From this fortified position, all challengers were excluded, including psychologists. As a consequence, psychoanalysis laid the groundwork for its own demise. Over the course of the next fifteen years, American psychoanalysis ascended into a cultural force, becoming the dominant paradigm. However, the first cracks appeared during the 1958 New York University Institute of Philosophy symposium, in which it was determined that psychoanalysis was not "scientific" (Hook, 1958; Popper, 1959). Despite the criticism, it was another 25 years before a significant treatment challenge arrived in the form of cognitive behavioral therapy. Paired with the advent of managed care in the late 1980s, significant alienation of others in related fields and the failure to grasp the central components of the philosophy of American pragmatism more or less guaranteed the loss of primacy of the psychoanalytic endeavor in the United States.

The formation of pragmatism as a school can be historically located as beginning 25 years prior to the turn of the 19th century. Beginning in 1872 at Yale, a group of young men, enthused about challenging the status quo, or alternatively obscenely bored while in the possession of first-class minds, formed the Metaphysical Club. Its purpose was to explore the state of the art in the field of philosophy and to challenge the European dominance of American philosophical thought. Among others, the club included Charles Sanders Peirce, John Dewey, and William James. Dewey went on to work at the University of Chicago, impacting both Sapir and Meade, both of whom would become seminal figures in their own fields, not to mention figures of importance in the thinking of Sullivan. In turn Adolf Meyer, himself largely responsible for the introduction of Krapelinian nosology to the American psychiatric scene, was strongly influenced by the brand of pragmatism practiced in Chicago (Silver, 2002). This club met regularly to write, debate, argue the contemporary philosophy of the day, and, one presumes, have drinks (Dewey, 1907; Peirce, 1902). Yet in the meeting of the club, something of a brotherhood formed, a commitment to the budding philosophy of pragmatism—a rejection of Kant, and inasmuch as possible, European modes of understanding. This brotherhood would last the entire lives of many of the main figures of the group. James supported Peirce financially till his death. It is worth noting that this formation of a brotherhood, with a purpose, is something of a more wholesome forerunner, be it ever so distant, of the same brotherhood forming under the generalship of Freud, several decades later.

The earliest proponent of pragmatism was Charles Sanders Pierce. Pierce was a dedicated logician and scientist by training who published papers on a wide array of topics. In that curiously unjust way reserved for academic and artistic pursuits, the brilliance of his ideas was largely restricted to a limited audience. He received little attention during his lifetime with the significant exception of William James (Dewey, 1931/1970; Mounce, 1997). His lack of success encouraged for Peirce, among other things, poor investments, poverty, and substance use. With his semi-tragic history, Charles S. Peirce is something of an interesting figure in the loose pastiche of what should not considered a singular "school" of pragmatic philosophy. Perhaps he is accurately described as writing in a more rigorous style than his later peers, with a greater formalism than his counterparts. Indeed, later in his career he strove to distance himself from his peers in the domain of philosophy due to his view on the nature of truth. Peirce constructed his philosophy in the context of British Empiricism and Continental Rationalism, both of which he levied the staunch attacks against.[4]

Peirce's great contribution to the foundation of pragmatism was to challenge the metaphysic basis for knowledge, or the metaphysic experience as a framework for understanding. As a reaction to Kant's attempt to unify empirical and rationalist philosophies (Dewey, 1931/1970; James, 1890/1970), Peirce's pragmatism embraces Kant's definition of human mind as interacting with reality in an active way. As a philosophy it rejects the Cartesian belief that the mind passively experiences reality. However, Peirce's pragmatism also eschews the spiritual level of experience as being generative of data that has relevance in the physical realm (and here he differed a great deal from his benefactor, James). Rather, Peirce deals with the metaphysical messiness generated by Kant's approach by regarding the practical effects of action taken on a belief. Consequently, *a priori* notions are ruled out in terms of the public sphere of discourse.

This position is most discretely summed up in what is called the pragmatic maxim. The pragmatic maxim, the cornerstone of pragmatism, was created by Charles Sanders Peirce as a way of establishing the best method to clarify understanding. Its function is to introduce a reliable way of communicating, in the most objective manner possible, an idea. By *idea*, what is meant by pragmatists is: what a thing is. The objectivity of this communication is grounded in the practical effects of that idea. To illustrate the meaning of the pragmatic version of "idea," let us conduct a thought experiment. Consider two ideas labeled x and z. The first idea x produces a result of y. The second idea z also produces a result of y. In such a case, both ideas, by the pragmatic maxim, are the *same* thing. To state this another way, a thing (idea) is what its observable effects are, and nothing else. Perhaps this might be termed the "whatever works" maxim, though this is a woeful understatement of the power and elegance of the pragmatic maxim. Perhaps more accurate would be to label it "whatever has an effect that we both agree upon the particulars of." In any event, the pragmatic maxim, as formulated by Peirce, served as the backbone for the newly budding philosophy, and his writings had a profound effect on his fellow pragmatists.

If Peirce was the progenitor of pragmatism as a philosophy, then William James was its public champion, popularizing it in the American landscape. An opportune time it was for such a purely American endeavor. Like the art world, philosophy was a domain in which Americans still had yet to come into their own, especially in the eyes of the Europeans. There was no long history, no philosophic tradition. Despite its newly forming economic and military wherewithal, intellectual peerage with the Europeans continued to escape the American academic community. It is likely that this factor played an extremely significant role in the embrasure of pragmatism, lock, stock, and barrel, by the American academic community. William James's academic superstardom both in America and Europe only furthered the popularity of pragmatism.

James was many things that Peirce was not. A clean, efficient writer, his social wit and interpersonal connections allowed him to further pragmatism's cause among the literati. Appointment to professorship at Harvard went no small way towards adding significant intellectual heft to his works, and having a famous and accomplished author as a brother was not negligible. Conversely, William James was often troubled by feelings of insecurity, existential angst, and overwhelming depression. It is not untoward to suggest that this was his foundation of brotherhood with C. S. Peirce, beyond the philosophical one. James approached pragmatism from a different perspective than Peirce. Rather than a reaction to Kant, or a break with European tradition, James saw pragmatism as the logical conclusion of empiricism if pushed to its logical limits (Thayer, 1982). James wrote:

> Radical empiricism consists first of a postulate, next of a statement of fact, and finally of a generalized conclusion. The postulate is that the only things that shall be debatable among philosophers shall be things definable in terms drawn from experience. [Things of an unexperienceable nature may exist ad libitum, but they form no part of the material for philosophic debate.] The statement of fact is that the relations between things, conjunctive as well as disjunctive, are just as much matters of direct particular experience, neither more so nor less so, than the things themselves. The generalized conclusion is that therefore the parts of experience hold together from next to next by relations that are themselves parts of experience. The directly apprehended universe needs, in short, in short, no extraneous trans-empirical connective support, but posses in its own right a concatenated or continuous structure. (James, 1890/1970, p. 199)

But pragmatism is a uniquely American philosophy, perhaps the only philosophy produced by Americans. Wholly conceived of in the United States, its major proponents and theorists were American. More importantly, the central idea of pragmatism is that reality is based on agreement. In other words, it can be seen as an application of democratic compromise to the domain of philosophy. This American-ness of the philosophy is important to note (Mitchell & Harris, 2004), especially as it is in reaction to Kant and his later followers, an eschewal of what the idea of reality as being anything other than what is in relationship to the human mind, as represented by language. It is not a surprise, then, that years later, when introduced to the cadre of European intellectuals fleeing the Nazis, it naturally seemed to be combative and inimical to the predominant continental philosophies in which they were steeped.

If Peirce is the intellectual father of the movement, and James its populist, then John Dewey must be considered to be its archivist, cataloguing the philosophy, annealing it to the pages of history. Dewey labored greatly in constructing the narrative, the backbone of American pragmatism. In doing so, Dewey inculcated the philosophy of pragmatism in the sphere of academe, arguing forcefully for its primacy, giving shape and a notion of contiguous shape (if not canon, though it is traditional to note that pragmatism has no true canon). It is he who popularized the philosophy, ensuring its adaptation particularly in the social sciences, through the use of his academic prowess and reputation.

FOUNDATIONS OF INTERPERSONAL PSYCHOANALYSIS

It is in this ferment of pragmatism that interpersonal psychoanalysis began to take shape. To say that interpersonal psychoanalysis is influenced by pragmatism is a bit like saying Andre Reed was influenced by Jim Kelly (or Jerry Rice by Joe Montana). Naturally, this is well known to be the case, and hardly anything interesting can be got from having mentioned it at all. It is de rigueur to mention this connection (Chodorow, 2004; Chrzanowski, 1977; Mitchell & Harris, 2004), superficially perhaps, in any article about the early days of interpersonal psychoanalysis, the degree to which Meyer influenced Sullivan, for instance, or the role that pragmatism played in forming the American approach to treating mental illness. Indeed, later classical pragmatists such as Edmund Sapir and George Mead heavily influenced Harry Stack Sullivan (Silver, 2002).

Like the school of pragmatism, interpersonal psychoanalysis, in its earlier forms, was a loose collection of individuals. Its lineage can be traced to Adolf Meyer, a seminal figure in the early American psychiatric scene, and initially a strong proponent of both Kraeplin and Freud. Meyer was at

University of Chicago with, among others, Sullivan, Sapir, and Mead. His work at the New York State Psychiatric Institute inspired William White, whose 1907 book *Outlines of Psychiatry* stood as a seminal work in the field of psychiatry for 30 years. But the connection between pragmatism and interpersonal psychoanalysis is not limited to this single filament. Notably, Clara Thompson, who can be seen as serving a similar role for interpersonal psychoanalysis as Dewey did for pragmatism, was analyzed by Sandor Ferenczi. He was considered to be by Sullivan, if not a guiding light, at least a legitimate member of Freud's inner circle (Grey, 1994; Ortmeyer, 1995).

I take time to point out these connections in order to address a misunderstanding or misconstrual of the basis of interpersonal psychoanalysis. Later, more relationally oriented readings of the interpersonal tradition have described it as beginning from a position of disputing classical Freudian metapsychological theory:

> Harry Stack Sullivan, Erich Fromm, Karen Horney, Clara Thompson, and Frieda Fromm-Reichman knew each other and worked together, and their individual contributions reflect considerable cross-fertilization. They began at a common starting point: a conviction that classical drive theory was fundamentally wrong in its basic premises concerning human motivation, the nature of experience, and difficulties in living and, therefore, that drive theory provides an inadequate and essentially misleading foundation for psychoanalytic theorizing.[5] (Greenberg & Mitchell, 1983, pp. 79–80)

The veracity of this assertion about the beginnings of interpersonal psychoanalysis can most likely be judged based on the degree of one's orthodoxy. It is also demonstrably wrong. The interpersonalists were not immediately concerned with drive theory (or structural theory for that matter) or interested in its adequacy to explain any particular experience. Rather, they were concerned with science, and, as adherents to pragmatism, they believed that they were obligated to do away with the metaphysical underpinnings of psychiatric theory. Expunge them then, and begin anew, with a focus on experience, practicality, and social interaction. Sullivan, at least, did not object to the notion of an unconscious; he just thought it was of little or no importance clinically and of specious utility operationally (Sullivan, 1953).

As desirable as it would seem to lay the blame of later invective against the interpersonal school entirely at the feet of its roots in pragmatism, this badly underestimates the political climate into which psychoanalysis in general, and interpersonal psychoanalysis in specific, was birthed. On one side, psychology in general faced strong resistance from the medical community and its tendency to see mental disorders as an extension of physiological ones (Goldberg, 2002). On the other side lay medicine's hierarchy regarding specialization, on which psychiatry fell quite low. Finally, there was the potential threat of that most reliable of American traits, puritanical reaction. The sexual theories of classical analysis, which in Europe may have been only worthy of a raised eyebrow (and perhaps a sidelong glance), were in America certainly beyond the pale of civilized company. In the context of desire for legitimacy, independence, and proper regard in the scientific community, Freudian orthodoxy was a difficult position to take for a practitioner. Again, no small part was then played by the "psychoanalytic Diaspora" and the event of bringing orthodoxy to American shores. Now, some may comment that Heinz Hartmann (ego psychology), Loewald (Kleinian), and Heinz Kohut (self-psychology) are all American analysts, but often they are defined as fitting into largely European traditions. Incidentally, Erick Erickson, arguably the most popular and commonly taught psychoanalyst outside of Freud, often seems to have gone unclaimed by any particular school. This is despite the fact that his writings on lifespan development remain consistently popular and are taught at the undergraduate level. Though he considered himself to be an interpersonalist, he may be a better representative of the British Middle School (Chodorow, 2004).

In other words, in its very formation, the interpersonal school faced not only the risk of reactionary moral-religious opprobrium, to a far greater extent than did Freud in Europe, but also the difficulty in achieving social, cultural, and professional legitimacy in the medical community. As in Freud's case, the establishment of a beachhead of respectability and legitimacy within the medical community was to be the primary prize. In this landscape, then, science became an attractive way to legitimize, in a cultural manner, efforts to apply a deeper method of treatment, a more nuanced way of seeing patients to the field of mental health. Unfortunately, interpersonal psychoanalysis was unable to fully escape the outcome of the 1958 New York meeting in which psychoanalysis was determined to be to be "unscientific" (DeRobertis, 2001). This did not prevent the school, and American Psychology as a whole, to maintain a rigid pursuit of scientific legitimacy, primarily by framing knowledge in a particular manner.

THE POLITICS OF KNOWING

The questions of what it means to know something is, in general, an ancient one usually attributed to Plato. However, epistemology did not exist as a separate field of direct philosophic inquiry for centuries. It was not until James Fredrick Ferrier coined the term in 1854 that it became a distinct area of philosophic inquiry, theory building, and debate.

Epistemology, simply enough, refers to the domain of knowledge. As with many things in philosophy, discussion of simple things becomes quickly complicated. For instance, there are various "modes" of knowledge. This includes the distinction between knowing through acquaintance, and knowing about. The former can be loosely defined as knowledge that arises from one's actual experience in the real world. Through one's experience of something, he becomes acquainted with it. The latter, knowledge about, on the other hand, defeats loose definitions. Epistemological considerations at their root address how it is we acquire knowledge, how we know what it is we know, and what indeed is knowledge itself. It is necessary here to note that knowledge does not equal truth (James, 1907; Mounce, 1997), a seemingly very fine but quite important point. It was commonly held for centuries that knowledge equaled truth. By this definition, knowledge cannot be false, as it corresponds accurately to what might be known as a true state of affairs. However, this understanding does not match some contemporary perspectives. The contemporary view contains something of a paradox. That which we might consider knowledge, either derived through logic (a priori) or through experience (a posteriori), is not equivalent to the truth per se. Instead, it may be better to see knowledge as a set of beliefs, and that these beliefs act as the bearers of truth. However, what is believed to be true may not actually conform to reality. Indeed, we now understand there is no commonly agreed upon definition of truth, but rather theories that may be categorized in terms of the availability of a reality to reference, and the nearness of the reference to actuality. It is easy to see here that, in essence, epistemological questions ultimately devolve to questions regarding the nature of actuality, or being. Parenthetically I will note here that questions regarding the nature of being belong under the heading *ontology*. This is primarily because knowledge about is only achieved through internal elaboration on something that one has experienced. In essence, one must think about something directly for there to be knowledge about it. However, since knowledge must apply to *something*, if not truth, we will see the ways in which both pragmatism and interpersonal psychoanalysis understand the acquisition of knowledge similarly, that something as corresponding to a state of observable reality (DeRobertis, 2001).

EPISTEMOLOGY AND INTERPERSONAL PSYCHOANALYSIS

For our intents and purposes, such as we have them, it is helpful to take a moment to consider an important, perhaps ultimately *the* important element of pragmatism: namely, that in the popular interpretation, pragmatistism as a philosophy eschews anything that smacks of metaphysics. To simply state this issue: Any phenomenon that can be ratified in the real world through the use of an observable measure falls in the domain of physics (meaning the action or property of a physical body). Anything that is unable to be measured in the real world, or cannot be directly observed, falls to the domain of metaphysics. One way to think about this difference is to recall that "meta" means above, and thus you have "above that which deals with the real." Doubtless you can already see the difficulties inherent in such a proposition, the greatest of which is that in its very definition, metaphysics implies a directional relationship, above, between the observable and the unobservable, which in some circles is tantamount to saying "god." This anathema, in the eyes of the pragmatists, was to be dealt with strictly and harshly (for the most part) by excising all mention of the metaphysic. If that came at a cost, then so be it. Evidence of this attitude can be found when one considers Peirce's initial formulation of his reaction to Cartesian abstraction:

> Thus our action has exclusive reference to what effects our senses, our habit has the same bearing as our action, and our belief the same as our habit, our conception the same as our belief: and we can consequently by wine other than what has certain effects, direct or indirect, upon our senses and to talk of something as having all the sensible characters of wine, yet in reality being blood, is senseless jargon. (Peirce, 1902/1970, p. 88)

Caution pays here at this juncture in that it cannot be said that pragmatists did not rule out the existence of God. Indeed, both Peirce and William James indicated discretely the opposite, writing several seminal works on the nature of the religious experience (Mounce, 1997). It was not James's opinion that the metaphysic did not exist. Rather, it is more accurate to say that in regards to what can be discussed with any degree of certitude, God cannot be talked about in any way that appeals directly to the senses (i.e., sensible). For James, there can be no model that spans a satisfactory epistemological gamut and consequently is not a rational-scientific dialogue. So much, then, for the "senseless jargon" with which is framed all knowledge. The metaphysic has been neatly and logically stuffed into a closet, and the key conveniently lost.

This understanding of the pragmatic stance towards metaphysics becomes important for our purposes when discussing the nature of its impact on American psychoanalysis. As I hope is clear at this point in the chapter, in embracing pragmatism, interpersonal psychoanalysis was constrained in particular ways leading naturally to a position at disunion with classical psychoanalysis, and by extension both ego psychology and the British Middle School. Most importantly, due to the constraints of the pragmatic maxim, interpersonal psychoanalysis reaches a crisis when encountering the concept of the unconscious as proposed by Freud.

Further, and perhaps more importantly for Harry Stack Sullivan, is that non-rational theories, under this definition, were not able to be investigated by scientific means. Thus they were to be avoided by psychiatry. Sullivan wrote:

> The third definition of psychiatry, which is the one relevant here, may be approached by considering it as an expanding science concerned with the kinds of events or processes in which the psychiatrist participates while being an observant psychiatrist. The knowledge which is organized in psychiatry as a science is not derived from anything special about the data with which the psychiatrist deals. It arises not from a special kind of data but from the characteristic actions or operations in which the psychiatrist participates... of all the actions or operations that the psychiatrist participates as a psychiatrist, the ones which are important are those which are accompanied by conceptual schematizations or intelligent formulations which are communicable. (Sullivan, 1953, p. 13)

Note the emphasis on science, the scientific method, organization, intelligence, and the consignment of psychiatry to all of the same. Rationality, using the lay definition rather than philosophic,[6] is the restless captain treading the boards on the ship of interpersonal psychoanalysis. Worthy also of notice is something that psychiatry is not. Namely it is not special, meaning personally idiosyncratic, there is nothing symbolic, metaphoric about what is going on in session. The process is then shorn of mystery, the psychiatrist avoids performing as an oracle, and theory of mind is freed of the thrones and powers of such concepts as id, ego, and superego. There is merely the analysand, the psychiatrist, and the operations (whatever they may be) that occur between them, delimited by the notion that all is understandable. What is known is agreed upon, under the bearing of the pragmatic maxim.

What I would like emphasize here is that the pragmatic objection to the unconscious is not an objection to the idea of an unconscious, or even to the more controversial construct of developmental conflicts; it is a natural extension of the demands of the basic driving philosophy of interpersonal psychoanalysis. There can be no true discussion of the unconscious, or more directly, debating of its existence. To put the dilemma another way, the unconscious (and indeed later the id/ego/superego) are by definition *a priori* concepts, and are discretely out of bounds for scientific investigation.

Now perhaps to some degree, Freud would agree and would respond by pointing out that the unconscious can only be known by drive derivatives and the like. Ego psychologists might equally respond by indicating that the unconscious is knowable only through observation of transference. A Kleinian might likely respond that the primitive fantasies that govern the unconscious are never truly knowable.

Indeed, to relate this discussion back to clinical concerns, it is worth returning to our question of how a patient goes about acquiring knowledge through the course of treatment. If the interpersonal position, driven by the requirements of the pragmatic maxim, is inherently a two-person position, where does that knowledge come from? It is fair to say that there is some validity to the claim that this position leads to a reduction in the scope and nature of knowledge that a patient-analyst dyad might achieve. If some of what we know is not symbolic, then what? Mead, a highly influential figure within early interpersonal psychoanalysis, argues that the fundamentally important and necessary parts of personhood arise from interaction with others in the social sphere. Inasmuch as there is a private self, this is a collection of habits rather than the psychic reality of personhood. Indeed, Sullivan quite strongly asserts this position that 50 years later is something of a shock to read:

> Psychiatry studies, as I see it, activity in the public mode and also that part of activity in the private mode which is not in any sense inviolably isolated. Let me say that insofar as you are interested in your unique individuality, in contradistinction to the interpersonal activities which you or someone else can observe, to that extent you are interested in the really private mode in which you live—in which I have no interest whatever. The fact is that for any scientific inquiry, in the same sense that psychiatry should be, we cannot be concerned with that which is inviolably private. The setting up of the psychiatric field as a study of interpersonal relations is certainly necessary if psychiatry is to be scientific; furthermore by this simple expedient of so defining psychiatry, we weed out from the serious psychiatric problems a great number of pseudo-problems—which, since they are pseudo-problems, are not susceptible of solution. (Sullivan, 1953, p. 19)

Setting aside the idea of pseudo-problems for a moment, let us acknowledge that this position introduces particular difficulties in regards to the acquisition of knowledge. To engage in a brief thought experiment, is it possible for a patients to know something about themselves that they do not report to their analyst? If so, without discussion, does it ascend to the status of knowledge? It cannot be said that the classic interpersonal position satisfactorily answers these questions outside of the application of clinical technique. Again, we are called to note the emphasis on scientific inquiry as a basis for clinical approach and theoretical underpinnings. It is clear then why understanding the historical context of this statement becomes so important. We as readers simply cannot do without it.

By way of addressing these questions it is useful here to take the opportunity to point out an ironic dualism: namely, the similarity between methods of treatment in both ego psychology and interpersonal psychoanalysis in the domain of knowledge. I refer here to the method of close questioning during a patient's narrative, respectively called tracking and the detail driven enquiry as noted in both traditions (Blanck & Blanck, 1993; Cooper, 1995). This technique of close questioning is not far, if removed at all, from the pragmatic approach to obtaining knowledge of Dewey (1938/1970, p. 316), who states, "Inquiry is progressive, addressing a situation of problematic indeterminacy and converting it to a soluble problem."

Neopragmatism and Psychodynamic Consensus

American pragmatism proper has had its day. Merging with logical positivism, it fell into disfavor in the face of European influences such as deconstructionism, a philosophy that answers epistemological challenges in a vastly different manner. It has been somewhat revived in a newer form by thinkers like Richard Rorty (1981), under the moniker *neopragmatism*. Likewise, interpersonal psychoanalysis has gone through significant changes. While the strong stance on pragmatism remains within the discipline upon American shores, the understanding of dynamic process is quite different. The unconscious, once a bugaboo, is now accepted, if not warmly[7] (Chodorow, 2004; Goldberg, 2002). Publications regularly refer to transference rather than parataxic distortion, and individuals from one institution regularly lecture at another. It begs the question: Has interpersonal theory been co-opted, and if so, is this a bad thing? We are in an era of mutual cooperation and acceptance between psychoanalytic schools. This is probably more attributable to external threats more than anything else. Invective has been reined in, and the appearance of a "big tent" approach is in favor (Wallerstein, 2002; White, 2001). It brings to mind a photo of an extended family, all smiling tightly and perhaps a bit insincerely, masking the deep family conflicts and divides for the sake of appearance. The following quote on interpersonal psychoanalysis by Goldberg nicely illustrates this phenomenon:

> In an effort to understand why a Kleinian and an interpersonalist can explain a patient in totally different vocabularies and help a patient in what may seem to be totally different methods, we would do best not to try to translate the workings and language of one into the other. That is often a leveling process that aims to reduce the one into the other. That is a search for a common ground, a pursuit that serves to ignore what is distinctive about each theoretical stance.... Such a respectful stance that recognizes commonality is more wholesome than one of insisting either that the others have gotten it wrong, or that you are the one who knows what is really going on. (Goldberg, 2001, p. 245)

Perhaps co-opted is too strong a term, but certainly its inclusion into the relational position has minimized much of its stark differences with the multitudinous schools of dynamic thought. It remains popular in many papers to quote neopragmatists like Richard Rorty and other proponents of neopragmatism. And perhaps Rorty is not so far from the classic American Pragmatic position: "Nothing counts as justification unless by reference to what we already accept, and that there is no way to get outside our beliefs and our language so as to find some other test than coherence" (Rorty, 1981, p. 178).

Alternatively, Nancy Chodorow has herself made a claim for intersubjective ego psychology as a basis for a communality between schools. While these things may be true, this does not resolve the fundamental difficulty resting at the heart of the dialogue between pragmatism, interpersonal psychoanalysis, and the rest of the psychodynamic literature: namely that the metaphysical elements of experience that are not verifiable through immediate introspection and agreement in community have little place. Perhaps, upon due consideration, we can see this conflict as emerging from two very different traditions, one American, and one European. I think it is worth noting that the appeal of European modes has not necessarily abated:

> In the present period, relational as well as ego-psychological institutes seem endlessly eager to host European (and occasionally) Latin American visitors. Those institutes are convinced, like the characters in a Henry James novel, that what is European must be better and that European critique and dismissal of naïve, provincial American thought and practice must have been right all along. (Chordorow, 2004, p. 215)

To end, let us return to the question of what it is that we know about a patient. Setting aside for a moment an argument about the existence of something like an unconscious, or repository of conflict, is not the immediate experience of seeing something about the patient that they themselves have little or no awareness of meaningful? If we believe that we are aware of something true about a patient that they themselves are ostensibly not, does this count as true knowledge?

NOTES

1. Actually, I freely acknowledge that this may not be the case. There may very well be clinicians who do not feel compelled to answer questions regarding what is "true" in the narrative of the patient.
2. For readers who are unaware of the historical splits between psychoanalytic schools, further detail will be provided later in this chapter.
3. Hartmann's work seems to be defined as both American in character (Mitchell & Harris, 2004) and European (Chodorow, 2004).
4. Amusingly, he describes the works of Spinoza, a prominent Rationalist, as a "dry rubbish heap" (Peirce, 1902/1970, p. 54).
5. Nota bene: They also say that reading Sullivan is difficult, challenging, and an acquired taste. I am not entirely sure this is a fair description.
6. Ironically, calling something rational means quite the opposite from what we would think philosophically. In rationalism there is a private mind that appeals to something greater than itself as opposed to empiricism, in which all is a blank slate.
7. I do not wish to be heedless here. Old habits die hardest.

REFERENCES

Blanck, G., & Blanck, R. (1993). *Ego psychology: Theory and practice.* New York, NY: Columbia University Press.

Chodorow, N. J. (2004). American independent tradition: Loewald, Erikson, and the (possible) rise of intersubjective ego psychology. *Psychoanalytic Dialogues, 14*(2), 207–232.

Chrzanowski, G. (1977). *Interpersonal approach to psychoanalysis: Contemporary view of Harry Stack Sullivan.* New York, NY: Gardner Press.

Cooper, A. (1995). The detailed inquiry. In M. Lionells, J. Fiscalini, C. Mann, & D. Stern (Eds.), *Handbook of interpersonal psychoanalysis.* Hillsdale, NJ: The Analytic Press.

DeRobertis, D. (2001). Notes for a definition of the concept of psychoanalytical epistemology. *International Forum of Psychoanalysis, 10*(2), 133–143.

Dewey, J. (1907). The development of American pragmatism. In H. S. Thayer (1970). *Pragmatism, the classic writings, Charles Sanders Peirce, William James, Clarence Irving Lewis, John Dewey, Gorge Herbert Mead* (pp. 352–357). Indianapolis, IN: Hackett. (Original work published 1931)

Dewey, J. (1970). *Logic: The theory of inquiry.* In H. S. Thayer (1970). *Pragmatism, the classic writings, Charles Sanders Peirce, William James, Clarence Irving Lewis, John Dewey, Gorge Herbert Mead* (pp. 101–119). Indianapolis, IN: Hackett. (Original work published 1938)

Galdi, G. (2007). The analytic encounter, a scene of clashing cultures. *American Journal of Psychoanalysis, 67*(1), 4–21.

Greenberg, J. R., & Mitchell, S. A. (1983). *Object relations in psychoanalytic theory.* New York, NY: Harvard University Press.

Grey, A. (1994). Ferenczi and the interpersonal school: A study of political climates in psychoanalysis. *International Forum of Psychoanalysis, 3,* 103–106.

Goldberg, A. (2002). American pragmatism and American psychoanalysis. *The Psychoanalytic Quarterly, 71*(2), 235–250.

Hook, S. (1958). *Psychoanalysis scientific method and philosophy: A symposium.* New York, NY: New York University Press. Retrieved from http://archive.org/stream/psychoanalysissc02newy#page/n5/mode/2up

James, W. (1970). *The principles of psychology.* In H. S. Thayer (Ed.), *Pragmatism, the classic writings: Charles Sanders Peirce, William James, Clarence Irving Lewis, John Dewey, George Herbert Mead* (pp. 221–223). Indianapolis, IN: Hackett. (Original work published 1890)

James, W. (1974). Pragmatism. In R. B. Perry (Ed), *Pragmatism and four essays from the meaning of truth.* New York, NY: The New American Library.

Jones, E. (1955). *Sigmund Freud life and work, volume two: Years of maturity 1901–1919.* The Hogarth Press, London

Jones, E. (1961). *Sigmund Freud: Life and work* (L. Trilling & S. Marcus, Eds.). New York, NY: Basic Books.

Lacan, J. (1977). The Freudian thing or the meaning of the return to Freud in psychoanalysis. *Ecrits: A Selection.* New York, NY: Norton. Retrieved from http://www.lacan.com/frameXIV2.htm

Komprides, N. (2006). *Critique and disclosure: Critical theory between past and future.* Cambridge, MA: MIT Press.
McWilliams, N. (2004). *Psychoanalytic psychotherapy: A practitioner's guide.* New York, NY: Guilford Press.
Mitchell, S. A., & Harris, A. (2004). What's American about American psychoanalysis? *Psychoanalytic Dialogues, 14*(2), 165–191.
Mounce, H. O. (1997). *The two pragmatisms: From Peirce to Rorty.* New York, NY: Routledge.
Ogden, T. H. (1992). *The primitive edge of experience.* Lanham, MD: Jason Aronson.
Ortmeyer, D. H. (1995). History of the founders of interpersonal psychoanalysis. In M. Lionells, J. Fiscalini, C. Mann, & D. Stern (Eds.), *Handbook of interpersonal psychoanalysis.* Hillsdale, NJ: The Analytic Press.
Peirce, C. S. (1902). The definition of pragmatic and pragmatism. In J. M. Baldwin (Ed.), *Dictionary of Philosophy and Psychology* New York. p. 321-323. In: Thayer, H. S. (1982). *Pragmatism, the classic writings, Charles Sanders Peirce, William James, Clarence Irving Lewis, John Dewey, George Herbert Mead.* Indianapolis, IN: Hackett Pub Co Inc.
Popper, K. (1959). *The logic of scientific discovery.* New York, NY: Routledge
Quinn, S. (1987). *A mind of her own: The life of Karen Horney.* New York, NY: Summit.
Rorty, R. (1981). *Philosophy and the mirror of nature.* Princeton, NJ: Princeton University Press.
Silver, A.-L. S. (2002). Psychoanalysis and psychosis: Players in American history. *Psychoanalysis and History, 4*(1), 45–66.
Simon, R. I. (1967). Great paths cross: Freud and James at Clark University, 1909. *American Journal of Psychiatry, 124*(6). Retrieved from http://www.scribd.com/doc/18796908/Freud-and-James
Sullivan, H. S. (1953). *The interpersonal theory of psychiatry* (H. Perry & M. Gawel, Eds.). New York, NY: W.W. Norton.
Taylor, E. (1999). William James and Sigmund Freud: "The future of psychology belongs to your work." *Psychological Science, 10*(6), 465–469.
Wallerstein, R. S. (2002). The Growth and Transformation of American Ego Psychology. *Journal of the American Psychoanalytic Association, 50,* 135–168.
White, R. S. (2001). The interpersonal and Freudian traditions: Convergences and divergences. *Journal of the American Psychoanalytic Association, 49,* 427–454.
White, W. (2011). *Outlines of psychiatry.* Seattle, WA: Ulan Press. (Original work published 1907)

COMMENTARY

REFLECTIONS ON THE WAYS PRAGMATIC PHILOSOPHY AND INTERPERSONAL PSYCHOANALYSIS ARE "RELATED"

Cory K. Chen
VA NY Harbor Healthcare System–Manhattan Campus
William Alanson White Institute

Where we come from impacts where we go—our origins orient our perspective. So by way of introduction, I would like to describe my intellectual "family of origin." I am a clinical psychologist and psychoanalyst trained at the William Alanson White Institute (WAWI). The White Institute was founded by the progenitors of the interpersonal psychoanalytic movement—Harry Stack Sullivan, Clara Thompson, Freida Fromm-Reichmann, and Erich Fromm. It is historically considered the center of interpersonal thinking. The White Institute is also analytic home to many of those who went on to become pioneers in relational psychoanalysis. The complex distinction between the interpersonal and relational perspectives is beyond the scope of this chapter, but the White Institute is a key contributor to the historical and contemporary ideas on which the authors of this volume

Making Our Ideas Clear, pages 195–212
Copyright © 2015 by Information Age Publishing
All rights of reproduction in any form reserved.

comment (Ehrenberg, 2006; Frankel, 1998; Mitchell, 1999). My teachers and supervisors at White taught me to appreciate and take pride in the diversity of perspectives that exist within the interpersonal school—a sort of antidogmatic dogmatism. Thus, I won't pretend to represent an "official" interpersonal stance (if such a thing exists). The ideas I express are my own although based on my experience as shaped by my training at White. In describing myself and one part of my interpersonal history (that of my training), I am also attempting to begin my comments by emphasizing a crucial aspect of interpersonal thinking—an attention to the details of the interpersonal particular.

I want to say upfront that in reading the chapters by Sergio Salvatore, Michael Mance, Mayer Bellehsen, and Jon Weidenbaum, both the breadth and density of their ideas make commenting in a comprehensive way impossible. I find much that is familiar—ideas with which I feel a resonance—approaches to material that are close cousins of one another. In other instances, the ideas or tone are more removed, evoking the feeling that I am a distant relative or outsider attempting to understand and interpret something from a distinctly foreign perspective. In this commentary, I hope to acknowledge the similarities, note useful questions that these chapters inspire, and perhaps more importantly, I strive to highlight some of the differences in the hope that clearer explication of these contrasts will facilitate new understandings.

The overarching theme of this commentary is that a tension exists between the general and the specific. I believe that a dialectic must be held between the big picture ideas discussed by the authors and the importance of attention to the details, or "the pursuit of the particular" (Levenson, 1988). This theme will be illustrated by focusing on differences in how self-experience is defined and expanded given our assumptions about the nature of the field that organizes our experience.

CLOSE COUSINS

As these chapters explicitly attempt to draw parallels between a pragmatic understanding of human experience and interpersonal psychoanalysis, or to illustrate the philosophical foundations of the interpersonal approach, much in these chapters evoke a sense of kinship. For example, Michael Mance's description of the pragmatic approach to gaining knowledge that formed the basis of the detailed inquiry and consensual validation are resonant with my own understanding and approach (Sullivan, 1970). Similarly, both Mayer Bellehsen and Jon Weidenbaum discuss and elaborate on contemporary pragmatic conceptions of multiple selves, which obviously parallels and (even precedes) Bromberg's work on multiple self-states (Bromberg, 1996).

There are instances where similarities are subtle. For example, Bellehsen's description of interpersonal dynamics highlights the role of contrast. He writes: "This process of adopting the other's I-position highlights an externalizing-internalizing-externalizing dynamic in which one individual embodies an I-position for the partner, the partner finds a way to internalize it, and the partner can then embody it for the other" (this volume, p. 109). This reminded me of Sandra Buechler's notion of the importance of providing contrast for our patients and that through provision of a contrasting way of being, we facilitate the process of expanding the range of experiential possibilities that our patients can know: "Contrast is inherently freeing because it says, implicitly, there is more than one way to be human" (Buechler, 2008, p. 23).

Lastly, in instances where accusations of "gaps" in psychoanalytic understanding were expressed, those issues have also found footing within contemporary interpersonal literature. For example, compare Sergio Salvatore's discussion of the problems inherent in conceptions of meaning as preexisting with the similar issues that Donnel Stern has been grappling with over the past 30 years. Salvatore writes:

> Contemporary psychoanalysis is still based on a conception of meaning that has a glorious past (Bühler, 1934/1990; De Saussure, 1916/1977; Frege, 1892/1980; see also Eco, 1975), but that needs to be radically updated.... The traditional conception assumes that meaning is an autonomous entity, pre-existing its private and/or public representation. According to this assumption, individuals have a given content in their mind (a concept, an image, a representation—a significance) and this is why they can express it. (Salvatore, 2012)

Thirty years ago, Donnel Stern (1983) similarly stated:

> According to Freud, each experience is recorded and stored more or less permanently in the unconscious, much like a film or tape library. Conscious memories and other experience are the result of the distorting effects of drive and defense on the permanent unconscious record. This leads to the familiar psychoanalytic concept of self-deception. Deceiving ourselves means convincing ourselves that we do not know something when we actually do know it. The Freudian defensive processes are always processes of masking, or disguise, or outright expulsion and banishment of (fully formed) experience from consciousness. (p. 79)

Stern goes on to offer an alternative approach to understanding the nature of meaning:

> Unconscious clarity rarely underlies defense. On the evidence of our observations of them as they emerge in awareness, the perceptions, ideas, and memories we prefer not to have, the observations we prefer not to make, are most often murky and poorly defined, different in kind than they will be when the

> process of completion has progressed to the level of words. "Unformulated experience" is the label I have chosen to refer to mentation characterized by lack of clarity and differentiation.... [Thus] [m]eaning becomes creation, not discovery. (Stern, 1983, pp. 71–72)

Additionally, Salvatore's statements about exploring and expanding the conditions under which patients can have access to a broader range of thoughts and experience are similar to Stern's more recent writing. Salvatore writes, "The interpretation is always *genetic*—not in the historical sense, but in the sense of aiming systematically to understand the condition of thinkability governing whether a certain pattern of mental content comes to be involved."

Similarly, Stern (2009) writes:

> The appearance in the treatment of mutually accepted new content or newly organized content... is the sign that change has taken place. It is true that a new understanding is the fulfillment of possibility; but it is to the creation of that possibility, not the shape of its fulfillment, that we must look for the source of change. The important thing about a new understanding... is less its novel content than the new freedom revealed by its appearance in the analytic space, a freedom to feel, relate, see and say differently than before. (p. 712)

These similarities illustrate instances where our approaches connect in meaningful ways. As I recognize the overarching compatibility of our worldviews, I am hopeful that continuing to explore the ideas of the pragmatic philosophical tradition will fruitfully provide ways of expanding my work with patients.

Experiencing With New I's Through New Relationships

Exposure to the ideas and traditions of other families, even closely related ones, can be enlightening. In my clinical work, I've been struck by the frequently encountered phenomenon of patients gaining new insights from their experience of entering into the families of their romantic partners. The nature of these insights can range from discovering novel ways of understanding their own experiences, recognizing different possibilities or ways of connecting, or gaining a new appreciation for their own family of origin. Sullivan wrote of the usefulness of interpersonal connections outside of one's family for similar reason (Sullivan, 1953). Similarly, these chapters were exciting in the ways they inspired different ways of thinking about how my "family" approaches the clinical problems we grapple with. Due to limited space, I want to focus on one idea in particular that is briefly presented by Bellehsen (this volume)—the development of "new self-states."

> There is a multiplicity of selves that the individual may come to embody, and the threat of trauma is that it challenges the overall system to adapt in ways that force a reorganization of the dialogical self system or demand *the development of new selves* in that system. It is the dialogical relations between I-positions that become strained. Dominant I-positions or hierarchies may become dislodged such that the individual feels in unfamiliar territory. Yet, as will be seen below, *the resilience of the individual lies in the ability of the dialogical self system to recruit other or new I-positions, as well as establish new dialogical relations between I-positions.* This is possible because of the multiplicity in the system. (p. 106, emphasis added)

At the heart of the interpersonal literature is the belief that "we are all much more simply human than otherwise" (Sullivan, 1953, p. 32). When we discover parts of our patients that we struggle to understand and connect with, our task becomes searching to connect with those unfamiliar parts of ourselves in the service of reaching our patients. It is a call for clinicians to not allow anything in the human experience to "be alien to us." This idea has always been compelling to me as it speaks to the responsibility and opportunity that comes with the work we do—to examine ourselves and grow in order for the work with our patients to progress (Wolstein, 1959). The struggle to access those parts of ourselves that we experience difficulty connecting with has sometimes been conceptualized as a painful process of reclaiming aspects of ourselves relegated to the realm of experience that is "not me." These parts of ourselves become disowned due to interpersonal trauma, where shame forced a turning away from those parts of us that threatened important connections with others. This narrative makes the implicit assumption that within us is the full range of human experience, a full complement of all potential self states and that it is trauma that raises the barrier of access to certain experiences.

In thinking about Bellehsen's statement above, I became intrigued by the idea of *new* self-states (not just newly accessible ones) as an important aspect of growth. Perhaps unformulated experience could include both: (a) those ways of being that have been unattended to and thus never coalesced in perception (and thus remained incoherent) as well as (b) those moments when a person is faced with something so foreign that it lacks coherence, not because of shame-derived dissociation, but because of its novelty. A patient of mine once spoke of participating in an interpersonal process group for mental health professionals. My patient is an extremely intelligent, sensitive, and perceptive young man. He is also highly educated, from a wealthy family, the very epitome of privilege in class, race, SES, and gender. In this group, my patient described being verbally attacked by a young African American woman who challenged his view of himself, the extent to which his achievements were deserved, and his assumptions about his relationship between himself and those around him. My patient described feeling disoriented by the experience. Making reference to Piaget, he reported being "unable to assimilate or accommodate" the information into existing narratives of himself. He left the group session feeling angry and misunderstood. Yet he was also able to sustain an impressive degree of curiosity. Much like the subtle tugs/snags that Stern (2004) described analysts experiencing when recognizing the presence of an enactment, my patient had the inkling that there was some other way of experiencing the world that teetered on the edge of his awareness. Within the context of a relationship where he felt respected and safe, he began to examine the familiar narratives that he had used to organize his experience around race, gender, and power. In doing so, he began to recognize inconsistencies and previously unattended to data that slowly coalesced into new narratives that could incorporate his growing awareness of the privileged place he holds within our society.

For my patient, this was an unfamiliar, disorienting, and disturbing experience. He described the odd (for him) feeling of being seen as "other." He spoke of an assault of assumptions that resulted in his prior sense of himself being annihilated. He further described a sense of powerlessness and invalidation in the face of another's perspective, which, in that context, was seen as more "valid." In some ways, that moment induced for him an experience recognizable and common for many marginalized individuals. Of course, any experience will have some reverberations to aspects of one's history and so for this patient, being experienced as the "other" was not entirely without a frame of reference. That said, despite his recognition of the ways this moment was reminiscent of some aspects of his history, he described experiencing it as a moment that evoked something previously unknown. The new narratives required to organize this previously unknown experience were not comfortable as they forced him to question his view of himself and the reasons behind the ways that others interact with him. Thus, this new way of experiencing himself and his relationships was, for him, "I" opening.

Moments like these can take many forms. They can range from the painfully traumatic, when a person's illusions of safety and security in his or her world is shaken to the opposite end of the spectrum, experiences like falling in love for the first time or the feelings that arise when one becomes a parent. I had a recent conversation with a colleague who posited that one of the reasons many people can feel so frightened of parenthood is that the stresses are all experiences that most people have some frame of reference for (e.g., sleep deprivation, responsibilities that limit freedom, interacting with irrational and/or frustratingly petulant people), but the joys are entirely different from anything previously known. More often, these experiences that expand the range of who we can be are less dramatic—a natural and subtle part of the process of "growth." Perhaps the experience of "fakery" that Dodi Goldman discusses can be thought of as a reflection on one part of this phenomenon (Goldman, 2007). In one of my favorite papers, Goldman discusses the anxiety that comes with the experience of transition between who we are and who we sense we can become. He describes the struggle with one's sense of inauthenticity that can accompany transitions and growth. Perhaps that new place one strives to reach could be considered a new "self-state."

My point, and the idea sparked by Belleshen's chapter, centers on the question of why experiences may be inaccessible. Certainly, there are those cases when an experience becomes dissociated because of the anxiety or shame that was evoked at some point in our development, where inattention prevents a coalescing into coherence. There may be other instances where experience is new because of a lack of exposure—whether because of one's luck at avoiding some of life's misfortunes or the ways one's cultural/societal/interpersonal experience has constructed a world view that has limitations or that a person has not yet lived through that part of being human.

DISTANT RELATIVES

Despite the similarities and new directions that these chapters inspired, there are also differences in understanding, tone, or emphasis between our approaches that I want to highlight. These differences are to be expected when looking across fields (and continents). Sometimes I felt a sense of disorientation reading material from a new field, and that must certainly have contributed to a sense that some of the ideas I encountered were alien. That said, as best as I am able to grasp them, there are instances where I think I see a genuine difference between how we hear, understand, and interact around the material a patient might bring to the consulting room. In the spirit of the interpersonal tradition, I hope to pursue and contrast the particulars of these differences.

Expanding Different Boundaries of the Self

In Chapter 4, Bellehsen describes his conception of "I positions" and examines parallels to Bromberg's idea of self-states. He labels these various positions in the following ways: "caretaker," "physician," "therapist," "parent, spouse, employer, businesswoman," "husband," and "anchor." As I read these labels, I wonder what it *feels* like to be that particular person at that particular moment. For example, "caretakers" may at some moments experience affection and devotion, at other moments they may feel resentment and anger, and in other moments that role may evoke feelings of mastery, power, powerlessness, guilt, loss, frustration, sadism, masochism, and so on. In fact, the individual caretaker will almost inevitably experience some complex and shifting admixture of these feelings depending on the context of what is happening in a particular moment and what it evokes for that particular individual. Thus, the experience of being a "caretaker" will vary significantly across person and time. What felt different about Bellehsen's "I positions" from Bromberg's self-states was the emphasis that Bromberg's concept places on *individual felt experience in a specific moment.* The concept of self-states, as I understand it, comes out of an exploration of the nature of self, specifically the illusion of cohesion and a movement towards a, "view of the self as decentered, and the mind as a configuration of shifting, nonlinear, discontinuous states of consciousness" (Bromberg, 1996, p. 112). Although the idea of delineating categories of self is theoretically interesting, what has always been most compelling to me about the concept of self-states is the emphasis it places on the importance of attending to the particulars of moment to moment *felt experience.* To me, self-states emphasize experience, particularly *affective* experiences in a particular instant, and contrasts with the more static social role of "I-positions." In my view, many of these "I-positions" require unpacking to explore the nature of the person's felt experience within that role at a particular moment. The self-state is not the role itself; rather, it represents a range of experiences accessible to the patient in that role at that time.

Many interpersonal theorists have identified the expansion of experiential possibilities as a key aspect of therapeutic change. Being cut off from aspects of our experience limits the range of ways that we can relate to the people in our lives. But the question of what is expanded must be grappled with. What we strive to expand guides the nature of the therapist's interactions and inquiry. When Bellehsen talks about role expansion, I hear it as an expansion of behavioral repertoires. This may in fact be incredibly useful, and some writers suggest that behavioral change can be a key ingredient in sparking new insight (Wachtel, 1993). Nonetheless, I see this as distinct from the idea of developing a capacity to hold multiple self-states simultaneously. For example, at one point Bellehsen (this volume) describes one patient adopting a "good patient" I-position so that when considering how to interact with his doctors he thought about

> how to be a *good patient.* How to ask the right questions? How to assess whether this doctor with whom I was meeting was a good person to go with?... How much to honor timeliness and pursue the surgery quickly versus go through a really methodical set of consultations?

Rather than defining the patient's self by these identified behaviors, I would feel drawn to unpack these behaviors associated with "goodness" and define the self based on the patient's subjectively felt experience (i.e., I would ask what it *feels like in that moment* to be a "good patient"). Does it bring a greater sense of power in taking charge of his care *or* does it bring a sense of panic, confusion, and uncertainty about how to proceed? Does it evoke fantasies of being cared for by his doctors as a reward for being so good *or* of being the one who is the decision maker and does not "need" anyone else? What is it like for the patient to be panicked or methodical? And what is going on when the patient begins to feel this way? What is the context in the patient's life or in his conversation with me that results in movement to this particular mode of experience? Does it happen in a moment when he feels misunderstood by me and thus represents an attempt to reconnect and elicit my help? Does it represent a communication about just how hard he's trying to be a good patient for me because he's worried about my capacity to stay with him in his despair (perhaps in a way that parallels worries he has about other relationships in his life)?

To return to my question of what is expanded, I think that the central difference between "I-positions" and "self-states" is the difference between an ability to take on additional "roles" ("I-positions") versus the capacity to have access to a broader range of felt experiences ("self-states"). It may be useful to expand the range of roles available but working with "self-states" focuses on the nature of the patient's experience around these roles. Perhaps in Bellehsen's clinical work, he does help elaborate on the specifics of the patient's experiences beyond what is ambiguously implied by these role labels. In fact, Bellehsen (this volume) does state that these models can be seen as "maintaining sensitivity to the felt experience of the whole individual, [as] it allows for addressing the nuances of experience through the parts of the self"; however, the case descriptions left me longing to know more about his patients' felt experiences. From my perspective, an inquiry designed to help patients articulate, elaborate, and expand the range of their experiences is not just part of what's done, it's at the heart of what's done.

The View From Different Fields

Above, I focused on my perception of differences in how to define the self that we strive to help our patients expand. I argued for an emphasis on the details of moment-to-moment felt experience over social role. But what aspect of felt experience is focused on and how does that felt experience arise?

Part of the reason I was drawn to the interpersonal literature is that I understand experience to be formed out of the feelings, hopes, beliefs, and desires that exist between people. This belief situates the *interpersonal field* as the context out of which all other experience is understood. In contrast, Weidenbaum's chapter discusses James' conception of "the field" where he states that the field is "a broader network of connections underlying and shaping our more explicit acts of cognition." He goes on to trace a shift that occurs in James' view of the field from "a structure of our mental life . . . the halo of felt relations surrounding our thoughts" to "the one complex substance from which the mind and the external world are constituted." Although the goal of this discussion is to explore a way of reconciling the notion of a decentered, contexualized self and an individualized, centered self with agency, this explication of James's notions of field are relevant to my point. In exploring the implications of this way of conceptualizing the field on the experience of self, Weidenbaum describes the notion that there's a material and spiritual self that is separate from the social (or interpersonal) self. This is not consistent with my view. The nature of my exploration of a patient's "material" or "spiritual" self would emphasize an attempt to understand the interpersonal context of material and spiritual aspects of that individual's experience. For example, I would wonder how the feelings evoked in the context of material or spiritual life serve as ways of guiding or reacting to anticipated interactions with others in one's present relationships or of remaining connected in some way to figures in one's relational past. Weidenbaum does discuss the *importance* of our "encounters with others," but this is different from experience being *defined* by encounters with the others.

The discussion of "external I" positions and "internal I" positions further illustrates the difference between a pragmatic perspective where "the interpersonal" is important to the field and my own perspective where "the interpersonal" constitutes the field. Bellehsen writes:

> The external I-positions are those that are felt to come from the environment, like an I-position of my daughter, while the internal I-positions are those that are felt as a part of the self, like an I-position as a parent. One can imaginatively embody either of these positions when negotiating the environment, such as purchasing a toy (feeling and considering the competing desires and demands as one moves from the daughter to parent I-positions). Additionally, the collective voices of culture may also be internalized as I-positions.

I would like to posit that the "external I-position" of "my daughter" is based on a construction of my daughter's experience arising from the details of *my* experiences with others. When my daughter is sad, my understanding of that sadness is driven by my own experience of sadness, longing, or loss with significant people in my life. Our capacity and experience of empathy is directly related to our experience of past relationships that evoke the feelings that need to be empathized with. Selma Fraiberg's

(Fraiberg, Adelson & Shapiro, 1975) moving account of helping mothers at risk of abusing their children illustrates this well. They write:

> We began with the question to ourselves: 'Why can't this mother hear her baby's cries?' This was a mother whose own cries have not been heard. There were, we thought, two crying children in the living room. The mother's distant voice, her remoteness and remove we saw as defenses against grief and intolerable pain. Her terrible story had been first given factually, without visible suffering, without tears.... She had closed the door on the weeping child within herself as surely as she had closed the door upon her crying baby. (pp. 395–396)

It is through the details of our own interpersonal histories that our experiences are constructed.

These experiences may not cleanly line up with one specific relationship. For example, my conception of "father" is constructed out of my experience with my own father and my reactions to him (e.g., rejection of or striving towards particular internalized aspects of that relationship), other fathers whom I observe, cultural constructions of what being a father means communicated through people in my life, and so on. It is through these consciously or unconsciously imagined relationships with others that my sense of "father" forms. I emphasize this point to encourage an inquiry into the details of a patient's interpersonal experiences that inform their sense of a particular "I-position." If we take for granted what "father" means to a particular person at a particular moment, if that line of inquiry is foreclosed too quickly by labeling "father" as a category of experience rather than the class of experiences to be explored, the nuance of what the experience of being a father for that particular person at that particular time will be lost. Bellehsen (this volume) does state that:

> The model of the dialogical self is one that is not only multiple but also socially constituted. In the above delineation of adaptive I-positions, one sees this social constitution through the adoption of positions like therapist, oncologist, husband, physician, parent, employer, and so on. The individual has developed these I-positions through interactions with others. Additionally, they are social in that they carry cultural representations that guide the actions and feelings of the individual.

This is an important point, but there is inconsistency between this insightful description of the social origins of the dialogical self and a lack of exploration of those origins. How do those *relationships* define the nature of that position for this particular patient? What does being a therapist, oncologist, husband, physician, parent, employer, and the like *mean* to this specific patient at this specific moment?

I argue for an approach to the individual's experience as multiply defined based an extremely nuanced sense of self, arising from specific interpersonal experiences. With this conception of self, one does not need to rely on the sources of novelty and uniqueness that Mead's concept of a "generalized other" is dependent on (i.e., different organizations based on their different position to the social whole or the uniqueness of the response of the "I"); rather, uniqueness arises from the fact that moment-to-moment interactions within relationships are unique and always changing. I believe it is real interactions, what really happens between people that define us—not a "generalized other" conception. Larger cultural systems act through individual (interpersonal) interactions and are viewed through the lenses created by earlier interactions. Thus, race, ethnicity, gender, sexual orientation, and so on may be approached this way. The "general" does not define one's experience (e.g., being an Asian American male can be experienced an infinite number of ways moment to moment and across different people); rather, the general serves to orient clinicians to an aspect of a person's interpersonal history to inquire into *in order* to understand that person's experience.

For example, Bellehsen (this volume) points out, "one's experience as a husband represents the internalization of the set of culture's attitudes and responses as a husband along with adjustments of the experience and expectations of engaging one's particular wife." Bellehsen suggests a particular organization of experience around a culturally defined social role, but to me culture is mediated by specific real relational experiences. So the experience of being a husband, father, or Asian American male is always based on the nuance of the specific feelings that are aroused in the specific context given my specific interpersonal history rather than being constructed out of culturally defined social roles. In some ways, this approach is alluded to in Salvatore's chapter (this volume) where it is stated that "meaning is a matter of positioning within a field of possibilities." I understand him to mean that potential meanings are defined by the combination of both the specific experience being evoked and the range of possibilities that the individual has access to given their unique history. So I would ask: What is that specific individual feeling in that role and how does their interpersonal history define the limits of what is felt?

THE VIEW FROM MY ANALYTIC HOME

Below, I present a case that focuses on the particulars of the interpersonal field in the hopes of illustrating some of the points discussed above. Beth, a 34-year-old Caucasian woman arrived in my office for consultation during my first year of training at the White Institute. She was in treatment with me throughout my five years at White, where my experience of her was constantly being shaped by the relationships I had with my teachers, supervisors, and my own analyst. The first time we met, I remember thinking of Beth as edgy—edgy in multiple meanings of the word: she had multiple tattoos; her hair (which evolved in color over the course of our work) was at the time an unnaturally bright, fiery red. Her clothes conveyed an attitude of combativeness that I associated with an artsy/creative crowd. But the look on her face revealed something else—a childishness, almost as if she was a kid playing dress up. Here is where the other meaning of "edgy" comes in—there was a skittishness to her and the sense that she seemed lost. The look on her face evoked in me a flicker of a memory of how I felt at 5 years old on my first day of elementary school, unsure of my ability to communicate, lost and scared, unsure of where I was supposed to go or what to do—my understanding of Beth's experience arising from my own history of related feelings.

When I asked her why she'd come to therapy, Beth said that she had been on antidepressant medication since college. She told me that the medication had been relatively successful at managing her anxiety and depression, but she did not understand why she was anxious or depressed. She began to cry:

> "What's going on for you right now?" I asked.
>
> With a shaky voice, she responded, "I don't know, I get this way whenever I have the space to feel anything, but I don't know why . . . "

During that first session Beth described often feeling confused about both her current experiences and her history. When I asked about the nature of her anxiety, she described being afraid she'd end up like her "crazy aunt." When I asked for details about her aunt, she said that she did not know what her diagnosis was or any details about her symptoms or care. When I asked about her family history, she told me that her mother had divorced her father because he was gay. When I asked for additional details about what had happened or the impact it had on her, she again said that she wasn't sure. In fact, she was not even sure how old she was when they divorced—"Maybe 2 or 3?" she said with a tone more question than answer. She said the fact that he was gay had been kept from her until she was in her late teens, but she could not remember how she had understood her parents' separation before then.

As we examined her experience in greater detail, we noticed a pattern in her narratives where her recognition of her own lack of knowledge would precipitate feelings of acute confusion and anxiety. As a teenager, she realized that she was supposed to do something to maintain the new BMW given to her by her father but never having been told what and afraid to ask, she felt constantly panicky each time she drove. She recalled not being told about sex so that at twelve she was terrified that she might get pregnant from masturbating. One of Beth's earliest memories was of wandering around her home, anxiously looking for her father and coming to discover that he had vanished. Beth's experience was of a world where she rarely understood how things worked, and the things she did not understand were far from trivial—people she loved could disappear without explanation.

In spaces of not knowing, Beth created fantasies, what she called "backstories" to make sense of the world around her. Often these backstories were not fully in awareness, but could be felt in ways that were disturbing because they were decontexualized. Beth filled these spaces of the unknown with terrifying backstories of rejection and abandonment. Following any rupture in her relationships, Beth would describe intense fear—a terror that if she did something wrong, even some small infraction, those she cared about most would reject and abandon her. Slowly, Beth began to recognize and articulate the backstory she had created about her father's leaving. A part of her had always believed that she had been unwanted in her family and that things were left unspoken to protect her from learning that her father's leaving was Beth's fault—a rejection of her. These beliefs had remained largely unformulated, too dangerous to fully acknowledge in part because they *felt* so true. What Beth saw was that asking questions, particularly about her father's absence, made her mother anxious. In these moments, the familiar backstory rushed in to fill the void of uncertainty formed in the wake of her mother's ambiguous anxiety. Later, we would come to understand that the more likely source of her mother's anxiety was the highly conservative community they lived in where the secret of why her parents were no longer together (her father's homosexuality) brought with it dangers of her family's communal rejection. For Beth, these realizations came much later and could not undo the ways that her backstories had informed how she continued to experience herself in relation to those around her. Exacerbating these anxieties was the family atmosphere where fear of knowledge was pervasive, so the clarity that would have relieved Beth's anxieties and guilt never came. Instead, she learned to refrain from asking the questions that would make those she loved nervous and to pretend to not recognize the gaps in her knowledge.

The Therapeutic Relationship and Curiosity

Donnel Stern (2012) has written about the importance of having a partner in thought, a witness that can be internalized to help make sense and meaning out of a person's experience. This is a concept that resonates with me. For Beth, it wasn't so much that she did not have a witness, but rather that the approach to witnessing that her parents took had a particular quality that impacted the nature of the meanings she could create. She internalized a relationship with a father whose love she believed was so fragile that any additional burden threatened to break their tenuous link. And she internalized a relationship with a mother whose concern was not an invitation to share and receive help understanding the world around her, but rather was a demand for reassurance that Beth was "fine." In fact, pressing for that understanding could evoke anxiety in her mother that in her mind threatened her mother's love and could lead, Beth feared, to being left utterly alone. We explored the unspoken rules that Beth believed existed in her family: the rule that she was supposed to figure things out on her own; that questions were not allowed because they made others anxious; that distress was something dangerous, something to be controlled and was devoid of meaning and needed to be eliminated rather than understood. Identifying these rules was a slow process, in part because they were not concrete things—they did not exist as a list posted on a bulletin board—rather these rules were communicated implicitly in ways far more confusing and insidious. My task involved helping her to make meaning of her feelings, to inspire curiosity about them. The underlying belief was that at the heart of psychoanalysis is, "The progressive awakening of curiosity, a movement from familiar chaos to creative disorder... the emergence, through curiosity and the acceptance of uncertainty, of constructions which may never have been thought before" (Stern, 1983, pp. 93–94). The creation of meaning and the stimulation of curiosity in and of themselves modify the nature of the feelings experienced. For Beth this meant that her experiences were no longer without a context and that rather than needing to run away from them, we could look at them together. In treatment, we strove to reignite Beth's capacity to think of questions and take a stance towards knowing that emphasized jointly creating meaning but holding that meaning lightly—an approach similar to that discussed by Salvatore (this volume). In my view, part of what inspires curiosity is one's attention to the details of the particular.

The Therapy Relationship and the Opening of the Patient's "I's"

Two years into treatment, Beth began a session talking about what on the surface seemed to be core issues of anxiety about fully investing herself in her work and relationships. Edgar Levenson writes about the frequent parallels between the content of the patient's material and the interpersonal process in the room with the therapist (Levenson, 2009). This useful idea has become so associated with Levenson that it's often referred to as a “Levensonian moment.” Thus, in that moment, despite the seemingly compelling nature of the content, I began to notice a lack of affect—the sense that neither she nor I were particularly invested in what we were talking about. I shared my impression with her and initially she expressed indignation,

> “I thought we were talking about important stuff.” I responded, “You’re right that the ideas we are talking about are very important, but I was noticing that you didn’t have much feeling as you talked. I notice myself really trying to get at what you were feeling, to imagine it as you’re speaking and I can’t seem to get there. And when I ask you about it, it seems like it’s hard to open up about the feelings you’re having. And I started to wonder if it’s hard to invest yourself fully in here, to really put yourself out there, just like what you said you’re struggling to do that in your other relationships and with your work.”

To her credit, Beth was able to recognize and acknowledge that she was keeping herself emotionally distant from me. We wondered together why that might be, and in exploring this, Beth began to inch towards connecting with and describing the pleasure she gets in having others “chase her” when she creates distance from them. She described their chase as reassuring. Beth also began to talk about her desire to have me chase her but with the caveat that she must never be caught, must always keep a certain distance. The thought of fully investing was terrifying to her. As we explored this further, Beth explained that fully investing would require being fully known, and in her fantasy to be fully known was to risk abandonment because the part of her that she could not tolerate me knowing, the part that she believed would drive me away, was the part of her that needed me. “I’m afraid that you’ll see me as needing help, that I’ve got serious problems, and I’ll need more help than you can give, that you’ll feel like I’m too much to handle and then you’ll have to send me to someone else; you’ll abandon me.”

Thus, her maintaining a distance was actually a way to remain connected, to demonstrate that she was “all right” and that she wasn’t going to be a burden and thus I need not abandon her. I recalled a fantasy that she described earlier in the treatment. After she saw another patient leaving my office, Beth told me that she imagined herself as one of my “easy patients.” Beth imagined my other patients as much sicker and requiring more care, and that our meetings were a “nice break.” This fantasy now made new sense as a reflection of her terror at burdening those she needed. She began associating to her aunt whom no one could help and who she ultimately saw as unreachable, abandoned and alone. “I’m so afraid of ending up like her. Even though I know I’m different.” Beth talked about trying to build a wall between her experience of herself and her fantasy of her aunt’s experience, disowning those experiences in an effort to protect herself. I encouraged her to expand on and explore this fear. In doing this, it became clearer that

Beth's aunt was her personification of "not-me," the aspects of herself that she could not and would not tolerate.

The emergence of those aspects of herself led Beth to psychically flee in terror as she "recognized" those feelings as harbingers of a breakdown like her aunt's. This is partly why her experience of her own affect could be so frightening. Feelings of anxiety and depression would evoke this underlying terror of an annihilation of herself and her connection to others. This terror overwhelmed her capacity to create other meanings and perverted the underlying wisdom Beth's feelings were trying to communicate. As she began to recognize that anxiety, despair, joy, and craziness are aspects of being human that exist in all of us, Beth began to own those experiences in fuller ways. Here, by keeping one foot in her newly gained sense of self and tentatively dipping a toe in this other, scary part of herself, Beth attempted to peer over the wall separating her from her aunt and to reclaim those parts that had been disowned. I believe that it was through inquiring into the details and particulars of her experience and helping Beth to articulate these specifics that she was able to look at the parts of her experience that she had previously ignored, create a more comprehensible narrative of her life and a greater connection to a broadened range of "her self."

REFERENCES

Bromberg, P. M. (1996). Standing in the spaces: The multiplicity of self and the psychoanalytic relationship. *Contemporary Psychoanalysis, 32,* 509–535.

Buechler, S. (2008). *Making a difference in patients' lives: Emotional experience in the therapeutic setting.* New York, NY: Routledge.

Ehrenberg, D. B. (2006). The interpersonal/relational interface: History, context and personal reflections. *Contemporary Psychoanalysis, 42,* 535–550.

Fraiberg, S., Adelson, E., & Shapior, V. (1975). Ghosts in the nursery: A psychoanalytic approach to the problem of impaired mother infant relationships. *Journal of the American Academy of Child Psychiatry, 14*(3), 387–421.

Frankel, J. B. (1998). Are interpersonal and relational psychoanalysis the same? *Contemporary Psychoanalysis, 34*(4), 485–500.

Goldman, D. (2007). Faking it. *Contemporary Psychoanalysis, 43,* 17–36.

Levenson, E. A. (1988). The pursuit of the particular: On the psychoanalytic inquiry. *Contemporary Psychoanalysis, 24,* 1–16.

Levenson, E. A. (2009). The enigma of the transference. *Contemporary Psychoanalysis, 45,* 163–178.

Mitchell, S. (1999). Letter to the editor. *Contemporary Psychoanalysis, 35,* 355–359.

Salvatore S. (2012). Social life of the sign: Sensemaking in society. In J. Valsiner (Ed.), *The Oxford handbook of culture and psychology* (pp. 241–254). Oxford, UK: Oxford University Press.

Stern, D. B. (1983). Unformulated experience— from familiar chaos to creative disorder. *Contemporary Psychoanalysis, 19,* 71–99.

Stern, D. B. (2004). The eye sees itself: Dissociation, enactment and the achievement of conflict. *Contemporary Psychoanalysis, 40,* 197–237.

Stern, D. B. (2009). Partners in thought: A clinical process theory of narrative. *The Psychoanalytic Quarterly, 78*(3), 701–731.

Stern, D. B. (2012). Witnessing across time: Accessing the present from the past and the past from the present. *Psychoanalytic Quarterly, 81*(1), 53–81.

Sullivan, H.S. (1953). *The interpersonal theory of psychiatry.* New York, NY: W.W. Norton.

Sullivan, H. S. (1970). *Psychiatric interview.* New York, NY: W.W. Norton.

Wachtel, P. (1993). *Therapeutic communication.* New York, NY: Guilford.

Wolstein, B. (1959). *Countertransference.* New York, NY: Grune & Stratton.

SECTION III

PRAGMATIC METHODOLOGY IN CLINICAL WORK

CHAPTER 8

THE PSYCHOSEMIOTIC MODEL FOR UNDERSTANDING THE BODY–MIND CONTINUUM

Implications for Epistemic and Psychotherapeutic Applications

Matti Keinänen
Finnish Student Health Services

The human mind is not a vase to be filled, but a flame to be lit.
—Plutarchos

In spite of the intensive study on the connections between the body and mind, their relationship has until now remained a dilemma (e.g., Damasio, 1999; Kandel, 1998, 1999). Different theoretical approaches touch on the mind–body problem, which are well described in recent articles (e.g., Damasio, 1999; Kandel, 1998, 1999; Kendler, 2001). These philosophical positions (Kendler, 2001) include: substance dualism, property dualism, type identity, token identity, functionalism, eliminative materialism, and explanatory dualism. However, there are no explicit and widely accepted answers to such issues as the origin of intentionality and meaning in the body–mind

Making Our Ideas Clear, pages 215–241
Copyright © 2015 by Information Age Publishing
All rights of reproduction in any form reserved.

problem. By the same token, the idea of a causal relationships between the body and mind and also the interconnections between the body and mind and psychotherapy have become unsettled.

This chapter discusses in depth a major psychiatric issue: namely, the understanding of the body–mind continuum and its connection to epistemology and psychotherapy practice from the viewpoint of psychosemiosis (Keinänen, 2001a, 2003). Psychosemiosis considers the human mind emerging through a coding method of signs in mutual interaction with the significant others. The four-stage symbolization-reflectiveness model has been developed to study the psychosemiotic process and its evolution in the human mind (Keinänen, 2001a, 2003). According to the symbolization-reflectiveness model, if the development of the psychosemiotic process is inhibited and/or disturbed, mental health disorders may result. Psychoanalytic psychotherapy offers the opportunity to work through the inhibited and/or disturbed psychosemiotic process. In this collective study of seven separate journal articles (Keinänen, 1997, 1999, 2000, 2001a, 2001b, 2002, 2003), the development of the stable personality from the borderline personality disorder in psychotherapy is examined.

The aim of the chapter is to show that:

1. Psychosemiosis offers a key to understanding the dilemma between the human body and mind.
2. The human mind emerges through the development of psychosemiosis, which means that the human mind binds the emotionally meaningful interaction with significant others by means of a coding system of signs.
3. The four-stage symbolization-reflectiveness model is suited for the study of the psychosemiotic process and its evolution in the human mind. Psychoanalytic psychotherapy has a curative effect on the development of the psychosemiotic process in the human mind.

Interconnections between the body–mind problem and psychotherapy have not been thoroughly explored. Accordingly, an additional goal of this chapter is to show how the body–mind continuum develops in psychosemiotic processes and, further, how to understand psychotherapy's curative effect. This is necessary, because psychotherapeutic treatment is the main treatment method for helping young adults develop a mature, coherent personality, which helps them function as an independent individual able to encounter the challenges of the adult life.

In the Practice Guideline for the Treatment of Patients with Borderline Personality Disorder (American Psychiatric Association, 2001), psychoanalytic psychotherapy is evaluated by means of the evidence-based methods as the treatment of choice. Patients with borderline personality disorder will need extended psychotherapy to attain and maintain lasting improvement in their personality, interpersonal problems, and overall functioning (APA, 2001). The APA concludes (p. 43) that the following is one main specific question that needs to be addressed by future research: What components of psychodynamic psychotherapy are responsible for its efficiency?

Psychosemiosis, creating the body–mind continuum, is one relevant component of the efficiency of psychodynamic psychotherapy, which in turn promotes the capacity for self-regulation. The capacities for self-regulation and meaning formation are the instruments of human mind that he/she uses to integrate the self experience and the experience from the outer reality, the significant other persons (Keinänen, 1997, 2001a).

THEORETICAL BACKGROUND

The Four-Stage Symbolization-Reflectiveness Model to Describe the Self-Regulation and the Meaning Formation in the Human Mind

One goal of psychic development is the ability to apply the basic skills of self-regulation, which is thought to be learned in relation to our first caregiver (usually the mother) (Kernberg, Selzer, Koenigsberg, Carr, & Appelbaum, 1989; Ogden, 1989; Stern, 1985) to other social relationships. These skills are internalized by means of psychic binding (symbolization) (Green, 1986; Keinänen, 1999, 2000; Peirce, 1960; Segal, 1957). Psychic binding means primarily that the person is able to contain information coming from inside and from outside the body together, creating first the affective base of the human mind. Thereafter, it is possible to label this affective base by means of symbols creating the emotional–cognitive part of the mind; this is clarified in detail in the following section.

The word "symbol" derives from the Greek word "symbolon," which literally means "a sign." Accordingly, this concept refers to the connection of two initially separate parts (symballein = to throw, bring together, connect) that creates a new entity. By means of a sign we try to describe a certain state of affairs or phenomenon. The sign itself is not related to the afore-mentioned phenomenon. It may be by nature either a completely private sign or decided by common consent (i.e., it is conventional) like linguistic signs. By symbolic function we mean the use of symbols, the fact that somebody, by using a symbol, aims at presenting some state of affairs or phenomenon with the help of it.

Charles S. Peirce (1960) put forth a tripartite division of signs describing the presentation of symbols and their different functions. The three types of representing signs are an index (an indicator or deictic element), an icon (a picture) and the symbol per se—a conventional symbol (e.g., a linguistic verbal or gestural sign). It must be noted that, while Peirce concentrated on the relation between a sign and sign's referent (object) in the outer world in creating his terminology, my present approach has a different point of view, namely focusing on the intrapsychic use of the signs. In this chapter the concept *symbol* is also used in a broader sense to cover all three types of signs. The term "conventional symbol" or "verbal symbol" is specifically used for the linguistic sign that Peirce called "symbol."

The three types of symbols are the instruments of the human mind, and they are clarified in more detail in the following section. The psychosemiotic model is visualized in Figure 8.1 to illustrate it schematically. We have also recently operationalized the four psychosemiotic modes of experience in order to make the model more understandable in order to specify the concepts so that they could be valid and reliable for use in scientific work (see Table 8.1, The operationalization of the four psychosemiotic modes of experience; Keinänen & Martin, 2010).

1. The *indexical experience* is the first mode of experiencing (Keinänen, 1997, 2000, 2001a). In this mode, the physical sensation in the body is transformed into an equivalent psychic form, which parallels the physical sensation, as smoke is related to fire. This means that the person is able to bind the information coming from inside and from outside the body together, creating the undifferentiated affective base of the human mind (see Figure 8.1 and Table 8.1).

The indexical way of experiencing does not differentiate between the self and the object, and it is estimated to have its origin in the first half year of life in the interaction with the mother. Stern (1985) speaks about generalized interactional experiences, which are, for example, created when the needs of the infant are repeatedly satisfied in the early interaction between the mother and the child. These generalized interactional experiences or the indexical experiences form the basic substance, the affective basic matrix of the human mind, so being all-inclusive (global) bodily affect states of mind. The indexical way of experiencing is also equivalent to the early body ego functioning of the mind (Freud, 1923/1961), the dream screen described by Lewin (1946), and the emotional tone described by Bucci (1997a).

2. The second mode of experiencing is *iconic experiencing.* This could be described as a continuous flow of pictures in the mind, like a silent film. This way of experiencing is represented by internal object relations such as our dreams (Lewin, 1946), in which the prevailing element is the visual-iconic nature of the mental imagery. So iconic experiencing includes immediate need-specific emotional mental images of self/other, expressed, for example, by fantasies and dream images. This immediate iconic mode of experiencing equally concerns oneself and the other and their emotional relationship.

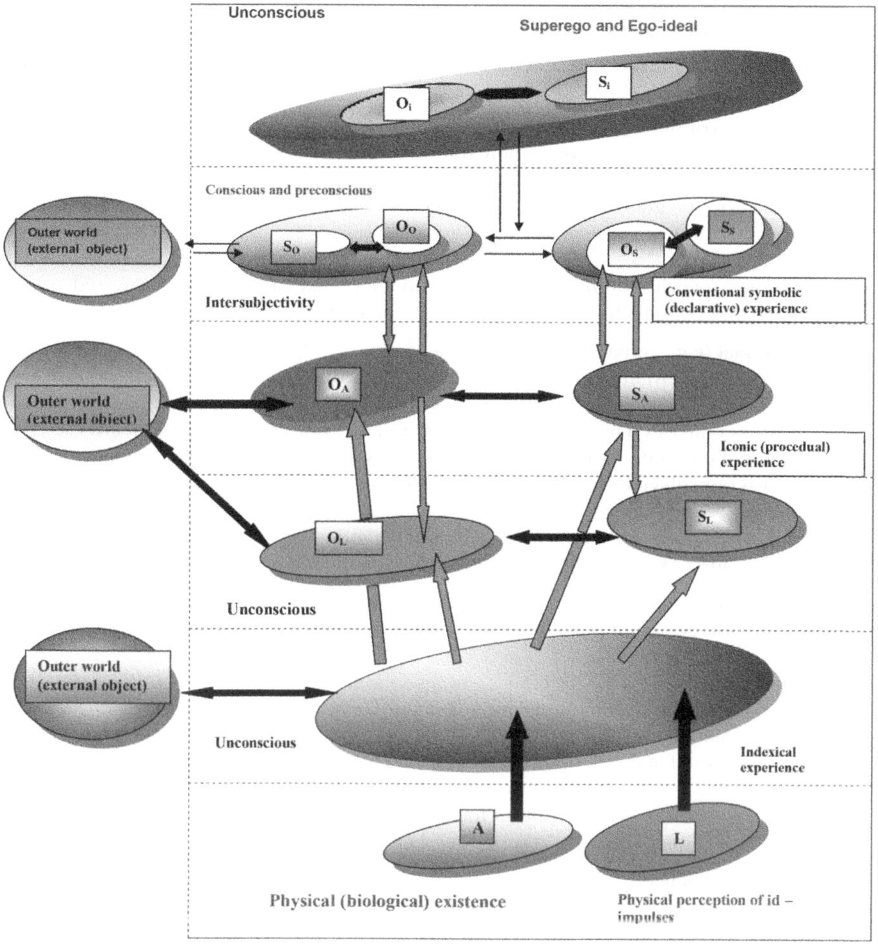

Figure 8.1 The psychosemiotic model of the human mind. Abbreviations: id-impulses; L = libido, A = aggression, S = self, O = object, S_L = iconic loved self, O_L = iconic loved object, S_A = iconic aggressive self, O_A = iconic aggressive object S_S = subjective self, O_s = object of the self, S_o = self of the object, O_o = object of the object, S_i = self-ideal, O_i = object-ideal.

The iconic mode of experiencing is similar to the procedural memory described by Fonagy (1999) and the introjects—that is, internal mental images of oneself and the other in the mind, which are frequently reviewed in the psychoanalytic literature (e.g., Tähkä, 1993,). Stern (1985) hypothesizes that the infant has the ability to differentiate experience already at the age of two months and relates this to the development of a core of the self. The iconic mental image level of experiencing can also be considered the

TABLE 8.1 The Operationalization of Four Psychosemiotic Modes of Experience

4. Reflective-integrative function

The capacity to consider the separate mental states of self and other in the mutual interaction with another person in time dimension.

Including

The capacity to integrate different experiences, including the ability to compare one's experiences with the experience of the other person.

Not including

Behavior and speech without reflective focus on affect states and verbally expressed emotional states of self and the other person in the mutual interaction

3. Conventional (e.g., verbal symbolic) experience

The mind creates conventional symbols to affects, emotions and thoughts.

Including

Verbal symbols are used by the subject to bind and describe different kinds of affects, emotions and thoughts. By means of verbal symbols one creates concepts, by which we can express our subjective (self serving) experience.

Not including

Behavior and speech without focus on affect states and need-specific, verbally expressed emotional states of self and the other in the therapeutic relationship.

2. Iconic experience

Emotionally laden iconographic, relationally bound mental states of self and the other triggered by the affect state.

Including

Immediate need-specific emotional mental images of self/other, expressed e.g., by fantasies, dream images and automatic behavioral patterns expressed e.g., by symptoms like cutting oneself and clothing styles expressing identity.

Not including

Behavioral patterns or speech without focus on affects and need-specific, nonverbal emotional states of self and the other in the therapeutic relationship.

1. Indexical experience

All-inclusive (global) bodily affect states of mind. The person expresses affectively in the therapeutic relationship how he/she is doing.

Including

Undifferentiated bodily affect states of pleasure (e.g., well being, gratification) or unpleasure (e.g., generalized anxiety, panic anxiety, oppression).

Not including

Behaviour or speech in the therapeutic relationship without focus on bodily affect states of mind.

equivalent of the visually perceived action in dream contents, taking place on the dream screen (Lewin, 1946). Also, iconic mental image experiencing corresponds with Segal's (1957) symbolic equation, the paranoid-schizoid position of Klein (1957/1975), and also the emotional tone described by Bucci (1997a). Once developed, there is a differentiation between the self and the object in contrast to the earlier undifferentiated indexical, affective experiencing.

3. The conventional (verbal) symbols can be integrated into the iconic mode of experiencing. *The conventional (verbal) symbolic experience,* for example, is represented by spoken or sign language, when verbal symbols are integrated with iconic images of oneself and the other; for example, this happens when we describe by words our manifest dreams. So this way of experiencing gives expression to immediate iconic emotional mental image ways of being. Thereafter, these three modes of symbolic experiencing are integrated in the mind to form a representation of oneself and/or the other.

Segal (1957) has distinctively separated the immediate symbolization (corresponding to the iconic mental image phase) and the symbolization proper (corresponding to the verbal symbolic phase and the depressive position of Klein (1957) in the psychic development of the child). The symbolic functioning proper (Segal, 1957) is related to the first separation–individuation phase of the child's psychic development and the achievement of a verbal capacity between 12 and 18 months of life in the interaction with the mother. Stern (1985) calls this phase of the psychic development the sense of a subjective self, to which the sense of a verbal self is integrated. The capacity for the full use of verbal symbolization is an important prerequisite for the individualization of the child (Keinänen, 1997, 1999; Tähkä, 1993). Also, the declarative memory function (Fonagy, 1999) is based on the capacity for verbal symbolic experiencing.

This *psychosemiotic* process takes place *epigenetically,* which means that the development of the previous mode (e.g., iconic experiencing—remaining also existing) is a precondition for the development of the following mode (e.g., verbal symbolic experiencing). Thus, in *symbolization, all the three described modes of symbolic experiencing are included (and remain existing),* emphasizing the evolving binding process in the body–mind continuum.

The abstraction capacity of Bucci (1997a, 1997b) corresponds with the conventional (verbal) symbolization. The three types of symbols are the instruments of the human mind, while the continuity of symbolic function as a whole is the breathing of the human mind.

The Reflective-Integrative Capacity

In order to understand how the meaning of symbolic function is manifested in the psyche, *the mind's reflective, observing capacity* (e.g., Keinänen, 1997, 1999) must be considered. During the development, the child learns the empathic manner the mother uses to relate to him/her and begins to apply this empathic capacity, to the introspection of the self and the internal world of the mother. The child thus develops a capacity to observe his/her own fantasy world and the psychic world of the other. Further, the child is able to integrate the representations concerning him/herself into one unity, the self. The separate representations concerned with the other are integrated into a unity, the object, usually the first representation being the representation of the mother (the emotionally important person of the child). Integrated images from separate self- and object representations are developed (see Figure 8.1 and Table 8.1; Keinänen, 1997, 1999; Kernberg et al., 1989).

The emergence and formulation of the reflective-integrative capacity in psychic development allows the child to observe his/her self and the other with his/her feelings and needs. The reflective-integrative experiencing separates him/her from the immediate, iconic mental image by way of symbolization (Keinänen, 1999, 2001a, 2003). This enables the development of the capacity to endure waiting and the ability to reflect oneself (Fonagy, Steele Moran, Steele, & Higgitt, 1991; Keinänen, 2003; Ogden, 1989, 1994b). The capacity to use historical memory also becomes possible at this time, which is central for time and history conceptualization. It is generally agreed that these capacities develop from 2 to 2½ years of age, and Stern (1985) relates them to domains of verbal and narrative relatedness. Thus, the reflective-integrative function includes the capacity to observe the indexical, iconic, and verbal symbolic ways of experiencing. It integrates them into a unity, forming a symbolic continuity (scc Figurc 8.1 and Table 8.1). The important property of the reflective-integrative function is the ability to reflect on the different ways of experiencing and the relational mutuality, unlike the indexical way of experiencing, which is only one-sided, deictic. The concept of reflective-integrative experiencing aims at describing the intersubjective, dialogical examination mode, similar to what Fonagy and his fellow workers (Fonagy, 1999, 2003; Fonagy, Steele, et al., 1991; Fonagy, Edgecumbe, et al., 1993; Fonagy, Gergely, Jurist, & Target, 2002), Ogden (1994a, 1994b), and Bollas (1987) have emphasized. The referential activity described by Bucci (1997a, 1997b) also corresponds with reflective-integrative function.

The modes of operating symbolic function, reflective-integrative capacity, and the formed internal object world, remain constant in the mind and are in a continuous dialogue with each other in a normal psychic process. It is the mobility between these three modes of symbolic function and the reflective-integrative way of observing the modes of symbolic function (Bollas, 1987; Ogden,1994a, 1994b), which constitute the prerequisite for and the indicator of psychic flexibility and adaptability (Keinänen, 2001a, 2003).

RATIONALE FOR STUDYING UNIVERSITY STUDENTS

Approximately 2% of the general population is thought to meet the criteria for borderline personality disorder (BPD) (Bateman & Fonagy, 2004).

The amount of BPD in the clinical psychiatric population is 10% and 15% from hospitalized patients. The proportion of BPD from personality disorder patients coming to treatment is 30–60%. Thus, BPD is clinically a serious problem.

BPD is a typical disorder having a deficiency of self-regulation capacity. Therefore, there is a great need for adequate psychiatric and psychotherapeutic help in this disorder, especially when the patients are young and have their adult life in front of them. All patients selected for the study were diagnosed according to the DSM-IV-TR as having BPD. In addition, they were also diagnosed according to Kernberg's classification (Kernberg et al., 1989) of having the borderline personality organization (BPO), which includes three main criteria: identity diffusion, primitive defences located around splitting, and the normal reality testing.

In the practice guidelines for the treatment of patients with BPD psychoanalytic psychotherapy is evaluated as the treatment of choice (APA, 2001). Patients with BPD need extended psychotherapy to attain and maintain lasting improvement in their personality, interpersonal problems, and overall functioning (APA, 2001). Thus, the treatment method for BPD in this study was psychoanalytic psychotherapy. The treatment frequency ranged from one to three sessions per week, and the duration of treatment was on average three years, but also longer if necessary (Keinänen, 2003, 2006).

The four-stage symbolization-reflectiveness model was used to evaluate the developmental stage of symbolization-reflectiveness capacity of the patients in the various phases of the therapy (Keinänen, 1997, 1999, 2000, 2001b, 2002, 2003, 2006; see Figure 8.1 and Table 8.1). A qualitative case research approach was used; each patient in the study (Keinänen, 1997, 1999, 2000, 2001b, 2002, 2003) was his/her own control. The developmental stage of symbolization-reflectiveness capacity in the various phases of the therapy was compared to that in the initial phase of the therapy, so it was possible to follow the progress of the treatment process.

The Scientific Basis of Psychotherapy: Qualitative Evidence Based Medicine, Circular Epistemology and Psychotherapy

The linear causality principle is currently the preferred epistemological vantage point for the prevailing trend of evidence-based medicine (EBM). The philosophy of EBM is logical empiricism, and the basic scientific conception is physical. The research method is according to natural sciences quantitative, using quantitative statistical methods (the qualification preconceives a great number of objects researched). Prospective randomized controlled double-blind studies are carried out. The influence of the researcher is essentially eliminated (at least that is the goal) with all kinds of methods in order to get reliable results with this approach. The empirical-experimental research method is indicated in psychiatry for research of biological psychiatry in which causality principle is linear: such as medicine studies. However, as will be shown, this principle is not applicable in psychotherapy research. The human mind and mental health are understood as a wholeness having psychic, biological, and social dimensions. The intrapsychic world constitutes the immediate basic experience, which includes the human being's ability to verbally communicate. Mental disorders are primarily disorders of experiential world (especially affects) independent of which frame of reference (biological, psychological) is used as the vantage point in the research (Bateson, 1979; Keinänen, 2006; von Bertalanffy, 1968). These issues are also illustrated in more detail in the thorough clinical case presentation in the following section.

According to the general systems theory (von Bertalanffy, 1968) the wholeness of a system is more than the sum of its parts. If one then tries to explain the phenomenon of experiential level merely by localizing it in some disorders in brain functions of metabolism (independent on how excellent the measuring device is, like positron emission tomography), there is an epistemic error: It is not possible to assign one part a causal influence vis-a-vis another, or put any linear markers on all. The anthropologist Gregory Bateson was known to say, "The brain does not think. What thinks, is a brain inside a man who is a part of a larger system residing in balance within his environment" (Bateson, 1979, p. 41).

New features of systems emerge at higher level of complexity that cannot be predicted from the more basic levels. With these new features come new properties. We need both the brain (the body) and the psychic functions to explain the wholeness of human mind: The mind without brain is brainless and the mind without psyche is mindless (Keinänen, 2006).

Bateson (1979) takes another example of the difference between kicking a stone and kicking a dog. In the case of the stone, the energy transmitted by the kick will make the stone move a certain distance, which can be predicted by the heaviness of the stone and by the force of the kick. But if a man kicks a dog, the reaction of the dog does not depend wholly on the energy of the man. Because the dog has its own source of energy, the outcome is unpredictable. What is transmitted is news about a relationship—the relationship between the man and the dog. The dog will respond in one of a number of ways, depending on the relationship and how it interprets the kick. It may cringe, run away, or try to bite the man. Furthermore, the behavior of the dog in turn becomes information for the man, who may modify his own subsequent behavior according to the dog's behavior. If, for instance, the man is bitten, he may think twice before kicking that particular dog again.

Communication and the relationship between the human beings come now to a crucial role. Bateson says that we need a new nonlinear grammar, a new language, to depict what is going on in the living world. This grammar Bateson (1979) defined as circular, giving the basis for *circular epistemology*. In this world the influences are not linear having causality: from *A* derives *B*. Instead, *A* may exert influence on *B*, but *B* thereafter may (or may not) influence on *A*. The reciprocal influences are interactive, recursive, and self-reflective, as was shown previously by Bateson's example of the individual emotional relationship between man and a dog.

These ideas have extraordinary implications for psychotherapy. The therapist can no longer be seen as impacting on the patient and the patient is no longer an object. Both are part of a system in which the therapist and the patient act and react upon each other in often unpredictable ways, because each action and reaction continually changes the nature of the relationship in which the therapeutic system resides. A circular epistemology forces the therapist to take account of the fact that he or she is inevitably part of this system, an inextricable element of that which he attempts to change (Bateson, 1979; Keinänen, 2006).

Therefore, we cannot conduct psychotherapy research using the linear epistemology of natural sciences. As we observe the psychic and lived experience phenomena, which are outside the direct observations of physical, sense monitored phenomena, *a circular epistemology, having interactive, recursive and reflective nature, is needed, because we observe the emotional fitting of both parties, the mutuality, the complementarity of feelings and the coevolution in the psychotherapeutic process* (Bateson, 1979). We need reflective consideration both in relational and in intrapsychic dimensions.

The transference-countertransference dialogue of the therapist and the patient now creates the basic structure of the treatment (Keinänen, 2006; Kernberg et al., 1989; Ogden, 1989). The research approach must be hermeneutic trying to understand the relationship between the patient and the therapist. From this position, idiographic qualitative research methods must be used, such as psychoanalytic psychotherapy case research studies. The scientific conception is humanistic, and the interest of knowledge is hermeneutic and emancipative (Habermas, 1971).

Because the nature of experiential phenomena is interactional and unique, we cannot directly observe large samples, but we must first observe single psychotherapy processes. Then it is possible to gather knowledge from the same kind of phenomena. Recurrence of the same kind of processes gives inductively generated knowledge of phenomena, which thereafter may be generalized and validated.

Each treated patient is at the same time the control patient. The change in the capacity level (the patient's ability to move in different levels of indexical/iconic/verbal symbolization- reflectiveness) is observed (see Figure 8.1

and Table 8.1). The gained research knowledge is received through a naturalistic research approach.

Linear diagnostics of symptoms (DSM) in psychotherapy is in the same position as pain and fever are in somatic medicine; if we treat the fever with medicine, we may lower the fever, but the background disease (the structural pathology) remains untreated. That is why it is important to understand the mind ontologically as a dialogic organ. The mind develops by means of psychic binding (symbolization) through the internalization of emotionally significant object relations. The emerged level of internalized object relations (the level of symbolization-reflectiveness capacity) determines the level of personality structure, which in turn is the relevant clinical vantage point for the realization of psychoanalytic psychotherapy.

RESULTS

The Psychosemiotic Development: The Development of Symbolization-Reflectiveness Capacity in a Typical Psychotherapy Process of Borderline Personality Disorder

A Clinical Example of Psychoanalytic Psychotherapy: The Lack of Developmentally Appropriate Self

Maria (pseudonym) was 19 years old when she came to therapy for the first time. She had moved away from home one year earlier. Maria is the youngest of the three children in the family; she is almost ten years younger than her older siblings. Her relations with the primary family have always been very close. She remembers her mother calling her the evening star and baby of the family. Despite this, her early childhood was tinged with a strange, endless feeling of emptiness. The only recurring image is that of her relationship to her mother; she is in a room with her mother, who is sewing or knitting something, but Maria cannot make contact with her, even though she tries very hard. She does not see her mother's face.

Moving to live on her own had been difficult for Maria from the very beginning. Although she wanted to begin her studies, she had a very conflicting attitude towards the choice of her special field. She found it very difficult to be alone in her flat, and she often went home to her parents in the middle of the week to escape the oppressive feeling. Consequently, Maria sought her way to the healthcare center for students in order to get rid of her anxiety.

We went through the evaluation phase, during which Maria described her extensive, oppressive feeling very openly. She felt that there was nothing but emptiness inside her, and when she was alone, her mind became seized with this emptiness, confusion, and fierce panic attacks. At that time, she did not have any peer relationships. Also, her contacts with previous schoolmates had broken. She felt that she was not strong enough to have contact with men, and especially not heterosexual relationships. The only contacts were with her family members.

Maria decided to start intensive therapy, and we agreed on a continuous therapy with two sessions per week. After her decision to come to therapy, Maria felt better for a while. During the therapy sessions, she described her overwhelming, oppressive feeling in many ways. Maria felt that she was empty, she was good for nothing and she would never become anything. She was unable to concentrate on her studies, and she spent her days waiting for the evening and going to bed. However, the oppressive feeling grew stronger in the evenings, and she could not sleep. In these situations, Maria often went home in the middle of the week.

In therapy, Maria did not feel strong enough or even willing to understand what caused the oppressive feeling. She wanted to get rid of it. The feelings of wanting to get rid of everything grew stronger towards the coming summer. The overwhelming, oppressive feeling appeared in two different ways—on the one hand, she suffered from a paralyzing, empty depression, in which nothing meant anything. On the other hand, the situation culminated in an explosive panic anguish, and she felt she was going to pieces. I connected these circumstances to her difficulty in being alone and to the coming summer holiday, but Maria's reaction was disparaging. She was not interested in what causes the circumstances—she wanted to get rid of them, whatever the price.

As the summer holiday approached, Maria remained in her flat lying and staring at the ceiling for several days. She canceled her therapy sessions, stating she was tired. Also during the therapy sessions, she occasionally sank into a state of stupor, staring with glazed eyes. I felt I had to pull her out of these circumstances: in general, by describing verbally what was going on in the therapy session at that moment. My own feelings after these sessions were mixed, and tinged by a deep feeling of helplessness and powerlessness. Our therapy was at a dead end. How could I help Maria, whom I felt to have a lack of age and developmentally appropriate self that would be able to deal with and master the demands of the female adult sexual identity? I decided to recommend that Maria visit another therapist in the hospital outpatient department during my holiday. This would also offer the opportunity for hospital treatment if necessary. After careful deliberation, Maria agreed to this.

How to Bear the Unbearable?

During my summer holiday, Maria visited the outpatient department of the hospital. There she was given bentzodiazepine medication when needed, which continued during the holiday. When the therapy continued in the autumn, she wanted to stop the medication. Maria told me about new symptoms that had appeared during the summer: she had begun to throw up. The bad feelings brought on by being alone culminated in her packing in all the food she could and then throwing up. After vomiting, she felt completely empty and feeble, but the oppressive feeling was gone for a while. In the middle of the dead-end feelings she was also thinking of suicide; she planned to take an overdose of medicines. I showed her the connection between throwing up, thinking of suicide, being alone, and the dead-end feelings. In an emergency, she could use them to get rid of the oppressive feeling that she thought was extremely difficult to process and work through in therapy. Maria listened to what I said and made a comment: she had two alternatives—she would either kill herself slowly by vomiting or do it quickly by taking a medicine overdose. I thought that there was also a sexual content in her vomiting because she could not let herself masturbate. Her sexuality was mainly oral, enabling the need satisfaction through bulimic symptoms.

I repeatedly felt overwhelmed by total irresolution and helplessness: I am observing an inevitable course towards destruction, and I cannot do anything. I was pushed forward by only one feeling: there was no alternative. If we gave up, Maria would then be more likely to kill herself. I decided to follow her into this unbearable emptiness by verbally describing how I understood her emotions. My identity as a therapist was put on trial in many ways. Am I doing the right things in her therapy? Am I a poor and unsuccessful therapist, since I cannot help her in a more concrete way? I find it particularly clarifying that these thoughts taxing my self-esteem are informative. They describe what the patient feels, and we can use them to give an image of Maria's undifferentiated anxiety.

The Creation of a New Structure

During the winter of the second year of therapy, we went through the psychic empty space of Maria. During this time, she attended the therapy regularly, but she aimed to show—in a variety of ways—how she had lost all the opportunities of her life and there was only the question of how she would die. Nevertheless, I occasionally had a feeling that talking about death involved a new kind of tone—she needed these thoughts to find her way to new things. Maria denied such confrontations and usually reacted by being absent from the next session or showing bulimic symptoms.

Therapy breaks were difficult. She either caught a cold before them and was absent from the session, or she caught a cold just after the therapy break. In these situations, she continued to go home to her parents.

However, now she had at the university two female friends whom she met rather regularly. She was also charmed with a male study mate, but he was dating another girl. Being outside from their relationship was for her very difficult to think about and to accept. She thought the man did not like her, which is why they could not be together.

Before the second summer holiday, the blood curdling feelings of anguish came back. On many days, she remained lying in her bed, staring at the ceiling and thinking of death. I connected the anguish and wishing to be dead with the coming summer holiday from therapy and the crisis of being apart and being alone. It is better to die than to go through the hard feelings related to separation from me. I also found that it was difficult for her to trust that her therapy would continue after the summer holiday. Maria listened to what I said but then said indifferently—that doesn't affect me. We agreed that she would visit the hospital outpatient department during my summer holiday. All the time during our sessions, I had the feeling that Maria could not yet contain her feelings of emptiness as a manifestation of separation anxiety from therapy.

The Feeling of Emptiness as a Mental Image Guiding the Treatment—Maria's Break into the Experience of Self

When Maria came to therapy after the second summer holiday, she was different. She was depressed, but simultaneously present in herself in a new way. For the first time, I had a feeling that she understood what I said, while stopping to listen to her own inner world. Depression radiated from Maria in a variety of ways: she was pale and spiritless. The therapy sessions now became hard in a different way. During many sessions, she was quiet for a long time and did not talk spontaneously. Although the sessions were full of melancholy and tinged with feelings of loneliness, I felt relieved about the change that had taken place. I had a feeling that Maria participated in the therapy as a subject—from then on we were two partners. Only later did she tell me that she had just met Jack, her husband-to-be. I thought that the meeting of Jack gave Maria a possibility to begin to contain and to process her earlier uncontrolled separation anxiety in addition to her work in the therapeutic relationship.

I spoke about the change with her. She had had the courage to settle down in a heterosexual relationship with Jack. I also pointed out how it has been difficult for her to speak about her affects towards me. I said, "Could it be possible that you are afraid of me because I am a man?" She identified the feeling of fear of me and the urge to run away. I had a feeling that the urge to run away was related to a new kind of fear, the fear of nearness. She could now be in contact with affects elicited in the therapy relationship. I described to Maria that she seemed to be listening to her feelings in a new way—at the same time, therapy has become important for her in a new way, which may frighten her. Maria commented on her vulnerable feelings: If she talks about them, she's afraid that they will turn against her. I said: "You're wondering whether you can trust me. If you come closer, if you venture to need, will I receive you or will you be rejected?" Maria was moved to tears by my comments, and I let her unburden herself. Although I did not at that moment say anything, there was a feeling that we understood each other. Even though the subsequent therapy was also tinged with feelings of loneliness, I felt that we could now study loneliness feelings together to find out about the nature and cause of them.

The above-mentioned change in therapy was epochal in many ways. Maria had ventured to settle into herself. She no longer needed to escape her inmost feelings, although she had a long way to go in analyzing the feeling of emptiness, the core affect of identity diffusion and depression. The question that now came into focus was how we could understand Maria's feeling of emptiness.

Her mind was flooded with memories from her childhood, especially memories connected with her relationship to her mother. She saw her mother either doing something on her own or sitting frozen, keeping to herself. I interpreted to her, how during the evaluation phase of the therapy, Maria described this same scene. Maria remembered that she could not get a contact with her mother. A noteworthy fact about these mental images was that she could not catch her mother's face, and there was no feeling of togetherness and attachment between them—this was the endless feeling of emptiness. I asked her what she thought about not remembering her mother's face. Maria experienced something very oppressive in it. She looked at the floor, she turned pale and started feeling nauseous. I asked her whether she was possibly afraid of looking her mother in the face, because she would have seen her being depressed. Maria momentarily managed to catch an image of her mother's face, which looked gloomy and inexpressive. She felt that at that time, she did not mean anything to her mother—everything was empty and purposeless. Maria then had a feeling that she was a burden to her mother. We were familiar with such transference feelings in our therapy sessions. Maria felt that she was a burden to me, too, and therefore it would be better if she were dead. These findings in the therapy created a feeling of relief and satisfaction in her for the first time during the working process. This sense of relief was a recurring feeling thereafter for her when finding new matters in the therapy process, such as when studying her relationships to other family members. Although the findings as such were not pleasant, it came to my mind that a person may take pleasure in finding the truth.

Diagnostically one can say that she moved from a borderline personality organization to a neurotic inner world. I saw that Maria had found a core adult identity in her closing the adolescent development. She had reached the psychic individuation and the adult sexual identity, which provided a new kind of an enduring pleasure in her.

DISCUSSION

The First Part of the Therapy—The Indexical and Iconic Symbolic Process

At the beginning of the therapy, Maria was in an imminent adolescent breakdown situation. She was unable to keep in mind and to process her own separateness in her internal object relationships when she was alone. This indexical way of experiencing (see Figure 8.1 and Table 8.1; Keinänen, 2000, 2006) was expressed as an unspecified, overwhelming, oppressive feeling, which seized her when she was on her own. To eliminate this feeling, she tried to empty her mind (Keinänen, 2000, 2006). In therapy, attacks on linking (Bion, 1959) appeared as the feelings of emptiness and culminated in states of stupor prior to the separation from me for the summer holiday. She expressed this by staring with glazed eyes during the sessions—by withdrawing from our therapy emotional relationship. Another important factor in Maria's wish to get rid of indexical feelings was to eliminate the dangerous instinctual—that is, sexual and aggressive—contents of her mind. Thus, at the beginning of the therapy, she mainly experienced things through indexical symbolization—or by eliminating feeling emptiness. Wilma Bucci (1997a) has illustrated the same mode as the subsymbolic nonverbal emotional schema.

Being unable to experience her own separateness, she was lacking an age- and developmentally appropriate self that would be able to deal with and to master the demands of the female adult sexual identity. During the second year of therapy, Maria began to show new symptoms by throwing up and using suicidal images. By vomiting, using her physical ego indexically, and by suicidal images she aimed to actively eliminate the feelings of separation and isolation that seemed unbearable. Compared with previous total attacks against her own experiences, her vomiting and suicidal mental images now included an attempt to process the feelings caused by separation at an iconic level of the symbolic process (Figure 8.1 and Table 8.1; Keinänen, 2000, 2006). Vomiting seemed to be clearly connected with the handling of separations, and it was no longer just a random, physical enactment. At the same time, as a compromise solution, she also could get a certain satisfaction to her sexual needs through oral route, by means of bulimia, because she could not masturbate and she had no heterosexual relationships.

Wilma Bucci (1997a) has also systematically described these same indexical and iconic phenomena. In her multiple code theory, she calls the corresponding modes subsymbolic nonverbal (in my work indexical) and symbolic nonverbal (in my work iconic) modes of communication.

The Transition to Using Reflective-Integrative Function and its Therapeutic Significance

The transition to using reflective-integrative function is preceded by certain signs, and the actual transition in the psychotherapy process appears more clearly after the second holiday break. In the spring of the second year of therapy, there were hints of a change in her manner of speaking, although she still talked about suicide as a way of getting rid of her painful feelings of isolation and separateness and also from her sexual desires.

Maria now became capable of controlling her anguish in a new way. The tone of her voice and her way of using words took on a new emphasis. They no longer had the same, nonverbally sensed tinge of hopelessness and no alternatives, which was characteristic of her previous manner of speaking. The change in Maria's voice involved a first clear sign of her evolving feminine body self. These iconic ways of using the voice and speech (Figure 8.1 and Table 8.1), which are significant in the therapy and analytic process, even if difficult to reach, have also been described with distinction in the psychoanalytic literature by Bollas (1987) and Ogden (1989, 1994a, 1994b).

The actual transition to the use of the reflective-integrative function came clearly to the fore after the second holiday break. It is often connected with situations where there is some crisis in the psychotherapy—however, this change need not necessarily be as dramatic as in Tim's therapy (Keinänen, 1997, 2006); the gradual change is seen in Maria's therapy. She began to use the reflective self (Keinänen, 2000) after my second summer holiday.

Where had this crucial change in psychic development originated? In a psychic and psychotherapeutic process, the different levels of the symbolic process are present all the time (Keinänen, 2000). Each therapy session is stored in the patient's mind through internalizing symbolization and they form the basic matrix of mind, including indexical feelings of both pleasure and oppression. My calm and clear basic attitude as a therapist was stored in Maria's mind as an indexical feeling of well-being. The iconic images of herself and me differed from this indexical matrix (Figure 8.1 and Table 8.1). The iconic images were in the therapy relationship bound to the direct and immediate experience of my presence (good iconic images of me) or absence (bad iconic images of me) during the second individuation process. Corresponding good and bad images of herself and the mother were already intrapsychically present in her, deriving from her first individuation process with her mother. During the two years of therapy, these images were gradually developed, strengthened, and balanced in a new way in Maria's mind. During the second year of the therapy process, she developed especially bad self icons and object icons of me with bulimic and suicidal symptoms.

As a therapist, my role in this therapeutic dialogue was to describe Maria's experience empathically as exactly as possible (Keinänen, 2000, 2006) while keeping my calm attitude all the time. At first, Maria internalized my attitude from repeated therapy sessions as a generalized, tranquilizing experience of interaction, which during the second year of therapy began to appear as softer iconic tones in her voice even before any change could be observed in the contents of her speech and in the development of reflection. The internalization of my empathic way of imaging was connected to this process and influenced on the emergence of Maria's own reflectiveness. Consequently, she could herself grasp and give a name to the previously chaotic, unidentified feelings of oppression.

The above-illustrated internalization which proceeded epigenetically through a symbolic process (Figure 8.1) culminated in the second break for a summer holiday. At that time, Maria initiated a heterosexual relationship with Jack, which contributed to her better integration offering a possibility to the full sexual satisfaction in a love relationship. The relationship with Jack assisted in her settling into herself and so in her adopting the reflective self (Keinänen, 2000).

When Maria could simultaneously find me sufficiently reliable as a therapist—as a result of my return after repeated breaks as agreed and of my putting up with her aggressions and despair, while maintaining the role of a therapist—she began to reflect her feelings, internal object relations, and inner world herself after the second summer holiday. This change took place while Maria was identifying with my reflective-integrative function. Thereafter, she adopted it permanently as her own structure. Since then, the changes achieved were also the result of the verbal interpretations, especially of Maria's fear of abandonment and non-acceptance in the therapeutic relationship.

The psychic change was impressive in many ways. From that moment on, Maria lived inside herself and was present in the therapeutic relationship as herself. She was calmer, more considerate and stable. Nevertheless, Maria still suffered from depression, which was now different, less tense, and also involved opportunities. Maria developed an ability to listen to and to study her personality here and now, as well as on a time axis. For example, she began to explore the origin and history of her depression, which was illustrated by the important findings of her relationship to her mother. Remembering mother's depressive face showed that she could now integrate verbally and reflect the iconic mental images of her depressive mother and herself when she was child: After working through this, she could recognize the psychological presence of the depressive mother in her childhood.

Feelings of sorrow and happiness became significant to Maria in a new way. She constructed realistic views of her parents in her mind and could compare them to her earlier created internal images. She realized what she had lost during the early years of her development and could genuinely and realistically examine the defects in her parents, but also their limited ability to show love and affection.

The reflective-integrative ability adopted by Maria was a relieving experience for both of us, as well as giving me pleasure as a therapist. From that point on, I had a partner to cooperate with in a shared world of experience (Keinänen, 2000, 2006) continuing until the agreed termination of the therapy.

Two and half years after the termination of the regular therapy, Maria contacted me. She had become a mother of a son who was now four months old. She had temporary difficulties in handling with all the responsibilities of motherhood, but otherwise she was doing well. She had maintained the mobility to use symbolization-reflectiveness freely when working with her psychic difficulties. So, she had gone through the closing phase of the adolescent development that she was undergoing during her therapy.

Symbolization-Reflectiveness Model and the Borderline Personality Organization

In the treatment of BPD, the other person (therapist, the caregiver) becomes bound to the patient's mind by means of the symbolic process and her mind stabilizes: The symbol draws to the mind the caregiving other and the patient can now keep the therapist in her mind independent on his physical presence. Verbal symbolic function contains within the mind the present experience of the other person, which may then be recalled (see Figure 8.1 and Table 8.1). A person becomes capable of waiting for the physical seeing of the significant other without being always physically present. She can by symbolization-reflectiveness transform her bodily needs into psychic desires, wishes and longings for another person. Separation anxiety of a borderline personality patient is from this viewpoint an insufficiency of the internalization of the tranquilizing other by means of symbolic function, as described in detail in the previous clinical section.

The capacity for self-regulation develops so that the mind binds the immediate experience first in the undifferentiated, indexical form, and then in the iconic, pictographic form, where the self and object are differentiated according to patient's need states. When the patient adopts the capacity to use reflection and verbal symbols for his feeling states of neediness, the mind disentangles itself from the chains of immediate experience. In the treatment of BPD, the person can differentiate his own immediate experience as his own experience by means of developing reflective function (Keinänen, 2000, 2006). This is crucial for the development of self-regulation. The patient no longer needs the other person to be present all the time: The capacity to be alone develops, when he can by means of symbolization call to the mind the absent person and maintain his psychic balance (Keinänen, 2006). So we can understand psychoanalytic psychotherapy's effect as a curative treatment of personality disorders, which offers a possibility to adopt the appropriate symbolization-reflectiveness capacity and therefore the capacity to self regulation and to the integrated identity.

The achieved psychotherapy knowledge becomes a vantage point when we are going to treat a new patient of the same category.

CONCLUSIONS

D. Sackett, one of the founders of EBM, hoped that it could trace the best possible evidence, by means of which we can ourselves evaluate our treatment practices and then be responsible for the adequacy of treatment methods (Sackett, Richardson, & Rosenberg, 1997). The aim of EBM is to connect the best available evidence to the clinical experience so that we can select for our patients the treatment which is most appropriate for them.

Thus, the following methodological conclusions for EBM from this work are drawn:

1. The descriptive diagnostics of psychiatry (today DSM-IV) describe symptoms, not background factors behind them. Therefore, it is problematic to use changes of symptoms as a substantive form of evidence when one evaluates evidence in all kinds of psychiatric treatments, especially in psychotherapy.
2. Using diagnosis according to symptom categorization of the DSM, EBM today uses the gold standard principle that one can study the object objectively without being a part of the observed phenomenon. In the psychotherapy research this is not true, because the observer is always a part of the observation. The therapist (and also the outside observer, if used in research) always influences to findings obtained with his own action/reaction.
3. We must take into account in psychotherapy research the structure of the human mind from the viewpoint of internalized object relations, which means that the mind is ontologically a dialogic organ. The human mind belongs to the area of circular epistemology, sepa-

rate from natural sciences, which often belong to the area of linear epistemology.

4. Due to the difference of epistemology, we must use principally qualitatively based methods of evidence in psychotherapy research in contrast to principally quantitatively based methods of evidence in natural sciences (Keinänen, 1997, 1999, 2000, 2001b, 2002, 2003, 2006).

The Four-Stage Symbolization-Reflectiveness Model for the Understanding of the Body–Mind Continuum

Scientific knowledge is based on unification, not on fragmentation of knowledge. The life sciences form two major domains: one extending from molecules to organism, the other from psychology to sociology. The aim of this work has been to present a scientific model to bring together the body and the mind, the body–mind continuum.

Representations in neuroscience (e.g., feature maps of the parts of the body, like the brain) and those in psychotherapy (e.g., body images) are distinctive. Thus, their data-coding mechanisms are different. My aim has been to present a new psychosemiotic model to describe how in the body–mind continuum the information is coded.

How is it possible to understand the body–mind continuum by means of the psychosemiotic model? At the bottom is biology: The body can be mindless, at least without consciousness, but the mind cannot be without a body, which is the base for the emerging body–mind continuum. The coding system of three signs (index-icon-conventional symbol) has a central role in the binding of originally physical perceptions into a psychic form. The lived experiences of our relationships with our significant others are stored into memories of mind by means of the epigenetically developing capacity for symbolization-reflectiveness. The aim of this study of symbolization-reflectiveness has been to construct a map to describe the continuum between body and mind. In normally functioning mind, there is a body–mind continuum, contrary to mental health disorders where this continuum fails.

Some Implications of the Four Models of Experiencing in the Body–Mind Continuum

1. The Indexical Experiencing

The indexical experiencing is formed by means of conaesthetic function (described by Spitz, 1965), which collects together the information coming from the inner world (internal tensions through the proprioceptive sense) and from the outer world (through the five senses of sight, hearing, smell, taste and tactile sense; see Figure 8.1 and Table 8.1).

The example of this elemental experience is the gratification that an infant experiences when being breastfed. The warm milk (from the mother sensed by the tactile sense) transforms the tension of the body (hunger sensed through the proprioceptive sense) into the undifferentiated indexical pleasure experience—creating gratification through the relief of tension. From these repeated good sucking experiences, a permanent indexical memory structure is created.

This same phenomenon has been described by Salonen (1989) by means of the concept of primary identification. Primary identification is formed by the mutual identification of infant and mother. This identification is thereafter intensified in parallel with the emergence of the first autonomous self-experience, when the organization of the core self begins to detach itself from the maternal environment. Salonen emphasizes that primary identification can be seen as a threshold phase from undifferentiated towards differentiation, and it forms the step that creates coherence and leads the infant to an integrated personal unity.

Disorders of indexical experience may implicate themselves in specific psychotic disorders. In schizophrenic psychosis, the experience of the primary identification (a coherent indexical experience) is broken down, and it must be restored in a good relationship between the therapist and the patient.

2. The Iconic Experiencing

The prototype is the diacritic function (Spitz, 1965), which forms the iconic experience and further, by means of conventional symbol (cognition), the conventional (verbal) symbolic experiencing (see Figure 8.1 and Table 8.1). The iconic mental image world of experiencing contains the person's private world of her needs and wills, and it is immediate, unconscious, without proper reflection. When this mode of experience prevails, the person acts immediately, impulsively, and without a capacity to differentiate herself from the experience. In this work, the aim has been to describe that when there is not yet a fully developed verbal symbolic capacity with the capacity for reflection of iconic mental image mode of experiencing, one consequence is borderline personality organization. When this occurs, the iconic mode of experiencing prevails (including of course epigenetically indexical experience). In the successful psychotherapeutic process borderline personality disorder is transformed into a more stable personality configuration (Keinänen, 1997, 1999, 2000, 2001b, 2002, 2003) when the patient gradually adopts the symbolization-reflectiveness capacity by means of psychotherapist.

3–4. The Conventional (Verbal) Symbolic Mode of Experiencing With Reflecting-Integrative Capacity

The capacity for the full use of verbal symbolization is an important prerequisite for the individualization and the capacity for object constancy of the child (Keinänen, 1997, 1999, 2000, 2001b, 2002, 2003). So the continuity of symbolic function is the breathing of the human mind: the essential part of the body–mind continuum. The reflective-integrative experiencing separates a person from the immediate symbolization. The capacity to endure waiting is created, as well as the ability to reflect oneself and the other here and now, as well as the changes in oneself and the other in a time dimension. The capacity to use historical memory becomes possible, which is central for time and history conceptualization (Keinänen, 2006).

Thus, the reflective-integrative function includes the capacity to observe the indexical, iconic and verbal symbolic ways of experiencing. It integrates them into a unity, forming a symbolic continuity. Its important property is the ability to reflect the different ways of experiencing and the relational mutuality, unlike the indexical way of experiencing, which is only one-sided, deictic (see Figure 8.1 and Table 8.1).

The classical example of the reflective function is Rene Descartes' *cogito ergo sum*—I think, therefore I am. This expression is reflective, but it does not yet take into consideration the other person—the dialogical nature of human mind, which becomes possible in the proper verbal symbolic experiencing. Thus, the problem in *cogito ergo sum* expression would not be the body–mind dualism but that it does not reflect the reality of significant others. In the dialectic world of the mind Rene Descartes' *cogito ergo sum* can be transformed to a new variation (Fonagy, 1999, 2003; Fonagy et al., 2002): "My caregiver thinks of me as thinking and therefore I exist as a thinker."

The emphasis, in the concept of the reflective-integrative function, is intersubjective, dialogical examination mode. Reflective functioning may recognize also only iconic experiencing (without words): then the reflection is from inside, like the contents of a dream. However, when dreams become verbally reflected, icons become conscious forms (symbols), contrary to unconscious iconic experiencing (described in the mode of iconic experiencing earlier having no availability to reflection, like in borderline states). Correspondingly, Freud (1923/1961) speaks about manifest and latent dreams. In the unconscious mode of iconic experiencing, they are in the normally functioning mind out of reflection. As described in this work, in borderline personality organization iconic experiencing may express itself, for example, in an immediate action.

The disorders of the mode of verbal symbolic experiencing with the capacity for reflection include neurotic disorders; there is the developed capacity to symbolization- reflectiveness (including integrated identity), but there are intrapsychic conflicts (Freud, 1923/1961) that inhibit the normal function of the human mind. Then the aim of psychotherapy is by means of symbolization-reflectiveness capacity to get insight into these (often sexual) repressed intrapsychic conflicts, and when the patient becomes aware of these conflicts he can disengage from them.

It is important to remember that the three modes of experiencing described are precisely that—modes of experiencing; they do not as such tell anything about whether there is a mental disorder or not. The normal functioning of human mind includes all these three epigenetically developed modes of experiencing and the reflective-integrative capacity as a functional continuum, the body–mind continuum.

In conclusion, the whole body–mind continuum evolves according to the epigenetic emergence principle. We can compare the evolution of the human mind to weaving fabric, which metaphor of mind Enckell (2002) has also used. The psychic matrix (weave) is woven by means of symbolization like a fabric. The previous mode of the symbolization (like the iconic mode) is a warp to which a weft of words (conventional symbols) is integrated: so the mind (weaver) weaves the web and the body–mind continuum is created. By these means, the originally physical needs are transformed in the mind into psychical desires and wishes.

The symbolization-reflectiveness capacity and the internal object world thus formed remain constant in a normal psychic process. It is the reciprocal mobility between the three modes of symbolic function and the reflective-integrative way of observing the modes of symbolic function that constitute the body–mind continuum and is the prerequisite for and the indicator of psychic health.

This work, which offers the psychosemiotic key by means of which we may conceptualize and map the bridge between the body and mind and understand the body–mind continuum as well as its development in a successful psychotherapy, is thoroughly presented in the book *Psychosemiosis as Key to Body–Mind Continuum. The Reinforcement of Symbolization-Reflectiveness in Psychotherapy* (Keinänen, 2006).

ACKNOWLEDGEMENTS

Grant support: the grants from Finnish Student Health Service and from Finnish Psychiatrist Association. I wish to express my deepest gratitude to Docent Ilpo Lahti, MD; to the chief psychiatrist Kari Pylkkänen, MD; to Prof. Johannes Lehtonen, MD; to psychologist Minna Martin; and to Prof. Yrjö Alanen, MD. They have cooperated, helped, and supported my work in many ways and given constructive criticism during the whole study process. The operationalization of the four psychosemiotic modes of experience was made together with psychologist Minna Martin.

REFERENCES

American Psychiatric Association. (2001). Practice guideline for the treatment of patients with borderline personality disorder. *American Journal of Psychiatry, 158,* 1–52.

Bateman, A., & Fonagy, P. (2004). *Psychotherapy for borderline personality disorder. Mentalization-based treatment.* Oxford, UK: Oxford University Press.

Bateson, G. (1979). *Mind and nature.* New York: E.P. Dutton.

Bion, W. (1959). Attacks on linking. *International Journal of Psychoanalysis, 40,* 308–315.

Bollas, C. (1987). The shadow of the Object. Psychoanalysis of the Unthought Known. New York: Columbia Universities Press.

Bucci, W. (1997a). Patterns of discourse in good and troubled hours: A multiple code interpretation. *Journal of the American Psychoanalytic Association, 45*(1), 155–187.

Bucci, W. (1997b). *Psychoanalysis and cognitive science: A multiple code theory.* New York, NY: The Guilford Press.

Damasio, A. (1999). *The feeling of what happens: Body and emotion in the making of consciousness.* San Diego, CA: Hartcourt Brace.

Enckell, H. (2002). *Metaphor and the psychodynamic functions of the mind.* Kuopio, Finland: Kuopio University Publications.

Fonagy, P. (1999). Memory and therapeutic action. *International Journal of Psychoanalysis,* 80, 215–223.

Fonagy, P. (2003). Attachment and borderline personality disorder. *Journal of the American Psychoanalytic Association, 48*(4), 1129–1146.

Fonagy, P., Steele M., Moran, G., Steele, H., & Higgitt, A. (1991). The capacity for understanding mental states: The reflective self in parent and child and its significance for security of attachment. *Infant Mental Health Journal, 12*(3), 201–218.

Fonagy, P., Edgcumbe, R., Moran, G., Kennedy, H., & Target, M. (1993). The roles of mental representation and mental processes in therapeutic action. *Psychoanalytic Study of the Child, 48,* 9–47.

Fonagy, P., Gergely, G., Jurist, E., & Target, M. (2002). *Affect regulation, mentalization and the development of the self.* New York, NY: Other Press.

Freud, S. (1961). The ego and the id. *Standard Edition, XIX,* 1–59. (Original work published 1923)

Green, A. (1986). *On private madness.* London, UK: Hogarth Press.

Habermas, J. (1971). *Knowledge and human interest.* Boston, MA: Beacon Press.

Kandel, E. R. (1998). A new intellectual framework for psychiatry. *American Journal of Psychiatry, 155,* 457–469.

Kandel, E. R. (1999). Biology and the future of psychoanalysis: a new intellectual framework revisited. *American Journal of Psychiatry, 156,* 505–524.

Keinänen, M. (1997). The meaning of the symbolic function in psychoanalytic psychotherapy: Clinical theory and psychotherapeutic applications. *British Journal of Medical Psychology, 70,* 325–338.

Keinänen, M. (1999). The evolution of the internal dialogue during the psychoanalytic psychotherapy process. *American Journal of Psychotherapy, 53,* 529–543.

Keinänen, M. (2000). Internalization and symbolization in the process of psychoanalytic psychotherapy: a case study. *Nordic Journal of Psychiatry, 54*, 347–354.
Keinänen, M. (2001a). The evolution of the psychosemiosis in the psychic development of the child. *Semiotica, 135*, 25–39.
Keinänen, M. (2001b). On symbolic function and its role in psychoanalytic psychotherapy. *Psychoanalytic Psychotherapy, 15*, 243–264.
Keinänen, M. (2002). The transformation of the internal dead mother into the internal living mother in the psychoanalytic psychotherapy of anorexia nervosa. *Israel Journal of Psychiatry, 40*, 220–231.
Keinänen, M. (2003). Charles Peirce´s sign terminology, psychosemiosis and psychotherapy. A clinical approach. *Semiotica, 146*, 213–236.
Keinänen, M. (2006). Psychosemiosis as Key to Body-Mind Continuum. The Reinforcement of Symbolization–Reflectiveness in Psychotherapy. New York: Nova Sciences Publishers.
Keinänen, M., & Martin, M. (2011). Mielen hengitys paniikkihäiriön psykodynamiikassa ja psykoterapiassa. *Psykoanalyyttinen Psykoterapia, 7*, 68–83.
Kendler, K. S. (2001). A psychiatric dialogue on the mind-body problem. *American Journal of Psychiatry, 158*, 989–1000.
Klein, M. (1975). Envy and gratitude. In *Envy and gratitude and other works, 1946–1963* (pp. 176–235). New York, NY: Delacorte. (Original work published 1957)
Kernberg, O., Selzer, M., Koenigsberg, H., Carr, A., & Appelbaum, A. (1989). *Psychodynamic psychotherapy of borderline patients.* New York, NY: Basic Books.
Lewin, B. (1946). Sleep, the mouth and the dream screen. *Psychoanalytic Quarterly*, 15, 419–434.
Ogden, T. (1989). *The primitive edge of experience.* Northvale, NJ: Jason Aronson.
Ogden, T. (1994a). The analytic third-working with intersubjective clinical facts. *International Journal of Psychoanalysis, 75*, 3–20.
Ogden, T. (1994b). *Subjects of analysis.* Northvale, NJ: Jason Aronson.
Peirce, C. S. (1960). *Collected papers of Charles Sanders Peirce.* (A.W. Burks, Ed.; Vol. VI). Cambridge, MA: Harvard University Press.
Sackett, D., Richardson, W., & Rosenberg, W. (1997). How to practice and teach EBM. London, UK: Churchill, Livingstone.
Salonen, S. (1989). The restitution of primary identification in psychoanalysis. *Scandinavian Psychoanalytic Review, 12*, 102–115.
Segal, H. (1957). Notes on symbol formation. *International Journal of Psychoanalysis, 38*, 391–397.
Spitz, R. (1965). *The first year of life.* New York, NY: International Universities Press.
Stern, D. (1985). *The interpersonal world of the infant.* New York, NY: Basic Books.
Tähkä, V. (1993). *Mind and its treatment.* Madison, CT: International Universities Press.
von Bertalanffy, L. (1968). *General systems theory.* New York, NY: Braziller.

CHAPTER 9

THE DYNAMICS OF CONTROL IN THE CASE OF MRS. C

A Pragmatic Study of the Patient/Analyst Dialogue

Georgia Lepper
University of Exeter, UK

INTRODUCTION

Pragmatics, now a widely used empirical method, has its origins in a theory originally developed by the philosopher Charles Sanders Peirce in the late 19th century. Peirce aimed to provide a realist account of how as sentient beings we relate to the world of objects, and others, through the continuous, developmental process of "perceptual judgments," mediated through interactions with others in the sign-rich world of human communication. If pragmatics is to be "explained by means of the word, it must be public experience that we speak of consisting of public operations, and public in the sense that a scientific experiment is" (Buchler, 1939/2010, p. 117). Peirce provided the philosophical foundation for the development of American

Making Our Ideas Clear, pages 243–273
Copyright © 2015 by Information Age Publishing
All rights of reproduction in any form reserved.

pragmatics, subsequently applied to psychology (James, 1890), education (Dewey, 1916), and social psychology (Mead, 1934).

Earlier chapters in this book outline the evolution of pragmatics and its influence on the interpersonal school of psychoanalysis. A second strand of its evolution is the development of empirical methods. The invention of the portable tape recorder in the 1950s provided the tool for a broad field of inquiry into the phenomenon of everyday communication. While focusing on spoken language and situating itself in the discipline of linguistics, empirical pragmatics touches on many adjacent disciplines: sociology, social and developmental psychology, anthropology, and cognitive science. (See Enfield & Levinson, 2006, for a cross-disciplinary overview of these developments.)

This chapter demonstrates a pragmatic approach to the study of therapeutic interaction. The focus is on how speakers coordinate their actions, in the turn-by-turn flow of the talk, and how they interpret each other's actions, as observed in the following turn. The first part of the chapter provides a brief introduction to the development of pragmatic methods for the study of interaction. This is followed by a study of some interactions in the analysis of "Mrs. C," which was recorded and archived for the purposes of research. Finally some thoughts about the relevance of pragmatics for the systematic study of some core psychoanalytic concepts will be offered.

A PRAGMATIC APPROACH TO THE STUDY OF THERAPEUTIC INTERACTION

Consider the following exchange between an analyst and his patient:

<A1> you mention that you had not liked my referring to your job or your task here/
<P2> /job is/
<A3> /as talking.
<P4> the word (chuckle).
<A5> yes.

In this exchange, patient and analyst align closely to each other's utterances. In turn 1, the analyst refers to a previous turn, and his understanding of it. In an overlapping turn (P2), the patient links to the word "job"—while the analyst completes his turn, clarifying that the "job" he is referring to is "talking." In turn P4, the patient builds on and extends the topic, by introducing a further modification: "the word" (with a chuckle, which, it turns out, is a frequent accompaniment of these speakers' communicative pattern). This sequence finishes with an agreement token: The analyst confirms the patient's hearing of his communicative intention.

The properties of human social interaction have been summarized by Levinson (2006, p. 54) as consisting of five elements, an "interaction engine" as Levinson styles it:

1. *Attribution of intention*, or "mind reading" based on
2. The ability to attribute *mutual salience for us right now* (at the neurophysiological level of mirror neurons)
3. *Gricean intentions*: intentional behaviors whose function is to be recognized
4. All underpinned by the *cooperative nature of human interaction*, which is required for
5. *Turn-taking*—the observable communicative practices of talk, which, on the evidence of a large body of empirical evidence, appear to be universal.

A foundational object of study for the study of interaction is the turn sequence. "It may be thought of as the cradle of meaning" (Hendriks-Jansen, 1996, p. 277). The minimum condition for a conversation is a speaker, a hearer, and two turns. Such interactions are observable between infants and their carers within the first days of life and form the foundation of the development of intersubjectivity (Trevarthen, 1998). Infants come neurologically equipped to look for and engage in turn taking. A conversation is organized by universal rules of hearing, obeyed by the partners to any interaction (Sacks, Schegloff, & Jefferson, 1974), procedures of conversational order that are learned by infants and children in the ordinary unremarkable course of their care (Beebe & Lachmann, 1988).

Schegloff (2006, p. 86) identifies five observable properties of turn-taking:

1. *One turn at a time:* Talk is orderly, governed by a universal rule: one speaker at a time. Exceptions, such as overlaps and interruptions, may require mutual repair to restore the turn sequence.
2. *Each turn related to the one just prior:* Each turn is ordinarily heard as a response to the prior turn, unless there is an indication to hear it otherwise.
3. *Nextness:* A turn at talk is characterized by words, parts of words, or sounds that provide cues, both affective and cognitive, as to how the recipient is to hear the utterance. The principle of nextness also produces basic sequences, such as questions and answers, which are reciprocal: A question must be responded to in some way by the hearer.
4. *Speakers listen for and orient to the next sound to assess the progress of the talk:* Speakers and hearers listen to others' words, parts of words, or

sounds in order to make inferences about the others' intentions, and to manage the direction of talk.

5. *When the turn sequence breaks down, a repair will be initiated:* Speakers will normally work to maintain orderly talk. If there is a breakdown in the talk, efforts will be made to restore the progress of the conversation. For example, not to answer a question is "accountable," and will result in a rupture in the talk, which will normally be repaired by one of the speakers.

This underpinning orderliness is the minimum requirement for the maintenance of everyday interaction, the foundation of intersubjective relating, and constitutive of the social order in which the interactions take place. At the same time, the interactions take place, and their patterns are transmitted to learning infants and new speaking partners, in the immediate context of the culture. The wider culture, its child rearing practices, and the local culture of the particular family, the immediate setting in which the conversation takes place, all provide the context in which a particular interaction has meaning. What goes in one social domain may be very different in another, even if the "language" is the same. The immediate context of the interaction shapes its possibilities and outcomes. This characteristic leads to a further property of talk:

6. Turns are *recipient designed:* Speakers shape their utterances in relation to the immediate context and with reference to who the hearer is, what his or her state of knowledge is or intentions might be, and regulate their communicative actions in relation to the response.

This order of reality provides a second level of pragmatic attention: the way in which the foundational rules of talk are used to achieve specific interactional goals in the context of the talk, and the way in which local constraints are observed and, sometimes, subverted by speakers.

To learn to talk is to enter into a world of shared meaning, on the basis of which inferences can be made about what is going on in a particular context, and what is going on in the mind of the other.

What is to be made of the context of the talk in this turn sequence? Evidently, the analyst is referring to the framework of the analysis—a specific context in which talk *is* the task, and the focus of attention—a communication about communication. It is the "job" of the patient to talk about whatever is on her mind, and the "job" of the analyst to observe and comment on this. His observation seems to be about a reluctance on the patient's part to have this made explicit. We will examine the wider context of this exchange in the analysis that follows. For the present purpose, it is sufficient to observe that in the context of the talk, the intervention of the analyst takes on another color. He is addressing what seems to be a potential area of disagreement: that the patient does not like his talking about "your job." His asking the question suggests that there is a potential for conflict. What is import of her reply (P4): "the word"? Is it really a reply? Taking the context into account reveals another dimension to this exchange. Despite its smooth surface of collaboration and agreement, a hint of challenge is observable. Just as much as cooperation, disagreement and conflict as speakers pursue their communicative objectives are achievements grounded in the interactional order that operates at the level of the turn.

If talk is work, and it is the work that is at the heart of the psychoanalytic enterprise, then taking a close look at the work of talk in the turn-by-turn interaction of an analyst and his patient may turn out to be a productive approach. The following pragmatic analysis will focus on the systematic production of turns, drawing on research from three sources: (a) the large body of findings on turn-taking from the discipline of conversation analysis (Sacks 1992; Sacks et al., 1974; Schegloff, 1992, 2006); (b) studies of the ways in which phrases and grammatical constructions function to provide cues to the hearer(s) for interpreting the communicative intentions of the speaker (Caffi, 1999; Schiffrin 1987); and (c) the means by which grammatical constructions create affective and conceptual "mental spaces" that underpin instersubjective communication (Caffi & Janney 1994; Jayussi, 1984; Verhagen, 2005). It will also set the investigation in the clinical context in which these utterances take place, and its significance for the unfolding talk.

BACKGROUND TO THE RESEARCH

This study is based on the case of "Mrs. C," a psychoanalytic case dating from the 1960s, recorded and archived for research purposes. Mrs. C was a recently married woman, a teacher in her twenties at the beginning of the analysis, in the course of which she gave birth to a daughter. The presenting issues were her adjustment to her married and professional life, and later to motherhood. The analyst was an experienced practitioner and an active researcher who recorded the case in order to provide data for research purposes. Permission to use the material was sought and granted by the custodian of the data archive at Hunter College, of City University of New York. The full data set, which has been archived, consists of 101 sessions, sampled in blocks at regular intervals across the whole length of the analysis consisting of 1,114 sessions, which took place over four years. This study will concentrate on just two blocks of sessions from the corpus—the first ten sessions, and the second set of ten sessions between sessions 91 and 100. On reading through the full data set, I noticed a topic of clinical interest that featured strongly. This observation provided the starting point for the analysis.

In several previous studies of psychotherapeutic interactions (Lepper & Mergenthaler, 2007, 2008), I observed a phenomenon that interested me: The topic of "control" was a frequent issue for both patients and therapists. Patients frequently brought material relating to being "in control," or being "out of control" of their lives, feelings, and reactions to others. Difficulties relating to control were also among the topics of interest in the interpretations offered by the therapist. In some cases, these difficulties were directly referred to in the context of the session: interpretations about the patient's wishes and attempts to control the therapist himself. The very practice of interpretation itself embeds the epistemological issues that are the primary concern of pragmatics: *how* can we know what is in the mind of the other?

To explore this, I take as my starting point Levenson's (1982) proposition: "The transference is the way that the patient and therapist will behave around what they are talking about in the framework established by the constraints of the therapy" (p. 13).

The concept of the transference, developed by Freud through his lifetime of clinical research, refers to psychical reality—the unconscious fears and desires of the subject, expressed in symbolic form in dreams and in the "transference neurosis"—the fantasies of the patient projected onto the person of the analyst and enacted in the context of treatment. The concept has been subject to much debate and revision in the subsequent development of psychoanalysis. Levenson's articulation of the concept of transference takes as its focal point the concept of "enactment" as a two-person process (Gill, 1982; Greenson, 1965; Searles, 1978): The transference is instantiated in the patient's communicative actions, both verbal and nonverbal, in the here and now of the analytic session. These communicative actions will shape the communicative actions of the therapist in response. The following analysis of the analyst/patient interaction will investigate if, and how, the dynamic turn-taking properties of the communicative actions of therapist and patient reflect the core topic of "control." Is it possible to observe an enactment of "control" in their communicative actions?

The Method

The study of naturally occurring talk always leaves the researcher with a dilemma, very similar to that faced by the analyst: how to select what is salient from the wealth of material available for observation and study. As a participant in the interaction, the psychoanalyst is most likely to draw on the theoretical framework of psychoanalysis to focus attention on aspects of the patient's utterances that may be of interest to the ongoing project of the analysis. A drawback of this approach was observed by Watzlawick and colleagues, who noted that in classical psychoanalysis, the focus is on the effects of person A on person B, "without taking equally into account that whatever B does influences A's next move, and ... they are both largely influenced by, and in turn influence, the context in which their interaction takes place" (Watzlawick, Beavin, & Jackson, 1968, p. 35). Levenson (1979) makes a similar point: "The transference arena is a subtle ongoing dialogic discourse between the two participants even when the therapist is totally silent" (p. 280).

Observing the therapeutic interaction from a pragmatic perspective means taking into account the reciprocal effects of the speakers' communications on each other and the ways in which they jointly create the communicative context. It is with this conceptual step that the move can be made from a clinical, experience-near perspective, to an observational stance that examines the meta-communicative properties of the clinical exchange. This is not to propose a movement from a "subjective" to an "objective" stance—the polarization so frequently generated by researchers to condemn psychoanalytic investigations, and by psychoanalysts to dismiss a research stance towards the psychoanalytic process. A pragmatic approach provides a rigorous solution to this epistemological problem. The focus of attention is neither on what is "really happening" nor on purely subjective phenomena (ineffable experience)—but rather on the observable actions of speakers in their coordinated attempts at joint meaning-making in the immediate context of the talk. The investigation starts from a phenomenon of interest and from there constructs a method for its detailed observation. The analysis of individual sequences, combined with comparative analysis of similar sequences across different contexts, provides for the building of a robust observational framework (Lepper, 2000; Schegloff, 1992; Schiffrin, 1987).

The first step in undertaking a pragmatic analysis is immersion in the text, with a questioning stance: What kinds of interactional phenomena are present here? What is the context of the talk? From the first reading of the sessions, the issue of control/being out of control quickly surfaced as a significant topic. In previous studies (Lepper, 2009; Lepper & Mergenthaler, 2007, 2008), using a quantitative strategy to map core themes in the discourse, the topic of control was observed in several different therapeutic pairs, in different therapeutic contexts. The topic seems to be one that frequently emerges in therapeutic discourse. The second consideration was informed by my own clinical experience: Control seems to be a salient dynamic in therapeutic interaction. So it was with the case of Mrs. C. What is said, to whom and by whom, and how much, is a theme which comes up throughout the analysis.

TABLE 9.1 "Control" as a Topic in the Case of Mrs. C

Session #	P Control Self	P Control Other	A Control Self	A Control Other
1–10	15	10	1	
91–100	27	4		5
259–268	4	2		
316–332	10	3		
404–409	7	3		
427–437	4	1		2
596–605	2	6		
726–729	4	4		
765–774		8		
936–944	3	3	2	
1112–1114		3		

The first task was to track down and identify any interactions in which "control" was the overt topic of the talk (the "word"). No doubt "control" was an implicit theme in all kinds of sequences where the word itself was not used. Nevertheless, sampling the sessions in this way provides a crude map by which to find a way through the text and discover what patterns might emerge (see Table 9.1).

Working my way through the text, I began to notice that quite a lot of the discourse around the topic of control also had to do with talk itself. Having noticed this, and to further reduce the amount of data for analysis, while at the same time sampling the text rigorously, leaving no instances out, the search was narrowed to identifying those interactions between analyst and patient in which "control" of "self" or "other" in relation to "talk" was the topic. Pursuing Levenson's proposal—that the transference is a semiotic process that will be evident in the actions of the parties to the talk—the specific question emerged: Can a pragmatic analysis reveal *how* the dynamic of control of talk is enacted in the sessions?

Text Analysis

The following analysis of 11 exchanges from 9 sessions (1, 3, 4, 5, 6, 9 and 94, 98, 99) explores *how* the properties of turn-by-turn talk are employed in the patient/analyst dialogue around the topic of "control," making use of findings from the substantial corpus of empirical pragmatics research.

The first exchange occurs in Session 1:

> <P> and I again could be imagining this, that uhm, neither of my parents particularly wants to hear anything that I have to say,

which always gets very upsetting to me. And usually I end up, up, feeling like having a tantrum. I don't have one (chuckle) but I end up just feeling I can't control myself. So I always have to leave.

<A> at the thought that they don't want to really listen, you mean?

<P> yes

Observation

The feeling of not being listened to in a conversation is linked by the patient to not being able to "control myself." This is accompanied by a "chuckle," which turns out to be a significant feature of these two speakers' talk. The analyst's response is affirmed: "yes." Note that the analyst's question is delivered in an open format. It is designed in a way that asks for confirmation of his hearing, and, through the use of the phrase "you mean," hands the privilege of "knowing" over to the patient. She could equally answer "no." Phrases like "you mean" are a foundational means of constructing intersubjectivity—creating a shared focus on a conceptual domain of mutual interest (Verhagen, 2005). The analyst makes sure that he has listened accurately.

Here (this is the first session) the analyst is working to establish the analytic framework and to build a mutual understanding of the local context of their talk. Listening will certainly be one of the important issues, though the listening complained about (in the ordinary interactions of the home) will be very different from the talking and listening required by the framework of analysis. Notice that he doesn't pursue what could be a transference interpretation about being listened to in the here and now of the session or not (this will come up later); rather he enacts a listening to, through his use of the confirming question.

The theme of "talk" and listening continues in Session 3:

<P1> I think I still feel, uhm, I have to have some kind of interchange in order to do this. Because, I don't know, I just think sometimes if I am talking to my husband and (pause) its not the same as this, but it's almost, some things upset me and I'm just talking about anything that's coming into my mind in relation to what's upset me and really all he can do is listen. He can't say very much except, "I'm listening" but I get very demanding that he make a response and extremely upset if he doesn't just make a response, even if I don't even listen to it or pay any attention to anything he may add as advice or comment. I still feel I have to sort of formulate my (chuckle) thoughts before I put them into words (pause) . . .

<A2> so, are you feeling upset that I didn't respond?

<P3> no, I just feel as if my mind suddenly goes blank (chuckle). and I, something might come to my mind and then I'll think like, well, that seems kind of silly to say or well, that's not quite the way to say it or, you know, things like that. So then I don't say it. Or else it's sort of vague and I'm not too sure exactly what it is I'm thinking. (pause) I think, maybe I don't remember. Before, probably yesterday too, I got, I was feeling rather sort of antagonistic to you because I knew you wouldn't respond but I kept thinking you should or I wanted you to so I wouldn't be able to go on. And although I don't I didn't feel I could say things some of the times, I mean just, I couldn't find the words or I don't know, I might have been feeling too tense or something but sometimes I was almost thinking I think, well, I'll just say nothing. (pause)

Observation

In this exchange, the analyst makes an intervention, which links the previous story about her husband to himself and his actions in the immediate context of the session. The analyst's intervention (A2) changes the terms of the talk. "So" is a pragmatic marker (Schiffrin, 1987)—a word with no substantive meaning, which is used to mark the speaker's intentions in the following utterance. "So" signals a change of register. It marks a shift the epistemological distance from experience—distant (other) to the experience—near (you and me) of their talk. The patient responds (P3) with a denial—"no"—accompanied by a "chuckle," and then proceeds to elaborate on the theme of saying what's on her mind (obeying the analytic injunction—the "job" is talking) in a rather roundabout way. This utterance is preceded by a series of "hedges" (Caffi, 1999)—"I think, maybe I don't remember, before, probably yesterday . . . "—that reduce the patient's commitment to the utterance that follows. This turbulent series of qualifying phrases leads to a new word, and a new phase in the talk: the admission that she "was feeling rather antagonistic to you." In this way, she enacts, in the here and now of the talk with the analyst, the very thing she was reporting: her wish to get the other to speak, while she doesn't pay any attention. The remainder of the utterance is very turbulent, and accompanied by significant pauses. Each pause represents a potential turn handover, and each failure of the analyst to take a turn means the patient has to keep the talk going. Not to take a turn at a potential handover is "accountable"—that is, it engenders a potential rupture in the interaction, which needs to be "repaired."

In the context of the analytic session, it is made explicit that it is the patient's "job" to talk, whether or not there is a response. It becomes clear that for this patient, at least, this is causing difficulties. Also observable are the two chuckles (P1 and P3), which seem to act as nonverbal markers of potential areas of conflict or disagreement. In one case, the way she has to "formulate my thoughts before I put them into words" is a contravening of the analytic injunction to "say what is on your mind." The second, in P3, precedes an open disagreeing about the analytic frame, and the therapist's silence. She "was almost [a hedge reducing commitment to the statement] thinking I think, well, I'll just say nothing." With the marker "well" [notice this] she throws down the gauntlet: "I'll just say nothing."

The analyst's silence—his failure to take up a turn in the natural sequential order of ordinary talk—poses a challenge to the patient's normal communicative strategy. Who is going to control the talk in this interaction?

In the following session, the subject of talk within the analytic frame resurfaces in another form.

Session 4

<P1> I was talking with mscz [her husband] last night about the fact that at the end of each session I feel very upset partly just because when I do talk, I, I do get very emotional and very tense, and then suddenly to stop right in the middle even if I, even if it isn't right in the middle of an emotional reaction, I find it very hard.

<A2> to sort of regain control, you mean?

<P3> uhum. (pause)

<A4> I gather from what you say that you must wonder whether or not to tell your parents that you've started analysis.

<P5> no, I think, well, sometimes I guess I have wanted just because they still are my parents and they have a right to know what's happening to me. But on the other hand, my decision right now is not to tell them . . .

Observation

Here the patient brings her immediate response to the context of the analysis to the fore, though reporting it in a "third person" distant sort of way in the form of talk with her husband. The analyst uses the

> word "control" for the first time, picking up on the aspect of "control" of emotions, in the form of an open question, with the tag "you mean" leaving to the patient the option of elaborating on her theme. The question, with its tag, "you mean," offers a thought about what might be on the other's mind, in a form that is open to negotiation, denial or reformulation by the recipient. His question, however, receives a minimal response (P3), leaving him with the task of continuing the talk. He responds to the challenge by turning the talk away from their immediate intersubjective engagement, using what on the surface appears to be a statement, though in fact it is heard as a question, as can be seen in her response (P5). Here it is the analyst who shifts the focus away from the us/here/now. Such an objectivizing move can be seen as a "shield" (Caffi, 1999), a pragmatic device by means of which the emotional content of the exchange is reduced in tone. Once more the patient's response is preceded by a denial, subsequently hedged and elaborated in the longish turn that follows. Both partners back away from the implications of the patient's talking directly about her response to the analyst ("stopping right in the middle... I find it very hard").

Does the analyst's backing away signal his avoidance, or perhaps his empathic recognition that she is not yet ready to engage at this level? The answer to this might emerge in an extended study of patterns of interaction of this type across the analysis. For the moment, talk and control seem to be intimately entangled in this interaction. As we shall see, intimate entanglement becomes a source of much talk and conflict. In the subsequent session the analyst returns to the topic of who should talk and where the talking should happen.

Session 5

<A1> you mentioned yesterday o- or the day before that uh things would occur to you during the day/
<P2> / mm.
<A3> /that you had looked forward, as a matter of fact, before you started the analysis to be able to come in and talk about them. What strikes me as you tell me this is that you went home after you left here and talked to mscz [her husband] about it;
<P4> mm.
<A5> wanting reassurance, but not here.
<P6> you mean not seeking reassurance here?
<A7> I mean, yeah, it's one of the things that apparently didn't occur to you (chuckle) to mention here. (stomach rumble) I

don't know what to make of it, except to just; I, I, I take note of these (chuckle)/

<P8> /mm.

<A9> / different things that you've said that you, ahead of time, wanted to be able to have a place to talk about, things like that, for example, that trouble you.

<P10> mm. now, well, I don't think I, well, that's not true. I do seek reassurance wherever I talk, (chuckle) even here, but I don't think that; I think if, if I bring something up here I, I already know that/

<A11> /you won't get it.

<P12> uh, that's not the point. Yeah, and so even though I would like to get it;

<A13> could that be in; one of the reasons it didn't come up? (chuckle) that's really what I'm getting;

<P14> (interrupting) I can't remember whether it even, you know, did come into my mind yesterday. It may have, but uhm, you know, sometimes I, especially when. . . .

Observation

In this exchange, analyst and patient refer back to the previous conversation about her wish to have someone to talk to, and the way in which she avoids bringing her thoughts to the analytic conversation. The analyst offers an observation that she seeks reassurance, but not from him. Note again the open form in which he couches his utterance: "I don't know what to make of it—I just take note of these things." Here a "taking note" is not a private affair, but an interactional "noting"—making inferences about the other's intentions (what is in the mind of the other). In the context of an analytic session, this becomes more than an interactional matter (something we all do all the time) but a part of the analytic frame: the "job" of the analyst is to take note. An overlap, with a neutral acknowledgement for the patient (mm), is accompanied by his chuckle before he completes his turn—"different things that you've said that you wanted to have a place to talk about things like that, for example, that trouble you." The chuckle perhaps suggests that he senses (and communicates) that he is moving into delicate territory and potential for disagreement.

The analyst's "noting" elicits a turbulent negation: "mm, now, well, I don't think I, well, that's not true. . . . I do seek reassurance wherever I talk, even here . . . " Another chuckle: This is a delicate matter. In the subsequent turn the analyst completes her sentence—"you won't get it"—making an inference about what is "in her mind." Voicing the thoughts or experiences of the other by completing an utterance is a means of eliciting agreement or disagreement about the inference made (Lerner, 1996). His inference is again rejected: "that's not the point" (P12), before she agrees ("yeah"). This is followed by another overlapping turn in which the analyst pursues his point (A13). Note the chuckle that accompanies his direct question. A pattern seems to emerge, in which the patient initially responds to an utterance of the analyst with disagreement, only then to produce an agreement, usually with some degree of hedging and turbulence. Here this occurs in the three turns P10, P12, and P14. It's clear from this sequence that both speakers are highly oriented to each others' talk, at the level of the turn; at the same time, there is an ongoing tussle about the ownership of her beliefs and intentions: Whose noticing is going to hold sway?

Later in the session, returning to the theme of talking, the patient remarks:

<P> I've noticed, sometimes in conversations too, that I'll either try to anticipate what somebody's going to say and then continue on with what I'm thinking, or keep talking when I should stop because they're about to say something and then they won't, then they'll never say it. And that way I control the conversation. But the conversation might not get anywhere, or certainly nowhere near where it could have if I had stopped talking when it was time to. (sniff) and the other thing I was thinking of when I was speaking of my reaction to psychoanalysis being, well, a questionable thing for all the money that it costs . . .

In this session, a long interaction between analyst and patient around the topic of control of the talk results in the patient "noticing" how she manages to control conversations. The talk of the session, within the analytic framework, is a different kind of conversation, and one that she may not be able to control in her usual way. At the point of the (sniff), a potential turn point for the analyst, the patient then changes tack (following the analytic injunction to say whatever comes to her mind?) to express her thought that analysis is "a questionable thing." The hint of trouble is out in the open.

Another exchange about controlling the talk occurs at the beginning of the next session, with the analyst's response to P's reflection on being late:

Session 6

<P1> I was thinking about the fact that I was late today but then I kept thinking, I'm really thinking about that so I won't have

to think about something else. (pause) but just in terms of my being late, it, whether or not it's something that I could have avoided. I always feel as if I have to make a great thing about why I was late, so, so I won't be held responsible. I guess I, I feel guilty whenever I am, no matter what. (silence)

<A2> I get the impression you uh, have been describing to me how you save stacks of things, piles of things. I get some impression sometimes when you are silent here, it's as though you're saving a pile of something to say later.

<P3> what I was thinking then was, when you, when I have uh, some idea of what it is I don't want to say, how much I should play the game (chuckle), that my mind's playing, and how much I should try to stop it. (pause) I think what's on my mind is the fact that I want your role to be something much more active than it really is and what I understand it should be. and I was thi- , thinking in terms of the, uhm other incidents I mentioned before of people who are in the position of being, well I don't know exactly the word, but I looked upon them as helping me.

Observation

In response to her opening reflection—what is on her mind—the analyst (A2) changes the direction of the talk, with a reference back to the previous session, with its discussion about her avoiding talking in the sessions. Again, he puts his turn in the form of a "noticing"—"I get the impression . . . " With a chuckle, the patient (P3) characterizes her *mind* as "playing a game"—the game of avoiding the analytic injunction to say what is on her mind. Her "mind" plays a game—but *she* could stop (control) it. She then, after a pause (no uptake on the part of the analyst to take up a potential turn of talk), offers what is on her mind: what she wants and what she understands the analyst *should* be: his role to be more active, like other people "helping me" (or not?). Here, she takes up the analytic injunction to say what is on her mind. Once more, as in the previous session, what is on her mind is a criticism of the analytic frame. While the criticism is more direct than the previous complaint (session 5), it makes use of the subjunctive "should be," and refers away to "other people" who "help me"—creating once more a "shield" that displaces the origin of the utterance and downgrades its emotional force. Caffi (1999) suggests that "when shields increase the emotive distance, as they do in the majority of cases that I have studied, this is due to the margin of uncertainty about the definition of the relationship: Who is speaking to whom? Whose project is enacted by the utterance?" (p. 904).

Then at the end of the session we find this exchange:

<P1> when I was talking to this mother it was something that we're both interested in and then I didn't know how to end it, and I do this so often, I just sort of will almost leave without ending it. and then after I've left I realize that I really hadn't ended it and then I'm not sure whether I did end it and that it doesn't have, the ending doesn't have to keep dragging out or whether I really did just sort of abruptly walk away. But I know I'm so busy thinking about myself and how awkward I'm feeling I stop thinking in terms of the other person and maybe, what (chuckle) they would consider an ending, I don't know, it's just, you know, I always feel after that I've done something wrong.

<A2> our time is up.

A story about ending a conversation (in her role as teacher) appears at the end of the session, with the comment that ending a conversation abruptly makes her feel "after that I've done something wrong." This reflection, accompanied by another chuckle, seems to mark a further potential for conflict. The "game," as she expressed it at the beginning of this session, is about her mind (not her) controlling how she participates in the analytic task. Just who is in control of the analytic task? Here we see another enactment around the framework of the analysis: the endings of sessions, without the customary bringing-to-an-end of a conversation or interaction in ordinary discourse is painful to her, and leaves her in a childlike position, not knowing what is coming next.

Session 9

It is a few days later, in session 9, that the exchange about the "job" of analysis that was introduced above occurs. Now it is possible to set it in a wider context of the developing interaction.

<P1> I knew anyway that certain things would not be approved of and certain things would be and I didn't know where I stood, where, how I felt about the things that were approved of or disapproved of and I wasn't sure that what my parents approved of, such as working hard and keeping your nose to

the grindstone and things like that were things that I really wanted to do.

<A2> you mention that you had not liked my referring to your job or your task here/

<P3> /job is/

<A4> /as talking.

<P5> the word (chuckle).

<A6> yes. is there any connection between that and your feeling I would be impatient if you didn't talk?

<P7> I suppose so. because I suppose I then think well, this is what I'm supposed to be doing here. and I think sometimes I'm wondering if, well, sometimes I get self-conscious about what I am saying and wondering if, if I'm just saying stupid things or irrelevant things or something like that.

Observation

The ongoing discussion of talk, set in the context of the analytic frame, and the analytic injunction to "say whatever comes into your mind" becomes an open topic in this exchange. The analyst responds obliquely (A2) to P's comment that "working hard and keeping your nose to the grindstone" was required to bring approval. Bringing the talk from the narrative about her parents (experience distant) to the immediate context of the session (experience near), he raises the topic of "your job"—the work of analysis, the injunction to "say what is on your mind." Note the close alignment of the speakers—their overlapping turns (P3 & A4) and A's confirmation (turn A6) of her hearing of his proposition—that the "job" is the "word." His proposal to "make a connection" (an epistemic connection) gets the response "I suppose so." To suppose that something is the case is to generate a potential shared mental space between the speakers (Verhagen, 2005). However "suppose so" (contrast it, say with "think that") reduces the force of the commitment to the shared, "intersubjective" space, opening up a potential space in its own turn for further development, and possible disagreement. A "job," she makes clear, is something you are "supposed" to do (P7)—that is, "keeping your nose to the grindstone" (turn P1). Close management of the turns generates at the same time agreement (their mutual orientation to the context of the talk, what is supposed to happen in the "work" of analysis) and conflict (the injunction to "say what is on your mind" leaves her open to "saying stupid or irrelevant things"). A pair of morally implicative "versions" of the self (Jayussi, 1984; Lepper, 2002) emerges: the "guilty one" who is *supposed* to be on time, to say what is one her mind, to say relevant and important things (the "good" girl);

and the "rebellious" one who doesn't know if those are things she really wanted to do.

By the end of these first ten sessions, a link between talking and how I feel has been constructed in the therapeutic conversation. The topic of "control" has established two linked thematic streams: (a) control of the talk; and (b) control over myself (feelings). To be in control of the talk parallels being in control of myself; not to be in control of the talk parallels feeling "wrong," "stupid." Minds and selves can even "play games" with each other. The construction of a "self" with its "mind" is not simply a matter of subjective experience; it is a discursive matter. Here we find evidence of the 'self' as an active intersubjective agent, which draws on well-learned resources available to speakers in order to create versions—"good," "bad," "stupid," "wrong"—of itself for the immediate purposes of the talk. Both analyst and patient are highly attuned to these possibilities.

The topic of control of self/of other/of talk continues in the next block of sampled sessions.

Session 94

The patient has been talking about an incident with her husband, in which they go through a process of deciding what play, or movie, to go to. In the course of reflecting on the event, she returns to the theme of "control":

> **<P1>** . . . I have a very unreasonable feeling of disappointment, and, well, I was going to say anger. Anger I don't know what at, but that I can't control the circumstances and whatever the emotions are, I I think I just ended up feeling it's better just not to get involved so much that I'll have these emotions. Because somehow I feel as either they're too strong to control, or else I feel that it's unreasonable that they are so strong. (pause) . . . I think that must be why, too, if mscz says, "what would you like to do?" I often don't want to just tell him. Because he might want something different and then we'll have to work out a compromise and I find that very difficult too once I decided what I want to do. (pause)
>
> **<A2>** and that would work the same way, I suppose, if, uhm, when you have the idea it would be better if he would just decide and then you'd go and you wouldn't have to worry and think about it, then you never face what you really want and feel the disappointment of not getting it.

<P3> umhmm.
<A4> that would protect you there, too.
<P5> umhmm. well, it just goes back and it just occurred to me it's that basic, well, pattern that I have of either having to be in control completely, making all the decisions or else being completely the follower and, and being told exactly what I'm doing. (pause)

The patient goes on to relate this to the way her parents interacted: "my father always yelling at my mother and being very aggressive, and my mother always being very passive." She continues, noting "and I remember at that time it (clears throat) that I was caught in the middle between seeing these two different roles and perhaps copying both of them at different times." She goes on to link this recollection with present interactions between her and her husband.

Observation

The two versions of control—"in control"/"out of control" take on a more specific form and function: what I want to do (don't tell him) versus compromise (if I tell him). The analyst's response to this (A2) takes up the thematic stream "control feelings"—"feel the disappointment of not getting it"—referring back to the "unreasonable feeling of disappointment" described by the patient in the previous turn. In the context of the initial self-reflection—"I think that must be why I don't want to tell him"—the analyst offers the thought "and that would work the same way, I suppose"—leaving room open for negotiation of the shared construction of the "why." He gets a positive response token, umhmm (P3) but must continue with a next turn in order to get the reflection he is soliciting. This is forthcoming in P5, where the patient responds with a further reflection on the experience: "it's occurred to me that is a basic, well, pattern that I have . . . " Here, observably, there is a negotiation—analyst and patient together construct a shared understanding of the matter to hand—her reluctance openly to say what she wants. How is this achieved?

In turn A2, the analyst "supposes." The use of a mental predicate with its complementary clause ("I suppose that") (Verhagen 2005) invites the recipient to talk about what is in her mind. Here, the analyst says what is on his mind about the state of mind of the patient. The phrase prefaces an indirect question: This is what I think; what do you think? By taking a second turn, he keeps the exchange going, perhaps giving the patient time to reflect upon and respond to his "supposing." In contrast to a mental state verb like "I think that . . . " which references the point of view of the speaker, in this turn, the predicate

> "suppose that [something]" offers an open invitation to join in a mutual thinking about something.
>
> Contrast this with the "suppose" expressed by the patient in the previous extract (Session 9, P7): "I suppose so." Here, the verb appears in response to the direct question, "Is there any connection between that and your feeling I would be impatient if you didn't talk?" Questions and answers are powerful interactional devices much studied in the CA literature (Heritage, 2002; Sacks, 1992). A question sets the topic for the next turn. Not to answer is "accountable" and would result in the breakdown of the turn-taking sequence. To change the topic would threaten the ongoing progress of the talk. It follows that the options open to the recipient are very much constrained by the form of the question, which can be constructed in a variety of ways in order to modulate the degree of control imposed on the hearer. Direct questions ("who," "what," where," "when" are the classic examples) constrain the potential response more than indirect questions. Often indirect questions are prefaced in a way that extends the options for reply. For example, a preface like "I wonder [if there is any connection . . .]" would leave far more room for the recipient's reply to expand on the thought, rather than to be required to respond "yes" or "no." Sometimes apparent statements are in fact indirect questions ("and that would work the same way, I suppose"), leaving open the possibilities for the next turn; while indirect questions can be heard and responded to more as statements. The dynamic consequence of the question's format is observable in the response.
>
> The form of the analyst's question "Is there a connection . . . " (more like a statement than a question) implies its answer. The patient's response—"I suppose so" (Session 9, P10)—works to provide a response, without true agreement or disagreement. The subsequent "suppose" expands on this, with an implicit mental state description: "suppose I then think well, this is what I'm supposed to be doing here." Her supposing describes her inference about what is in the mind of the analyst: what she is supposed to be doing here (what he expects of her).

Exercising power in talk is often pursued through the use of questions. Take, for example, the cross-examination of witnesses in courts of law: Questions are used to constrain responses, draw out inferences that the interrogator wishes to reveal and the witness to conceal. Yet, at the same time, the question is an important tool in the creation of intersubjective space. To ask for another's point of view is the primary form of saying: You have thoughts which may be different from mine. Questions are highly sensitive actions in the analytic process.

A few sessions later, the matter of direct talk gets opened up in the session. The analyst addresses the issue of who is in control of the talk in their own interaction.

Session 98

<P1> it made me feel as stupid as if I couldn't even judge the situations. And so then I began thinking, when my supervisor was talking, well, I should be able to, I should have been able to put it into those words or see it in that way. So it was combination of feeling angry at the parents [of a pupil], mainly the father, and feeling angry at myself.

<A2> are you saying now you felt angry at him because I said so or because you did, in fact, feel it?

<P3> well, no, I felt it because I, well, I just can't quite see it the way you said it but I know I did feel angry at him. (silence) if I'm really honest, I think I said at, that, about being angry at them mainly because you had said that, regardless of how I felt.

<A4> afraid of me too?

<P5> excuse me?

<A6> are you afraid of me too?

<P7> (pause) I just somehow can't answer that. Because it's almost like I don't let myself look at it in that way so;(silence) I almost make a separation, I don't quite understand what it is I do. But I can readily think I'm afraid of what you might think of me. But somehow it seems different from just saying I'm afraid of you because if I say it that way, that directly, then it doesn't make sense. (silence)

Observation

A's direct question (A2) addresses the patient's state of mind, but in a form that leaves little room for negotiation: did you, or did you not, feel it? There is an initial denial on the part of the patient (P3)—similar to those denials already observed in the first block of sessions. The denial is, however, hedged by the "Well"—a device that signals that a change in the terms of the talk is upcoming. By this means, she develops a response that neither denies nor affirms, until, after a silence (a potential turn opportunity that is not taken up by the analyst) she "admits" that his "saying so" has shaped her response. The exchange continues in turn A4, with a further question that likewise suggests

> a preference for a yes or no response—it is soliciting a "fact" about her inner state, rather than creating an intersubjective space for its exploration. The response to this is a question of her own—responding to a question with a question is one way of avoiding the requirement that questions impose: an answer. Has she really misheard? The analyst takes her at her word, and repeats his question. The response (P7), following a pause, is a moderated refusal to reply—"I can't answer that... " followed by reflection on her experience. However, the upshot of the exchange is that to her "it doesn't make sense," and it is fair to say that despite the analyst's intention to explore her feelings about him, the result is a failure of shared sense making.

Once more, the use of questions seems to play a significant role in the analyst/patient interaction. Control of the talk is intimately linked with how the talk is managed at the level of the turn, and both speakers can be seen skilfully to pursue their agendas in the exploration and concealment of motives and intentions, in the way that they manage this fundamental conversational device. The analyst draws attention to an emerging pattern in which the patient avoids a direct expression of her own thoughts and feelings, instead adapting to what she believes the analyst thinks or wants—and successfully secures her agreement. At the same time, the form of his subsequent question (A4, 6) has the effect of closing down exploration, resulting in further evasive actions on the part of the patient (P5, P7). Does her evasiveness elicit his controlling questioning? Or does his controlling questioning elicit her evasiveness? It seems that a pattern that she is reporting in the conversations she has elsewhere is being enacted in the turn-by-turn dynamic of their here-and-now interaction.

Talking about their relationship in the immediate context of the session comes up again in the next session and brings the topic of control directly into their interaction.

Session 99

<A1> what you don't mention is what you first mentioned, which was that you, ah, wanted to avoid feeling foolish. But you didn't say what you would have felt foolish about or what you were afraid you would feel foolish about, which aspect of it.

<P2> I did think of that one point. I think I thought of that, not exactly that way but in terms of when I felt so determined to keep on doing what I was doing. I'd made up my mind not to have intercourse so I wasn't going to. And I just wouldn't respond to mscz at all. I think I was feeling foolish then some of the times because it just seemed so ridiculous, the way I was acting. And I don't know, just the whole thing now seems, in one way, to be a ridiculous thing to have happened but in another way it doesn't.

<A3> but you were afraid I would feel it was foolish, that is, that you would sound foolish to me.

<P4> yeah, and, and this is another level, I was just thinking of this, that somehow I guess I'm thinking people just don't do this kind of thing. (pause) so if in my married life things happen that I think aren't normal things to have happened, I don't want anybody to know about it.

<A5> anybody?

<P6> well, beyond mscz and me. Because we have to know about it. (pause) I suppose I's even more, well, it was more direct in that the only person who even might know about it would be you because I would say it here. So then it would be, I didn't want you to know about it. But I think it's a, it's that feeling is just a reaction to having anybody outside of mscz or me hearing about it. (pause)

<A7> if I understand you, you must have felt, when you said you had a certain feeling of triumph and this morning you didn't feel angry with mscz at all and then you described, in one sense, how you, you really controlled the situation quite thoroughly, then, last night because it went in accordance with your wishes and your plans, so to speak. You were really in control.

<P8> well, in one way. But I had wanted just to say to mscz, "no, we're not going to have intercourse." And sort of, "look how upset I'm feeling" that type of thing. Or, "I'm tired and look how late it is." and to have him just leave me alone, which he didn't do. Because he kept insisting that I really did want to. And so then I had to just keep my point and I, and I felt very angry at him then. Because he wasn't doing what I wanted. So in that sense, I didn't control it. (pause)

Observation

In turn A1, the analyst interrupts the patient's utterance, which seems to be taking a rather directionless turn, with an observation (it is an open-ended, indirect question) about her avoiding talking in the here and now about "feeling foolish." This brings an affirmative response from the patient, followed by a reflection on her actions in relation to her husband's demands for intercourse, leading to an evaluation of the events: "the whole thing" seems on the one hand

> "ridiculous" but on the other, it doesn't. With this open ended expression of her thoughts, the way is opened for further reflection, which the analyst takes up in the next turn (A3). He follows his investigation of "foolishness" in the light of her opening response, using the mental predicate "be afraid [that] I would feel it was foolish," this time opening the door to an exploration of what she is able/prepared to talk about with him. The turn is again an inference about what might be on her mind, but it brings about a more open exploration of her feelings than the direct questions about what she feels about him in the here and now which he used in the previous session (98: A4 & A6). Then, in turn A7, the analyst prefaces his response with "if I understand you,"—a mental state predicate that hands over to the hearer the right to confirm or disconfirm his hearing. He responds to the topic of "control of others," with an observation about how she has "controlled the situation quite thoroughly" between her and her husband, having refused his demands for intercourse. The comment is not "empathic"—it is, rather, quite challenging. Yet it receives a positive uptake. The response to this invitation to a shared understanding is the patient's further exploration of the issues around control, and how, though she "kept to her point," her husband "insisted that she really did want to." She nevertheless felt that, because her husband didn't do what she wanted, she was "not in control." Twice, the patient prefaces her response with "well," signaling an adjustment to the relevant context (Zucker, 1993), taking charge of the direction of the talk without going off topic. Given the opportunity to build on the analyst's qualified "understanding" (he wasn't insisting on knowing what was in her mind), she produces neither "thinking what you say I should," nor an evasion away from the topic at hand. She says what is on her mind, and even though it rejects, to some extent, the analyst's proposition that she "controlled the situation thoroughly," nevertheless, in this case it seems to be a product of a joint sharing of thoughts, rather than a refusal/denial.

The analyst was pursuing, in both of these exchanges (Sessions 98, 99) the objective of talking about the relationship between them (the transference). In each case, the content addresses what she might be afraid of in saying what is on her mind—that is, talking freely, rather than controlling her thoughts and actions. Is she afraid of him? Is she afraid that he might think her foolish? However, the micro-outcomes of the two exchanges are quite different. The first exchange ends in a retreat; while the second exchange brings a new dimension into their developing relationship: the beginnings of a shared understanding of her wish to control others and what it means in the day to day course of her life. In session 98 (A4, A6) the analyst turns abruptly from the topic at hand—her compliance with his view of her state of mind—to the topic of "being afraid of me." From her response, it could be said that the question frightens her, and she quickly takes cover, an enactment of interactions between her parents reported in session 94, and the link she has made to her relationship with her husband. Contrast this with the return to the topic in this session, where the use of mental state verbs (A1 and A3) opens up an exploration about what might be in the other's mind, rather than an enactment of denial and flight.

The shape and form of the analyst's explorative questions seems to have a very different effect in the two exchanges, the one closing down the progress of the talk, and the other opening up space for shared thinking. Do these observed dynamics in the turn-by-turn interaction shed light on the processes of mutual regulation in the analytic discourse?

FINDINGS

Returning to the starting point of this study, does this pragmatic investigation shed any light on Levenson's (1982) proposition that "The transference is the way that the patient and therapist will behave around what they are talking about in the framework established by the constraints of the therapy"? My response to this is to suggest that Levenson's insight provides a valuable starting point for a systematic, pragmatic investigation of the transference, and how it works. Such a study, however, requires a shift of perspective, described by Enfield (2009) in the following way: "Relationship thinking defines individuals in terms of their relationships, not the other way around. The very notion of a social person (and self) is defined in terms of one's position in a patterned system of (interrelated) relationships" (p. 75).

This shift of perspective involves, I suggest, a shift from the focus on the content of the patient's narratives about self and other that classically characterizes the analytic exchange, to a focus on *how* the analytic relationship defines the position of the participants, and shapes their patterns of relating in the context of the analytic session. If the self is fundamentally intersubjective and shaped in relation to other, then how this unfolds in the analytic session is as important as the content. Furthermore, as this detailed, though limited, study of the analyst–patient interaction has demonstrated, these patterns are observable, using the methods of empirical pragmatics.

A dynamic process around what is in the other's mind, and who controls the talk, was a powerful dynamic in the talk between patient and analyst. In this novel situation, the patient is in the position of a child in relation to an adult. It is a principle of psychoanalytic method that the frame places the patient in a highly special context, "saying whatever comes to mind," which opens a window on how the patient will try to create familiar patterns of relating through the "transference neurosis." Observed through the lens of pragmatics, the patterns of relating analyst and patient create in the here and now of the session have consequences for both the micro-outcomes of individual exchanges and for the extended patterns that will contribute to the overall outcome of the analytic relationship. This close analysis of some exchanges around the single topic of control has revealed phenomena at several levels of interest to the clinical practice of psychoanalysis.

What Impact Does the Analytic Injunction to "Say What Is On Your Mind," and for the Analyst to "Take Note" Have on the Process?

An element at the heart of the analytic enterprise, in its classic form at least, is the injunction to "say what is on your mind," while at the same time, the therapist reserves the right not to take turns at points in the discourse where taking a turn would be the natural next step. There is a powerful dynamic at the heart of this basic frame that has implications for the unfolding of the therapeutic interaction. One aspect of that dynamic is observable in the negotiation between analyst and patient about the demands of the analytic frame. By *not* responding in the usual way, the analytic frame sets up a novel situation, which clearly the patient found disturbing. On the other hand, the universal properties of turn-taking necessarily involve both analyst and patient in a deep and mostly unconscious process of inference-making, in order to achieve the kind of joint understanding that is the ultimate objective of analysis. The communicative actions of the analyst can be seen to have influenced the progress of this objective of the talk in different ways, sometimes opening up the intersubjective exploration and sometimes seeming to shutting it down.

It is observable in the dialogue between them, especially in sessions 5 and 99, that the use of mental predicates and verbal constructions that tend towards the production of a shared intersubjective space resulted in productive sequences in which both speakers get a hearing. Do the actions of the speakers, analyst and patient, reveal anything to us about the developing patterns of relationship by means of which we look to discover the transference? How did the constraints of the analytic framework play a part? This study has revealed some of the ways in which the turn-by-turn interaction is shaped by the constraints of the classical psychoanalytic frame: on the patient (to say what is on your mind) and on the analyst (to interpret the transference). Close analysis of the turn-by-turn progress of the talk revealed that both speakers were alive to the issue of control of the talk in the here and now at the more conscious level of their lexical choice, and management of the topic. At a less conscious level of the turn by turn sequences, a patterned system of denial followed by compliance could be observed in the patient's responses to the analyst's interventions. Some of this patterning was also reported in the patient's talk about other relationships in her life. For example, in session 98, analyst and patient stumble into a reflection on the way she complied with the analyst's view (A2 and P3) before the analyst responds, enacting the injunction to "interpret the transference" (his "job"), with his direct question "afraid of me too?" With this action, he shifts the focus of attention away from her acknowledgment that she said she was angry "just because you said that," and loses the potential for creating a shared reflective space in which to explore her compliance.

In the following session (99), talking about her battle with her husband over intercourse, the patient reveals at a more conscious level that she is highly attuned to, and in a battle with, the way others make inferences about her thoughts, feelings, and wishes. Here, we see evidence of how her participation in "outside" interactions and her engagement with the turn-by-turn interaction with the analyst contribute to the "game" her "mind" plays with him around what she will and won't say, and how she will engage with him to share thoughts about her feelings. The "what is being talked about" is intimately linked to the communicative actions of patient and analyst in this therapeutic dialogue.

How do patient and analyst behave around what is in their mind and their inferences about what is in the mind of the other? What is the outcome of these exchanges?

From the evidence of this analysis of the topic of "control," it seems that the topic, so frequently encountered in many therapeutic settings, is also a dynamic process, centred around issues of a subjectively experienced "self"—seat of intentions, fears of intrusion, wishes for autonomy—that has its origins in patterns of relating that are in a continuous state of dynamic instantiation in the here and now communicative patterns of relating. Control of my thoughts, and the inferences made about them, is a highly charged matter.

Freud (quoted in Sacks, 1992), in a comment on a paper by Tausk (1933) on schizophrenic thought processes, provides an interesting thought on how this phenomenon might come about:

> After all, when you learn at least your first language, you learn it from your parents, from adults. And children must take it that adults, giving them the concepts, know how they're being used; know how the child is using them. So the problem is not that people come to think that others know their thoughts, but how it is that people come to think so deeply that others don't know their thoughts. (Vol I, p. 114)

Tausk and Freud were interested in the process by which normally we come to recognize (or not, in the case of schizophrenia) that our thoughts are private. Freud seems here to point to the ways in which, as we know now from contemporary research in developmental psychology, interactions between caregivers and children shape the child's understanding of self and other, and other minds, through the dynamic process of learning to talk. It turns out that the continual process of gauging what is going on in the mind of the other is a universal property of all human interaction, and it is built into the form and function of turn-by-turn interaction.

This has implications for the practice of interpretation, particularly of the transference. Making inferences about what is in the mind of the other is a universal phenomenon of everyday interaction. As the analyst makes an interpretation (articulates his inference), so the patient is herself making inferences about the intentions of the analyst and acting to accept, reject, conceal, or obstruct his intentions in ways specific to the immediate context of the talk. Interpretation is an active, two-way process. Turning again to session 98, A4—"afraid of me too?"—we observe the patient's retreat, though she then (turn P7) goes on to reflect that "can readily think I'm afraid of what you might think of me. . . ." In session 99, in response to the patient's reflection that she felt foolish about how she was acting (a narrative of self and other) the analyst replies (A3) "but you were afraid that I would feel it was foolish, that you would sound foolish to me." This turn has a positive receipt on the part of the patient, and a further self-reflection (P6): "It was more direct in that the only person who even might know about it would be you because I would say it here, so then it would be, I didn't want you to know about it. . . ." Note that the way in which it was phrased echoes the way the patient herself phrased her response, in the previous session—in the form of what you might be thinking is in my mind—a pattern quite different from that which the interaction reported in the initiating story, in which she reported her husband "knowing that she wants to have intercourse." Could this be the way she experienced the analyst's interpretation, in its form of direct question, "Afraid of me too?" Is this perhaps evidence of an enactment of patterns of relating on the analyst's part? If so, it would seem that they escaped this enactment and discovered a novel pattern of relating in the following session. These are empirical questions that invite further study.

Does any of this have relevance for clinical practice? Some preliminary observations arising from this study are useful to pursue in the empirical investigation of what kinds of interventions may enable, or impede, the intersubjective process and the development of a shared reflective space:

- Direct questions tended to close down intersubjective space.
- Indirect questions, especially those phrased in the form of mental state predicates, tended to open up reflective space.

- Privileging the interpretation of content without close attention to the immediate process of the turn-by-turn talk had the effect of a refusal to hear/pursue the thought/topic proposed.
- The making of inferences about the mind of the other is a pragmatic, rather than a theoretical/conceptual matter. The ways in which inferences, or interpretations, of the other's mental state are expressed can enable, or impede, the intersubjective process.

It would be impossible for any speaker to become totally aware of his or her contribution to the turn-by-turn sequencing of talk. However, just as through training and supervision the psychoanalytic practitioner learns to attune to the dynamic play of transference, so it is possible to learn to tune into the dynamic play of the turn-by-turn patterning of relationship, by listening to and reflecting on the next turn: How did the other respond to what I just said? Was there a retreat? Was there shared reflection—or was it compliance? How did the way that I spoke affect the response? What was I responding to? What made me change the topic then?

CONCLUSION

This study of some of the interactions between a patient and her analyst around issues of control, and in particular, around issues of control of what can or could be said, to whom, is just a single thread in a complex tapestry of relating, which covered many topics and took many turns over the course of this analysis. Any, or many, other threads might have been followed: The researcher is in the same position as the analyst in this respect. However, I would argue that the stance of the pragmatic investigator is different from and supplementary to the findings of an analytic case study. For, by casting a more distant eye on the interaction, and by drawing on the findings of many observers of naturally occurring interaction, the pragmatic investigation offers the opportunity to slow down and to examine in detail the lively dynamic process by which the participants in the analytic project make use of what are perfectly ordinary, though marvellously complex, resources in their efforts to understand each other, to fashion a rich intersubjective field in which the analytic process can prosper. These perfectly ordinary skills are ones we learn and can go on learning about as patients and as therapists. Pragmatics offers the potential for the gradual enrichment of the analytic framework through the systematic study of its primary tool: It is, after all, the "talking cure." Its findings can offer a nuanced understanding of the psychoanalytic process, which has potentially rich implications for the training and supervision of clinicians.

REFERENCES

Beebe, B., & Lachmann, F. M. (1988). The contribution of mother–infant interactions to the origins of self and object representations. *Psychoanalytic Psychology, 5*(4), 305–337.

Buchler, J. (2010). *Charles Peirces's empiricism.* New York, NY: Routledge Taylor Francis. (Original work published 1939)

Caffi, C. (1999). On mitigation. *Journal of Pragmatics, 31*(7), 881–909.

Caffi, C., & Janney, R. (1994). Towards a pragmatics of emotive communication. *Journal of Pragmatics, 22*(3&4), 325–373.

Dewey, J. (1916). *Democracy and education: An introduction to the philosophy of education.* New York: Macmillan Books.

Enfield, N.J. (2009). Relationship thinking and human pragmatics. *Journal of Pragmatics, 41*(1), 60–78.

Enfield, N. J., & Levinson, S. C. (Eds.). (2006). *Roots of human sociality: Culture, cognition and interaction.* Oxford, UK: Berg.

Gill, M. M. (1982). *Analysis of transference I: Theory and technique* New York, NY: International Universities Press.

Greenson, R. (1965). The working alliance and the transference neurosis. *The Psychoanalytic Quarterly, 34,* 155–181.

Hendriks-Jansen, H. (1996). *Catching ourselves in the act: Situated activity, interactive emergence, evolution and human thought.* Cambridge, MA: MIT Press.

Heritage, J. (2002). The limits of questioning: Negative interrogatives and hostile question content. *Journal of Pragmatics, 34*(10-11), 1427–1446.

Jayussi, L (1984). *Categorization and the moral order.* London, UK: Routledge and Kegan Paul.

James, W. (1890). *The principles of psychology.* London, U K: Macmillan & Co.

Lepper, G (2000). Categories in text and *talk.* London, UK: Sage.

Lepper, G. (2009). The pragmatics of therapeutic interaction. *International Journal of Psychoanalysis, 90*(5), 1075–1094.

Lepper G., & Mergenthaler, E. (2007). Therapeutic collaboration as interactional accomplishment. *Psychotherapy Research, 17*(5), 576–588.

Lepper G., & Mergenthaler, E. (2008). Observing therapeutic interaction in the 'Lisa' case. *Psychotherapy Research, 18*(6), 634–645.

Lerner, G. H. (1996). Finding 'face' in the preference structures of talk-in-interaction. *Social Psychology Quarterly, 59(4)*, 303-321.

Levenson, E. (1979). Language and healing. *Journal of the American Academy of Psychoanalysis*, 7, 271–282.

Levenson, E. (1982). Follow the fox: An inquiry into the vicissitudes of psychoanalytic supervision. *Contemporary Psychoanalysis, 18,* 1–15.

Levinson, S. (2006). The human interaction engine. In N. J. Enfield & S. Levinson (Eds.), *The roots of sociality: Culture, cognition and interaction* (pp. 39–70). Oxford, UK: Berg.

Mead, G. H. (1934). *Mind, self and society.* Chicago, IL: University of Chicago Press.

Sacks, H. (1992). *Lectures on conversation* (Vols I & II). Oxford, UK: Blackwell.

Sacks H., Schegloff, E. A., & Jefferson, G. (1974). A simplest systematic for the organization of turn taking in conversation. *Language, 50*(4), 696–735.

Schegloff, E. (1992). Repair after next turn: The last structurally provided defense of intersubjectivity in conversation. *American Journal of Sociology, 98,* 1295–1345.

Schegloff, E. (2006). Interaction: The infrastructure for social institutions, the natural ecolofical niche for language, and the arena in which culture is enacted. In N. J. Enfield & S. Levinson (Eds.), *The roots of sociality: Culture, cognition and interaction* (pp. 70–97). Oxford, UK: Berg.

Schiffrin, D. (1987). *Discourse markers.* Cambridge, UK: Cambridge University Press.

Tausk, V. (1933). On the origin of the influencing machine in schizophrenia. *Psychoanalytic Quarterly, 2, page reference to follow*

Trevarthen, C. (1998). The concept and foundations of infant intersubjectivity. In S. Braten (Ed.), *Intersubjective communication and emotion in early ontogeny.* Cambridge: University of Cambridge Press.

Searles, H. F. (1978). Concerning transference and countertransference. *International. Journal of Psychoanalysis, 7,*165–188.

Verhagen, A. (2005). *Constructions of intersubjectivity: Discourse, syntax and cognition.* Oxford, UK: Oxford University Press.

Watzlawick, P., Beavin, J. H., & Jackson, D. D. (1968). *Pragmatics of human communication: A study of interactional patterns, pathologies and paradoxes.* London, UK: Faber & Faber.

Zucker, A. H. (1993). The discourse marker well: A relevance-theoretical account. *Journal of Pragmatics, 19*(5), 435–432.

[illegible]

CHAPTER 10

CHILDREN'S DREAMS

A Novel Interpretation

Yariv Orgad and Yair Neuman
Ben-Gurion University of the Negev

A student seeking to understand the meaning of pragmatism would be naturally led to Wikipedia where she or he will find the idea of linking theory to practice. In the context of psychology, this means that psychological theorization and research should be grounded in real-world problems that shake our stable pattern of behavior, what Peirce has described as *habit*, and may motivate us to produce hypotheses to better explain a given state of affairs. In this context, the study of dreams and dreaming seems remote from the motivating turbulence described by pragmatism.

Freud's seminal work on dreams seems like a comfortable theoretical habit. Freud established our modern understanding of dreams as a form of symbolic disguise of repressed unconscious content seeking its expression when its warden, the ego, is off duty. Given the Freudian legacy, dreaming, at least as a psychological phenomenon inviting the researcher to find meaningful regularities in mental content, seems a closed case. Is it?

This chapter presents a meeting point between theory and practice that aims to examine the Freudian dogma. The first author (Yariv Orgad) is a kindergarten teacher. During his work and for several years he collected

Making Our Ideas Clear, pages 275–293
Copyright © 2015 by Information Age Publishing
All rights of reproduction in any form reserved.

the kindergarteners' dreams, organized them in a book, and read them to the kindergarteners. This practice was not motivated by a clear theoretical rationale, but it attracted the attention and curiosity of the children, who were fascinated to share and listen to other children's dreams. After several years, Mr. Orgad decided to complete his MA degree in education and participated in a university course taught by the second author (Yair Neuman). This was a graduate study course dealing with psychoanalysis, and the practice of collecting and sharing the dreams naturally intermingled with the theoretical discussions during the classes. The result is this chapter, in which we introduce a new interpretation of children's dreams.

Basically, while Freud believed that we dream in order to sleep, a rivaling hypothesis by Bion was that we sleep in order to dream. According to Bion, dreaming is necessary for mental functioning and growth through the transformation of unstructured, fragmented, and emotionally loaded particles of experience into a "digestible" and meaningful form. The way this transformation is conducted is far from trivial. Our work suggests that dreams involve a process of "symmetrization," described by Matte Blanco as the hallmark of the unconscious. This process of symmetrization, in which the "I" is equated with threatening imaginary beings such as monsters, is a process through which the "self" emerges as a hypothetical and ever-changing pattern. This interpretation follows C. S. Peirce's idea of the self as an invented construct, not in the sense that it emerges *ex nihilo*, but in the sense that it is hypothesized as an explanatory tool rather than as a metaphysical entity. This thesis is detailed below, starting with a short reminder of Freud's seminal work.

FREUD'S DREAMS

Freud (1900) argued that the purpose of dreaming is to protect sleep from the threat of overwhelming anxiety that may be caused by repressed impulses originating in childhood. As a repressed mental activity, these impulses are ever emerging and trying to regain access to the consciousness, exerting pressure on it. The reason they are seeking their way out is not clear in Freud's writing, and one may question the dynamics resulting in the ever-existing threat of impulses seeking their way out of the Pandora's box in which they are locked.

Since sleeping is a physical need, and since sleeping is the time when the ego's defense mechanisms are weakened and loosened, it must be guarded against interruption. Freud argued that dreams are the "guardians of sleep" (Freud, 1901, p. 678), whose purpose is to censor, distort, and disguise the repressed pressing content, converting it into a bearable one that will not interrupt sleep. Therefore, following Freud's line of thinking, dreams are also the way an analyst may get access to this content with which mental work can be done in order to relieve pressure on the ego. Dreams thus emerge as material not within reach of the subject but only for the analyst to interpret according to a well-defined scheme that aims to turn the mask out of the dream work. The subject will keep trying to disguise the pressuring repressed impulses while an analyst, by interpreting the "codes" of the dreams, will try to "decode" them, to go in the reverse direction of dreaming and to excavate hidden meanings in order to solve unconditioned stimulus (UCS) complexes originating in childhood.

Freud (1900) considered children's dreams as basic, primary, and under-developed material with which the more developed material (adult's dreams) could be more fully understood. This developmental view is present in contemporary studies of children's dreams wherein these are grasped as containing primal aggressiveness and anxiety (Muris, Merckelbach, Gadet, & Moulaert, 2000; Siegel, 2005).

From a developmental perspective, several studies have examined the relation between age and dream content (e.g., Lillard & Flavel, 1992; Sharon & Woolley, 2004; Simard, Nielsen, Tremblay, Boivin, & Montplaisir, 2008; Woolley & Wellman, 1992). It seems that dream content represents the basic Eros–Thanatos dynamics, which is at high levels in childhood, and the attempt to reduce levels of anxiety and allow some "good-enough" sleeping.

As argued by Schneider (2010, p. 522), "Freud's towering legacy dissuaded subsequent theorists from reconsidering dream-work from new perspectives that require of contemporary analyst nothing less than a paradigm shift." One important challenge to Freud's theory of dreams emerges from the work of W. R. Bion.

BION'S CHALLENGE: WE SLEEP IN ORDER TO DREAM

Bion proposed that dreaming is a process through which raw impressions are transformed into meaningful/digestible patterns (Bion, 1994). The main shift here is the relationship of the subject to his own dreams. Dreams are not merely analytical material for an analyst, but also for the subject's own thinking process that he may be able to use, either by himself or with the help of an analyst (Bion, 1989). Thus, what is needed is dreaming itself (rather than sleeping), which is secured through sleeping; hence we sleep in order to dream, and not vice versa.

In contrast to Freud, the most important "instinct" for Bion was the *truth instinct* of which thinking, dreaming, and mental growth are the main manifestations (Grotstein, 2007). Bion's subject is ever-trying to grasp the ultimate truth—O, which is always beyond her grasp. This truth is the primordial matter of experience, what Kant has described as the *Ding-un-Sich*, C. S. Peirce as the "*Dynamical object*," and Lacan as the "*Real*."

For the experiencing subject, life involves the never-ending task of reaching out toward the matter of life and reaching in by transforming this raw material into a "digestible," emotionally meaningful, and usable form. This process of transformation operates on various levels of the system. Just as the visual system faces the challenge of transforming light regularities in the external environment into the experience of vision, the "self" is attempting to convert the totality of his experience into a meaningful narrative, an act of integration and "meaning making" (Neuman, 2008) that stands at the heart of each living system. This general logic implies a process of learning from experience that transforms the subject and his reality—that is, experiencing reality induces making meanings out of it, making it meaningful in a very personal and individual way.

Bion (1989) suggested that the three main relations or "zones of interaction" of a subject with his world are love (L), hate (H), and knowledge (K), with which he can grasp the ultimate truth about reality and transform it into one's own. Hence, knowing reality, K → O, means that a subject constructs different sorts of emotional relations to reality and with it. Thus, knowing is not a rational and static situation, but rather an emotional and dynamic process that affects both subject and object. The subject's emotional relations are mediators for O, the "tools" with which to capture and manipulate reality. But since O is ever-evolving and cannot be captured or privatized, that which is mediated is no longer O. It is the subject's own creation, its unique, personal, and private "affair" with O, which gives private meaning to it and transforms it into one's own truth about reality.

For example, there is no such thing as an objective "mother," but rather the very private and individual experience of a baby (and his mother) that is being fed and nourished by his own unique mother. This provides the baby with his own perceptions of reality (being secured, persecuted, related, dependent, etc.) that are based on emotional-relational experiences—these transform his emotional-cognitive perception of reality, and the relational process also transforms the mother and the relationship itself. Thus any moment, any perception, is true for the very moment in which it is captured. The experiences to come will always be based on/consist of them, but ever different.

In Bion's words, it is an incarnation of O in one's inner world (Grotstein, 2007) that makes the world sensible. This incarnation brings the subject's evolvement through experience and to the emergence of the self as a useful and usable system. This system is developed as a "self-sufficient" one in the sense of making its own unique meaning out of its experiences. We can look at this process as one of self-construction in which the subject evolves and integrates in accordance with its object relations (Neuman, 2009). Namely, consolidating K links with objects (inner object relations) is a process by which the self's identity is integrated and then used to find one's own way for dealing with O. This point is relevant to the dream analysis that follows.

Epistemologically, Bion (1967) separated thinking, and the mind that operates it, from thoughts themselves. Thoughts exist in O prior to thinking, mainly as preconceptions. These are "thoughts without a thinker," incomprehensible and meaningless experiences and phenomena deriving from O's imprints on a subject's sensory and mental apparatus, waiting to be mentally processed ("digested") (Grotstein, 2009, p. 337)—for example, a hungry baby is craving for a breast while it is absent. Feelings of anxiety (lest it may not get fed) are incorporated into the hunger, thus printing a conjoined raw impression (of hunger and anxiety) on the baby's experience. This raw impression is yet meaningless for the baby and cannot be assessed, associated, and comprehended. But there are preconceptions in the baby's mind waiting to be filled in with meaning, as containers waiting to be filled with meaningful content (Bion, 1970). The baby has a (as yet meaningless) preconception of a nurturing breast. Under the hegemony of reality principle, which helps to manage frustration (Freud, 1900), the hunger experience may induce thinking. This thinking process is analogous to pouring content into a container, thus filling it with personal meaning, transforming the preconception into a concept. Thinking about a nurturing breast by fantasizing it can calm the baby until his mother will come to feed him. The experience of hunger and anxiety thus establishes an idea, symbolized by the fantasized breast, of the reality as it is for the baby, wherein it can survive via its nurturing mother. Thus the way one approaches reality is based on the very individual way one has transformed these raw experiences and constructed one's emotionally based symbols. Thinking as symbolizing is the very fundamental process of relating raw experiences to meaningful signs and constructing the organizing narrative of the self.

According to Bion, the process by which these relations are being worked out is the dreaming/α function (Grotstein, 2007). Although in Bion's writings there is sometimes confusion between dreaming and alpha function, Grotstein suggests understanding α function as a theoretical model for dreaming as the mental process (2007). While Bion eventually separated the two, the model and its mental application are interrelated and actually cannot be separated. Dreaming is *where* and *when* α function is at work, and it is also the function itself. It is a transformation of β ("raw") elements into α ("digested") elements, producing the very basic particles of knowledge in Bion's epistemology. Alpha elements constitute the emotional foundation upon which one's very personal reality is built. These elements are extracted by the self from its experiences, that is, from its contexts. The very unique ways in which a subject connects and relates between α elements constructs and reflects his unique character and ways of dealing with reality. It is as though there is a matrix of emotional associations (Salvatore & Freda, 2011) that produces private and unique inner meaning that enables the subject to apprehend and construct reality in accordance to his own needs and experiences.

Take for example a three-year-old child in the wilderness under a sky full of stars. It is a matter of emotional associative process what impression this experience may leave for the child to posses. It is possible for the child to sit with his father by the fire and to transform this experience to one of wonder, warmth, and courage. On the other hand, this could be an experience of horror. One may associate wilderness with opportunities and freedom, another with danger and impotence. The realm where symbols are being loaded with such meanings is the dreaming/alpha function (while sleeping and awake alike) where prior experiences provide emotional associations.

Furthermore, for Bion (1994), dreaming occurs in sleep as in wakefulness, where it is also a relational process that Bion termed *reverie*—that is, dreaming together or between people, a very primary and basic process of which the very early expressions can be found in the baby's relations with its mother. In the very early experiences of reverie the baby internalizes the way his mother handles him.

Internalizing, in this context, means that the baby transforms the relational processes to his own mental posture and ways of coping with his own reality (inner and outer). Thus, relations between subject and object transform into inner relations. In this context, mirroring is a very basic and functional process for the baby to internalize in order to develop a reflective stand, a "second person" perspective inside himself (Neuman, 2009). Dreaming enables this internalization through meaning-making processes in relation to a subject's experiences. One can see the importance of dreaming for one's own ability to configure one's place in a context. This may be a way of developing separation in a relational context. Nevertheless, the dynamics that constitute this process of transformation remained mysterious. A brief review of Matte Blanco's (1975) theory of the UCS is used here to clarify this point.

MATTE BLANCO'S BI-LOGIC

Matte Blanco argued (1975) that the system UCS has its own unique logic that differs from that of the system conscious, which he then termed "scientific" logic. To recall, Freud defined five characteristic of the UCS:

1. Absence of contradiction and negation
2. Displacement
3. Condensation
4. Absence of time
5. Replacement of external by psychical reality (Matte Blanco, 1975, pp. 36–37).

Matte Blanco argued that these characteristics conform to a well-defined logic, which differs widely from scientific logic. He writes: "We may conclude that the special characteristics of the system UCS described by Freud reveal the operation of a logic peculiar to this system, whose fundamental distinguishing mark is to treat as symmetrical relations which in scientific logic are not so considered" (1975, p. 47).

For Matte Blanco (1975, p. 13), "psychical life can be viewed as a perpetual dynamic interaction... between two fundamental types of being which exist in the unity of every man"—the conscious and the unconscious. In order to grasp the human psyche one must understand both parts of it and the relationships between them. For that purpose Matte Blanco strived to define the UCS and its rules. He stated two fundamental principles of its logic:

1. *The principle of generalization.* This principle suggests that the UCS considers any object as a part of a class that contains other objects and that the class in its turn is treated as a part of a wider class, and so on. There is a "propositional function" (1975, p. 27) that defines objects and their relations, and according to which objects are chosen to be integrated in a class. For example, while using the general category "predators," we may refer to a wide set of particular elements (lion, dinosaur, crocodile, etc.) in which the propositional function that joined them together (e.g., an animal that preys) still maintained their particularities. This idea is in line with Bion's (1994) concept of "selected fact," which identifies feelings and attributes of wholeness, meaning, and unity with a collection of elements not necessarily related. Otherwise, without the selected fact, this collection will be meaningless. This principle serves a process of abstraction as it enables, in its more developed stages, approaching a single object as an abstracted representation of widely ranged meanings. Matte Blanco showed how this principle of the UCS helps organize its chaotic nature. Since this principle also affects consciousness, it cannot be a special characteristic of the UCS by itself.
2. *The principle of symmetry.* This principle means that the UCS considers any relation as identical to its inverse. Hence, all relations, even asymmetrical relations, are treated as though they were symmetrical. This principle completely transforms the rules of scientific logic and is the main characteristic by which Matte Blanco describes the logic of UCS. For example, if $x < y$ it is also true that $y < x$. For instance, in the UCS it is acceptable that the son is younger than his father, and at the same time that the father is younger than his son, so they become interchangeable with each other while remaining different from each other. The difference between interchangeable elements is maintained by the unique and separated identity of each element.

> This last point is most important since it is relevant to separation–individuation processes through which a subject may separate and relate himself in a relational context. Furthermore, the separated and well-defined identity of each element is a precondition for interchanging processes. Only if there is a difference between *X* and *Y* would it be possible to construct an equation such as $X = Y$, meaning that *X* and *Y* are at the same time identical and different. This point is important for understanding the interpretation to be introduced later according to which dreaming involves the identification and differentiation of the emerging self. (Matte Blanco, 1975, pp. 37–38)

Matte Blanco realized that in its ultimate expression, the logic of symmetry will produce a chaotic reality in which there is no differentiation or meaning, only an "all-embracing infinite set in which nothing is distinguishable" (1975, p. 54). This is very similar to Bion's definition of O as a chaotic and infinite reality comprising nondigested elements that bear no meaning and cannot be differentiated (Grotstein, 2007). It also fits the realization of the state of "primordial self" (Neuman, 2009), in which symbol formation capability has not yet roused and the self comprises unknowable elements—in the sense of Bion's K—meaning they are not named or symbolized and cannot be used for mental growth.

Matte Blanco described psychic reality as a perpetual dynamic interaction between the UCS and the consciousness, between the symmetric logic and the asymmetric logic, which comprise together what he termed "a bi-logical system" (1975, p. 58). In bi-logic, the UCS, which may be described by the logic of symmetry, is ever-pressing upwards, looking for its expression, but being blocked by scientific logic because of the anxiety it rouses. This point is very important because it explains the urge to block unconscious materials from reaching the surface in epistemological and emotional terms. According to our reading of Matte Blanco, what threatens the self *is not the content of the repressed material but the dynamics of symmetrization.* Ultimate symmetrization is actually death. Think about a living organism versus a crystal. A crystal has a well-defined symmetry, but a living organism exists on the boundary of symmetry and asymmetry, order and chaos. For the organism, whether on the biophysical level or the mental level, the ultimate phase of symmetry is death, where the second law of thermodynamics is expressed as the system's maximization of entropy. In sum, the theory proposed by Matte Blanco provides an alternative explanation to the importance of constituting the boundary with the UCS.

The bi-logic is the logic that characterizes dreaming wherein processes of translation and duplication (Matte Blanco, 2005, p. 12) of symmetrical reality into asymmetrical reality occur. Matte Blanco suggested that epistemologically we may think of the very basic state of psychic reality (UCS) as symmetrical, chaotic, and one that we must transform into an asymmetrical and differentiated state of affairs in order to comprehend (Matte Blanco, 1975). Some parts of the original state may be left as they are, not transformed. Hence not all that is symmetrical/UCS is repressed, but rather it is in its original state—its primordial emotional experience. This is the very emotional (symmetrical) basis of the human sensory system upon which meanings are built (see Salvatore & Freda, 2011, for discussion of this idea). Thus, the dream is the medium where one mediates between these different levels, where one activates the bi-logic, where mental activity of connecting emotional and intellectual experiences and meanings is enabled. This is just another way to describe Bion's "*contact barrier*" (Bion, 1989), which is the mental mechanism that regulates the movement of particles both ways between the UCS and consciousness, thus enabling the transformation of raw β elements into meaningful α elements.

Matte Blanco (1975, pp. 140–141) described a few characteristics of the way the UCS operates, which may help us to observe dreaming.

1. Any object represents an aspect of a person and the person's relationships with the object (e.g., a lion may represent an aspect of a person associated with anxiety).
2. A singular object represents an abstraction and becomes identical to the propositional function of this abstraction (e.g., the lion in the above example turns out to be identical to the anxiety factor).
3. The UCS can recognize groups only. Any object (or element of a set) is treated as though it was the set itself (e.g., the lion is treated as the whole category of all creatures that provoke anxiety; namely it is an abstracted symbol of the emotional experience of anxiety).
4. Any set may be treated by the UCS as though it had human qualities (e.g., a lion may represent humans, and not animals, meaning the threatened/threatening aspect of a person's relationships with others. Home may represent such a containing aspect).

These points show how an object (e.g., a lion) may turn out to be identical with a propositional function (e.g., that which provokes anxiety). This means it represents the relations by which separated elements are conjoined and integrated into a dynamic unity of meaning. Thus "lion" may represent the endless emotional potential of meaning that "anxiety" entails. In the same way, "breast" may represent the endless emotional potential of meaning that "motherhood" entails. As a result, every set is a dynamic set that widens the potential meaning that it entails according to the accumulating experiences of the subject.

The theory of Matte Blanco's urges us to examine dreams as meaning-making fields, meaning that could not otherwise be made. This is where by symmetry, on the one hand, emotional existence is enabled with a very "real" relation to the primordial emotional experiences (I *am* lion—with all its consequences), and on the other hand, symmetry may result in separation and differentiation of the self from its objects as a consequence of the very singularity of one's own experiences (I *am different* from the lion by which I am knowing myself).

According to the above interpretation, the self emerges, unites, and identifies with "him-self" out of symbolizing, naming, and visualizing his experiences. The symmetrical experience enables the self to look at himself from different perspectives and to emerge as a whole that is different from the sum of its parts (Neuman, 2009). Thus dreams make the self known and meaningful to it, distinguished and separated from outer/inner reality while related to it. Symmetrization is revealed here as the mechanism of dreams, or of α function, that enables the enrichment of the self and the emergence of self awareness out of organization of inner object relationships.

We have contrasted Freud's and Bion's theories of dreaming (i.e., dreaming in order to sleep as opposed to sleeping in order to dream) and showed how symmetrization may play a major role in dreaming as a process through which authentic emotional existence and growth is enabled. It must be emphasized that this conceptualization did not emerge *a priori* to our analysis of dreams, but through a "recursive-hierarchical" process in which theorization and analysis emerged together step-by-step. We will turn now to kindergarteners' dreams. We have analyzed these dreams in a novel and structural methodology. The data, the methodology, and the emerging themes are presented in the next section.

METHODOLOGY

We have analyzed 155 kindergarteners' dreams that were collected over a period of four years in a kindergarten of 3–6-year-old children in Israel. The original purpose of telling and writing dreams was to serve as a method for dealing with language development (spoken and written) while relating it to representations of the kids' inner emotional worlds. All dreams were told voluntarily in the morning hours. Each child who wished to do so presented his dream without intervention by the kindergarten teacher. The kindergarten teacher wrote the dream and the only information he added was the date on which the dream was told and the child's name. One hundred and one dreams were told by boys and 54 by girls. The number of dreams per child varied with a single dream for few of the children and up to 15 for others.

Siegel (2005) shows how methods for collecting children's dreams are largely diverse and asserts "that no standardized method for collecting children's dreams has been established" (p. 148). This methodological diversity of dream collection and analysis naturally led to the question of whether the children's dreams we have collected are valid in the sense that they represent the experience of dreaming rather than the child's creative invention of dream-like stories or interpretation of dream content. This question is inevitable, as the ability to differentiate between reality and fantasy starts to appear around four years of age and is rarer in younger children (Sharon & Woolley, 2004; Woolley & Wellman, 1992). To address this methodological issue we would like to return to Bion.

Bion (1967) used the term *"reverie"* for describing conjoined wakeful thinking—a joint process in which both mother and baby are involved. In this process, the mother introjects the baby's projections, "digests" them, and transforms them for him into a bearable and meaningful matter. The baby then introjects the transformed material—not just as it is, but rather as the transformational function. It is the function itself that is introjected by the baby and enriches inner object relations. It is a highly developed α function in which α elements are being transformed (by the mother, for the baby) into functions; that is, the elements are being loaded with functional meaning; they are now used to manipulate relationships between themselves. In other words, α elements are being "elevated" into functions as the baby constructs K links between them; inner object relations become meaningful and transformable. These links with objects are the expressions of a subject's very individual way of mental growth. Thus one can see how one's very inner world of object relations is rooted in relatedness. In this light, aspects of credibility, authenticity, and reality and fantasy differentiation in relation to the dreams' stories become irrelevant. The process of telling dreams in the kindergarten, writing them, and reading them in front of the whole group turned them into sort of shared "private mythology" of this group of kindergarteners. This was a multiparty joint process of projecting, digesting, introjecting, and meaning-making. It constructed a semiotic matrix in which "dynamic configuration of sign-use that is constituted by individual minds and constitutes the minds of the individuals who compose it" (Neuman, 2011, p. 324) occurs. This matrix is a dynamic joint process that enables the individual to design and define his own and unique inner object relations in an intersubjective environment. The accumulated dream corpus actually creates an unconscious foundation of matrices of stories—signs characterized by symmetrical relations. After clarifying the methodological issue concerning the "validity" of the dream telling, we now turn to the analysis.

For the analysis, each dream has been represented as a *semiotic map* that was used to characterize links and relationships between the dream's objects. Sketching these maps has been motivated by the use of *category theory* as a formal perspective for analyzing psychological phenomena (Neuman,

2011, 2013; Neuman, Assaf & Cohen, 2012). Category theory is a mathematical framework that emphasizes the greater importance of objects' relationships over the objects themselves. Thus this theory enables the sketching of maps that depict the structures of psychological categories as relationships.

According to Matte Blanco (1975) the symmetry that characterizes dreams and the UCS is expressed through object relationships. Hence category theory was used to examine object relationships that characterize the dream corpus, trying to reveal the meanings that children construct by linking objects.

The maps are composed from objects/signs and their relations, graphically presented as arrows that connect objects: for example, for the utterance "a monster preyed on me," we sketched a map comprised of an arrow (the predicate "preyed") leading from the object "monster" to the object "me" (Figure 10.1).

To identify important symmetries between dream objects we have used category theory's idea of a "point." In Euclidean geometry a point is a "primitive," the most basic entity, albeit in a different sense. In category theory, a point involves two types of objects described as *initial* and *terminal.* An object in a given category C is described as "initial" if for every other object of the category there exists precisely one arrow pointing from this initial object to the others. The complementary term "terminal object" is used to denote a given object in a category to which all the other objects point with exactly one arrow.

We have used this abstract idea, albeit in a free sense, to identify dream objects with many relations to the rest of the objects as well as "terminal" objects toward which the other objects point. In this context, a *point* as a primitive unit of the category involves a reciprocal relation between objects that are both initial and terminal. The above map illustrates *a point,* the relationships between a self (me) identified in the dream story through the child's implicit use of a second-person pronoun and an object (i.e., monster).

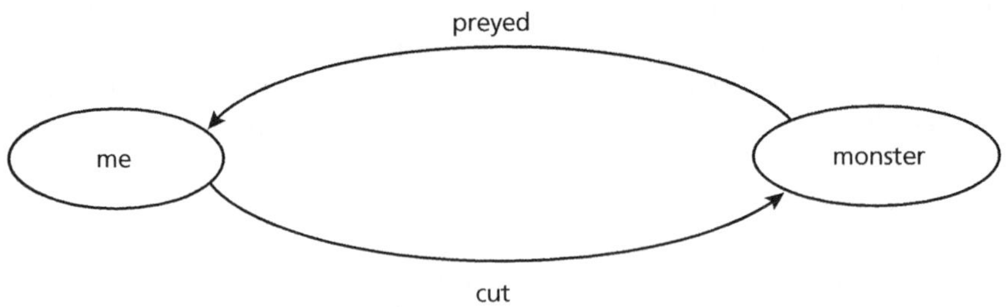

Figure 10.1 A semiotic map for the dream"I dreamt that a monster preyed on me and I cut it."

Both objects are initial and terminal. Thus category theory helped us to focus our attention on the part of the map in which hidden meanings were found and to excavate them.

In the above map, the self may be seen as both the victim and the aggressor as the child is being preyed upon by the monster, but he also "cut" it. Taking the symmetry principle into consideration, we can interpret the above "point" as follows: self = monster; the inverse of a relation is identical to the relation and both parts of the equation are interchangeable.

As a result of the analysis, we have identified several clusters of objects. The objects and their frequency appear in Table 10.1, which enables us to identify those objects that are most prominent in the dream corpus. For each of these objects, we sketched a map that relates to the whole corpus, which is a map that presents the object's relationships with *all* other objects that exist in the whole dream corpus as opposed to appearance in a single dream of a specific child. Such a collective map of dreams enables us to extract a wider volume of relations than those that exist in a single dream.

Following our sociocultural approach to psychology, with its emphasis on the semiotic and collective mediation of the human mind (Valsiner, 2007; Volosinov, 1986), this choice, which contrasts typical approaches to the analysis of dreams, is considered by us as legitimate.

For example, a semantic map for the object "lion" would present its relationships with all other objects that exist in the dream corpus as a whole, as it emerges out of the very peculiar experiences and understandings of different children who shared their dreams. Such reference to an object enables us to present it as a mediating sign in a semiotic matrix that is a "dynamic web of signs that emerges out of local interactions" (Neuman, 2011).

The individual, from his very beginning, experiences dialogical and interpersonal dynamics that constitute his peculiar personality. The interpersonal interactions provide the individual with mediating signs, with "tools"

TABLE 10.1 Frequency of Appearance for Different Dreams' Objects

Real Animals	Imaginary Animals	Family Relatives	Places/Arena
Lion (18)	Monsters (26)	Mother (33)	Home (26)
Dinosaur (9)	Dragons (22)	Father (26)	Room (11)
Elephant (8)	Witches (5)	Brother or Sister (24)	Garden (7)
Bear (5)		Grandparents (10)	Bed (6)
Mouse (5)			Forest (5)

for understanding and dealing with his experiences. In this way, these ztools are the means by which these interactions can be worked out, and at the same time they are the products of it.

These ideas fit Bion's (1967) model of α function and reverie, which is the very basis for the development of thinking. In this model the individual introjects and internalizes from his mother α elements and the ability to use them for α function in order to be able to confront reality, to apprehend it, to make it meaningful to himself, and to be able to grow mentally. Additionally, Bion asserted that experiences are narrated into a mythic-cultural frame that limits, directs, and guides human thinking (Grotstein, 2007). This frame constitutes the individual and is being constituted by him at the same time. Dreaming organizes chaotic experiences and impressions of O into mythic narratives that inspire the individual with a sense of coherence, meaning, and unity. Thus, while the dreams are accumulated into a corpus, they develop an unconscious foundation of the signs–myths matrix. We will now turn to discuss the major theme that emerged thorough this analysis.

THE MAJOR THEME IDENTIFIED IN THE DREAMS

While analyzing the maps, we identified an interesting theme: *Points*, or reciprocal relationships between initial/terminal objects, were limited to relationships of objects with the self only. All other objects were related to other objects by a one-direction relation, being initial *or* terminal objects only. Hence the maps pointed to the fact that what we could assume as expressions of UCS or representations of symmetrization in relationships was evident only in relations with the speaking I—the self.

What is the explanation of this emerging theme? A possible interpretation is that the self is constructed by being identified as well as contrasted with other objects. Take for example the map of the object "monster" previously presented. It equates the self with monster (i.e., self = monster) while it necessarily maintains through this symmetrization the separation of the self and the object (self ≠ monster). After all, symmetrization necessarily entails differentiation. Therefore, we read the symmetrization of the "talking perspective"—the self—with dream objects as a process through which the self emerges as a differentiated construct.

We should recall that Ogden (1985) discusses the potential space as a "process in which two opposing concepts each creates, informs, preserves and negates the other, each standing in a dynamic (ever changing) relationship with the other…integration is never complete" (pp. 130–131). This eternal tension constitutes the potential space for mental growth in which dreaming is only a specific expression. We propose that the process of symmetrization is at the heart of the mental growth as it induces this eternal tension, hence contributing to the development, integration, and identity of the self.

A look at the "monster" map may reveal a process of dealing with anxiety in which the experience must be symbolized and then manipulated in order to be able to cope with it. Anxiety is being symbolized, reified, and objectified as a monster, and then situated in the inner world of object relations. A child may feel anxious as his self is both physically and psychologically a self-organizing system in which a sense of functional coherence emerges from fragmented pieces of experience. After all, achieving, for instance, eye-hand coordination, control over secretions, and regulation of anxiety are tasks yet to be achieved rather than completed achievements. In this context, a general anxiety of defragmentation is a natural threat facing the subject. Symbolizing this anxiety as a monster and symmetrizing this symbol through the use of the first-person perspective, the child may feel that *HE is the monster*, that *HE contains it*, and that he can manipulate this emotional experience. By uniting with the emotional experience and objectifying it, by confronting the sign and using it, the self is enriched and strengthened, its boundaries are expended.

An introjected and symbolized object is a meaningful and useful object for α function, for mental growth, for experiencing, and dealing with reality. In other words, it is a fundamental element of Bionian thinking that enables transformations in O, K → O, influencing O, and being influenced by it. The recognition of the incarnation of O in oneself brings mental growth. In this light, symmetrization may be seen as a liberating aspect of dreams in the self's interaction with reality, an aspect that liberates and transforms the self through a perpetual striving outwards towards emotional perception of reality, and inwards towards emotional recognition of itself.

The maps that we have sketched show how, according to the characteristics of the UCS, the chaotic existence (in which the self and all other objects might be assimilated as an undifferentiated whole) is organized by propositional functions. Delineating relationships between objects enables objects' categorization according to their relationships. For example, as opposed to self = monster/lion/dragon, we were able to point to the propositional function "all those that prey" and to characterize a category with which the self could be equated. In this sense, the monsters represent not only the child's aggression as theorized by Melanie Klein, but also the attempt to face the chaos from which the self has emerged and to which one day it will return. This configuration serves Kleinian (Segal, 1973) depressive mechanisms of enrichment that allow the self to integrate as a whole and organized system that contains ambivalence towards its inner object relationships. Here symmetrization may explain how specific aspects of the depressive position are constructed.

To recall a main character of the depressive position is the ever-growing capacity of integration, meaning the growing ability of containing opposites, or paradoxes (e.g., approaching the mother as a whole, containing both good *and* bad breasts). The self (by symmetrization) is capable of equation with monster (aggression) but also of negation of it, separating from it, thus perceiving the quality of "aggression" as multivocal, the essence of itself as multidimensional.

The process of self-construction enabled by symmetry is infinite. Since the self is defined by propositional functions that characterize ever-widening sets, the perception of the term "self" becomes deeper, multidimensional, and abstracted constantly. Every experience can potentially contribute to the dream work a new concrete meaning for a sign, a new association, or a new way for linking objects. Thus, dreaming helps the self in his quest for truth, in his attempts to comprehend O and himself. Dreams translate and symbolize O into meaningful and individual experiences embodied in a sociocultural linguistic and semiotic matrix: that is, in signs. These signs remain dynamic forever in order to preserve the potential space of experiences. This dynamic quality enables further growing, further dreaming, and innovative use of symbols. This aspect of symmetrization guarantees an endless process of abstraction in relation to the self as a perceptual object. As Sanchez-Cardenas (2011) puts it, "the symbolism used by the psyche is the vehicle of infinite possible meanings . . . each unique symbol may represent infinite number of objects or situations" (pp. 819–820). Bion's (1989) idea of a preconception that develops into a concept, of a container waiting to be filled with meanings, can be used here to understand the way the self is being constructed through dream work. *The self is a preconception*, a container that children are ever pouring emotional content into, ever trying to construct and define as a dynamic concept that would fit their experiences.

Symmetrization also contributes to the process of separation and differentiation of the self from its objects in another and deeper sense. Freud (1925) argued, "By the help of the symbol of *negation*, the thinking-process frees itself from the limitations of repression and enriches itself with the subject-matter without which it could not work efficiently" (p. 368). When something is negated, it is no longer threatening to the consciousness, hence it can evade repression. Negation for Freud was the expression of Thanatos, the death force as expressed in the separation of the self from its objects. Symmetrization is seen in the dream corpus as integrating the accepted with the negated, as it enables the self to be equated with and opposed to the same object: self = monster and self ≠ monster. It brings to the separation and differentiation of the self from the same objects with which it identifies. Symmetrization is the dialectics that characterize the potential space in which the paradox of simultaneous acceptance and negation can exist. From this dialectical existence emerges the separated and differentiated united self, which can be apprehended by its comprising elements.

To summarize the function of symmetrization in dreams as it emerged from our analysis of the kindergarteners' dreams:

1. Symmetrization helps to organize the emotional experiences of the self by enacting categories of abstracted symbols through which thinking and mental growth are possible. It transforms the chaotic reality into a dynamic web of meaningful signs in which the self may feel and find its own and unique perspective.
2. Symmetrization brings separation and differentiation of the self from its objects. The self emerges as an autonomous object that consists of its inner objects but whose meaning extends beyond them.
3. Symmetrization is an attribute of the potential space in which the ambivalence of inner object relations may contribute to the enrichment and development of the self. Symmetrization enables the coexistence of identification and differentiation in the self's relations to its objects.
4. In light of the above suggestions, symmetrization helps to transform paranoid–schizoid mechanisms such as projection and splitting into depressive ones such as introjection. The self manages to introject and tolerate its experiences thereby widening the limits of its world of object relationships.
5. In a related context, symmetrization consolidates a reflective stand for the self with which to construct its own subjective perspective.

Following Bion's theory of dreaming and thinking, our analysis of dreams suggests the interpretation of dreams as the process by which mental growth is enabled and perpetuated. Analyzing the dreams, symmetrization emerged as a dominant expression of object relationships with which the self-perspective and boundaries are being constructed. Here the importance of symmetrization of relationships comes to the fore; it enables feeling and being in touch with emotional life and with the experience of existence.

As our thesis suggests a reconsideration of dream-work as theorized by Freud, we bear in mind the "epistemological pluralism in psychoanalysis" (Sanchez-Cardenas, 2011). We must remember that "when we turn our attention towards mental life, we are not dealing with a direct subject of observation... the knowledge of facts is hypothetical rather than final and remains constantly open to correction" (Sanchez-Cardenas, 2011, pp. 820–821). In this light, the way we applied symmetrization to the interpretation of dreams is viewed here as a suggestion and a call for further consideration of the way it works.

CONCLUSION

Let us conclude by linking our interpretation to the work of C. S. Peirce. In his seminal paper, "Questions Concerning Certain Faculties Claimed for Man" (1868), Peirce reflects on self-consciousness, which he considers the "recognition of my private self" (p. 108). The emergence of the self according to Peirce is deeply embodied, as for the child "the body is the most important thing in the universe" (Ibid). Embodied sensorial experiences are fragmented and do not comprise a "self." The self is inferred as an explanatory construct. For instance, a child hears that the stove is hot. However, if he has not directly touched it and then directly touches it, he becomes aware of his ignorance, the place where habit collapses. In this context, "It is necessary to suppose a *self* in which this ignorance can inhere." That is, an "error" can be explained only by "supposing a *self* which is fallible." As elaborated by Lincourt (1976, p. 37), "For Peirce, the self is not to be viewed as an insular, atomic, and static entity sufficient unto itself. The self is general, interactionist, and social." It is therefore a symbol "in the process of becoming." Dreams play a crucial role in this process of becoming, as the realm of dreaming is the realm through which the self is hypothesized and formed as a symbol through processes such as symmetrization, generalization, and separation. Pragmatism does not only urge us to link theory with practice but, according to some of Peirce's ideas, to carefully weave the threads through which our selves are in the process of becoming. We have proposed that dreaming is an important process in becoming and in this sense we are not only star dust, as some naïve physical reductionists would like to make us to believe, but the matter from which dreams are made and the dreams that "matter"—our selves.

REFERENCES

Bion, W. R. (1967). *Second thoughts.* New York, NY: Aronson.

Bion, W. R. (1970). *Attention and interpretation.* London, UK: Tavistock Publications.

Bion, W. R. (1989). *Learning from experience.* London, UK: Falmer.

Bion, W. R. (1994). *Cogitations.* London, UK: Karnac.

Freud, S. (1900). The interpretation of dreams. *Standard Edition, 4–5,* 1–621.

Freud, S. (1901). On dreams. *Standard Edition, 5,* 633–686.

Freud, S. (1925). Negation. *The International Journal of Psychoanalysis, 6,* 367–371.

Grotstein, J. S. (2007). *A beam of intense darkness.* London, UK: Karnac.

Grotstein, J. S. (2009). *"... But at the same time and on another level ... ".* London, UK: Karnac.

Lillard, A. S., & Flavel, J. H. (1992). Young children's understanding of different mental states. *Developmental Psychology, 28,* 626–634.

Lincourt, J. M. (1976). Peirce and psychiatry. *Transactions of the Charles S. Peirce Society, 12,* 33–45.

Matte Blanco, I. (1975). *The unconscious as infinite sets.* London, UK: Karnac.

Matte Blanco, I. (2005). The four antinomies of the death instinct. *The International Journal of Psychoanalysis, 86,* 1–14.

Muris, P., Merckelbach, H., Gadet, B., & Moulaert, V. (2000). Fears, worries, and scary dreams in 4 to 12-year-old children: their content, developmental pattern, and origins. *Journal of Clinical Child Psychology, 29,* 43–52.

Neuman, Y. (2008). *Reviving the living: Meaning making in living systems.* Oxford, UK: Elsevier.

Neuman, Y. (2009). On love, hate and knowledge. *The International Journal of Psychoanalysis, 90,* 697–712.

Neuman, Y. (2011). A novel semio-mathematical technique for excavating themes out of group dynamics. *Semiotica, 187,* 323–336.

Neuman, Y. (2013). A novel generic conception of structure: Solving Piaget's riddle. In L. Rudolph (Ed.), *Qualitative mathematics for the social sciences* (pp. 255–279). Abingdon, Oxford, UK: Routledge.

Neuman, Y., Assaf, D., & Cohen, Y. (2012). Automatic identification of themes in small group dynamics through the analysis of network motifs. *Bulletin of the Menninger Clinic, 76,* 53–68.

Ogden, O. H. (1985). On potential space. *The International Journal of Psychoanalysis, 66,* 129–141.

Peirce, C. S. (1868). Questions concerning certain faculties claimed for man. *The Journal of Speculative Philosophy, 2,* 103–114.

Salvatore, S., & Freda, M. F. (2011). Affect, unconscious and sensemaking: A psychodynamic, semiotic and dialogic model. *New Ideas in Psychology, 29*(2), 119–135. doi:10.1016/j.newideapsych.2010.06.001

Sanchez-Cardenas, M. (2011). Matte Blanco's thought and epistemological pluralism in psychoanalysis. *The International Journal of Psychoanalysis, 92,* 811–831.

Schneider, J. A. (2010). From Freud's dream-work to Bion's work of dreaming: The changing conception of dreaming in psychoanalytic theory. *The International Journal of Psychoanalysis, 91,* 521–540.

Segal, H. (1973). *Introduction to the work of Melanie Klien.* New York, NY: Basic Books.

Sharon, T., & Woolley, J. D. (2004). Do monsters dream? Young children's understanding of the fantasy/reality distinction. *British Journal of Developmental Psychology, 22,* 293–310.

Siegel, A. B. (2005). Children's dreams and nightmares: Emerging trends in research. *Dreaming, 15,* 147–154.

Simard, V., Nielsen, T. A., Tremblay, R. E., Boivin, M., & Montplaisir, J. Y. (2008). Longitudinal study of bad dreams in preschool-aged children: Prevalence, demographic correlates, risk and protective factors. *Sleep, 1,* 62–70.

Valsiner, J. (2007). *Culture in minds and societies: Foundations of cultural psychology.* New Delhi, India: Sage.

Volosinov, V. (1986). *Marxism and the philosophy of language.* Cambridge, MA: Harvard University Press.

Woolley, J. D., & Wellman, H. M. (1992). Children's conceptions of dreams. *Cognitive Development, 7,* 365–380.

CHAPTER 11

HOW EMPIRICAL RESEARCH CAN HELP CLINICIANS EVALUATE PSYCHOANALYTIC THEORY AND PRACTICE

A Pragmatic Approach

Jean Knox
University of Exeter

One of the defining features of psychodynamic psychotherapies, regardless of theoretical orientation, is their focus on working with unconscious processes. But this common purpose is not matched by an equally coherent ontological understanding of the unconscious (what its essential properties are and how it is formed), nor by a shared epistemological approach (how we best investigate its characteristics and determine what we can know about it). The differing opinions on such issues can be held with great passion and conviction, and this has often led to acrimonious disagreements and splits within the psychotherapy profession, from the initial vitriolic rupture between Freud and Jung (McGuire, 1961), through the controversial discussions (King & Steiner, 1990), to the contemporary disagreements between relational and classical psychoanalysis (Aron, 2006; Benjamin, 2009; Wachtel, 2010).

Making Our Ideas Clear, pages 295–316
Copyright © 2015 by Information Age Publishing
All rights of reproduction in any form reserved.

Charles Sanders Peirce (1877), one of the founding fathers of pragmatics, argued that there are four ways of dealing with such differences of opinion: first, the method of *tenacity*, holding to a belief without wavering and ignoring any evidence that might contradict it. Peirce argued that the peace of mind this brings is the main goal of this approach, like an ostrich burying its head in the sand and remaining oblivious of reality. A development of this approach is the method of *authority*, where the state or an institution enforces "correct" doctrines and represses all disagreement, keeping individuals ignorant of alternative views and reinforcing the doctrines by coercion, fear, or violence. The third method is that of *congruity*, where beliefs are agreed upon because they seem "agreeable to reason" (Peirce, 1877, p. 10)—they are what people want to believe and are not based on observed facts or any form of experimental evidence. Peirce suggested that this is the methodological basis of historical metaphysical philosophy. The problem is that the differing views reflect personal tastes or fashions in ideas and so remain a matter of preference, without any reliable method for choosing one such *a priori* belief over another. Finally there is the method of *science*, which relies on the "regular laws" (p. 11), such as the laws of perception, by which reality affects our senses; so "reality" is discoverable and independent of particular opinion. Unlike the other methods, the scientific approach inherently tests and criticizes assumptions and beliefs, and Peirce argued that this not only makes it a more reliable basis for knowledge but also a more moral one: "to avoid looking into the support of any belief from a fear that it may turn out to be rotten is quite as immoral as it is disadvantageous" (1877, p. 15).

Peirce (1868) placed the scientific method in opposition to Cartesian philosophy, which, he suggested, trusts to "a single thread of inference depending often upon inconspicuous premises" (p. 140). Peirce's view was that we should "[c]onsider what effects, that might conceivably have practical bearings, you conceive the objects of your conception to have. Then, your conception of those effects is the whole of your conception of the object" (1878, p. 293).

Peirce implied that tenacity, authority, and congruity exert a powerful hold on us because they help to quell the anxiety that accompanies any search for knowledge. Although science opens up that anxiety by taking away the certainty inherent in the other forms of knowing, it also provides a method for managing that anxiety by studying the effects of a theory—how useful, applicable, and comprehensive it is in explaining the phenomena (or as Peirce puts it, the objects) we are observing.

An iconic historical example of this pragmatic approach is that of Galileo, whose view that the sun is at the center of the solar system was based on empirical observation of the phases of Venus, using the telescope, which he invented. His finding, that Venus exhibited the same full set of phases as the moon, could only mean that Venus was orbiting round the sun, since the orbit of Venus around the sun would cause its illuminated hemisphere to face the Earth when it was on the opposite side of the sun and to face away from the Earth when it was on the Earth side of the sun. His concept of the solar system was based on studying the consequences of the rotation of Venus, and it is this study of effects that is the essence of the pragmatic approach, as Peirce described. But Galileo was found guilty of heresy in 1633 by the Inquisition, because his experimental findings rendered as untenable the Ptolemaic model that the earth is the center of the universe and does not move. Galileo's scientific approach was a direct threat to religious authority, which was based on belief in statements in the Bible that the earth does not move.

THE IMPLICATIONS OF A PRAGMATIC APPROACH FOR PSYCHOANALYTIC THEORY

Peirce's discussion of the ways in which we settle differences of opinion and the confrontation between Galileo's scientific method and the "method of authority" of the Inquisition raises important questions for psychoanalysis. Peirce (1877) stated that "wherever there is an aristocracy, or a guild, or any association of a class of men whose interests depend . . . on certain propositions then the method of authority will be in operation" (p. 9). So should psychoanalysis be found guilty of this charge? Do psychoanalysts rely overly much not only on authority but also on the methods of tenacity or congruence in response to challenges to their theories? Examples of each of these attitudes can be found in the psychoanalytic literature. For instance, the method of tenacity seems to be exemplified in Ernest Jones's comment, "To tell a psychoanalyst that the phenomena he is dealing with all day long do not exist leaves him as little impressed as a chemist would be by the argument that oxygen and hydrogen, being invisible, cannot exist" (British Medical Association, 1929, p. 17).

Sylvia Payne, in a paper given at the British Psychoanalytic Society, propounded the method of authority in writing: "The basic conceptions of psychoanalysis were laid down by Professor Freud, and this Society and this Institute were founded on them" and that "only those analysts adhering to the conceptions of Freud had the right to call themselves Psycho-Analysts" (King & Steiner, 1990, pp. 53–54). The method of congruence underpins Donald Meltzer's argument (1973) that clinical observation and analytic theory confirm each other in the consulting room:

> On the basis of validated hypotheses about the here-and-now transference and using his inference from the compulsion to repeat, the analyst may con-

> struct the development of the unconscious object relations of the patient. From a wide experience of individual patients he may then generalize and propose a theory of development which he believes to be biologically founded on the deep levels of the psyche and not fundamentally different in varying races, or circumstances of life. (p. 12)

This illustrates what Fonagy and Tallindini-Shallice (1993) have called "enumerative inductivism," the finding of ever more examples consistent with the theory being used. There is no recognition of the fact that there may be other hypotheses that explain the clinical material equally well, and psychotherapists who rely on this method have no means of testing, modifying, or discarding their preferred theories.

Numerous critics of psychoanalytic theory have suggested that such attitudes fatally undermine the claim of psychoanalysis to be taken seriously both ontologically, as a theory of the way the human mind works, and as an epistemological method, which has at its core the undoing of repression by free association and interpretation (Grunbaum, 1984; Popper, 1962). Grunbaum (1984) concluded that "the reasoning on which Freud rested the major hypotheses of his edifice was fundamentally flawed" (p. 94). Such critiques have led to a steady erosion in the authority of psychoanalysis as a clinical treatment because psychoanalysis is not considered to be open to modifying both theory and practice in the light of new information obtained by use of observational tools such as tape and video recorders and fMRI scans, which allow much more detailed observation both of human interaction and of the brain, just as the greater magnifying power of the telescope revolutionized astronomy.

Although many psychoanalysts have increasingly accepted the value of such empirical research, there remain significant groups who argue that clinical phenomena can only be "observed" within the psychoanalytic clinical setting. For instance, Blass and Carmeli (2007) argue that any other form of observation is "irrelevant to psychoanalytic aims and practice" (p. 34) and that "biological explanation will not deepen our understanding of the influence of latent meanings or psychic truths—the domain of psychoanalysis" (p. 35). Similarly, Danielle Quinodez et al. (2006) write, "If patients are to develop the capacity to understand their unconscious internal world, they must have the experience of doing so in their relationship with the analyst" (p. 330). But such authors seem to fail to recognize that psychoanalysts' understanding and interpretations of the patient's unconscious internal world are based on preconceptions that are derived from psychoanalytic theory about psychic contents and processes and that do not take into account alternative perspectives on the origins, nature, and purpose of a patient's communications.

In marked contrast, two key psychoanalysts to recognize the urgent need for psychoanalysis to open itself to empirical enquiry were Harry Stack Sullivan and John Bowlby. Both adopted a pragmatic approach—Bowlby

(1988) clearly stated "my starting point in developing theory was the observation of behaviour" (p. 28). Sullivan likewise argued that clinically we can only effectively study "phenomena that go on between the observer and the observed in the situation created by the observer participating with the observed" (in Greenberg & Mitchell, 1983, p. 89). So he argued that we can have no direct knowledge of processes presumed by psychoanalytic theory to be taking place in the patient's unconscious.

On the basis of this pragmatic observational approach, both were highly critical of the untested assumptions of psychoanalytic drive theory. Greenberg and Mitchell write, "Sullivan suggests that every major tenet of Freud's drive theory can better be understood in terms of interpersonal and social processes. The Oedipus complex, he suggests, is an artefact of the prominence in our society of competitiveness, jealousy, prolonged dependency and sexual hypocrisy" (1983, p. 87).

Bowlby (1988) similarly argued that Freud's reliance on the biological theories of Lamarck and Haeckel meant that "much of his metapsychology and all his developmental psychology came to be founded on principles long since abandoned by biologists" and that "if psychoanalysis is to become the natural science that Freud intended, there are compelling reasons for drastic changes in some at least of its basic assumptions" (p. 66). Bowlby argued that the development of libido is a core psychoanalytic concept that is based on discredited biology and that there was no empirical evidence to support Freud's theory that sexual drive determines unconscious phantasy.

Freud regarded the Oedipus complex as a "phylogenetically inherited" schema, a view that Bowlby regards as a profound misunderstanding of the emergent nature of the development of the human mind and brain, which means that "selection pressures operate at all phases of the life cycle" (Bowlby, 1988, p. 66). To assert that our desires are predetermined by our genetic makeup fails to reflect the fact that both the physical and psychological—bodies and minds—emerge out of developmental processes that are both self-organizing and highly dependent on the environment and relationships, as Susan Oyama describes in her remarkable book *The Ontogeny of Information* (Oyama, 2000). An emergent model of development has at its core the view that a stream of current experience constantly reshapes and guides the development of the human mind and brain, continuously switching some genetic pathways on and others off in a highly interactive way (Deacon, 1997; Karmiloff-Smith, 1992). Developmental studies such as those of Ed Tronick support the view that experience changes genes and brain—that the influence is not just one way. Genes and brains are not static entities but change throughout development:

> It is necessary to recognize that experience, genes, and brain, as well as the structures and processes of all three, are not only fundamentally different

> at different ages, but their constant interplay is also different and makes for qualitative differences in the totality of the biopsychological organization of the individual in each moment of the lifespan. (Tronick, 2007, p. 6)

In these developmental and emergent models, there is no certain outcome of these complex interactive processes, and so they lack the certainty about the structure of the human psyche of some schools of psychoanalysis. Instead, they echo Peirce's view that "the mind is not subject to 'law' in the same rigid sense that matter is. It only experiences gentle forces which render it more likely to act in a given way than it would otherwise be" (Peirce, 1892, p. 554).

It seems that psychoanalysts sometimes try to sidestep the issue of empirical observation by staying in a hermeneutic bubble dealing with immediate here-and-now subjective experience. But whether we like it or not, we construct theories about the brain processes that underpin the phenomena we see in the consulting room, and our clinical interventions derive from those theories we hold about how the brain functions. There is enough empirical evidence from other disciplines to enable us to show that some of the core psychoanalytic theories about the nature of the human unconscious mind are based on inaccurate and outdated assumptions about neurobiology, genetic inheritance, and developmental processes. So as clinicians, we are faced with a choice between outdated neurobiological theories—innate mental contents, instinctual drives, and inherited collective unconscious—or empirical research that does give us more accurate working hypotheses about some of the neurobiological and developmental processes that might underpin the phenomena we see in the consulting room.

Let me draw on some clinical material to illustrate these issues by describing two different therapists' ways of understanding a dream that a patient had during a previous therapy and that she subsequently described to me.

> A woman dreamt that she was in the sea, in the midst of a number of sharks and people fighting. They were in pairs, with one shark and one person fighting each other. She was not clear if either the shark or the human was a victim—each seemed to be attacking the other. She was terrified that she herself would be attacked, so she sank slowly to the bottom, where she was able to breathe, and stayed there very still and quietly.

Her previous therapist had interpreted this as her choosing death over life, an interpretation that reflected the therapist's belief that innate instinctual drives directly determine the nature of unconscious fantasy (including dreams) and that the dream was an expression of the death instinct in action.

In contrast, my view of the dream was that it conveyed the impact on her of her parents' violent arguments when she was a child—her only defence being to withdraw from relationships into a dissociative observer position and to freeze emotionally so as not to draw their rage onto herself. This way of seeing the dream reflected my view that it is the internalization of real relational experience that creates unconscious fantasy and that a dream such as this represents the patient's internal working models of such relational patterns, including the emotions of terror and frozen withdrawal she experienced when her parents were fighting.

These two different interpretations of this dream directly reflect each therapist's assumptions about the neurobiology and developmental processes that underpin unconscious thought and imagery. So how are we to determine which one of us had the more accurate view of the dream? I do not think it is acceptable to take a postmodern approach and argue that all interpretations are equally valid. Although a postmodern approach embraces the absence of certainty of knowledge that Peirce highlighted, it avoids an active engagement with clinical phenomena through which we try to gauge the effects of one intervention or another—an empirical approach. I think it really does matter that our theories reflect the accumulating empirical evidence about the ways that the human brain and mind actually do develop and function. Peirce (1868) suggested that integrating a number of differing lines of inquiry offers the most robust way of reaching conclusions:

> Philosophy ought to imitate the successful sciences in its methods, so far as to proceed only from tangible premises which can be subjected to careful scrutiny and to trust rather to the multitude and variety of its arguments than to the conclusiveness of any one. Its reasoning should not form a chain which is no stronger than its weakest link, but a cable whose fibers may be ever so slender, provided they are sufficiently numerous and intimately connected. (p. 141)

This argument applies as much to psychoanalysis as to philosophy. So in relation to psychoanalytic explanations for the clinical phenomena we encounter in the consulting room, we need to construct the most plausible and logical hypothesis based on interweaving the evidence from different disciplines. In essence, this is a kind of meta-pragmatism (akin to the concept of meta-analysis in scientific enquiry), an integrated overview of a range of research findings.

Let me illustrate this approach by showing how research findings from different fields can be integrated into a working hypothesis about the causal role of early relational trauma in relation to chronic PTSD and related symptomatology in adult life. The research I shall draw on comes in four categories:

1. Clinical phenomena that constitute a regular clinical pattern that therapists can reliably identify and describe sometimes as chronic

posttraumatic stress disorder (chronic PTSD) or alternatively as borderline personality

2. Developmental research that shows
    a. the developmental role of early relational experience
    b. the long-term impact of negative attitudes of caretakers on their infant's sense of self
    c. the links between early relational trauma and chronic PTSD in adult life
3. Neuroscientific research demonstrating that neural pathways exist that link perception of emotion on another's face to self-experience
4. Psychotherapy outcome studies that demonstrate the link between relational experience with the therapist and the outcome of the therapy

Clinical Phenomena

All therapists are constantly confronted with the reality of the powerful unconscious hold that the past can have over our perception of the present, so that the past comes alive in the consulting room in the implicit relational and affective interactions that are activated in the therapist-patient relationship. Empirical evidence that supports this clinical experience that internalized models of our most important early relationships profoundly affect our experiences of and behaviors with significant others in the present comes from the study of internal working models (Bowlby, 1988; Sroufe & Waters, 1977) , the Core Conflictual Relational Theme (Luborsky & Crits-Christoph, 1990), and interpersonal scripts (Siegel & Demorest, 2010)

One of the most intractable problems all therapists encounter is that patients who have experienced early relational trauma often seem to persist in describing themselves as disgusting, bad, dirty and all the other words of self-loathing which reflect a deeply painful self-hatred that the person clings to in spite of all attempts to shift it. Together these are identified as borderline personality disorder (BPD), with some authors suggesting that BPD should always be seen as a form of chronic PTSD, resulting from neglect or abuse in childhood (Herman, Perry, & van der Kolk, 1989).

Shame is possibly the most corrosive and persistent effect of early relational trauma and, in many clinicians' experience, the most resistant to change in psychotherapy (Loewenstein & Welzant, 2010; Nathanson, 1992). This is partly because any attempt to work through a traumatic memory and reflect on the emotions thus aroused—to mentalize—quickly becomes hijacked by overwhelming shame, as though being vulnerable and powerless somehow permitted abuse or neglect. These feelings are often accompanied by self-harm of various kinds—repeated cutting or overdosing, alcohol or drug abuse, eating disorders—and by particular patterns of difficulty in affect regulation, mentalization, attachment, and sexuality. It often takes the form of persistent self-attacks, self-disgust, and self-hate.

But the theoretical explanations psychoanalysis offers for this clinical picture of shame accompanied by self-harming behavior are not themselves based on the method of science, but instead rely on authority or congruence. A Kleinian might consider this clinical picture to be an expression of the death instinct (Hinshelwood, 1989). In contrast, a Jungian might see these self-destructive patterns of behavior as manifestations of an archetypal "daimonic" internal figure that ruthlessly attacks any expression of vulnerability or dependence in order to protect the self from further trauma (Kalsched, 1996). A British object relations theorist might see them as an expression of the anti-libidinal ego attacking the libidinal ego (Guntrip, 1969). But all such theories are actually just examples either of the method of congruence that Peirce describes—they are the most "agreeable to reason" for that particular theorist, or of the method of authority, if they reflect an unquestioning adherence to the theories of a particular analytic institute.

This matters because in most psychodynamic theories, the model of the mind is closely coupled to and prescriptive of specific clinical techniques. For example, Klein's view of the nature of the unconscious is not just a theoretical model of the mind but also a prescription for a particular clinical technique, centered on deep and early interpretation, as Hinshelwood spelled out: "Since derivatives of the death instinct are the problem, aggression and destructiveness need to be brought into the transference for investigation and interpretation" (Hinshelwood, 1989, p. 16).

But if there is no way of evaluating how relevant these differing analytic theories are to any one clinical pattern, there is no sound basis for assuming that theory should determine the treatment approach. The only reliable way of establishing how such clinical phenomena can best be explained is an empirical pragmatic approach that seeks to establish whether there are in fact significant correlations between the range of clinical phenomena that characterize chronic PTSD or BPD with the research evidence that these are frequently linked to early relational trauma.

Developmental Research

The Developmental Role of Early Relational Experience

Vygotsky developed the concept of the "zone of proximal development" (Vygotsky, 1978) to refer to the distance between the child's independent problem-solving ability and her potential with assistance from more knowledgeable adults and older peers. He argued, for example, that mothers intuitively scaffold children's understanding of mind through their talk at a level more advanced than the child's independent ability level, but not so advanced as to be too distant from the child's experience.

Taumoepeau and Ruffman (2008) have refined this relational model of psychological development, suggesting that mothers provide a systematic scaffolding process in their choice of language, unconsciously structuring their communications to match the infant's current cognitive and emotional abilities and level of understanding. So mothers first talk to their children about the child's own desires, because the child has direct internal experience of those as bodily states, such as hunger or thirst. By describing these states in language, they help their child to connect these bodily experiences to mental states. Only later do mothers begin to focus on abstract concepts, such as thoughts and knowledge, because desire talk fits better into younger children's zone of proximal development—young children understand about desire before thoughts and knowledge. For children to receive maximum benefit, mother talk must be appropriately timed to fit with the child's existing understanding. Only talk of this nature can help to make explicit a child's underlying implicit understanding of mental states.

Fonagy, Gergely, Jurist, and Target (2002) describe another aspect of this process of Vygotskian scaffolding, suggesting that mothers do not just facilitate a preprogrammed development of mind understanding but play a more active role in the development of their infants' understanding of mind by attributing intentionality to behavior before the child has any sense of intentionality for him- or herself. So the meaning that the child attributes to her action is not really her own but reflects the meaning given to it by her main caregivers:

> The caregiver produces intentionality through complex linguistic and interactional processes, primarily through behaving towards the baby and child in such a way that it leads him eventually to postulate that his own behaviour may best be understood in terms of ideas and beliefs, feelings and wishes that determine his actions and the reactions of others to him. Unconsciously and pervasively, with her behaviour the caregiver ascribes a mental state to the child that is ultimately perceived by the child and internalized, permitting the development of a core sense of mental selfhood. (Fonagy et al., 2002, p. 286)

The caregiver attributes meaning and intentionality to the infant's actions before any such meaning or intentionality exists reflectively in the infant's own mind. A baby gradually internalizes the meaning attributed by the mother to his or her actions, so that, as Jungian analyst George Hogenson describes it the caregiver, "bootstraps the infant into the world of meaning" (Hogenson, 2009, p. 183).

The argument that early relational experience is internalized to become an enduring and powerful determinant of psychological and emotional development throughout life is not just an untested hypothesis but derives from careful observation of the predictors of patterns of attachment by Bowlby, Ainsworth, and more recently Beatrice Beebe and Peter Fonagy, among others. It has been supported by a number of longitudinal studies that demonstrate that patterns of interaction with caregivers in the first months of life have life-long effects (Beebe et al., 2010; Broussard & Cassidy, 2010; Sroufe & Waters, 1977).

The Effect of Negative Experience

Although the clinical picture I described above may be accompanied by a history of overt violence or severe emotional abuse, this is not necessarily the case. It can simply result from the hidden trauma of a caregiver's inability to give emotionally appropriate responses to the child—"to comfort and regulate the stress of fear-evoking events that are a daily part of the infant's experience" (Bureau, Martin, & Lyons-Ruth, 2010, p. 48). The infant's dependence on key attachment figures to give meaning to his actions makes him uniquely vulnerable to negative responses from the caregiver. This kind of parental mis-attunement, if regularly repeated, becomes a core part of the infant's relational experience, as Sullivan recognized. "In Sullivan's system . . . painful anxiety-provoking aspects of early relations with significant others are unavoidably structured into the self" (Greenberg & Mitchell, 1983, p. 103). Sullivan suggested that these create a sense of 'bad-me' in the infant, through the empathy with the mother's anxiety (Greenberg & Mitchell, 1983).

Empirical evidence supports this claim. For example, Broussard and Cassidy (2010) assessed the attitude of mothers to their newborn babies, using the Neonatal Perception Inventory (NPI), which measures the mother's perception of her baby compared with her view of an average baby. They showed that a mother's positive perception of her infant as "better" than average correlates with low risk for subsequent psychosocial problems, while her view that her infant is not better than average correlates with higher risk. In this latest follow-up, Broussard and Cassidy demonstrated that this negative effect continues right into adult life:

> The experience of having been viewed negatively by one's mother as a newborn, as assessed with the NPI, substantially increased the risk of insecure adult attachment. The odds of having an insecure AAI for adults whose mothers had held a negative perception of them at 1 month old were 18 times greater than for adults whose mothers had perceived them positively. (2010, p. 165)

These negative attributions are internalized to become a core part of the sense of self. Alicia Lieberman (1999) says that the child may become "the carriers of the parents' unconscious fears, impulses and other repressed or disowned parts of themselves" and that "these negative attributions become an integral part of the child's sense of self" (p. 737). The child becomes literally "ashamed of himself," of his or her self-agency and libido, because of the negative way these are responded to by the caregiver. I have suggested (Knox, 2007) that this is the basis for the "fear of love"—a kind of autistic defense against relationships in those who have experienced such colonization by the disowned parts of the parental psyche.

A key question is how the baby detects such negative attributions. A one-month old baby cannot mentalize about his mother's state of mind, cannot think "oh, she doesn't think I'm good enough." What the baby does see is the caregiver's reactions to her agency in the turn-taking that forms the core of human communication (see Lepper, this volume). A caregiver's negative attitudes show themselves in avoidant, aversive, or conflictual responses to the baby's agency so that, in the words of the Boston Change Process Study Group (BCPSG), the baby learns "what forms of affective relatedness can be expressed openly in the relationship and what forms need to be expressed only in 'defensive' ways, that is, in distorted or displaced forms" (BCPSG, 2007, p. 851).

For example, Beatrice Beebe and colleagues have found that many four-month-old infants who later show disorganized attachment have mothers who are preoccupied with their own unresolved abuse or trauma and cannot bear to engage with their infant's distress. Essentially, these mothers are unable to regulate their own distress when faced with their infant's distress and so are unable to allow themselves to be emotionally affected by their infants' distress; they "shut down" emotionally, looking away from the infant's face and failing to coordinate with the infant's emotional state, a self-protective dissociation, especially around the infant's need for comfort when distressed (Beebe et al., 2010).

If a mother's face shows disappointment, fear, or avoidance when she looks at her crying baby, her discordant aversive response is puzzling and distressing to her infant, as Beebe's research and Tronick's (2007) still face experiments have shown. Broussard and Cassidy's (2010) demonstration of the long-term impact of early relational experience justifies us in hypothesizing that this will have profoundly damaging long-term effects on an infant's sense of self in relationships, leading to the sense of self as bad, which our patients so often describe.

Research That Demonstrates the Links Between Early Relational Trauma and Chronic PTSD in Adult Life

Lanius et al. (2010) have drawn together the evidence that examines the clinical effects in adults of early life trauma. The theme that predominates in much of the literature cited is that "abuse and/or neglect experienced in childhood is particularly toxic" (Briere & Hodges, 2010, p. 207), leading to major difficulties in identity, affect regulation, and interpersonal relatedness. The book describes the hugely damaging impact that neglect or abuse by primary caregivers has on the psychological and emotional development of the human infant, creating life-long consequences in terms of brain development, attachment and affect dysregulation, altered stress responses, and a range of psychological symptoms from the flashbacks and hyperarousal of PTSD to altered perception, epileptic-type phenomena, and dissociative states of varying degrees of severity, including borderline personality and dissociative identity disorder. Insecure attachment, childhood separation, emotional neglect, sexual abuse, and dissociation are significant predictors of self-harm (Gratz, Conrad, & Roemer, 2002). It has been suggested that "the avoidance symptoms of PTSD can be conceptualized as avoidance of the shame that is an essential part of interpersonal trauma" (Loewenstein & Welzant, 2010, p. 261). As I indicated in the previous section, shame is one of the most prominent emotions that patients bring to therapy.

This compilation of evidence powerfully supports the argument that it is real-life experience rather than innate unconscious fantasy that determines most of the problems our patients bring to the consulting room. These research studies place the earliest relationship with caregivers right at the heart of human psychological and emotional development, and as clinicians we simply have to become aware of the impact of this kind of empirical evidence on our theoretical models and hence on our clinical practice (Schore, 1994). This evidence-based model directly challenges some psychoanalytic models, which attribute innate inherited mental content derived from the supposed biological forces of libido and the death instinct as the forces that shape unconscious content. Specifically, the psychoanalytic view that instinctual drive creates specific unconscious fantasy and the Jungian view of an inherited collective unconscious are both based on an implicit assumption that a ground plan or blueprint of the human psyche is inherited in our genes and that this blueprint contains specific desires, such as the infant's incestuous or destructive wishes, or the potential for specific types of imagery, such as the archetypes of the collective unconscious (Knox 2003).

But such theories are based on neurobiological models for which there is no empirical evidence and that are increasingly out of step with the detailed developmental research, such as that of Beatrice Beebe and colleagues, whose research suggests that the unconscious is co-constructed in relational interactions:

> In our view representations arise from interactions. We hold a dynamic process transformational model of representations in which a schema is constructed and transformed through the expected moment-to-moment interplay of the two partners. What is represented is the dynamic interactive process itself. (Beebe & Lachmann, 2002, pp. 147–148)

This co-construction is also an essential feature of the mentalizing approach to psychotherapy in which therapists "strive to engage the patient in a collaborative effort to find meaning and to create a coherent narrative" (Allen, Fonagy, & Bateman, 2010 p. 251).

Neuroscience

I shall now turn to another strand that forms part of the cable of evidence that Peirce proposed, namely the possible neuroscientific mechanisms that might contribute to the developmental and clinical phenomena I have outlined. First, there is the role of mirror neurons, found in specific parts of the cerebral cortex. The crucial characteristic that defines mirror neurons is that the same neurons fire both when carrying out an action and when observing another performing an action. Mirror neurons have different degrees of specificity, but they work together as a system to encode not just the observed actions per se, but the intention to perform those actions. So when mirror neurons fire, we know, in an unconscious embodied way, what we ourselves would intend if we performed that action and we therefore attribute the same intention to the person we observe (again, an unconscious embodied expectation). Mirror neuron activity provides a direct matching of the others' observed behavior to our own motor repertoire, a neurological mirroring process that functions automatically and does not require any conscious concept or inference. This "mirror system" integrates observed actions of others with an individual's personal motor repertoire and suggests that the human brain understands actions by motor simulation.

Vittorio Gallese explores this mirror matching process in relation to facial expressions, showing that when people observe pictures of emotional facial expressions, they show spontaneous unconscious and rapid firing in the same facial muscles as those involved in the other person's facial expression (Gallese, 2007, p. 149). He indicates that this rapid and automatic activation of facial muscles is probably triggered by activation of the mirror neuron system. Furthermore, an fMRI study (Carr, Iacoboni, Dubeau, Mazziotta, & Lenzi, 2003) showed that *both observation and imitation* of the facial expression of emotions not only activate the same facial muscles but also activate the same group of brain structures, including the ventral premotor cortex, the insula, and the amygdala, a mirror matching mechanism. This enables us to recognize the intention behind the facial expression, to know, for example, if a smile is affectionate and friendly or mocking and contemptuous.

For example, fMRI scans show that when one person (A) observes disgust on another's face, this activates the same parts of the insula that are activated when that person (A) directly experiences disgusting smells, suggesting that mirror-neuron activity occurs in the insula. So if the infant's communications are met by an expression of disgust or fear on the mother's face, the infant's mirror neuron system activates the corresponding networks in the baby's insula so that he or she presumably also experiences disgust or fear directly in response to his or her own emotional states.

But this is still not the whole story. How does this mirroring become so embedded in the child's sense of identity, the core sense of self? How does a person come to feel that she is irredeemably bad if she seeks to elicit a loving emotional response from another person? The answer I suggest may lie in the neurological links between the cortical mirror neuron system and the deeper midline structures in the brain.

Jaak Panksepp and colleagues (Panksepp & Northoff, 2009) have suggested that the most basic form of self is rooted in specific midbrain neural networks, which are linked to deep forebrain subcortical regions, together forming the subcortical midline system. Panksepp describes these midbrain and forebrain systems as constituting a core-SELF, the seat of specific motivational and emotional systems common to all mammals: those of *seeking, rage, lust, care, panic,* and *play* (Panksepp, 1998; Panksepp & Panksepp, 2000). This core-SELF (Panksepp & Northoff, 2009, p. 196) is a primitive form of consciousness, which at this level is essentially affective (emotional).

Now here is the key point—it has been suggested that the insula may be one critical relay from the mirror neuron system to the cortical and subcortical midline systems that underpin the core-SELF experience described by Panksepp (1998). Other direct connections between the mirror neuron system and cortical midline systems (inferior parietal lobe—precuneus, mesial frontal areas—inferior frontal gyrus) form other pathways by which the two networks may interact and coordinate their activity (Rizzolatti & Luppino, 2001). These pathways may provide the route by which an expression of disgust on a mother's face in response to her infant activates the infant's mirror neuron response in the insula, so that the infant experiences disgust, which then directly feeds into the infant's core-SELF system. It is a reasonable working hypothesis that this could slowly become transformed into a kind of self-hatred or self-blame—a sense of one's own emotions and intentionality as the cause of distress, disgust, or fear in another, a sense of badness at the core of one's being, which could form the basis for the experience of the "bad-me" that Sullivan proposed.

Uddin, Iacoboni, Lange, and Keenan (2007) suggest that it is likely that the direct connections between the mirror neuron system and the cortical and subcortical systems integrate information that is necessary for maintaining self–other representations across multiple domains. This brings me to the default network, a neural network that overlaps extensively both with mirror neuron areas, such as the inferior parietal lobe and parts of with the cortical midline system (CMS) such as the precuneus.

The default network is a network of brain areas (comprising the posterior cingulate and precuneus, anterior cingulate and medial-prefrontal cortex, and temporoparietal junctions) that show more metabolic activity when the brain is at rest than during attention-demanding and goal-directed tasks, consuming 30% more calories for its weight than any other area of the brain (Raichle, MacLeod, Snyder, Powers, Gusnard, & Shulman, 2001). The default network is active when individuals are engaged in internally focused tasks including autobiographical memory retrieval, envisioning the future, and conceiving the perspectives of others. Researchers (Northoff & Panksepp, 2008; Uddin et al., 2007) now believe that the default network stores and updates memories based on their importance from a personal perspective and their emotional quality and returns to its sorting process whenever the brain is not engaged in an active task. So one function of the default network is to act as a constant monitor of the self and its social relationships, a self-referential processing that goes on in a resting state.

So the activity of the default network is the process by which the brain integrates memories, emotions, and self-experience. A key contributor to this integrative work is imagination, which is attracting increasing attention from neuroscience researchers and derives from the activity of the default network (Uddin et al., 2007). It is the activity of imagining that seems to integrate the different neural networks that contribute to self-experience. We know clinically that one consequence of trauma is that precisely this capacity for imagination is destroyed (Affeld-Niemayer, 1995). The dissociative processes characteristic of trauma means that memories do not become incorporated into self-experience but intrude like alien objects into the psyche in the form of flashbacks and nightmares. Even when the trauma seems less severe, our patients also often find it far too distressing to imagine themselves back into their childhood relational experiences and it often triggers self-harm or dissociative states.

There is one final piece of neuroscience that might help explain why this is. Ruth Lanius and colleagues (Bluhm et al. 2010) have shown that at rest, spontaneous low-frequency activity in the PCC/precuneus was more strongly correlated with activity in other areas of the default network in healthy controls than in patients with PTSD. In other words, patients with chronic PTSD related to early-life trauma display significantly reduced functional connectivity within the default network during the resting state. The PCC may be a crucial node in the default network, linking past information with current environmental events and assessing these events with regard to their relevance to the self. Accordingly, Lanius and colleagues' evidence could indicate that altered forms of self-perception and consciousness accompanying more severe and chronic PTSD derive from the greatly impaired capacity for self-referential processing of the default network in these conditions.

The reduced default network connectivity in PTSD described by this group of researchers may explain the extraordinary difficulty people with a history of relational trauma have in developing a more positive sense of self and why the self-hate that I have described remains so intractable. Without the capacity for imaginative activity inherent in the default network, the patient cannot develop and maintain new stories to modify the self-hate and self-blame narratives nor imagine new ways of seeing him- or herself and a more positive sense of self and of self-agency in relationships. In this context, one of the major tasks of therapy is to create the safe relationship within which it becomes possible to imagine and build a new sense of self—Sullivan's "good-me."

Psychotherapy Outcome Studies

If this working hypothesis is correct about the developmental processes and neuronal pathways that underpin the destructive long-term impact of early relational trauma on a person's sense of self, then this would have important implications for our clinical practice. For example, we could argue that a "blank screen" therapeutic style can easily replicate the same confusion, distress, and shame in the patient that Tronick's still face experiment causes the infant, or it can be experienced by the patient as a therapist's aversive rejecting response to the patient's distress, like the babies in Beebe's study. We know from Broussard and Cassidy (2010) that such facial responses have long-term negative effects and our adult patients are describing how this remains alive for them in the here and now, through their subjective sense of badness, self-blame, and self-hate.

So psychotherapy outcome studies are the fourth strand of evidence we can use to support the hypothesis that it is real relational experience, not innate instinctual forces that determine the best treatment approach for the problems our patients bring to our consulting rooms, particularly those who have experienced early relational trauma. When researchers study the effectiveness of psychotherapy in general or compare one kind of therapy with another, a consistent finding is that psychological interventions of all kinds are better than no treatment at all—"the average treated person is better off than 80% of people who have not been treated" (Lepper & Riding, 2006, p. 9). The use of randomized controlled trials in an attempt to discover whether one type of psychotherapy can be shown to be better than another has so far failed to demonstrate any clear advantage of any one particular approach, a finding known as the Dodo effect: "Everybody has won and all must have prizes" (Lepper & Riding, 2006, p. 10; see also Luborsky, Singer, & Luborsky, 1975; Shedler, 2010). But although no one treatment approach has demonstrated universal effectiveness, a recently published meta-analyis by Jonathan

Shedler has shown that relational factors consistently predict the outcome of psychotherapy, whatever the supposed overt theoretical model the therapist uses, from CBT to psychoanalysis—the active ingredients of therapy are not necessarily those presumed by the theory or treatment model. The more effective therapists facilitated relational processes such as a positive working alliance, enabled the patient to "experience" (focus on emotions and thoughts about self), discussed interpersonal relationships, and explored relationships with early caregivers. All these are aspects of a relational approach that also facilitates the patient's own sense of self-agency both in relationship with the therapist and in terms of making sense of his or her own emotions and past relational experience.

CONCLUSION

Together these studies from different disciplines are like strands that form the cable of intertwined evidence that Peirce proposed, one that provides a convincing argument that early relationships are the primary determinants of later psychic life. The sense of "bad-me" that Sullivan identified is, in part, a defensive response to trauma. Trauma, especially that which arises in long-term relationships—parent to child, or adult sexual partners—is not just an experience of external events that are painful or distressing. Over time, it also gets right inside the psyche, profoundly damaging the sense of oneself as a subject with a capacity for agency, which is our sense that we can influence and modify the behavior and attitudes of others towards us. Instead, the person comes to take endless responsibility for their actions, leading to the state of self-blame. Self-blame narratives, created in imagination and fantasy, are attempts to find some meaning in the cruelty, rejection, or indifference from those whom we love and on whom we are most dependent. One aspect of these narratives is that the child feels that his or her own vulnerability, naivety, and dependence were the cause of the parental rejection and therefore unconsciously condemns and persecutes any such weakness whenever it emerges. This basic assumption remains unquestioned and unmodified, so that child grows up to believe that it is dangerous to enter into any relationship and that all emotional vulnerability or need for attention will trigger rejection. This, in itself, can create the sense of self-blame that is so resistant to change through insight.

So I argue that a pragmatic approach can help us to understand the clinical phenomena we work with in the consulting room better by studying the empirical evidence for the causal role of early life trauma. This evidence enables us to refine our clinical theories and to create the hypothesis that offers the best overall fit for the clinical phenomena we work with, including self-harm, eating disorders, and dissociative states, which are usually linked to a history of early relational trauma and for which a traditional analytic approach is often largely unhelpful. I also suggest that clinicians can also contribute to developmental and neuroscience research by a more active dialogue with researchers about some of the clinical problems that our patients bring to us. As clinicians, we urgently need to understand the neurological processes that both underpin the problems and that can contribute to developing more effective treatment approaches, based on the findings of neuroscience and developmental research and outcome studies that highlight the relational factors that actually seem to work.

REFERENCES

Affeld-Niemayer, P. (1995) Trauma and symbol: Instinct and reality perception in therapeutic work with victims of incest. *Journal of AnalyticaL Psychology, 40*(1), 23–40.

Allen, J. G., Fonagy, P., &Bateman, A. (2010). The role of mentalizing in treating attachment trauma. In R. Lanius, E. Vermetten, & C. Pain (Eds.), *The impact of early life trauma on health and disease: The hidden epidemic* (pp. 247–256). Cambridge, UK: Cambridge University Press.

Aron, L. (2006) Analytic impasse and the third: Clinical implications of intersubjective theory. *International Journal of Psychoanalysis, 87*, 349–368.

Boston Change Process Study Group. (2007). The foundational level of psychodynamic meaning: Implicit process in relation to conflict, defence and the dynamic unconscious. *International Journal of Psychoanalysis, 88*, 843–860.

Beebe, B., Jaffe, J., Markese, S., Buck, K., Chen, H., Cohen, P., et al. (2010). The origins of 12-month attachment: A microanalysis of 4-month mother–infant interaction. *Attachment and Human Development, 12*, 1–135.

Beebe, B., & Lachmann, F. (2002). *Infant research and adult treatment: Co-constructing interactions.* Hillsdale, NJ: Analytic Press.

Benjamin, J. (2009). A relational psychoanalysis perspective on the necessity of acknowledging failure in order to restore the facilitating and containing features of the intersubjective relationship (the shared third). *International Journal of Psychoanalysis, 90*(3), 441–450.

Blass, R., & Carmeli, Z. (2007). The case against neuropsychoanalysis. On fallacies underlying psychoanalysis' latest scientific trend and its negative impact on psychoanalytic discourse. *International Journal of Psychoanalysis, 88*(1), 19–40.

Bluhm, R. L., Williamson, P. C., Osuch, E. A., Frewen, P. A., Stevens, T. K., ... Lanius, R. A. (2010). Alterations in default network connectivity in posttraumatic stress disorder related to early-life trauma. *J. Psychiatry Neurosci. 34*(3), 187–194.

Bowlby, J. (1988). *A secure base: Clinical applications of attachment theory.* London, UK: Routledge.

Briere, J., & Hodges, M. (2010). Assessing the effects of early and later childhood trauma in adults. In R. Lanius, E. Vermetten, & C. Pain (Eds.), *The impact of early life trauma on health and disease: The hidden epidemic.* Cambridge, UK: Cambridge University Press.

British Medical Association. (1929). *Report of the psychoanalysis committee* (pp. 207–216). London, UK: Author.

Broussard, E., & Cassidy, J. (2010). Maternal perception of newborns predicts attachment organization in middle adulthood. *Attachment and Human Development, 12*(1-2), 159–173.

Bureau, J-F., Martin, J., & Lyons-Ruth, K. (2010). Attachment dysregulation as hidden trauma in infancy: Early stress, maternal buffering and psychiatric morbidity in young adulthood. In R. Lanius, E. Vermetten, & C. Pain (Eds.), *The impact of early life trauma on health and disease: The hidden epidemic* (pp. 48–56). Cambridge, UK: Cambridge University Press.

Carr, L., Iacoboni, M., Dubeau, M. C., Mazziotta, J. C., & Lenzi, G. L. (2003). Neural mechanisms of empathy in humans: A relay from neural systems for imitation to limbic areas. *Proceedings of the National Academy of Sciences, USA, 100,* 5497–5502.

Deacon, T. (1997). *The symbolic species: The co-evolution of language and the human brain.* New York, NY: Norton.

Fonagy, P., & Tallindini-Shallice, M. (1993). Problems of psychoanalytic research in practice. *Bulletin of the Anna Freud Centre, 16*(1), 5–22.

Fonagy, P., Gergely, G., Jurist, E., & Target, M. (2002). *Affect regulation, mentalization and the development of the self.* New York, NY: Other Press.

Gallese, V. (2007). Before and below "theory of mind": Embodied simulation and the neural correlates of social cognition. *Philosophical Transactions of the Royal Society, 362,* 659–669.

Gratz, K. L., Conrad, S. D., & Roemer, L. (2002). Risk factors for deliberate self-harm among college students. *American Journal of Orthopsychiatry, 72,* 128–140.

Greenberg, J. R., & Mitchell, S. (1983). *Object relations in psychoanalytic theory.* Cambridge, MA: Harvard University Press.

Grunbaum, A. (1984). *The foundations of psychoanalysis: A philosophical critique.* Berkeley, CA: University of California Press

Guntrip, H. (1969). *Schizoid phenomena: Object relations and the self.* London, UK: Hogarht Press.

Herman, J. L., Perry, J. C., & Van der Kolk, B. A. (1989). Childhood trauma in borderline personality disorder. *American Journal of Psychiatry, 146*(4), 490–495.

Hinshelwood, R. D. (1989). *A dictionary of Kleinian thought.* London, UK: Free Association Books.

Hogenson, G. (2009). Synchronicity and moments of meeting. *Journal of Analytical Psychology, 54*(2), 183–198

Kalsched, D. (1996). *The inner world of trauma: Archetypal defences of the personal spirit.* London, UK: Routledge.

Karmiloff-Smith, A. (1992). *Beyond modularity: A developmental perspective on cognitive science.* Cambridge, MA: MIT Press.

King, P. H. M., & Steiner, R. (1990). *The Freud-Klein controversies in the British Psychoanalytic Society 1941–1945.* The New Library of Psychoanalysis. No. 11. London, UK: The Institute of Psychoanalysis/ Routledge.

Knox, J. (2003). *Archetype, attachment, analysis: Jungian psychology and the emergent mind.* London, UK: Routledge.

Knox, J. (2007). The fear of love. *Journal of Analytical Psychology, 52* 543–564.

Knox, J. (2010). *Self-agency in psychotherapy: Attachment, autonomy and intimacy.* New York, NY: Norton.

Lanius, R., Vermetten, E., & Pain, C. (2010). *The impact of early life trauma on health and disease: the hidden epidemic.* Cambridge, UK: Cambridge University Press.

Lepper, G., & Riding, N. (2006). *Researching the psychotherapy process: A practical guide to transcript-based methods.* Basingstoke, UK: Palgrave Macmillan.

Lieberman, A. (1999). Negative maternal attributions: Effects on toddlers' sense of self. *Psychoanalytic Inquiry, 19,* 737–754.

Loewenstein, R., & Welzant, V. (2010). Pragmatic approaches to stage-orientated treatment for early life trauma-related complex post-traumatic stress and dissociative disorders. In R. A. Lanius, E. Vermetten, & C. Pain (Eds.), *The impact of early life trauma on health and disease: The hidden epidemic* (pp. 257–267). Cambridge, UK: Cambridge University Press.

Luborsky, L., & Crits-Christoph, P. (1990). *Understanding transference: The core conflictual relationship theme method.* New York, NY: Basic Books.

Luborsky, L., Singer, B., & Luborsky, L. (1975). Comparative studies of psychotherapy: Is it true that "Everyone has won and all must have prizes?" *Archives of General Psychiatry, 32,* 995–1008.

McGuire, W. (Ed.). (1961). *The Freud/Jung letters.* London, UK: The Hogarth Press/Routledge & Kegan Paul.

Meltzer, D. (1973). *Sexual states of mind.* Perthshire, UK: Cluny Press.

Nathanson, D. L. (1992). *Shame and pride: Affect sex and the birth of the self.* New York, NY: Norton.

Northoff, G., & Panksepp, J. (2008). The trans-species concept of self and the subcortical-cortical midline system. *Trends in Cognitive Science, 12,* 259–264.

Oyama, S. (2000). *The ontogeny of information: Developmental systems and evolution.* Durham, NC: Duke University Press.

Panksepp, J. (1998). *Affective neuroscience: The foundations of human and animal emotion.* New York: Oxford University Press.

Panksepp, J., & Panksepp, J. B. (2000). The seven sins of evolutionary psychology. *Evolution and Cognition, 6,* 108–131.

Panksepp, J., & Northoff, G. (2009). The trans-species core SELF: The emergence of active cultural and neuro-ecological agents through self-related processing within subcortical midline networks. *Consciousness and Cognition, 18,* 193–215.

Peirce, C. S. (1868). Some consequences of four incapacities. *Journal of Speculative Philosophy, 2*(3), 140–157.

Peirce, C. S. (1877). The fixation of belief. *Popular Science Monthly, 12,* 1–15.

Peirce, C. S. (1878). How to make our ideas clearer. *Popular Science Monthly, 12,* 286–302.

Peirce, C. S. (1892). The law of mind. *The Monist, 2*(4), 533–599.

Popper, K. (1962). *Conjectures and refutations.* New York, NY: Basic Books.

Quinodez, D., Aubry, C., Bonard, O., Déjusseland, G., & Reith, B. (2006). Being a psychoanalyst: an everyday audacity. *International Journal of Psychoanalysis, 87*(2), 329–348.

Raichle, M., MacLeod, A. M., Snyder, A. Z., Powers, W. J., Gusnard, D. A., & Shulman, G. (2001). A default mode of brain function. *Proceedings of the National Academy of Sciences, 98,* 676–682.

Rizzolatti, G., & Luppino, G. (2001). The cortical motor system. *Neuron, 31,* 889–901.

Schore, A. N. (1994). *Affect regulation and the origin of the self.* Mahwah, NJ: Erlbaum.

Shedler, J. (2010). The efficacy of psychodynamic psychotherapy. *American Psychologist, 65*(2), 98–109.

Siegel, P., & Demorest, A. (2010, March 23). Affective scripts: A systematic case study of change in psychotherapy. *Psychotherapy Research,* 1–19.

Sroufe, L. A., & Waters, E. (1977). Attachment as an organizational construct. *Child Development,* 48, 1184–1199.

Taumoepeau, M., & Ruffman, T. (2008). Stepping stones to others' minds: Maternal talk relates to child mental state language and emotion understanding at 15, 24, and 33 months. *Child Development, 79,* 284–302

Tronick, E. (2007). *The neurobiological and social-emotional development of children.* New York, NY: Norton.

Uddin, L. Q., Iacoboni, M., Lange, C., & Keenan, J. P. (2007). The self and social recognition: The role of cortical midline structures and mirror neurons. *Trends in Cognitive Sciences, 11,* 153–157.

Wachtel, P. L. (2010) One-person and two-person conceptions of attachment and their implications for psychoanalytic thought. *International Journal of Psychoanalysis, 91,* 561–581.

Vygotsky, L. S. (1978). *Mind in society: The development of higher psychological processes.* Cambridge, MA: Harvard.

COMMENTARY

THE LANGUAGE OF DREAMS

Dissociative Processes and Symbolic Functioning In Dreaming

Rhona Kaplan
Private Practice and William Alanson White Institute

In response to Yariv Orgad and Yair Neuman's chapter, "Children Dreams: A Novel Interpretation," it would seem valuable to clarify and expand on the ideas they present in their chapter, as they relate to dream interpretation. Orgad and Neuman assert that both Freud and Bion interpreted dreams based on their respective theories of the unconscious. The chapter refers to two theoretical constructs (a) structural theory/ego psychology and (b) object relations. Specifically, I will reflect upon particular ideas and thoughts as they relate to Bion's and Matte Blanco's theories of dreams. In the following discussion, I incorporate a developmental perspective along with an understanding of dissociative processes in adulthood. I consider both of the aforementioned theoretical constructs significant in working with dreams to the extent that they are connected with the capacity or limitations for

Making Our Ideas Clear, pages 317–324
Copyright © 2015 by Information Age Publishing
All rights of reproduction in any form reserved.

symbolic functioning and the development of self and other experiences. As Orgad and Neuman describe a particular technique of semiotic mapping of symbols in dreams, I will introduce general guidelines I find useful in working with patients' dreams. These guidelines are somewhat informed by a theoretical preference towards working within a dissociative paradigm. More significantly, they have been established through what I have found to resonate with patients when working with dreams. I will present a brief clinical vignette and a dream report, which illustrates the intermingling of theory and practice as it pertains to work with dreams.

CLASSICAL THEORY

As discussed in the chapter, Sigmund Freud believed that aggressive or sexual impulses might overwhelm a person leading to intolerable anxiety. As a result these impulses were repressed. The goal then of dream analysis, in adults, would be to uncover the meaning of the dreams to relieve the "ego," of these repressed impulses resulting in symptom relief. Orgad and Neuman describe Freud's psychosexual theory of development, which informed his ideas about children's dreams. Consistent with both Sigmund and Anna Freud's theories of child development: Steven Luria Ablon and John E. Mack (1980) consider children's dreams from both psychosexual and ego developmental perspectives. They suggest that children's dreams reflect stages of their personality development as well as the formation of ego defenses. In reference to Anna Freud's work with children, Ablon and Mack suggest that "the language of dreams utilizes certain defensive operations including repression, reaction formation, omissions and sublimations" (p. 191).

They further suggest that dreams reflect inner conflicts with which children struggle. For example, from a psychosexual perspective, dreams may reflect conflicts relating to toilet training, aggressive drives, and Oedipal conflicts.

It is significant to note that Ablon and Mack (1980) put forth the idea that children's retelling of the dreams, to adult caregivers, helps them to understand their wishes and conflicts. Verbal descriptions and/or other expressions (such as drawings) support a child's growing ability to differentiate fantasy from reality. The process of distinguishing fantasy from reality enhances a child's growing capacity to move from concrete thought processes to more abstract thought processes, as they are able to increasingly symbolize experience (Klein, 1932). The importance of their reference to symbolic functioning in the chapter is further expanded upon in the following discussion of object relations theory.

OBJECT RELATIONS THEORY

In contrast to Freud's theory, Bion's ideas are informed by object relations theory. Object relations theory posits that both reality and fantasy are central to personality development and emotional well-being. Bion asserts that dreams represent movement from the paranoid-schizoid position, where self-other representations are concrete, to a depressive position, which is a more highly integrated psychic state with the potential for increased symbolic functioning. In the depressive position one has the capacity to live with ambiguity and complexity. Orgad and Neuman introduce Bion's idea of the "truth instinct," or knowing parts of oneself and experiences that were previously out of one's awareness and thus unknown. In this way, dreaming serves a specific function to the dreamer. Through dreaming, one comes to understand parts of the self and experiences that were previously unknown. Further, symbols in dreams expand one's sense of knowledge about self–other experiences in an ever-evolving process. Exploration of dream symbols is significant in work with dreams. Specifically, Orgad and Neuman (this volume) state, "By uniting with the emotional experience and objectifying it, by confronting the sign and using it, the self is enriched and strengthened, boundaries are expended."

Matte Blanco's idea of symmetry and asymmetry is valuable and relevant not only to nighttime dreaming, but to any function in which there is potential to use symbolism and metaphor, which could also include daydreams, fantasy play, and artistic endeavors. Related to the idea of symmetry, one might also consider Peter Fonagy and Mary Target's (1996) ideas of psychic reality and psychic equivalence. Fonagy and Target (1996) theorize that small children generally operate in the mode of psychic equivalence or what Matte Blanco might refer to as "symmetry" in which "ideas are not felt to be representations but rather direct replicas of reality" (p. 219). Fonagy and Target (1996) assert the following: psychic equivalence in young children also refers to ideas children have about their own as well as other's thoughts. Fonagy and Target (1996) suggest that play is crucial in developing children's ability to symbolize and understand themselves in relation to self and other, as well as to begin to be able to separate their own desires, feelings, and thoughts from that of others. Orgad and Neuman (this volume) refer, for example, to the lion in children's dreams. One aspect of a child's development is her increasing capacity to understand symbolism, meaning the idea that objects stand for something else or have meaning. As suggested in their study of children in the kindergarten class, the lion is a characterization representing internal experiences and aspects of their feelings and thoughts. Children come to understand that they are not literally the lion; rather, the lion represents thoughts and feelings related to feeling aggressive and powerful and/or victimized and helpless.

SYMBOLIC FUNCTION AND DISSOCIATION

Symbolic functioning is an important aspect of a child's development and continues to be crucial throughout one's life. Based on Winnicott's (1971) ideas, play is the vehicle through which a child begins to develop a sense of self and other. In "Playing and Reality," Winnicott (1971) states, "Playing is inherently exciting and precarious. This precariousness belongs to the interplay in the child's mind of that which is actual or shared reality" (p. 47). Here, "play" describes various activities in which a space is created to use one's creativity and imagination, in the presence of another person or alone. This can include creating stories, storytelling, recalling of dreams, use of objects, and fantasy play. A limited ability to reflect upon or symbolize experience through play could be observed in heightened states of anxiety or fear in both adults and children. When attempts at symbolic play are obstructed as a result of traumatic experiences (including neglect, abuse, family violence, and depression/anxiety in caregivers), children's access to their feelings, thoughts, and experiences of self and other is limited. One must manage thoughts and feelings, which become overwhelming, by adapting ways to cope with experiences for which meaning cannot be made through symbolic functioning (such as play). One such way is through splitting off or dissociating self-states and experience (Bromberg, 2003). Where play promotes creativity, psychic growth, and development of self, dissociation limits access to experience that one needs in order to develop and know oneself. I emphasize that this is not a linear process. There is the possibility for certain experiences to be symbolized while others are not, throughout one's life. In considering the role of dissociation, it is important to note that dissociation is not always a pathological process and one that we often rely upon for survival and psychological well being. For the purposes of this commentary, I am referring to dissociative processes that are particularly pathogenic and, as a result, inhibit the capacity for creativity and psychic growth.

GUIDELINES IN WORKING WITH DREAMS

In considering dreams, I have a preference for understanding dreams as dissociated aspects of one's self and experiences, which are not accessible to an individual in his conscious, waking life. These experiences, thoughts, and feelings are yet to be symbolized and known to the dreamer. Along with understanding dreams from a dissociative paradigm, I also have come to view dreams and dream symbols as manifestations of aspects of current and past experiences, feelings, and thoughts about self and other relationships, and conflicts one might be struggling with at any given point in time.

I emphasize the word *symbolic* in that it seems that one commonality among varying theories is this: Dreams contain symbols and are symbolic. If one adheres to Freudian theory in dream work, symbols have a prescribed meaning related to a specific psychosexual stage or conflict, and the analysis of symbols is interpreted to the dreamer. In Bion's work, and consistent with my understanding of dreams, the symbol's meaning to the dreamer is of primary significance.

How one works with dreams varies widely among clinicians, based on theoretical leanings, preferred technique, personal style, as well as the analyst's relationship to his or her own dreams. It is crucial to inquire about what a particular symbol means to the individual reporting the dream. As a therapist hearing the dream report, I allow myself to at first silently associate to the content of the dream. These associations might be based on knowledge I have about the patient's current life experiences as well as their history, the dreamer's affect while reporting the dream, my own affective experience, and reveries I might have during the dream report. In addition to listening to an individual's particular associations to the dream, I further inquire about what a patient recalls about feelings they experienced in relation to the dream symbols. I am particularly interested in affects that seem in contrast to what the person is describing in the dream. For example, a patient is describing what seems to be a frightening image or experience in their dream and describe feeling unafraid and even having pleasurable feelings in the dream or while telling the dream. This is common in dream reports, and I might think of this discrepancy as some dissociated aspect of experience and/or a conflict the patient is currently working through.

Once I sense there is a space to discuss my ideas, thoughts, and/or associations upon hearing the dream, I will begin to share them with the patient. I often wait for a patient to communicate an interest in hearing these. A process of mutual exploration and engagement around the dream emerges in which there is a co-creation of meaning through "playing" with the dream.

DISSOCIATIVE PROCESS IN DREAM WORK

I will use a brief clinical vignette to illustrate consideration of dreams as dissociated aspects of the dreamer's experience as well as the process by which working with the dream promoted psychic growth:

Sally is a 22-year-old woman whom I have been treating in twice-per-week psychotherapy for four years. She was referred for treatment following a diagnosis of anorexia nervosa. During the first few years of treatment, Sally severely restricted food intake and described persistent preoccupation with her body, particularly her weight, and with food intake. With relentless precision, she counted and maintained records of calories and nutritional contents of food she ate. Despite developing medical conditions associated with malnourishment and low body weight, she struggled with allowing herself to eat intuitively and to gain weight. Sally's history contained experiences of sexual trauma, as well as emotional neglect. She was encouraged by parents be a "good happy girl," which meant not talking about her experiences, expressing unacceptable feelings, or asking for what she needed. Sally's anger and sadness were not permissible. She had very restricted space to express her internal world symbolically. Being overwhelmed with intolerable feelings of anger, confusion, and abandonment, she survived her childhood traumas by developing obsessive-compulsive rituals. At very specific times during the day, Sally would wash her hands in a very ritualistic manner. She reported believing that if she did not she would contract diseases from certain germs that she could not identify, but she was certain they would develop into an incurable disease. These rituals were concrete manifestations of her internal turmoil, since as a result of sexual trauma she experienced a violation beyond her control. Since Sally existed in a paranoid schizoid state, this violation was experienced as infesting her with something dirty and poisonous. She could not actually rid herself of intolerable and intrusive feelings, which threatened to overwhelm her and potentially lead to a psychic collapse (or psychosis). In addition, being emotionally neglected and silenced reified Sally's experience of herself as bad and dirty. These rituals helped Sally survive at a cost to her developing sense of self-other through symbolic play and other forms of self-expression. As an adolescent and young adult, these obsessive-compulsive rituals evolved into a persistent obsession about her weight and food intake. Sally's thinness protected her from being "seen" and thus vulnerable to being violated. Her restriction of food controlled the potential to be "poisoned" by external forces beyond her control. Her low body weight kept dangerous feelings at bay and impeded integration of affect and experience (Bromberg, 2003). Specifically, Sally could not allow for the experience of being a woman with sexual desire, need (hunger), and anger and aggression.

I found Sally likable and pleasant to work with (after all, she was a good girl), yet sessions were empty of affect and bogged down in Sally's preoccupation about her weight and food. Sally's capacity to reflect on the meaning of food restriction and her body weight seemed lacking during sessions. She continue to compulsively control her weight and expressed a concrete thought process which resulted in difficulty making contact with her emotional states. Sessions felt deadened by these concrete manifestations (food, calories, and her body weight) of her inner world and struggles. I often found myself feeling disconnected and bored, unable to make meaning myself. My own ability to form thoughts was impaired, and I experienced a limited capacity to guide Sally to a more meaningful and nuanced exploration of her struggles. Sally is a bright young woman and could understand that her difficulties with food and intense need to remain underweight were connected to her early experiences. Yet her insights seemed to be a rather linear, intellectualized narrative with little affective charge. Towards the end of her third year of therapy, Sally reported a dream, which was the first in her treatment with me. The dream was as follows:

> I was getting ready for a party, it was going to be this big feast. There were also going to be many children at this party. There was a long table, lavishly decorated with dishes of food set out in beautiful ornamental bowls. These women were telling me it was time for them to put on my makeup and get dressed. I felt kind of special, like maybe I was a guest of honor. After the makeup artists were finished, I could see in the mirror that I was made up to look like a character in a story who chooses children to be sacrificed and killed, and I realized the children were there to be chosen by me to be sacrificed, at first I was confused, but then I felt like, this weird sort of pleasure and felt very powerful. I was the character.

Sally reported this dream and described waking from it feeling horrified and guilty but also recalling the pleasure she experienced when she realized she was the villainess character. I asked her about her associations to this story, and she reported that she was actually quite fascinated with it and had an affinity for the heroine in the story (an adolescent girl) and so was surprised by the dream. It so happened that it was a story I was also familiar with and enjoyed quite a bit. In the process of beginning to discuss her associations and feelings about different symbols in the dream (the food, decorated table, children, villainess, etc.), it felt as if a space was created to begin to "play" with yet unknown aspects of herself and experiences. The boredom and deadness seemed to lift at those moments, and I could sense more emotion and life in her voice. "Playing" with the dream was fun for us, and co-creating meaning opened a potential space in which to interact. What was most significant to Sally was her experience of herself as the destructive and envious villainess (aggressor). We were able to begin to identify angry feelings—destructive, envious, and aggressive feelings—which she had previously dissociated from awareness, some of which she noticed she experienced towards me. She also began to notice that her needs and desires were often experienced as potentially dangerous. Food became an important metaphor for need. Desire—emotional, physical, and sexual—was frightening as Sally equated this with being both powerful (aggressive) and vulnerable (victimized). This was a very significant dream in Sally's treatment, and it was one she continued to refer to over the course of her treatment. Through both analyzing the content of the dream and the process of "playing" with the dream, Sally is able to develop and understand parts of her self and her experiences.

SUMMARY

I will conclude with a summary of the ideas presented in this commentary:

1. Dreams can represent dissociated aspects of self and experiences.
2. The process of working with dreams is akin to playing.
3. The process of co-creation of meaning is as important to working with dreams as the content of the dream report.
4. Reporting and analyzing dreams opens a potential space for new ways of understanding self and others.
5. Dreams have the potential to promote psychic and emotional growth for both children and adults.

REFERENCES

Ablon, S. L., & Mack, J. E. (1980). Children's dreams reconsidered. *Psychoanalytic Study of the Child, 35*, 179–215.

Bromberg, P. (2003). One need be a house to be haunted. *Psychoanalytic Dialogues, 13*(5), 689–709.

Fonagy, P., & Target, M. (1996). Playing with reality: I. Theory of mind and the normal development of psychic reality. *International Journal of Psychoanalysis, 77*, 217–233.

Klein, M. (1932). *The psychoanalysis of children.* New York, NY: Grove Press.

Winnicott, D. W. (1971). *Playing and reality.* London, UK: Routledge.

CONCLUSION

THE PRAGMATIC MAXIM AND THE GOOD LIFE

Philip J. Rosenbaum
Haverford College and William Alanson White Institute

CONCLUDING THOUGHTS

The goal of the current volume was to (re)introduce American pragmatism into the landscape of contemporary psychoanalysis, specifically the loosely organized relational movement. As stated in the introduction, contemporary psychoanalysis has undergone a "postmodern" revolution, distancing itself from more classical psychoanalysis. The revolution has led to reconsidering and reworking central topics such as how the self is understood, the role of the analyst's authority and influence, the nature of transference and countertransference, and the ubiquity of interpersonal enactments. Although no longer considered "revolutionary," as relational psychoanalysis is now safely "mainstream," analysts are still grappling with the clinical and theoretical consequences. This process has benefited from including ideas from a variety of fields, such as queer theory and chaos theory. Within this context, this project has argued that pragmatism and pragmatic theory has much to offer contemporary psychoanalysis.

Pragmatism may at first have seemed an odd choice; after all, its influence is generally considered historic. However, as demonstrated throughout

Making Our Ideas Clear, pages 325–329
Copyright © 2015 by Information Age Publishing
All rights of reproduction in any form reserved.

this volume, it is actually very well suited to the contemporary setting. The pragmatic emphasis on interpretation, active meaning making, and the primacy of subjectivity are consistent with today's analytic values. Not only does pragmatism share postmodern sensibilities about the illusion of an isolated and central self, the constitutive role of the other and culture, and the centrality of experience, but it also offers the advantage of the pragmatic maxim. Far from reducing experience to "whatever works" as is often associated with it, the maxim provides a way for considering the effects of an idea or thought. As a way to evaluate effect, pragmatism opens the door to considering ideas as better or worse, more compelling or less so, and more or less useful. In other words, pragmatism has a built-in tool for evaluating ideas, which provides a way of resolving thorny theoretical dilemmas and a way out of numerous philosophical quagmires. Just as William James settled his personal debate about free will by choosing to believe in it and then dealing with its effects, analysts can also ask what effects certain ideas may have. In this regard, the pragmatic maxim serves as a tonic to the metatheoretical stalemates that postmodernism sometimes leads to.

In this respect, this volume highlighted that the strengths of pragmatism as a tool for thinking and living in the world are well suited for today's uncertainty and postmodern anxieties. As a philosophy, pragmatism is concerned with how people practically live their lives. Pragmatic discourse meaningfully seeks to understand how meaning is made, how it is subjectivity experienced, and how relationships work. Its reapplication to the analytic field offers a broad and deep philosophy that compliments contemporary therapeutic and analytic efforts.

Some specific effects of reading the chapters compiled in this volume may have been reconsidering the historical relevance of key figures, encountering a new language for thinking about known phenomena, or discovering different ways of analyzing textual data and thinking about interactive moments. One effect that I consider important when reading this, or perhaps any other text, is an experience of an expansion upon previous thoughts. Put somewhat differently, the effect is a furthering of the flow of symbolization and signification. It leads to someplace new and different. This emphasis seems to mirror the shift in contemporary psychoanalysis: one that has moved the field away from a focus on resolving predetermined goals such as the Oedipal complex, working through a particular stuck developmental stage, or getting in touch with one's anger, towards expanding awareness, formulating and partaking in new experience, and developing greater insight into self and other.

This view implicitly structures what pragmatism considers the "good life" to be. The idea of the "good life" is of course one of the oldest, if not the oldest philosophical question—essentially, asking what are the requirements, expectations, values, beliefs, habits, feelings, and so forth one should emulate, adopt, and internalize in order to live a particular type of life. The Oracle of Delphi's proclamation "know thyself" represents one version of the good life, which is different than, say, Freud's idea about everyday unhappiness, and still yet different than more modern proclamations about living "authentically." For the pragmatist, the good life is intricately tied into the pragmatic maxim of considering effect. In the absence of a predetermined idea about what one needs to do, the maxim itself seems to represent some version of the good life. In other words, one needs to continuously consider effects. While this in of itself can become its own predetermined goal, I believe it does have the effect of moving the target of the good life away from accomplishing certain tasks towards living in a certain way.

Before moving forward, it is interesting to consider how the pragmatic maxim is already deeply embedded within the structure of relational psychoanalysis. Consider, for example, the question of interpersonal communication, which is a central topic of relational psychoanalysis. As many of the authors in this volume discussed, communication is a semiotic act. Namely, it involves a highly complex and coordinated series of signs (iconic, indexical, and symbolic) consistently moving and being exchanged at various levels of conscious awareness. Within a two-person situation, signs are exchanged from both self to other and also within the self (self to self, or self-state to self-state). From moment to moment, an overwhelming amount of information about the other, oneself, or both is communicated. Consider all the non- and preverbal information that gets exchanged upon first meeting. This includes what someone is wearing, how they appear, their smell, type of eye contact, hand motions, twitching, raised eyebrows, and so forth. It would be easy to quickly become overwhelmed by the potential communicative acts and the meanings that could be constructed from them.

Within this context—a first session, or the hundredth session—the communicative act is what the analyst or patient interprets of the other or of themselves. In this regard, noticing that something has happened or registering effect (this and not something else) constrains the realm of future interactions, while further structuring the field of inquiry. Analysts, not to mention their patients, regularly make such interpretations already, implicitly utilizing the pragmatic maxim of effect to conduct their practice. Further considering effect, one might wonder how a particular interpretation made either silently or verbally to the other, begins to shape what comes next. In this respect, being silent is not neutral, but rather one form of interpreting. Similarly, there is a difference between noting something and not saying anything about it—say for example, a patient's provocative t-shirt—and not noticing it at all.

When considering effect, we might ask, does the interpretation open up or close the inquiry? Does it free up or stop associations? Or does the patient become more or less emotionally grounded? Interestingly, the answer to each of these questions is also an effect, generating a type of data on a different level of abstraction that can be evaluated within the therapeutic situation. For instance, we might ask what about this question or observation enabled the patient to respond in one way and not another. In this regard, as Edgar Levenson often notes, as we talk with our patients we act with them. More specifically, we engage in a structured semiotic, sign-based relationship of interpretation, where how we talk and interact is closely connected to what is being discussed. This is not random. A patient talking about her fear of being abandoned by her mother who has recently passed away suddenly shifts the topic from her feelings, towards noticing a play kitchen in the corner of the room. In noting the shift, the therapist asks if the patient found it too emotionally difficult to talk about her deceased mother. The patient dismisses both the interpretation and her own, and the session moves to a different topic. From a different level of interpretation, looking at how the patient and therapist interacted, one could note the way the patient avoided emotional closeness with the therapist. At the same time, perhaps the patient also asked to be fed by the therapist, who did not get the message and so left the patient feeling abandoned?

From a pragmatic perspective, considering effects can be used to focus on the relationship between therapist and patient or how one or both parties makes meaning—in this case for instance how they interpret (understand) the communications of the other. Effects can, of course, be affective as well: the feelings and emotions we have with certain patients and theirs with us. A different therapist thus may have inquired more into the feelings that the patient had when looking at the toy kitchen, or their own feelings when the conversation was shifted.

It should be apparent that when the pragmatic sensibility is applied to the analytic situation, the focus is less on delivering a "correct" interpretation and more upon opening up the situation to increasingly complex and nuanced observations, thoughts, feelings, and so forth. This of course reflects the pragmatic idea of the good life. One considers effects and has conversations (dialogue) about them. That pragmatism is an invitation to dialogue about one's experiencing in the world seems fitting given its historical founding as the "Metaphysical Club." Furthermore, its emphasis on actively engaging in the world to grasp and make sense of experience seems to suit its American roots.

Of course, as asked earlier what stops the pragmatic maxim from becoming its own tautology—its own predetermined set of ideas and beliefs that analysis strives towards obtaining? On the one hand, the answer to this may be nothing beyond awareness of the possibility that this can happen. However, I think the history of pragmatism is instructive here: specifically, the tension that existed between William James's pragmatic pluralism and Charles S. Peirce's objectivist pragmatism. According to Peirce, there is an objective world that a dedicated committee of investigators may ultimately reach consensus on. Much like Freud, who argued for a causal and explanatory system, Peirce considered his pragmatic logic as working toward a theory describing an objective reality. In contrast, William James argued for the value of pluralism: that there are many realities and that causal explanations are not possible. Instead, he valued descriptive accounts of experience that are accordingly more relativistic. While attempts have been made to bridge this tension, the claim of relativism and what it means for knowing and psychoanalytic knowledge remains an area of debate.

Specifically, if we take Peirce's view of the objective world seriously, it argues that there is some concrete referrent that we can make mention of and know in at least some ways—that there is an actual something out there that we are making sense of and interpreting as are our patients. When working with them, our use of signs and interpretations connects us to them and to this reality in at least some basic ways. Peirce's idealistic belief that researchers could all agree to some aspects of this external reality contrasts with James's perspective that reality is inherently subjective. His pluralism predates more modern constructive ideas and in an interesting way is a precursor to postmodernism.

While the contrast in beliefs was a source of stress for Peirce, pragmatism, in its fragmented and non-unitary way, seems to allow the space for both exist. That there can be a dialogue (or dialect) between these ideas seems to enrich the conversation, rather than limit it. Thus, the pragmatic maxim, much like psychoanalysis, argues for the value of conversation as central to the good life. This of course can be subject to its own evaluation; some types of conversations seem "better" or "more interesting" than others.

Certainly, the chapters in this volume express the tradition of conversation and dialogue. By bringing a number of pragmatic principles to the discussion of psychological phenomena, it is my hope that they stimulated the reader's curiosity.

Hopefully, the chapters struck a balance between presenting ideas that are familiar and comfortable, but locating them in new historical and theoretical contexts, and offering new and challenging ideas and theories. As much of the theory is bound up in history and a philosophical discourse that may have been novel, it is my hope that readers fought through feelings of frustration and engaged with these chapters pragmatically—that is to say, that they not only considered the denotative aspects of the chapters, or what the authors may have been conveying, but also more importantly, the connotative aspects, what effects the chapters had on them—making it something personally relevant.

Printed and bound by CPI Group (UK) Ltd, Croydon, CR0 4YY

15/09/2026

14962370-0006